Transatlantic Literary Studies

TRANSATLANTIC LITERARY STUDIES:
A READER

Edited by
Susan Manning and Andrew Taylor

THE JOHNS HOPKINS UNIVERSITY PRESS
BALTIMORE

Printed in Great Britain on acid-free paper

First published in the United Kingdom by Edinburgh University Press, 2007
Published in the United States by the Johns Hopkins University Press, 2007
9 8 7 6 5 4 3 2 1

The Johns Hopkins University Press
2715 N. Charles Street
Baltimore, MD 21218-4363
www.press.jhu.edu

ISBN 10: 0-8018-8730-5 (cloth: alk. paper)
ISBN 13: 978-0-8018-8730-7

ISBN 10: 0-8018-8731-3 (pbk.: alk. paper)
ISBN 13: 978-0-8018-8731-4

Library of Congress Control Number: 2007921655

A catalog record for this book is available from the British Library.

CONTENTS

NOTE ON THE TEXTS

Sources are given at the beginning of the extracts; readers are encouraged to consult these for a full text. Editors' elisions appear as [. . .]. Punctuation and references have been standardised, and minor errors in the original sources silently corrected. For simplicity of reading and in the interests of brevity, notes have been reduced to references to works quoted within the extract, and placed at the end of each extract. Notes have not been supplied where they are absent in the original text. Terms which do not appear in the Concise Oxford Dictionary, or which require expansion, are marked *; asterisked words can be found in the Glossary at the end of the book. Some explanations are drawn from Julian Wolfreys (ed.), *The Edinburgh Encyclopaedia of Modern Criticism and Theory* (2002); [E] indicates where this text offers more information on the glossed term.

ACKNOWLEDGEMENTS

We would like to thank the participants of the STAR seminar at Edinburgh University for their helpful suggestions and comments during the course of our work on the *Reader*. In particular we want to acknowledge the work of Ashley Hales, whose research, editorial and general administrative skills have been essential for this book's completion. The editorial and production staff at Edinburgh University Press have been unfailingly efficient and helpful. In particular we would like to acknowledge the enthusiasm of Nicola Ramsey and Jackie Jones for the idea of this book, and their support in its realisation.

SLM
AT

PUBLISHER'S ACKNOWLEDGEMENTS

Grateful acknowledgement is made to the following sources for permission to reproduce material in this book previously published elsewhere. Every effort has been made to trace copyright holders, but if any have been inadvertently overlooked the publisher will be pleased to make the necessary arrangement at the first opportunity.

Extracts from 'Copywriting American History: International Copyright and the Periodization of the Nineteenth Century' by Claudia Stokes from *American Literature* 77.2, 2005. © 2005, Duke University Press. All rights reserved. Reproduced with the permission of the publisher.

Extract from 'The Transnational Turn: Rediscovering American Studies in a Wider World' by Robert Gross from *Journal of American Studies* 34.3, 2000. © 2000, Cambridge University Press. Reproduced with the permission of the publisher and Robert Gross.

Extracts from 'Nineteenth-Century United States Literary Culture and Transnationality' by John Carlos Rowe from *PMLA* 118.1, January 2003. © 2003, Modern Language Association of America. Reproduced with the permission of the publisher.

Extract from 'National Narratives, Postnational Narration' by Donald E. Pease from *Modern Fiction Studies* 43.1, Spring 1997. © 1997, Purdue Research Foundation. Reproduced with the permission of The Johns Hopkins University Press.

Extracts from 'Transnationalism and Classic American Literature' by Paul Giles from *PMLA* 118.1, January 2003. © 2003, Modern Language Association of America. Reproduced with the permission of the publisher.

Extracts from 'The Limits of Cosmopolitanism and the Case for Translation' by David Simpson from *European Romantic Review* 16.2, April 2005. © 2005, Taylor and Francis. Reproduced with the permission of Taylor & Francis Ltd. and David Simpson.

Extracts from 'Between Empires: Frances Calderón de la Barca's *Life in Mexico*' by Amy Kaplan and Nina Gerassi-Navarro from *Symbiosis: A Journal of Anglo-American Literary Relations* 9.1, April 2005. © 2005 Symbiosis. Reproduced with permission.

Extracts from 'Principles of a History of World Literature' from *The World*

Republic of Letters by Pascale Casanova, translated by M. B. DeBoivse, Harvard University Press, 2004. © 2004 the President and Fellows of Harvard College. Reproduced by permission of the publisher and Editions du Seuil.

Extracts from 'General, Comparative, and National Literature' from *Theory of Literature* by René Wellek and Austin Warren, Harcourt Inc., 1976. © 1949 by Harcourt, Inc. and renewed 1977 by René Wellek and Austin Warren. Reproduced with the permission of the publisher.

Extract from 'Notes Towards a Comparison Between European and American Romanticism' from *Scenes of Nature, Signs of Men* by Tony Tanner, Cambridge University Press, 1989. © 1989 Cambridge University Press. Reproduced with the permission of the publisher and the author's estate.

Extract from 'English Romanticism, American Romanticism: What's the Difference?' in *Theory, Now and Then* by J. Hillis Miller, Harvester Wheatsheaf/Prentice Hall, 1991. Reproduced with the permission of J. Hillis Miller.

Extracts from 'Cultural Time in England and America' from *Atlantic Doublecross: American Literature and British Influence in the Age of Emerson* by Robert Weisbuch, The University of Chicago Press, 1986. Reproduced with the permission of the publisher and Robert Weisbuch.

Extracts from 'Nature and Walden' from *Romantic Dialogues: Anglo-American Continuities, 1776–1862* by Richard Gravil, Palgrave Macmillan, 2000. Reproduced with the permission of the publisher.

Extracts from 'Introduction: On Beginning to Tell a "Best Kept Secret"' from *Golden Cables of Sympathy: The Transatlantic Sources of Nineteenth-Century Feminism* by Margaret McFadden, The University Press of Kentucky, 1999. Reproduced with the permission of the publisher.

Extracts from 'Network Analysis: A Reappraisal' by Jeremy Boissevain from *Current Anthropology* 20.2, 1979. Reproduced with the permission of The University of Chicago Press and Jeremy Boissevain.

Extract from 'Prospero and Caliban' from *Colonial Encounters: Europe and the Native Caribbean, 1492–1797* by Peter Hulme, Methuen, 1986. Reproduced with the permission of the author.

Extracts from 'Cultural Identity and Diaspora' by Stuart Hall from *Identity: Community, Culture, Difference*, edited by Jonathan Rutherford, Lawrence & Wishart, 1990. Reproduced with the permission of the publisher.

Extracts from 'The Black Atlantic as a Counterculture of Modernity' from *The Black Atlantic: Modernity and Double Consciousness* by Paul Gilroy, Verso, 1993. Reproduced with the permission of the publisher.

Extracts from 'American Literary Emergence as a Postcolonial Phenomenon' by Lawrence Buell from *American Literary History* 4.3, Autumn 1992. Reproduced with the permission of Oxford University Press.

Extracts from 'European Pedigrees/African Contagions: Nationality,

Narrative, and Community in Tutuola, Achebe, and Reed' by James Snead from *Nation and Narration*, edited by Homi Bhabha, Routledge, 1990. © 1990 Routledge. Reproduced with the permission of Taylor & Francis Books UK.

Extracts from 'Deep Time: American Literature and World History' by Wai Chee Dimock from *American Literary History*, 13.4, December 2001. Reproduced with the permission of Oxford University Press.

'The Task of the Translator' from *Illuminations* by Walter Benjamin, translated by Harry Zohn, Pimlico, 1968. Reproduced with the permission of The Random House Group Ltd and Suhrkamp Verlag.

Extract from 'On Linguistic Aspects of Translation' by Roman Jakobson in *Language in Literature*, edited by Krystyna Pomorska and Stephen Rudy, Belknap Press, 1987. Reproduced with the permission of the Roman Jakobson Foundation.

Extracts from 'The Hermeneutic Motion' from *After Babel: Aspects of Language and Translation* by George Steiner, Oxford University Press, 1975. Reproduced with the permission of the publisher.

Extract from 'The Tropics of Translation' from *The Translator's Turn* by Douglas Robinson, The Johns Hopkins University Press, 1991. Reproduced with the permission of the publisher.

Extracts from 'Gender and the Metaphorics of Translation' by Lori Chamberlain from *Signs*, 13.3, 1988. Reproduced with the permission of The University of Chicago Press and Lori Chamberlain.

Extracts from 'Jack Spicer's *After Lorca:* Translation as Decomposition' by Daniel Katz from *Textual Practice*, 18.1, 2004. Reproduced with the permission Taylor & Francis Ltd. and the author.

Extract from 'The French Caribbeanization of Phillis Wheatley: A Poetics of Anticolonialism' in *Transamerican Literary Relations and the Nineteenth-Century Public Sphere* by Anna Brickhouse, Cambridge University Press, 2004. © 2004 Anna Brickhouse. Reproduced with the permission of the publisher and the author.

Extract from 'The Foreign Policy of Metaphor' and 'The Frontier of Decorum' from *Poetics of Imperialism: Translation and Colonization from the Tempest to Tarzan* by Eric Cheyfitz, Oxford University Press, 1995. Reproduced with the permission of the publisher.

Extracts from 'Introduction: Rhizome' from *A Thousand Plateaus: Capitalism and Schizophrenia* by Gilles Deleuze and Félix Guattari, translated by Brian Massumi, The Athlone Press, 1988. Reproduced by kind permission of Continuum International Publishing Group.

Extracts from 'Traveling Genres' by Margaret Cohen from *New Literary History* 34.3, 2003. © New Literary History, University of Virginia. Reproduced with the permission of The John Hopkins University Press.

Extract from 'Introduction: History, Memory, and Performance' from *Cities of the Dead: Circum-Atlantic Performance* by Joseph Roach, Columbia University Press, 1996. Reproduced with the permission of the publisher.

Extract from 'Romance and Rational Orthodoxy' from *The Development of American Romance: The Sacrifice of Relation* by Michael Davitt Bell, The University of Chicago Press, 1980. Reproduced with the permission of the publisher.

Extract from 'The Failure of Genre Criticism' from *American and English Fiction in the Nineteenth Century: An Antigenre Critique and Comparison* by Nicolaus Mills, Indiana University Press, 1973.

Extracts from 'Empire and Occasional Conformity: David Fordyce's *Complete British Letter-Writer*' by Eve Tavor Bannet from *Huntington Library Quarterly* 66.1&2, 2003. Reproduced with the permission of The University of California Press and Eve Tavor Bannet.

Extracts from 'The Americanization of Clarissa' by Leonard Tennenhouse from *The Yale Journal of Criticism* 11.1, 1998. © Yale University and The Johns Hopkins University Press. Reproduced with the permission of The Johns Hopkins University Press.

Extracts from 'Reflections on Exile' by Edward Said from *Granta* 13 (Autumn 1984) and *Reflections on Exile and Other Literary and Cultural Essays*, Granta, 2001. © 2001 Edward Said, reproduced with the permission of The Wylie Agency.

Extracts from 'Ethno-Graphy: Speech, or the Space of the Other: Jean de Léry' from *The Writing of History* by Michel de Certeau, 1988. © 1988 Columbia University Press. Reproduced with the permission of the publisher.

Extract from 'Introduction' by Stephen Fender from *Sea Changes: British Emigration and American Literature*, 1992. © Cambridge University Press. Reproduced with the permission of the publisher and the author.

Extracts from 'The Rewards of Travel' by William Stowe from *Going Abroad: European Travel in Nineteenth-Century American Culture*. © 1994 Princeton University Press. Reproduced with the permission of the publisher.

Extracts from 'Introduction' and 'Alexander von Humboldt and the Reinvention of America' by Mary Louise Pratt from *Imperial Eyes: Travel Writing and Transculturation*. © 1992 Routledge. Reproduced with the permission of Taylor & Francis Books UK.

Extracts from 'Travel Writing and its Theory' by Mary Baine Campbell from *The Cambridge Companion to Travel Writing* edited by Peter Hulme and Tim Youngs. © 2002 Cambridge University Press. Reproduced with the permission of the publisher and the author.

INTRODUCTION: WHAT IS TRANSATLANTIC LITERARY STUDIES?

Susan Manning and Andrew Taylor

'American Studies' was an indirect product of the post-Second World War attempt to stabilise and propagate 'American values' in a world which had proved catastrophically volatile. Institutionalised as a cross-disciplinary field of academic study which aligned literature, history and politics, it became a tool of cultural imperialism in the Cold War era, and developed powerful (because radically simplified) descriptions of American identity clustered around a series of resonant phrases and images: manifest destiny, the frontier spirit, the 'American Adam', the credo of Progress. Its often unexamined equation of American with United States Studies underscored the geopolitical impetus of its inception. The classic texts or canon of American Literature, drawn up in the same years and responding to similar paradigms, perpetuated an image of the United States as 'different': enclosed, self-contained, isolated from cultural and intellectual currents emanating from the Old World. Isolation, indeed, was a mark of the classic 'American hero'. Exceptionalism of this kind shaped the scholarship of an early generation of critics in a disciplinary field that seemed to underwrite the politics of Cold War America. As Donald Pease has noted, 'The disciplines within the field of American Studies intersected with the United States as a geopolitical area whose boundaries field specialists were assigned at once to naturalize and police' (157).

Such a model of complicity, where literary texts are deployed to shore up and enforce a national self-image, has come under scrutiny by new conceptual orientations that resituate the United States – and the American continent more widely – in a global context. With the passing of the rigidities and binary oppositions of the Cold War, scholars began to read the Americas through different frameworks, prompted in part by developments within the academy as well as wider economic shifts: issues of migration and exchange that inform multi-cultural and postcolonial critiques, international trade in goods and ideas, the circulation of peoples and texts – all result in more fluid forms of comparative criticism. The image of the frontier as marking the outer reaches of American incorporation has been replaced by that of borders permeable to the reciprocal flow of cultures.

This shift may be regarded as an instance of an oscillation between active engagement with, and withdrawal from, the concerns of 'the world'. This has characterised the rhetoric of American history and politics at least since the Revolutionary War of Independence of 1776–83, and arguably since John Winthrop, preaching aboard the *Arabella* off the Massachusetts coast in 1630, declared the Puritans to be engaged on a mission to found a 'City on a Hill' – a pronouncement frequently cited as early evidence of American exceptionalism, but which in fact follows closely its doctrinal source in Christ's Sermon on the Mount. Despite the exceptionalist claims of earlier exponents of American Studies, American writing has always concerned itself with relations and dialogues. Even in the nineteenth century, the United States' nationalist interpretation of American culture continually competed against a transnationalist insistence that understanding of the United States can only take place in the context of a wider hemispheric or pan-American study. Recent work by Gretchen Murphy, Amy Kaplan, Felipe Fernandez-Armesto and James Dunkerley, for example, has sought to expand the geographical parameters in which the United States is located. Ralph Bauer's *The Cultural Geography of Colonial American Literatures: Empire, Travel, Modernity* (2003) argues, on the basis of comparative investigation of colonial prose narratives in Spanish and British America from 1542 to 1800, for the complete imbrication of the histories of white exploration and settlement of the Americas from the sixteenth century onwards. Anna Brickhouse, whose work is excerpted here, reminds us that 'the nation as imagined by the US writers of the dominant literary public sphere [. . .] proves uneasily tied to the larger hemisphere even in its most exceptionalist incarnations' (27).

Tempting though the neatness of a 'pendulum swing' interpretation of American self-conception might be, particular instances are always rooted in historical realities. If, in recent years, the pedagogical and institutional currency of 'Area Studies' disciplines has been progressively reshaped by an increasing critical awareness that we live in an era when national boundaries can no longer be regarded as viable categories for discrete study, this has happened in response to specific geopolitical shifts. The rise and continuing power of Atlantic civilisation has unquestionably been central to the modern world.

Complex interchanges between the Americas, Europe and Africa, with all the forces of 'global' markets and movements of people, are a fundamental feature of modern life, one that makes clear the futility of continuing with nation-based studies developed in a world whose parameters looked very different. The effects and implications of the global economy, and the communications revolution spearheaded by the internet, have resulted in the questioning of a largely Romantic and nineteenth-century idea of the nation-state as an unproblematic location of definition and character. This conception of nationhood as a culturally homogenous, organic whole with a shared language, history and environment was exemplified by the German poet and philosopher Johann Gottfried von Herder's (1744–1803) notion of *Das Volk* (meaning 'folk' or 'nation'), which contributed to the collective consciousness (*Volksgeist*) of a people.

Rather than seeing national identity in such terms, as the product of 'natural' facts such as language, soil or religion, the contemporary cultural theorist Arjun Appadurai has noted how modern nationalisms are constructed through acts of collective imagination (161; see also Anderson). They are created and sustained through narratives of belonging and affiliation that bind geographically distant peoples together. Our current global patterns of connection and interrelation suggest that the autonomously secure national space – whether defined through tangible *or* imagined characteristics – is no longer a viable category of self-definition. In a borderless world, homogeneity and singularity increasingly give way to transnational spaces of relation and hybridity that, as Paul Giles has commented, have the effect of 'pulling the circumference of national identity itself into strange "elliptical" shapes' (2002: 6). As we shall see, the implications of this for comparative literary history are profound.

The idea of the transnational is not without its critics or its troubling paradoxes: it should be asked, for example, to what extent the concept is intended to be critical of, or perhaps complicitous with, the consecration of global hegemony. To what extent does it endorse a middle-class cosmopolitanism, enfranchised to traverse national borders (Part I of the *Reader* addresses such issues)? Transnationalism may describe *both* the workings of a corporate capitalist economy *and* the projects of groups such as Amnesty International or Oxfam that are located outside of and across territorial borders. Appadurai has pointed out that transnationalism's interest in examples of mobility and circulation tends to privilege certain class, economic and racial groups. The other side of the transnational coin is an increased interest in localism, regional cultures and place-specific writing, what Rob Wilson has called 'the process of differentiation' whereby local cultures 'recognize the global design and world market and yet assert [the possibility of] alternative spaces' (11). Ecological and eco-critical perspectives often set themselves explicitly against global and transnational perspectives. Further, we must take into account instances of reactions against globalising perspectives, evident in commitment to, and renewed agitation for, nationalism and religious exceptionalism across the world from the Middle East to Europe to the United States itself.

There has been significant recent work, particularly by historians, on the fractal movements and rhizomorphic exchanges around the 'Atlantic rim': Bernard Bailyn's long-running Atlantic History seminar at Harvard has established the field in Historical Studies; also in 1997 the Ford Foundation, under its 'Crossing Borders: Revitalizing Area Studies' initiative, awarded Duke University $50,000 for its 'Oceans Connect' project. An important volume to emerge from the Harvard seminar was David Armitage and Michael J. Braddick's edited collection *The British Atlantic World, 1500–1800*. Armitage's essay in this volume advances 'Three Concepts of Atlantic History' (15), as follows:

1. *Circum*-Atlantic history – the transnational history of the Atlantic world.
2. *Trans*-Atlantic history – the international history of the Atlantic world.
3. *Cis*-Atlantic history – national or regional history within an Atlantic context.

In this *Reader*, we use the term 'Transatlantic' to encompass elements of all three of these categories, with specifically literary reference. The 'triangular trade' between Africa, Europe and the Americas of slavery, for example, or 'Oceanic' studies, have generated a vocabulary of circulation, flow, movement which has proved useful to some authors we include.

Transatlantic Studies draws attention to the ways in which, within the discipline of American Studies, ideas of crossing and connection have helped to rethink the ways that national identity has been formulated. The essays selected in this volume explore culture according to an explicitly intercultural, comparative perspective; their focus on reciprocal cultural exchange opens up the assumptions upon which national identity, and the critical paradigms it has fostered, are founded. The work brought together here suggests that the relationship between text and context, subject and nation, indeed nation and nation, is not transparent, but is rather refracted and distorted, transformed and made strange, by confluence. Points of intersection between Atlantic cultures and such processes as creolisation, hybridity and translation help to reveal how cultures have been reworked and reinscribed by the transatlantic movement of people, ideas and cultural artefacts.

Transatlantic *Literary* Studies, the particular concern of this volume, is the sub-field that concerns itself explicitly with transatlantic texts and comparisons. Cultural transatlanticism is, on the one hand, much discussed in relation to trans- and post-nationalist political and cultural studies, while on the other, comparative practice in transatlantic literary studies has to date been relatively unreflective about its methods and assumptions. What sort of models might be available for this new field of transatlantic literary studies? These are some of the issues that the editors hope to address through the establishment of the STAR (Scotland's Transatlantic Relations) seminar, and their editorship of the new Edinburgh Series in Transatlantic Literatures. The *Transatlantic Literary Studies Reader* is the first volume to bring together examples of the critical and theoretical models that have influenced and continue to define this rapidly expanding field; it offers a range of instances of comparative thinking that focuses some of these questions about literary history. As a geographic area, a location of material and economic exchange, and a metaphor for the transmission of aesthetic and ideological forms, the 'transatlantic' is an important framework through which literary texts can be explored. The *Reader* is structured around a series of theoretical and thematic groupings which combine internal coherence in helping to define available angles of approach, with an open-ended relation to one another. The arrangement creates a fluidity in the juxtaposition that allows individual excerpts to reflect upon each other to create a continuous dialogue. In this way, the *Reader* both selects important examples of what transatlantic literary criticism looks like, and offers a model for the kinds of plurality instantiated in transatlantic literature itself. It shows how theoretical paradigms drawn from comparative literature, postcolonial studies, and travel and translation studies are able to contribute interpretative possibilities to the field. Our selection allows students and academics to chart some of these contours as they have shaped the ways in which we continue to read literature. It is not a digest or a 'state of the art' compilation, but rather a rigorous selection drawn from a large body of disparate material in books, chapters and scholarly articles, chosen for their particular suggestiveness and resonance; one criterion for inclusion was whether the piece could be useful in providing a conceptual paradigm to someone looking at a different text or from another perspective. To this end, not all of our selections address the 'transatlantic' specifically; but we hope that each has the potential to generate connections and exchanges for those working in the field. Wellek and Warren, for example, are included for their classic and succinct statement of comparative literary theory, while Deleuze and Guattari's celebrated image of the rhizome exemplifies a way of 'thinking across' which seems singularly suggestive for transatlantic critical comparison.

The focus and criteria that shape this *Reader* are primarily textual rather than historical or political. We have sought indicative examples of major trends and approaches that seem to offer important models for the practice of transatlantic literary critique. Cosmopolitanism, for example, which is touched on in the first section, is a large subject with its own huge literature and extensive points of contact with other fields, such as comparative literature and translation studies.

David Simpson's fine essay 'The Limits of Cosmopolitanism and the Case for Translation', excerpted here, mounts a strong argument for an intrinsic relationship between a cosmopolitan viewpoint and a multi-lingual perspective. The case for literary cosmopolitanism is also implicit in the work of Pascale Casanova, J. Hillis Miller and Edward Said, to cite just three critics whose work is included in the volume. Inevitably, space constraints mean that many roads have not been taken; these include much pertinent work in interdisciplinary, material, sociological, anthropological and cultural studies. However, some selections included themselves draw heavily on other disciplines and we hope will help to point out further possibilities to the reader. Michel de Certeau's account of Jean de Léry's travels in Brazil borrows from the discourse of social anthropology; Casanova is indebted to Pierre Bourdieu's analyses of material culture; and Wai Chee Dimock's essay is conscious of the work of comparative linguistics in its account of 'deep time'. These disciplinary crossings are indicative of our wider concern to suggest the possibilities for intellectual and aesthetic migration that are inherent in the transatlantic paradigm.

While acknowledging the widened geographical and discursive parameters of Transatlantic Studies, it would be foolish to suggest that the nation-state, an organising political and ideological entity, has been made redundant in the rush to embrace global flows. As John Carlos Rowe puts it in the selection included here, 'imagining communities other than the nation is difficult, in part because of the powerful grip of nationalist rhetoric on our theoretical models, intellectual methods, and educational institutions'. His retrospective perspective calls our attention to the ways in which 'the national form is indeed compelling, perhaps even compulsive, not because it is inherent or natural to human beings – it is of recent invention – but because its history is so much a part of us'. The transatlantic literary space, then, represents the textual collision of the 'integral' nation and those forces – material, ideological or aesthetic – that resist or distort the authority of the national imaginary. Rowe's account helps to move us from the broader concerns of Cultural Studies towards some of the more particular issues confronting the practice of literary history in a transatlantic context.

Literary history as a chronological procession of writers and works, where ancestors and descendants slot neatly into succession, was an innovation of Enlightened progressive historiography, focused through an individualistic Romantic lens. As we noted above with Herder, ideas about the 'natural' or 'authentic' voice of a *volk* – narratives of national origins, in a word – gave particular contexts for individual works and writers. The concept of the nation, Claudio Guillén reminds us, 'regarded . . . as an organic whole, growing and developing in history, became the all-embracing principle of unity' in the nineteenth century (5). At the same time, interest in comparing national literary cultures at similar (or indeed different) 'stages of development' on this progressive march, was instrumental in the foundation of a new discipline, Comparative Literature. 'Comp. Lit.' used to be based in 'influence' studies of a very empirical kind; its presuppositions and expectations were initially drawn from the same Romantic cultural politics of northern Europe. Influence was, more often than not, taken to be demonstrable on the basis of library borrowings, citations, reviews, or other externally documented forms of 'literary relation'. The 'influence' story assumes hierarchical forms of connection that answer to a politically- and culturally-inflected historicism, in which a dominant (prior) position exerts power and imposes uniformity on a subdued other. The notion of literary influence has been in question at least since Henri Peyre's (influential) call for its re-appraisal in 1952; Hans Jauss's perception that literary history needs to be understood in terms of 'dialogue as well as process' would seem to lend itself well to transatlantic literary studies, which are sadly impoverished when formulated in terms of one-way influence, or reception (8). All are versions of a purposeful narrative with a teleological thrust; the national imperative is embodied in the historical method, and vice versa.

How may transatlantic literary history be released from the 'national narrative' of traditional literary history? What sort of model might enable an explicitly comparative historical critique that does not resort to the critical short-circuit of 'influence', or documentation of unexamined 'literary relations'? One possibility is offered by Dimock's essay 'Deep Time', excerpted here, which proposes a means of relating American literature to world history and of reconstructing its literary relations in a historicised but transnational context. 'Deep Time', in her words, 'produces a map that, thanks to its receding horizons, its backward extension into far-flung temporal and spatial coordinates, must depart significantly from a map predicated on the short life of the US'. Dimock's assertion that 'neither a single nation nor a single race can yield an adequate frame for literary history' is one of the working assumptions on which this *Reader* proceeds. But 'Deep Time' by itself cannot show us how to 'do' literary history transatlantically or transversely. Its insights may be supplemented by Paul Giles, who in the essay excerpted below describes a 'spatial turn' in literary studies. His terminology draws on recent developments in geographical studies, in which geographers have drawn attention to how space and place are constructed as much as they are discovered. In 1992 the 500th anniversary of Columbus's 'discovery' of America was marked by the publication of works arguing for recognition of the ways in which America – indeed the Americas – have historically been invented by Europeans for their own purposes and corresponding to their own expectations, a position previously argued by the Irish-Mexican historian Edmundo O'Gorman, in *The Invention of America: An Inquiry into the Historical Nature of the New World and the Meaning of its History* (1958). More recently, Anthony Pagden, a political theorist of empire, has written on European encounters with America from the

Renaissance to Romantic period, as well as a series of comparative studies of relationships between the peoples of Europe and those of the Atlantic and Pacific. Postmodern geography has advanced this relational agenda; as Doreen Massey notes,

> An understanding of the relational nature of space has been accompanied by arguments about the relational construction of the identity of place. If place is a product of practices, trajectories, interrelations, if we make space through interactions at all levels from the (so-called) local to the (so-called) global, then those spatial identities such as places, regions, nations, and the local and the global, must be forged in this relational way too, as internally complex, essentially unboundable in any absolute sense, and inevitably historically changing. (Quoted in Hones and Leyda: 1024).

Transnational cultural and political studies have built in various ways on such insights to move beyond single centre analysis. Their potential in helping to formulate transatlantic literary theory is apparent in several of our selections, including those of Gross, Rowe and Pease in Part I; critical demonstrations of their implications at the level of texts remain sparse, though they are implicitly at work in, for example, James Snead's vocabulary of the mutual 'contagion' of literary traditions encountering one another. Instrumental, too, has been postcolonialism's attempts to deal with what one of its foundational texts refers to as 'the problems of transmuting time into space, with the present struggling out of the past' (Ashcroft, Griffiths and Tiffin; 36). In this domain, Homi Bhabha's work has been immensely influential in signalling the ways in which colonial discourses are never perfectly achieved; instead, they are constantly hybridised by an inevitable relation of reciprocity with the colonial subject, such that a pure opposition between master and slave is impossible. The imaginative possibilities of relational identity have been explored by the Anglo-Guyanese writer Wilson Harris. Harris advocates literary relations that exercise a 'cross-cultural imagination' resistant to the kind of imperial homogeneity that 'tends to become an organ of conquest and division because of *imposed* unity that actually subsists on the suppression of others'. Instead of the artificial stasis of imperialism, he traces the 'cross-cultural capacity' of a literary text to sound 'the ceaseless dialogue it inserts between hardened conventions and eclipsed or halfeclipsed otherness, within an intuitive self that moves endlessly into flexible patterns, arcs or bridges of community' (xviii).

Transatlantic Studies is by nature eclectic; the literatures of the Caribbean, Canada and California have all been shown to benefit from a transatlantic approach. Although it is not practical in an anthology such as this to include material in languages other than English, some of our selections are themselves translations, and the section devoted to models made available from within Translation Studies indicate the inseparability of transatlantic literary studies from language studies. They share, after all, a common root term. At least as far back as the early seventeenth-century Puritan conversion narratives, the physical crossing of the Atlantic itself was the overwhelming, compounded agent and image of a comparative perspective. The Latin *transeo, transpire*, meaning to go over, cross, pass over, gives rise to *Translatio* which is not only the root term for translation but has a long pedigree to indicate a cultural transferring, handing over from one location to another. In 1787, with the outcome of the Revolutionary War which would establish the separate existence of America still uncertain, Thomas Jefferson suggested some 'doubt . . . whether nature has enlisted herself as a Cis- or Trans-Atlantic partisan' (189). Process, not state, is at issue. Jefferson's 'doubt' embeds the political and moral questions surrounding the patriot case within a much older rhetorical formula: the classical trope of *translatio studii et imperii*, which decreed that virtues flee a decadent civilisation for a simpler, regenerate one. The trope comprehended originality – newness – and authority; it encompassed linguistic translation, too, understood as skilful weaving of recognised (authoritative) patterns and elements into a new web of relationships (as discussed further in Part IV). Eighteenth-century observers of shifting relationships between Europe and her transatlantic colonies renewed the assumption of the *translatio* that civilisation consistently migrates from East to West. This is the thinking behind Jefferson's revolutionary 'doubt': would 'Nature' make the transatlantic crossing, to seal the victory for America and smooth the transport of Empire and cultural authority? The crossing here clearly implies the furtherance of imperial hierarchy and subordinative relation. By 1837, when Emerson delivered his Phi Beta Kappa address 'The American Scholar', which opens with a sweeping transitive panorama from Ancient Greece to the medieval troubadours, and from modern Europe to the here-and-now of America, the question of influence, which privileges origin and priority, has been transformed into a metaphor of relationships conceived spatially: 'What is nature to [the American Scholar]? There is never a beginning, there is never an end, to the inexplicable continuity of this web of God, but always circular power returning into itself' (85).

'The American Scholar' initiates a stylistics of comparison conceptualised spatially, horizontally. 'Transatlantic' and 'transcendental' are semantically imbricated through the common crossing root 'trans-'; a much older tradition of rhetorical analysis acquired new associations. The stylistic ramifications of this trope pervade American Romantic writing, as Tony Tanner shows in his 'Notes Towards a Comparison of British and American Romanticism', included here. It has, as he suggests, implications not only for a particular comparison of American and British Romanticism but perhaps some potential for a wider stylistics of comparison based in 'thinking across'. The excerpt in Part III from Peter Hulme's book *Colonial Encounters* represents an important example of what this kind of comparative, traversing criticism might look like. Since Leo

Marx's *The Machine in the Garden* (1964), Shakespeare's *The Tempest* has borne the soubriquet 'Shakespeare's American play'. In a detailed argument that engages with the Americanness of the work, Hulme picks up the term 'congener' to bring together texts that, without requiring justification of anteriority, or standing in an influential relation to one another, nevertheless may offer some purchase to a transatlantic literary history. Hulme's reading advances the possibility of reading across texts, transatlantically, without requiring the empirical or inter-textual evidence of relationship.

The Latin *translatio* is, in Greek, *metaphora* (*meta*: over, *phereia*: to carry). In Rhetoric (the study of the art of language use), the figure of metaphor traditionally embodied the 'handing across or over' of meaning. The excerpt from Eric Cheyfitz's book that we include in Part V develops the possibilities of metaphor as a structuring term for transatlantic critical comparison, and its relation to translation. Loss of confidence in the adequacy of the 'influence' story has fostered a general mistrust in transatlantic literary studies of texts as highly organised verbal artefacts; most recent work tends towards comparative cultural history that analyses texts in terms of context and situation, or deconstructs them to 'reveal' the ideological predeterminations of form. These strategies simply reproduce the structure of implied priorities and progressions. The selection included in Part V, with the additional list of further reading, brings together some suggestive examples of work that has attempted to rethink or move past this dilemma. Nonetheless, this kind of approach – crucial for a mature transatlantic *literary* studies – is perhaps, to date, the least well developed of those represented here.

One of the questions addressed in Part V is whether, and how, genre 'travels': what sorts of deformation or transformation are observable, and what critical conclusions may be drawn from the comparison. Travel literature and theory offers a variety of approaches to transatlantic literary studies, as Mary Baine Campbell's survey of the field, reprinted in our section on 'Travel' (Part VI), attests. Most obviously, travel insists on the inevitability of comparative criticism; to inhabit an unfamiliar space triggers estimations of affinity and/or dissonance. William Stowe's account of American nineteenth-century tour guides of European destinations suggests some of the strategies by which geographical difference might be accommodated into forms of textual stability. From Columbus's first accounts of the 'New World', transatlantic texts have rewritten alterity into the reassuring tropes and vocabularies of home. This kind of linguistic colonisation (also central to Part III of the *Reader*) is usefully complicated by Mary Louise Pratt's notion of travel as 'transculturation', in which the reciprocities of encounter are emphasised: travel allows for the establishment of zones of contact, permeable spaces that resist the conventional containers of identity.

Pratt's deliberately hybridised concept of the self, as prone to contagion and distortion, stands opposed to the Romantic model of agency and causality. As a governing principle of individual expression, as well as of literary historical narrative, it offered a rationale for evolutionary progression. Cutting into this mythological structure of self-authentication, Joseph Roach's study of transatlantic performance, excerpted in Part V, describes how 'improvised narratives of authenticity and priority' solidify into 'full blown myths of legitimacy and origin' in response to anxieties provoked by surrogation or substitution in the processes of cultural continuity. Faced with the spectre of their own obsolescence, Roach proposes, cultures like individuals attempt to reify their position. If the relationship between 'old' and 'new' is one of surrogation, their performance in relation to one another is crucial to any analysis. Roach's suggestive comment that 'performances . . . often carry within them the memory of otherwise forgotten substitutions' suggests how textual analysis may elucidate and reconstruct a historical relationship in dynamic form:

> The key to understanding how performances worked *within* a culture . . . is to illuminate the process of surrogation as it operated *between* the participating cultures. The key, in other words, is to understand how circum-Atlantic societies, confronted with revolutionary circumstances for which few precedents existed, have invented themselves by performing their pasts in the presence of others.

The performance of the past in the presence of others: this suggests, in a trans- or circum-Atlantic context, a renegotiated relationship between the two terms of our compound – the history in the literary as much as the literary in the history. At least as important, it multiplies the possible trajectories in which narratives are read, and construed (as J. Hillis Miller notes in Part II). The process of comparison elicits mutual self-definition, and undoes automatic assumptions of priority. But, as Roach makes clear, these mutually defining performances of difference can only be understood in relation to the conditions of an earlier performance: in a historicised framework, in other words.

What, then, might 'transatlantic literary theory' look like? For a start, as this introduction has implied and as all the selections that follow confirm, it neither could, nor should be, singular. The bipolarities and multiple possibilities that Modernist critics such as Edmund Wilson and F. O. Matthiessen found to constitute American Literature between the 1920s and 1940s refract and propagate themselves in a transatlantic framework. The key terms that resonate from the excerpts in this *Reader* – rhizome, congener, contagion, surrogation, translation, metaphor, web, network, circulation, flow – have in common assumptions about relation, and a framework of comparison, implicit or explicit. Beyond that, they suggest possibilities rather than prescriptions. Our aim has been to bring together a stimulating combination of possible ways of 'reading transatlantically'; the reader may focus on one kind of approach, or navigate across them, and the *Reader* will have served its purpose if it provokes further responses to literary texts that are alive to their ceaseless overlapping, intersection and convergence.

A word about the selection. In the interests of surveying as wide a range of approaches as possible, no writer is excerpted more than once in the *Reader*; within this, we have attempted to represent both the spectrum of possibilities in the field, and their most persuasive exponents. In the interests of focus (and because not to have done so would have produced an unworkably large anthology), we have in most cases chosen to excerpt particularly relevant selections from longer pieces which in their entirety do not necessarily offer the pointed and suggestive terminology and approaches we have sought. While we have endeavoured, in making our selections, not to misrepresent the original, in every case the reader is urged to seek out the complete text from which an extract is taken, in order to gain the full force and context of the author's argument. The introduction to each part attempts to contextualise the selections and indicate connections between excerpts. The introductions offer some examples of how we hope readers might approach the selection. We would stress, though, that these are intended to be indicative rather than prescriptive. The brief list of further reading which follows each section is again not intended to be exhaustive; each title has been chosen because we regard it as a foundational or key text in the particular area. This *Reader*, finally, is intended as itself the first half of a dialogue between theory and practice, the present and the past. It is to be followed by an anthology of primary sources that exemplify the transatlantic perspectives outlined here.

FURTHER READING

American Literary History 18.2 (2006) [a special issue devoted to the relationship between transnationalism and literary history].

Anderson, Benedict (1983; rev. edn 1991) *Imagined Communities: Reflections on the Origin and Spread of Nationalism*. London and New York: Verso.

Appadurai, Arjun (1996) *Modernity at Large: Cultural Dimensions of Globalization*. Minneapolis: University of Minneapolis Press.

Armitage, David and Michael J. Braddick (eds) (2002), *The British Atlantic World, 1500–1800*. Basingstoke: Palgrave.

Ashcroft, Bill, Gareth Griffiths and Helen Tiffin (1989; 2nd edn 2002) *The Empire Writes Back: Theory and Practice in Post-Colonial Literatures*. London: Routledge.

Beer, Janet and Bridget Bennett (eds) (2002) *Special Relationships: Anglo-American Affinities and Antagonisms, 1854–1939*. Manchester: Manchester University Press.

Bhabha, Homi K. (1994) *The Location of Culture*. London: Routledge.

Bauer, Ralph (2003) *The Cultural Geography of Colonial American Literatures: Empire, Travel, Modernity*. Cambridge: Cambridge University Press.

Brickhouse, Anna (2004) *Transamerican Literary Relations and the Nineteenth-Century Public Sphere*. Cambridge: Cambridge University Press.

Cutler, Edward S. (2003) *Recovering the New: Transatlantic Roots of Modernism*. Hanover, NH: University Press of New England.

Dunkerley, James (2000) *Americana: The Americas in the World, Around 1850*. London: Verso.

Emerson, Ralph Waldo (1985) *Selected Essays*, ed. Larzar Ziff. London: Penguin Books.

Fernandez-Armesto, Felipe (2003) *The Americas: The History of a Hemisphere*. London: Weidenfeld & Nicolson.

Giles, Paul (2001) *Transatlantic Insurrections: British Culture and the Formation of American Literature, 1730–1860*. Philadelphia: University of Pennsylvania Press.

Giles, Paul (2002) *Virtual Americas: Transnational Fictions and the Transatlantic Imaginary*. Durham: Duke University Press.

Guillén, Claudio (1971) *Literature as System: Essays Toward a Theory of Literary History*. Princeton: Princeton University Press.

Harris, Wilson (1983) *The Womb of Space: The Cross-Cultural Imagination*. Westport: Greenwood.

Hones, Sheila and Julia Leyda (2005) 'Geographies of American Studies', *American Quarterly* 57.4: 1019–32.

Jauss, Hans (1970) 'Literary History as a Challenge to Literary Theory', *New Literary History* 2.1: 7–37.

Jefferson, Thomas (1984) *Writings*. New York: Library of America.

Kaplan, Amy (2002) *The Anarchy of Empire in the Making of US Culture*. Cambridge, MA: Harvard University Press.

Macpherson, Heidi Slettedahl and Will Kaufman (eds) (2002) *New Perspectives in Transatlantic Studies*. New York: University Press of America.

Murphy, Gretchen (2005) *Hemispheric Imaginings: The Monroe Doctrine and Narratives of U.S. Empire*. Durham: Duke University Press.

Noble, David W. (2002) *Death of a Nation: American Culture and the End of Exceptionalism*. Minneapolis: University of Minnesota Press.

Pease, Donald E. (2002) 'C. L. R. James, *Moby-Dick*, and the Emergence of Transnational American Studies', in Pease and Robyn Wiegman (eds), *The Futures of American Studies*. Durham: Duke University Press, pp. 135–63.

Peyre, Henri (1952) 'A Glance at Comparative Literature in America', *Yearbook of Comparative and General Literature* 1: 1–8.

Verhoeven, W. M. and Beth Dolan Kautz (eds) (1999) *Revolutions and Watersheds: Transatlantic Dialogues, 1775–1815*. Amsterdam: Rodopi.

Wilson, Rob (2000) *Reimagining the American Pacific: From South Pacific to Bamboo Ridge and Beyond*. Durham: Duke University Press.

PART I
THE NATION AND COSMOPOLITANISM

THE NATION AND COSMOPOLITANISM: INTRODUCTION

Nations, and in particular the nation-state, are as categories largely the invention of a Romantic interest in origins and the organic integrity of identified groups. They tend to be imaged as monolithic, static entities with characteristic or essential features which may be compared (or more usually contrasted) with those of others, but are rarely affected by them. To imagine the transatlantic, on the other hand, is to conceive of spatial practices as dynamic and unfolding; it is to posit both a geographical area and an intellectual arena in which material and conceptual goods circulate and are exchanged. The prefix 'trans-' points at movement across and over conventional or expected categories, so that to speak of the 'transnational' in the context of transatlantic studies, as some of the critics in this section do, begins to conceptualise literary analysis beyond the bounded framing of national traditions. What happens when one nation's texts, attitudes, prejudices, modes of interpretation and generic expectations are brought into contact with a different national set? What is essentially – or 'purely' – English about English literature, or exceptionally American about writing from the United States? Randolph Bourne's coinage of the term 'transnational' in 1916 to characterise an American identity formed through the hybrid collation of diverse peoples anticipates current concerns to revise the essentialised status of the nation as the source and site of legitimate personhood. Transatlantic literary studies re-opens the assumptions underlying nationally-bounded literary histories by trying to show how the writing produced from within a particular national tradition is inevitably implicated in a network of *trans*-national choices and influences. By locating texts in wider networks of engagement, it is possible to uncover the often distorting strategies by which a particular idea of the nation-state is articulated and enforced. As Paul Giles notes here, 'in a world of transnational mobility and spatial dislocation, no enclosed community – neither university nor region nor nation – can define itself in a separatist manner'.

Benedict Anderson, in his influential 1983 book *Imagined Communities*, describes the manner in which national identities become constructed around certain powerful fictions of belonging or affinity. The conjunction of 'nation and narration' (a phrase made current by an influential collection edited by the postcolonial critic Homi Bhabha) is thus central to modern concepts of collective affiliation; in a special number of *Modern Fiction Studies* devoted to 'National and Postnational Narratives', Donald Pease identifies different kinds of stories told by postcolonialism and globalisation about nations in their 'postnational' state. His article, excerpted below, exemplifies the highly abstract discourse often employed by postnational theorists, as it describes the 'site' in between the nation and the state 'traversed by multiple and heterogeneous acts of narration' which may either accommodate or resist their global contexts. Pease implies that a sentimental fiction (or 'illusion') lurks at the heart of arguments such as Anderson's which read the nation as the product of individually and collectively imagined desire: for him (and, he believes, inherent in postcolonialism), national narrative is always a political instrument of state. Pease's dense discussion of the 'metanarrative aspects' of national narration will benefit from being read in conjunction with the postcolonial work excerpted in the following section. Their potential for transatlantic study might lie firstly in questioning the covert ideologies inherent in 'national' or exceptionalist literary histories; subsequently in its discussion of how such ideologies become naturalised and embedded as authentic through a collusive (imagined) relationship between nation and narrativity – stories always tell stories of nationality and national identity – and thirdly in raising questions of ownership: who is included and who excluded in such accounts, whether national or postnational in their perspectives (a point also taken up in Appadurai's argument that the international markets and free movement of people associated with globalisation are in fact available to a tiny minority of the world's population).

By focusing on the Atlantic, with its emphasis on mobility and migration, Transatlantic Studies challenges the security of static and bordered spaces of all kinds, none more so than the defining authority of the nation. Rethinking the geography in which literary study is undertaken, the critics selected here develop a scholarly practice that is *relational* rather than *territorial*, showing how the diverse networks of travel, exchange and contact entail new and diverse ways of imagining space, place, and identity. This is not to deny the continuing power of the nation-state as an organising structure: even if 'imagined', national affiliation continues to provide a focus for political, cultural and affective attachment. But, as Lawrence Buell has argued, nations display a combination of strength and redundancy that provokes interesting literary questions of affiliation and disjunction, sympathy and resistance. Nations, he writes, are 'utopian social fictions that are at once epistemologically suspect, economically obsolete, politically potent (since world order continues to recognize the sovereign nation as primary unit), territorially determinate (except in wartime), and culturally porous' (89). The contributions in this section explore the theoretical, literary and material implications of national formations that are residually and strategically powerful, yet are also simultaneously challenged by modes of encounter that highlight the contingency of that power.

Each extract locates aspects of literature or literary history in an expanded geographical space that unsettles the assumptions of the national imaginary. Claudia Stokes's article examines the transatlantic relationship from the perspective of the nineteenth-century campaign to institute an international copyright law that would protect English-language authors from pirated reprinting on both sides of the Atlantic. Stokes reads the history of this legislation – not passed until 1891, and therefore a huge issue in transatlantic literary relations throughout the nineteenth century – as providing the ground for opposed nationalistic perceptions of the authorial role: aristocratic and leisured in Britain, democratic and populist in the United States. 'In depicting themselves in conflict with Britain', she argues, 'American writers were able to reposition themselves in this dyad as the abused victims of a literary aristocracy'. The political desire for an equitable flow of intellectual goods, she points out, was tied to powerful reconstructions of literary history that affirmed 'the narrative and reperformance of American victory over Britain [. . .] A culture predicated on pedigree and Old World sympathies in conflict with a culture characterized by self-invention and self-creation'. The battle over copyright fed into the institutionalisation of a literary nationalism that, Stokes notes, was detached from the complex transnational exchanges that actually exemplified Anglo-American relationships at the turn of the century: in fact – as the correspondences of Thomas Carlyle and Ralph Waldo Emerson, and Walter Scott and Washington Irving; or Charles Dickens's *American Notes*, make clear – the battle for international protection of intellectual property brought writers on both sides of the Atlantic into mutual alliance against their respective national legislatures. Her essay is important for reminding us of the ideological as well as the political implications of the material exchange of literature.

Robert Gross's essay explores at a more theoretical level the features of a transnational world in which communication, trade and travel are performed seemingly without regard for national borders. While aware of the parameters of class, race/ethnicity and gender that determine (and might restrict) these possibilities of movement, Gross advocates the cosmopolitan sensibility of the transnational citizen. The 'outward-looking mood' of transnationalism, he suggests, generates 'rich resources for the voluntary fabrication of personal and social identities', identities that might resist the grand national narratives of exceptionalism and manifest destiny. John Carlos Rowe, in his essay, examines more closely the effects of transnational identity in the United States of the nineteenth century, a period 'when the nation and its sustaining, often generative imperialisms were the dominant forms of state organization'. For Rowe, the American transnational impulse at this time was imperial in its mission, seeking simultaneously to purify the nation internally of its Old Word vestiges and to expand beyond its geographical limits so that 'the borderlands of the United States are narratively imagined as requiring national incorporation for their realization as civilized or even natural'. He argues that the cosmopolitan authority of literary Transcendentalism (represented by figures such as Emerson) underwrote political projects of expansion such as the Mexican-American War – itself an indirect exemplification of powerful transformations of British and German Romantic ideologies that belies the national insularity of ideas. His essay is a useful reminder of the impulse to colonise that lies behind the exceptionalist agendas of the nineteenth century, where national self-definition is perpetuated through the negation of those elements of difference and strangeness that might threaten it.

Giles expands upon this idea in his essay, reminding us that one of the effects of situating American literature in a global perspective is to estrange those native discourses of manifest destiny and the 'Emersonian rhetoric of idealism that has worked consistently to underpin and institutionalize it'. Transatlantic literary study works instead to undermine the cherished shibboleths of national self-definition, whether American or European, eroding the sense of the nation as 'a privileged and protected space'. Giles is wary of proclaiming the demise of the nation in favour of the freedoms of transnational flow (he reminds us that globalisation has been seen as 'an extrapolation and sublimation of United States interests'); instead his essay focuses on those 'points of intersection' (at which the local might meet the global) 'where cultural conflict is lived out experientially'.

Cultural conflict of another kind is the subject of Pascale Casanova's piece, excerpted from her book *The World Republic of Letters*. She maps national literary traditions as sites of competing influence and shifting authority. With the emergence of the nation-state, literature is marshalled into a series of cultural battles that underscore a country's political dominance. Casanova, however, imagines 'the world of letters' as operating somewhat apart from the constricting and confining demands of political appropriation; hers is a *textual* space of contestation, one of 'incessant struggle and competition over the very nature of literature itself', that establishes forms of connection, distortion and migration as the literary history travels across and between geographical spaces. Even the most located of texts, she suggests, is defined – and to a degree deformed – by other national traditions in which it is read: literature never inhabits positions of pure autonomy. Later in her book, for example, Casanova focuses on how William Faulkner, the novelist of a rural American South, 'travels' to Spain, Algeria and Latin America, where his aesthetic and political concerns are put to different kinds of work. Casanova's taxonomy of national traditions inevitably caught in a nexus of competing *inter*-national forces points to the degree to which literary histories need to expand their parameters beyond the borders of the carefully delimited nation-state.

Elsewhere in *The World Republic of Letters* Casanova looks at the figure of the cosmopolitan as the purveyor of the fruits of international exchange. Rooted in the Greek Stoic ideal of world citizenship, exemplified in the Enlightenment ideal of the cultured traveller (see Part VI below), and central to the mobility of transatlantic cultures, cosmopolitanism has become an important term in discussions of intellectual and aesthetic connection. The figure of the cosmopolitan remains compelling because of the ways in which it tests parameters of belonging and identity, asking us to consider where the highest value resides – with the individual, the group, the nation, or the world. David Simpson's article details the contested nature of the term (its oscillation between connotations of detached sophistication and middle-class cultural tourism) and points out its imbrication with issues of translation (see Part IV below); drawing examples largely from Romantic poetry, he highlights the extent to which a cosmopolitan politics is intertwined with a national one that both regulates and is challenged by it: 'Cosmopolitanism is neither local/national or international, but both at once. The citizen of a town, a department, a country, is and is not a citizen of the world'. This denial of pure positioning, as Paul Giles's article also suggests, produces texts in which the national is always in a dynamic and dialectical relationship with that which lies beyond its borders. To situate a literary text in this more fluid and expansive sphere of influence is to be sensitive to how style and ideology might compete to unsettle the reading experience.

Amy Kaplan and Nina Gerassi-Navarro uncover the career of just such a cosmopolitan figure in their reading of Frances Calderón de la Barca and her work *Life in Mexico* (1843). Scottish-born and married to Spain's first minister in independent Mexico, Calderón was positioned amid three imperial systems – British, Spanish and American – allowing her to emerge 'as a migrating subject between these multiple and often conflicting frames'. Kaplan and Gerassi-Navarro's essay sets out to complicate the binary transatlanticism of European and North American connection; instead the authors consider the role that a decolonising Latin America has in relation both to the established empires of Europe and to the burgeoning and expansive imperialism of the United States. Calderón's cosmopolitan observer is located within a triangulated geometry perfectly in tune with her own 'lack of a distinct nationality and equal lack of conformity to the role of "lady traveler"'. The kind of relational geography that Kaplan and Gerassi-Navarro explore produces a dynamic transatlantic space that generates cosmopolitan sympathy for the instabilities and pluralities of place, and an awareness of the forces producing and distorting narratives of nationhood.

FURTHER READING

Anderson, Benedict (1983) *Imagined Communities: Reflections on the Origins and Spread of Nationalism*. London: Verso.

Appadurai, Arjun (1996) *Modernity at Large: Cultural Dimensions of Globalization*. Minneapolis: University of Minneapolis Press.

Bhabha, Homi (ed.) (1990) *Nation and Narration*. London: Routledge.

Bourne, Randolph (1916) 'Trans-National America', *Atlantic Monthly* 118 (July): 86–97.

Brennan, Timothy (1997) *At Home in the World: Cosmopolitanism Now*. Cambridge, MA: Harvard University Press.

Buell, Lawrence (1996) 'Are We Post-American Studies?', in Marjorie Garber et al. (eds) *Field Work: Sites in Literary and Cultural Studies*. New York: Routledge, pp. 87–93.

Cheah, Pheng and Bruce Robbins (eds) (1998) *Cosmopolitics: Thinking and Feeling Beyond the Nation*. Minneapolis: University of Minnesota Press.

Giles, Paul (2001) *Transatlantic Insurrections: British Culture and the Formation of American Literature, 1730–1860*. Philadelphia: University of Pennsylvania Press.

I

'COPYRIGHTING AMERICAN HISTORY: INTERNATIONAL COPYRIGHT AND THE PERIODIZATION OF THE NINETEENTH CENTURY'

Claudia Stokes

Between 1868 and 1891, writers across genres and even – in the terms of Parrington's* periodization – literary periods participated in concentrated activism in support of international copyright legislation. American domestic copyright laws, instituted in 1790, preserved an author's rights only within the nation's boundaries and neither protected the American author from unauthorized reprinting abroad nor guarded foreign authors from piracy within the United States. Without international protection, English-language writers on both sides of the Atlantic complained of unauthorized reprintings not bound by law to pay royalties; of the frequency and license with which pirates made changes to their writings, even altering endings and adding characters; and of having their names attached to ghostwritten books. After a few false starts before the Civil War, the copyright movement emerged as a fully organized campaign just a few scant years after the war ended. Writers as diverse as Twain, Oliver Wendell Holmes, Henry James, E. P. Roe, and Edmund Stedman were active members of the American Copyright League, which counted over seven hundred members and presided over a lengthy campaign that included petitions, boycotts, and lobbying. Writers testified before Congress, contributed to public readings, signed petitions, and wrote scores of testimonials and essays describing the injustices of

From *American Literature* 77.2 (June 2005): 291–317.

international piracy and detailing the moral, literary, and national benefits of international protection.

[. . .]

The copyright movement was perhaps the most important institutional sponsor of the production of literary history in the period. [. . .] [It] was exceedingly contentious, largely due to the outrage that often met authors' appeals; it was assumed that they were either already wealthy or came from the patrician class. The publication of any essay on authors' rights was sure to bring an outpouring of letters arguing opposing positions. Even activists in favor of international copyright were known to argue with each other, as the lengthy quarrel between [Thomas] Lounsbury and Henry C. Lea published in the *New York Tribune* in 1884 attests. But writing literary history seems to have provided copyright activists with a respite from such arguments and the threat of dueling in the press. In fact, activists quickly exhausted argument as a vehicle for the movement, so there are relatively few solely argumentative writings in the copyright archives. Instead, the vast majority of work published on the copyright question in the 1880s is limited to the recitation of data: histories of copyright, myriad reprints of the texts of copyright bills, and bibliographies of publications on copyright. These works allowed activists to keep the copyright movement in the public eye while avoiding the inevitable disagreements that threatened to make their efforts seem subjective and morally indefinite. This is not to suggest that the many literary histories published in support of copyright are without argument; rather, as one of the strategies by which activists were able to circumvent bitter public quarrels, the medium of literary history allowed argument to pass under the radar of detractors with ready pens.

This collateral benefit aside, literary history chiefly allowed writers to circumvent the ire of a public unsympathetic to the financial pleas of a constituency they believed to be aristocratic. Literary history, that is, proved instrumental in bridging class divisions that had interfered with public support of copyright protections for so long. Brander Matthews's telling, if disingenuous, explanation for the prominence of literary history in copyright literature neatly illustrates the usefulness of historical narration in this context:

> The struggle to secure the protection of our laws for literary property produced by citizens of foreign countries has been long and wearisome. To some it may seem fruitless. An ocean of ink has been spilt and a myriad of speeches have been made; and yet there are no positive results set down in black and white in the Revised Statutes of the United States. But the best cure for pessimism is to look back down the past, and to take exact account of the progress already made. This examination reveals solid grounds for encouragement in the future. The labor spent, although often misdirected, has not been in vain. Something has been gained.[1]

Matthews attributes the rise of literary histories to the need to take stock of past successes in order to retain optimism amid unremitting obstacles. But his designation here of the 'citizens of foreign countries' as the primary beneficiaries of copyright activism reveals the latent motives of literary history hiding in plain sight.

International copyright promised to protect not only American writers from piracy abroad but also foreign writers from piracy within the United States, where many imprints specialized in cheap reprints of foreign works, usually British ones. Copyright activists often discussed copyright within a moral and legal framework that allowed them to address piracy without the specificity of authorial nationality. Although the interests of foreign writers pirated in the United States did occasionally appear as terms of debate, copyright activists generally appointed American writers as unambiguous victims of a British publishing industry that belittled American literature even as it brazenly pirated it. In an interesting turn to the foreign author as the primary beneficiary of copyright law, Matthews displaces the onus of piracy – and the benefits of copyright law – away from himself and his peers. Matthews's own well-known wealth and aristocratic lineage tacitly underlie his decision to invoke the foreign writer, enabling him to deflect the criticism of self-interest leveled by skeptics and to reconstitute himself and the movement as altruists campaigning for the sake of others. It is fitting that Matthews would attempt to imbue the copyright movement with selflessness in a context that largely served that very purpose for copyright activists: literary history allowed activists to document the injuries of piracy without making themselves open to accusations of selfishness and money-grubbing.

Matthews's widely reprinted essay 'American Authors and British Pirates' offers a typical example. First published in the *New Princeton Review* in 1887 and issued as a pamphlet two years later by the American Copyright League, the essay responds to British protestations of innocence with a meticulous catalog of pirated American books for sale in Britain at the time. In opting for hard data over subjective argument, this essay conveys the widespread desire of activists to stay above the fray by allowing evidence to stand alone and speak for itself. Before beginning this inventory, Matthews briefly discusses the effects of piracy on earlier writers such as Cooper, Hawthorne, and Longfellow, substantiating his claims with evidence culled from biographies, letters, and diaries attesting to the wrongs these writers endured. This prefatory narration of the literary past primes readers to be receptive and sympathetic to the list that will follow, for it draws on a presumed affection for writers whose status was in the process of being fortified by the many literary histories published in the era. Matthews uses literary history to waylay accusations of self-absorption and envelop the movement with dutiful piety and filial respect. The result is the constitution of copyright activists as literary avengers redressing the wrongs endured by those who had been unable to act.

No figure of literary history appeared more frequently in this setting than Washington Irving, whose status as the nation's first internationally recognized writer made him not only central to any American literary history but also a suitable case study of copyright infringement, as his transatlantic celebrity made him particularly vulnerable to foreign piracy. His centrality to the copyright movement may have been facilitated also by the waning reputation and aristocratic pretensions of Cooper, Irving's most famous colleague in piratical injury in early American letters. In the preface to his collection *The Question of Copyright*, Putnam interrupts his discussion of the general inadequacy of copyright law to relate the bitter circumstances surrounding Irving's patrimony after his death. The brief extension of copyright after an author's death had made Irving 'unable to insure for his nieces (his adopted children) the provision which they needed, and which a continued copyright in their uncle's works would have secured for them'.[2] Putnam's heartrending account of displaced bequests and disinherited daughters reduces the complex matter of copyright to a simple moral calculus: copyright is necessary to protect the vulnerable and powerless, an argument that directly counters the arguments of those critics who intertwined authorship with hereditary power.

It is impossible to reconstruct the reception of such rhetoric, especially because copyright supporters controlled literary media and closely monitored the ways in which copyright was handled in the press. However, one must not discount the influence of the then quasi-academic genre of literary history in imbuing copyright rhetoric with legitimacy and erudition. Moreover, it bears noting that the authors – or circulators – of such rhetoric were themselves reputable writers, critics, and scholars whose reputations also helped lend it credence. But altering public perception of literary work required the proliferation of rhetoric not only about labor but also about the aristocrat, the apparition that has long stalked literary work in the West and that late-century American writers were at pains to cast off. And it is in pursuit of this aim that the rhetoric of international copyright mediated uneasily between the literary present, in its struggle to affirm authorial labor, and the literary past, in both its narration of literary history and its management of the aristocracy. I do not want to suggest that this occurred with the production of literary histories that inflected the American literary past with elitism and privilege. (On the contrary, literary historians – Matthews among them – took pains to depict antebellum writers such as Hawthorne as working men, establishing their character by documenting the financial burdens they endured.) I argue, instead, that the periodization of the nineteenth century was made possible by the entanglement of literary history with political history. The conflict at the core of the international copyright movement indeed pit the aristocrat against the populist, but in their struggle to divest themselves of the taint of aristocracy, copyright advocates manufactured narratives that displaced the immediate political and literary context of the copyright dispute onto the literary past, as reiterated by Parrington's peri-odization of the nineteenth century.

For explication, I turn to an example taken from early in the post-Civil War copyright movement, with the founding of the International Copyright Association, a precursor to the American Copyright League that disbanded in the wave of belt-tightening after the financial panic of 1873. At the first meeting of the Association, Presbyterian minister Samuel Irenaeus Prime – a founder and editor of the *New-York Observer* and manager of the 'Editor's Drawer' column in *Harper's Magazine* – proclaimed the movement 'a demand for *justice*. It is not asking for privileges; it is the assertion of rights'.[3] On the heels of this announcement, Prime tells a story meant to illustrate these wider polit-ical aims:

> In the year 1784, the year after our National Independence was recog-nized by treaty with Great Britain, an English publisher seized upon Morse's Geography, an American copyright work of great literary and pecuniary value, and published it without recognition of the rights of the author, and without making him the least compensation. That system of piracy thus begun has been relentlessly pursued by the British, with a dis-regard for our rights which has justified the remonstrances of authors and publishers, and which they have bitterly and often complained of, these many years.[4]

Prime's story of the first geography published in the United States by an American, Jedidiah Morse's *Geography Made Easy* (1784), gives way to a larger narrative of British tyranny. Situated in the aftermath of the American Revolution, this story treats the piracy of Morse's geography as the founding moment of a long-standing practice in which the British contravene American political as well as literary sovereignty. Within the logic of Prime's narrative, it is important that Morse's geography was published in the wake of the American Revolution, for he regards Morse's text as the cultural fruit of that political rupture. Prime also sees in this piracy, however, a continuity of British tyranny, although it has evolved from political to cultural and literary tyranny. British oppression endures in the literary arena, and the international copyright move-ment emerges as a modern version of the American Revolution in its pursuit of independence from Britain. Prime's rendering of the current dispute as an atavistic extension of the American Revolution is designed to assure activists of the successful conclusion to this most recent quarrel.

Prime's account points to the primary vehicle by which copyright advocates were able to affix aristocracy to the American literary past: the centrality of Britain and transatlantic literary relations in the copyright movement. Despite the movement's avowed internationalism, England and Scotland were its prin-cipal targets, as shared language made piracy easy and economical for British and American publishers alike. Hostilities toward Britain overwhelmed the movement; the literary histories produced in support of copyright were, like Matthews's essay 'American Authors and British Pirates', generally limited to incidents of British piracy endured by American writers. The very complicated matter of international copyright, which entangled international relations with class-based disputes between workers and authors in the publishing industry, was reduced to a transatlantic quarrel within what Matthews, borrowing from James Russell Lowell, called the 'community of blood, of law, of language, and of books existing between Great Britain and the United States'.[5] In a distillation that essentially revised Prime's account, F. A. P. Barnard, then president of Columbia University, wrote: 'Between Great Britain and the United States there has been a war in the literary field of a century's standing, signalized by incessant acts of pirateering on both sides'.[6]

Isolating Britain as the principal villain was astute, for it allowed copyright activists to revise somewhat the terms of authorship already in circulation. Eager to relieve themselves from the freight of aristocracy, late-nineteenth-century writers were able to map the populist-aristocrat dyad onto their literary grievances with Britain, whose prominent aristocracy made it an easy target. In depicting themselves in conflict with Britain, American writers were able to reposition themselves in this dyad as the abused victims of a literary aristocracy. In 1890, the *New York Times* published an editorial on copyright containing this rhetorical move:

> In American communities there is a well-grounded tendency to regard a man who is merely the heir to a fortune as one who has never endured the tests of labor and hardship, in contradistinction to the feeling in Europe, which makes people ridicule and belittle the 'self-made' man, whether or not his manners are such as deserve it. Authors are essentially self-made men, in the best sense of that abused term, and as such are often subject to a certain coolness on the part of fashionable folk at home and abroad, for the latter are taught to value most the descendents of ancestors raised by wealth above the struggle for existence.[7]

Britain and the United States stand in clear opposition here in their respective attitudes toward pedigree, and the article uses British reverence for aristocratic lineage as an explanation for their ill-treatment of American authors, especially in copyright matters. With the disingenuous announcement that 'authors are essentially self-made men', the article is able to make writers the apotheosis of the American values of self-reliance and self-invention and Britain the center of aristocratic operations. And this move leads inexorably to the alignment of copyright with democracy, as with Matthews's observation that '[i]t is pleasant for us Americans to know that this first feeble acknowledgment of copyright was made by a republic' in Venice in 1469.[8] Matthews saw more than coincidence in the simultaneous emergence of copyright and the rise of democracy in the English-speaking world, for, he argued, the legal protection of authorship is an indispensable step in the legal enfranchisement of all people. Twain, an avid copyright activist, concurred in *A Connecticut Yankee in King Arthur's Court* (1889), where Hank Morgan, a Connecticut foreman displaced to the sixth century, begins his campaign to dismantle Camelot's aristocracy by establishing intellectual property laws: '[F]or I knew that a country without a patent office and good patent laws was just a crab, and couldn't travel any way but sideways and backwards'.[9]

High-profile tours of the United States by British writers complicated Britain's public image within the copyright movement. Matthew Arnold, Charles Dickens, and Anthony Trollope were among the outspoken advocates of an Anglo-American international copyright agreement and all used their tours of the United States to generate interest among Americans. Dickens undertook two tours, the first in 1842 and the second immediately following the American Civil War in 1867, and both tours have been credited with invigorating the American copyright movement with his explicit, if awkwardly received, exhortation on the matter. These tours produced mixed feelings among Americans, who were disappointed by what they perceived as ingratitude, rudeness, and explicit cultural criticism from their guests. When Dickens famously addressed international copyright, he outraged Americans with his accusations of piracy and requests for remuneration, thereby consolidating copyright activism with greed, ingratitude, and anti-Americanism in the American consciousness, associations that thwarted later American copyright enthusiasts.

[. . .]

It is plain that the centrality of Britain in the American literary imagination of the 1880s allowed copyright enthusiasts to position themselves as populists locked in struggle with British hegemony. However, what has proved to be especially important and enduring is the incorporation of this ploy into a historical narrative of the nineteenth century promoted by Parrington and others. Indeed, the narration and reperformance of American victory over Britain circulated by copyright activists is, at its core, the same story as Parrington's periodization. Both narratives position a culture predicated on pedigree and Old World sympathies in conflict with a culture characterized by self-invention and self-creation, and both narrate the demise of lineage in favor of meritocracy, the decline of aristocracy in favor of populism. The discourse of Anglo-American political history that made the dyad of populist-aristocrat particularly weighty in the late century figures as an early avatar of the narrative of democratic ascendancy at the core of the periodization of the nineteenth century. Vital to the imbrication of these two narratives is a consciousness of the past, which offered a rubric for disentangling the untidy relations within the literary circum-atlantic and leaving late-nineteenth-century American writers free to define themselves as independent of these transnational, trans-historical relationships. Despite the martial rhetoric freely bandied about, Britain and the United States enjoyed stable political relations in the late nineteenth century and were mutually dependent trade partners; the late-eighteenth-century military engagements that figured in metaphors of the literary transatlantic were already swaddled in nostalgia and remoteness. The pastness that encircled this metaphorical conceit became the vessel that contained the Anglicized Old World, which had long fueled American suspicions of authorship. To the advantage of late-century writers, the past became the site onto which a literary aristocracy was displaced, as narrated by the periodization of the nineteenth century.

NOTES

1. Brander Matthews, in 'Open Letters', *Century* (July 1885): 488; quoted in Aubert J. Clark, *The Movement for International Copyright in Nineteenth-Century America* (Washington, DC: Catholic University of America, 1960), p. 148.
2. George Haven Putnam, preface to *The Question of Copyright. A Summary of the Copyright Laws at Present in Force in the Chief Countries in the World*, ed. George Haven Putman (New York: Putnam, 1891), p. viii.
3. 'Speech of S. Irenaeus Prime', in *International Copyright: Meeting of Authors and Publishers, at the Rooms of the New York Historical Society, April 9, 1868, and the Organization of the International Copyright Association* (New York: International Copyright Association, 1868), p. 18.
4. Ibid.
5. Brander Matthews, *American Authors and British Pirates* (New York: American Copyright League, 1889), pp. 14–15.
6. F. A. P. Barnard, 'Open Letters', *Century* (February 1886): 628.
7. Brander Matthews, 'Copyright Property', *New York Times*, 28 August 1890.
8. Brander Matthews, 'The Evolution of Copyright', in *The Question of Copyright*, p. 15.
9. Samuel L. Clemens, *A Connecticut Yankee in King Arthur's Court* (New York: Norton, 1982), p. 4.

2

'THE TRANSNATIONAL TURN: REDISCOVERING AMERICAN STUDIES IN A WIDER WORLD'

Robert A. Gross

Is transnationalism, then, simply a reflection of and upon changing times? Arguably, it represents an intellectual outlook born of new global realities and indispensable to their comprehension. Who could gainsay the far-ranging transformation of the world economy over the last two decades, as transnational corporations have brought about an unprecedented integration of finance, production, and distribution around the globe? As recent financial crises in Asia, Russia, and Brazil make plain, no nation-state can command its own economic destiny, though, of course, some have far greater power than others, especially in shaping the policies of the European Union and of the International Monetary Fund. And who has been untouched by the fundamental instrument of globalization: electronic communications? Information technology serves multiple ends. Like the telegraph in the nineteenth century, it 'annihilates time and space'. Through its medium, organizations, both large and small, in every field of endeavor, can pursue activities in the international arena. No government has yet succeeded in controlling the internet. For those with the means to enjoy unlimited access to cyberspace, especially in the academic community, desktop computers ease cross-national communications and research and foster cosmopolitan ties. It is in the realm of news and popular culture that global communications have made the most dramatic impact. Genocide in

From *Journal of American Studies* 34.3 (2000): 373–93.

Rwanda, war and refugees in Kosovo, floods in Bangladesh, Presidential scandals in Washington: television, led by CNN, fashions our image of the world, to which politicians are compelled to respond. Broadcasts track the price of interdependence for the environment: oil spills, nuclear accidents, global warming, the spread of AIDS. As for popular entertainment, we are fast becoming, in the words of a popular tune and exhibit at Walt Disney World in Orlando, Florida, a 'small, small world', thanks, in large measure, to the marketing power of mega-companies like Disney, which have made the sale of American 'software and entertainment products' abroad a $60 billion a year industry. 'America's biggest export is no longer the fruit of its fields or the output of its factories', according to the *Washington Post*, 'but the mass-produced products of its popular culture – movies, TV programs, music, books and computer software'.[1] No novice Fulbright* in Europe, surrounded by American images and sounds, could miss that fact.

The intertwining of American and global interests in this account should give pause to enthusiasts of transnationalism. Who actually benefits from the new world order? Is the push for 'post-nationalism' the self-serving stance of a cosmopolitan elite, centered in America and Europe and profiting, economically and culturally, from the ready flow of people, capital, and information across national borders? [. . .] Happily, within American Studies, the proponents of transnationalism have raised it themselves. Far from justifying the existing distribution of global resources, transnationalism is [. . .] a way to fuse domestic and international concerns into a critical tool for democratic change. For all the globalism, the new outlook retains the oppositional spirit that has animated American Studies since the 1960s.

The impetus for transnationalism marks the arrival of fresh voices in the field. Prominent among them are scholars from the diverse ethnic communities that have taken shape since 1965, when the United States opened its doors to immigrants from all over the world. As participants in that movement, they have an insider's view of life in the new transnational world. Others develop their ideas from outside the United States. Theirs is an international perspective, fascinated and bemused by an expansive American culture, most palpable in music and film, that captures the imaginations of millions around the globe. As superpower and symbol, 'America' enters into others' cultures, appropriated for purposes it never knew. To take account of that process, to assess, for example, the so-called 'Americanization' of Europe, has set a new, dynamic agenda for the practice of American Studies abroad. The transnational turn registers the growing influence of international scholarship about the US.

No single paradigm or politics governs transnational studies. Even so, we can trace the intellectual trajectory by which the new perspective has taken hold. For students of multiculturalism, the move has offered a way out of an ideological impasse. In the 'culture wars' of the 1980s, the multicultural approach was assailed for exaggerating racial and ethnic differences and thereby under-mining common bonds. To that charge, many responded quite reasonably that it was American experience – notably, the subordination of women and minori-ties, the practices of racism and exclusion – that had made difference central to American life. Exploring the history, literature, and cultures of groups long ignored could be exhilarating; from that effort has emerged a vast body of texts, previously neglected or unknown, documenting and expressing the cultural values and political consciousness of peoples once deemed 'inarticulate'. But difference is a social construction, not an abstract principle. In defense of their scholarship against partisan critics, some multiculturalists forgot that point. Hoping to show the unity of a chosen group, they were tempted to deny dif-ferences within. Seeking to demonstrate its distinctiveness, they overlooked connections to people without. Ironically, that approach reproduced the very failings of the white cultural nationalism it meant to overturn. But the sepa-ratist phase is largely over. It has given way to a new appreciation of the 'hybrid' character of American life. Out of the incessant interchange across the bound-aries of race and ethnicity have developed vibrant cultural forms, like jazz, and rich resources for the voluntary fabrication of personal and social identities. That circumstance is quintessentially cosmopolitan, and it has come to be valued as such. In the sophisticated analysis of David Hollinger, an historian at the University of California at Berkeley, this spirit of tolerance inspires a vision of America as a 'postethnic' nation. 'A truly postethnic America', he writes, 'would be one in which the ethno-racial component in identity would loom less large than it now does in politics as well as culture, and in which affiliation by shared descent would be more voluntary than prescribed in every context'.[2]

Transnationalism suits this outward-looking mood. If diversity on the home front deepens American culture and enhances personal life, all the more so for international encounters. Celebrating the link between the local and the global, multiculturalism carries on in the cosmopolitan spirit of Randolph Bourne, the Progressive intellectual who coined the term 'transnational' on the eve of American intervention in World War I. Appalled at campaigns for '100 per cent Americanism', Bourne castigated the self-styled 'Brahmins' who fancied them-selves arbiters of national character. *They* were the hyphenated Americans, still looking to the courtly muses of Europe and clinging stodgily to antiquated English ways. Owing to this colonial mentality, America had never developed an authentic culture of its own. In the Anglophilic milieu, 'the distinctively American spirit' of Emerson, Whitman, and William James 'has had to exist on sufferance'. By contrast, the waves of immigrants to the US from European shores, like the Germans and Scandinavians in the Middle West, invigorated American life with expansive 'political ideas and social energies'. These were the 'pioneers' of a new nationality, bringing a vivid heterogeneity to the cultural landscape, 'without the [intolerant] spirit that inflames it and turns all its energy

33

into mutual destruction' in the Old World. Bourne's ideal was a 'federated America', where natives and newcomers alike could elect their identities, in a process of mutual education. Let its members hold 'dual citizenship', at home and abroad, if they will. 'Only the American . . . has the chance to become that citizen of the world. America is coming to be, not a nationality but a transnationality, a weaving back and forth, with the other lands, of many threads of all sizes and colors'.[3] Bourne was silent about the racism that had belied his ideal from the nation's start. Until the 1940s, US immigration policies extended a welcome mat to white people only; Africans and Asians were refused the benefits of naturalization. Still, his vision has a modern ring. That is, in fact, what the skeptical transnationalist Frederick Buell detects in his essay for *American Quarterly*. In the discourse of diversity strengthening democracy, Buell discerns a Clinton-era strategy for advancing US power in the post-Cold-War world. Who better to represent American interests than the 'global cosmopolitans' of the latest immigrant streams, 'quintessential insiders for the new postcolonial global system'? In this perspective, multiculturalism looks far less radical than once thought. In the service of US empire, it represents a 'new postnational nationalism'.[4]

NOTES

1. 'Made in America', *Washington Post*, 25 October 1998.
2. David Hollinger, *Postethnic America: Beyond Multiculturalism* (New York: Basic Books, 1995), p. 129.
3. Randolph Bourne, 'Trans-National America', *Atlantic Monthly* 118 (1916): 86–97. Reprinted in Bourne, *War and the Intellectuals: Essays, 1915–1919* (New York: Harper and Row, 1964), pp. 107–23 (quotations pp. 110, 111, 113, 116, 121).
4. Frederick Buell, 'Nationalist Postnationalism: Globalist Discourse in Contemporary American Culture', *American Quarterly* 50 (1998): 558.

3

'NINETEENTH-CENTURY UNITED STATES LITERARY CULTURE AND TRANSNATIONALITY'

John Carlos Rowe

Transnationalism also suggests a weakening over the past fifty years of national sovereignties and geopolitical borders. In many contexts, *trans* is used instead of *post* to avoid the often vexing questions provoked by the term *postnational*. In some contexts, *transnational* is employed to cross national borders intellectually and abstractly without disturbing them. In this sense, the tourist is as transnational as the migrant worker, political refugee, or invading army; academic life, as in 'traveling theory', can also be a transnational phenomenon. From the outset, I want to reject this overly cautious use of *transnational*, especially as it is invoked as a way of avoiding the practical and theoretical paradoxes deliberately posed by *postcolonial* and *postnational*. Each of the latter terms calls attention to the negative heritage of colonial or national practices, suggesting that the critical study of these discourses can best be accomplished from a utopian postcolonial or postnationalist perspective. Neither approach assumes that colonialism or nationalism has disappeared (or will shortly do so); each works on the assumption that critical studies of colonialism and nationalism have as their aim the political as well as intellectual transformation of inherently exclusive and repressive systems.

All this suggests that we can and should push such critical study back into the eighteenth and nineteenth centuries, when the nation and its sustaining,

From *PMLA: Publications of the Modern Language Association of America* 118.1 (2003): 78–89.

often generative imperialisms were the dominant forms of state organization. Paul Giles has argued that 'transnationalism has a specific history, often connected to developments in communications technology and the various metaphorical displacements associated with them, and that canonical American authors often appear in quite a different light if they are examined through [this] matrix'.[1] If we identify transnationalism only with postmodern forces of globalization or with resistances to them, such as creolization and hybridization, then we are likely to forget the roots of these postmodern economic and cultural practices in modernization. Much as I disagree with many of the criticisms leveled against the 'presentness' of cultural and postcolonial studies, I admit that there is a tendency in these related approaches to alienate new global phenomena from their complex histories. Yet as we return to these crucial histories to understand better what we mean by postcolonial, postmodern, and transnational phenomena, we should also be cautious not to project such terms – framed in the current crises occasioned by the exploitative reach of transnational capitalism and by new modes of production and commodification – too unilaterally onto the related but different histories that have given rise to such circumstances.

By the same token, postcolonial studies of eighteenth- and nineteenth-century nationalisms and their processes of expansion – that is, modernization – should not lead us to conclude hastily that because the United States emerged from the eighteenth-century anticolonial struggle, it qualifies as a postcolonial state. We should be precise in defining the postcolonial perspective as thoroughly anti-imperialist and thus be as critical of the colonialism practiced by the decolonized as we are of that practiced by the original colonizers. If we maintain this high standard for the use of the term, we may find it impossible to speak of a postcolonial condition or achieved postcoloniality, insofar as most decolonized societies have practiced their own versions of territorial, human, and symbolic domination in the interests of consolidating national or other forms of state identity. As a consequence, most postcolonial studies focus critically on the colonial, national, and other state formations that have prevented the attainment of a postcolonial, postnationalist ideal. The historical fact that the United States pursued colonial policies in conjunction with its anticolonial revolution is an interesting subject of study for postcolonial scholars, and it gives further evidence that postnational and transnational phenomena deserve to be understood in the historical contexts of nationalism, including colonial expansions and anticolonial struggles, decolonization, re- and neocolonizations, and neo- and postnationalisms of various sorts. Such historical genealogies are complex and have only recently been the objects of intense scholarly inquiry. Yet even as we encourage such research and the theoretical models on which it depends, we must be careful not to confuse our methods, models, and terminology with geopolitical realities. Desirable as certain postcolonial and postnationalist states ought to be for those conducting postcolonial inquiries – as the utopian horizons of such historical interpretations – we would be hard-pressed to identify a successful example of such states, even if we took 'state' as a philosophical or psychological condition rather than as a geopolitical reality.

The postrevolutionary United States emerged as a coherent nation in many respects as a consequence of its colonial imaginary and the latter's deployment of a wide range of symbolic instruments. Culture was from the outset fantastically conceived as unified, in order to legitimate the indisputable fiction of a union of states previously held together primarily by means of British colonial foreign policies and laws, many of which varied drastically to regulate different regions and economies in British North America. It is possible to speak of early United States nationalism as itself a colonial project, insofar as the formations of the nation depended crucially on the transformation of British colonialism into national institutions and practices in a rapid, defensive manner. The urgency, even hysteria, of this nationalism is evident in the Alien and Sedition Acts*, anti-Jacobin sentiments in the widely rumored Illuminati conspiracy*, and general anti-European sentiments prompted by the feared anarchy of the French Revolution. The transnational imaginary of the early United States republic is significantly shaped by free-floating paranoia regarding wandering anarchists, dangerous foreigners, and murderous 'savages'. Charles Brockden Brown's novels are symptomatic of such cultural hysteria, and the remedy in both literary and geopolitical fictions seems to be the imposition of artificial borders to control such threatening foreignness. It is especially interesting that Brown's weird literary works should have been considered for so long the origins of the American novel.

Well before it was declared a national purpose, Manifest Destiny* begins in the social psychology of such defensive nationalism, so that the expansion of the national border functions as one means of controlling threats within an unstable, new, and contrived nation by projecting them outside or beyond that nation. From the journals of the Lewis and Clark expedition to Washington Irving's fictionalized travel narratives and Edgar Allan Poe's plagiarisms of fact-based narratives for his poetic fantasies, such as *Narrative of Arthur Gordon Pym* (1838) and *The Journal of Julius Rodman* (1840), the borderlands of the United States are narratively imagined as requiring national incorporation for their realization as civilized or even natural. Whether the territory west of the Mississippi is contaminated by the disease of Native Americans, as Poe represents it in *Julius Rodman*, or by the mongrelization of racial inbreeding brought by French trappers (and thus a flawed colonial enterprise), as Irving represents it in *Astoria* (1836), the wilderness must be purified by United States expansion.

Although it seems incredible today that nineteenth-century manifest destiny could be distinguished from other European imperial projects in the Western

Hemisphere – virtually all of which were being contested in various ways by native people and colonial emigrés – the United States transnational imaginary was rationalized by such philosophical rhetorics as American transcendentalism. However critical Ralph Waldo Emerson, Henry David Thoreau, Margaret Fuller, Walt Whitman, and other transcendentalists may have been of specific United States imperial projects, like the Mexican-American War* and slavery, transcendentalism relied on a rhetoric of transcendental expansion, internalization (and thus appropriation), and psychic progress and development well suited to the politics of Jacksonian America. The transcendentalist was intrinsically cosmopolitan and transnational, so much so that John Aldrich Christie could write an entire book on the paradox, *Thoreau as World Traveler*, arguing that Thoreau's lack of travel (his only foreign travel was to Montreal in 1844; his only other travels outside New England were to Fire Island, New York, in 1850 and to Minnesota in 1861) was more than compensated for by his careful reading and citation of travel writers. Indeed, the maps Christie includes in his study of Thoreau's global 'travels' and local trips are designed to suggest some impossible homology between microcosm and macrocosm.

[. . .]

The new comparative American studies must include Canada as a crucial and distinct multiculture, whose complex history includes not only the struggle between British and French imperialisms (and their consequences for revolution and nation building in the United States) but also the diaspora and subordination of native peoples ('First Peoples' in Canada), many of whom refused to recognize the national boundaries dividing Canada from the United States. Twentieth-century Native American writers, like Louise Erdrich in *Love Medicine* (1984; 1993) and *Tracks* (1988) and Thomas King in *Green Grass, Running Water* (1993), draw on the contemporary implications of their nineteenth-century ancestors' refusal to respect national boundaries. Frequent border crossings in their fiction are symbolic reminders of how the artificiality of national boundaries has had real consequences in Indian suffering. What such contemporary work teaches us is that the study of nineteenth-century transnationality must include not only the Canadian border but also the different and shifting borders imposed on native peoples by the systematic violence of enclosure we know as imperialism.

NOTE

1. Paul Giles, *Virtual Americas: Transnational Fictions and the Transatlantic Imaginary* (Durham: Duke University Press, 2002), p. 16.

4

'NATIONAL NARRATIVES, POSTNATIONAL NARRATION'

Donald E. Pease

With the intention of demonstrating that they authorize very different narrative protagonists, a distinction between national and postnational narratives might be provisionally drawn at the line demarcating the temporal from the critical inflection of 'aftering'. *Post*national narratives might, as a consequence, be understood either to constitute belated accommodations to global capital or to narrate forms of resistance. The narrative of global capital is accommodationist in that it simply recasts the state in the diminished role of manager. It redefines national narratives as instruments of state rule through the reproduction of the collective illusion that the state is an imaginative correlate of an individual's desires, the world s/he wants, rather than the world the state has already imposed.

When emplotted within a postcolonialist narrative, however, the nation undergoes a dramatic change in historical orientation. Its spatial and temporal coordinates reverse their relationship to the colonialism and imperialism that played the parts of protagonists in the accommodationist narrative of global capital. Postcolonialism sorts national narratives into at least three separate but overlapping categories: national, antinational, and postnational. In establishing interlinkages between proletarian anticapitalism and nationalist anti-imperialism, postcolonialism often deploys national narratives strategically as forms of local resistance to the encroachment of global capital.

From *Modern Fiction Studies* 43.1 (1997): 1–23.

Unlike the discourse of globalization, postcolonialism emerged, in part, through an immanent critique of the nation as an ideological mystification of state power. Its pervasive recharacterization of nationalism as the fictive invention of a civi-territorial complex that did not in fact exist resulted from an analysis of the narrative elements – the national metanarrative, narrativity, and the intentionality – that conveyed this fiction.

The metanarrative aspect of national narratives, as this critique might now be summarized, constituted a metaphysical mediation between the state and the lifeworlds of its subjects. Metanarratives recast the reason of state as a teleology (a horizon of narrative expectations emanating from a national origin and organized by a national purpose) and thereby induced the state's subjects to collude in their own subjection. National narratives were structured in the (metanarrative) desire (intentionality) to recover a lost national origin whose projection onto a national future organized an individual quest in the form of a sequence of purposive events (national narrativity).

National narratives might in retrospect be described as having constituted literary forms wherein official national fantasies were transmitted to a 'national people' that they aspired simultaneously to consolidate and represent. Narrativizing a relationship between a 'people' and a civi-territorial complex thereafter construed as 'natural', national narratives effected imaginary relations between national peoples and the states that secured them to their apparatuses. The conjunction of 'nationness' with narrativity activated a two-tiered process dividing the manifest organization of the state apparatus (wherein the Reason of State was Sovereign) from the latent fantasy (wherein state subjects imagined themselves granting this power to the state).

It was this fantasy's latency that supplied the power necessary to animate the national people's longing for an imaginary relation to the state. Various elements of the narrative process supplied different links between the modality of the state apparatus – its subject positions, preconstituted norms and assumptions, the cultural performatives whereby these norms became embedded as assumptions, and the relay of sites sedimenting their iterability – with the invariant contents of the national fantasy. The property of 'nationness' intrinsic to these narratives has been sorted into a range of categories whose variations on the relations – democratic, authoritarian, socialist, liberal, imperial, anticolonial – between the 'national people' and the state depend upon one or another modular version of the enlightenment grand narrative from which they derive their authority.

As collectively experienced fantasies, these narratives extended the reach of state regulatory mechanisms into the individual psyche where these fantasies have historically performed functions that are both extensive and complexly interrelated. They organized collective representations of the national people, transmitted the official scenarios wherein individuals were subjectivized as its citizen-subjects, and controlled the individual citizen's relation to the state. Overall, these narratives positioned a totalized community as the narratee of a story that structured the subject positions, actions, and events of that community within a masterplot that performed the quasi-metaphysical function of guaranteeing its perpetuity.

National narratives derived both their coherence and their claim to 'universal' value from their opposition to 'other' national narratives. These opposed narratives 'face one another like images gesturing from opposite directions toward a patriotic threshold, the reader who calls one image reality and the other a reflection is, in fact, declaring what side of the mirror he or she is on'.[1] The construction of the national Other produced a totalized image of the national community at the surface of this national mirror. A 'patriotic' national identity was subsequently structured in the imagined relation of absolute difference from this national enemy.

But the contradictory relation between difference and sameness out of which national narratives and national identities were fashioned could only be resolved into a unity through the state's intervention. When it exercised the power to make a unity out of difference, however, the state also threatened its individual subjects' relation to this unity with disruption at the paradoxical space wherein unification was accomplished. If state power was required to constitute (and enforce) the national unity that the individual presupposed as a property intrinsic to the nation, however, that accomplished unity would always lack at least one part. Since it required the intervention of the state's power as a force external to the (not-yet-united) nation, the unified nation would always lack the part played by the state in constituting its integrity. Contrarily, insofar as an individual could only consider him or herself as a part of the nation *after* recognizing his or her apartness from it, her (or his) national identity could only be achieved through an act performed by this part lacking the whole. When either the state or the individual performed the action(s) necessary to make a whole out of these part actions, however, the national unity and the national identity accomplished out of these performatives were manifestly the effect of this paradoxical social logic – the whole nation minus this part (action) or the part(ial national identity) in addition to the whole nation.

Etienne Balibar has invoked this (post)national paradox to ask whether universalism and racism are opposed or intertwined features of the nation-state. After asking this necessarily provocative question, Balibar discovers a 'fluctuating gap' between 'the representations and practices of racism and nationalism', symptomatic of the national narrative's effort to cover over this paradoxical space. This gap effects an externalizing action – the exclusion of national others – Balibar describes as necessary to effect the nation's internality. Racism, under this description, constitutes 'a supplement of nationalism or more precisely a supplement internal to nationalism, always in excess of it, but always indispensable to its constitution and yet always still insufficient to achieve its project, just as nationalism is both indispensable to and always insufficient to achieve the formation of the nation'.[2]

The operations nationalism required to produce for itself the illusion of universalism take place as supplemental scenes in its national narratives. These supplemental scenes effect elisions of the nation's lack of universality otherwise evident at the site of the state's unification of the nation. Racism, according to Balibar's model, effects a generalized misrecognition of the sovereign power the state exercised there by displacing the state's nation-making act (making 'one out of many') with representations of the national people's collective abjection of stateless (racialized) persons. These representations effect the related nation-making illusion that, rather than functioning as the precondition for the individual's act of identification with the nation-state, the condition of apartness refers only to non-nationals and results from the national people's abjection of racialized others. Racism, that is to say, effects the collective illusion of the nation as a concretized universal (of nationalism) through its occlusion of the paradoxes associated with the nation's unification (the whole nation plus or minus the part making a whole).

Understood in Balibar's terms, national narratives elide recognition of the paradoxical relation between the state and its subjects through their inclusion of these supplemental acts of abjection. National narratives encode these supplemental acts as at once political – racializing the national other – and psychic – internalizing the traumatic residua of these acts of abjection. In positioning an 'enemy within' as the tain for the imaginary mirror linking the individual psyche to the national narrative, paranoia and narcissism became interrelated state fantasies.

Paranoia enabled national identification with already existing subject-positions through the abjection of state aliens. In thereby disavowing recognition of the individual's own apartness, paranoia also effected the internalization of abjection as a latent national identity. After paranoia became inextricably intertwined with official state fantasy, however, it could only pass from the manifest phase of an opposition between national others to the latency required for the transmission of the nation's narrativity (the ongoing disavowal of national abjection) through its partial cathexis onto a narcissistic subject.

In the construction of abjectable and internal aliens as their shared precondition, national narratives effected a silent partnership between the nation and a state of paranoia. National narrative animated as manageable state fantasies the paranoia associated with psychic traumata – unavowable memories, repressed experiences, drives – then rechanneled them into the abjection of (racialized) 'aliens'. The overcoming of paranoia through these acts of abjecting accomplished a narcissism assignable to the state's as well as to the individual's sovereign powers of integration and control. Patriotism named the form narcissism assumed in its passage from an individual to a state fantasy. This structure of feeling thereafter promoted the illusion that the national patriot was also the putative center of state power.

NOTES

1. Doris Sommer, *Foundational Fictions: The National Romance of Latin America* (Berkeley: University of California Press, 1991), p. 112.
2. Etienne Balibar, 'Racism and Nationalism', in Etienne Balibar and Immanuel Wallerstein, *Race, Nation, Class: Ambiguous Identities* (London: Verso, 1991), p. 54.

5

'TRANSNATIONALISM AND CLASSIC AMERICAN LITERATURE'

Paul Giles

A wider perspective reveals, however, that there is nothing particularly surprising or unusual about what has happened recently to American literature, which is the same thing that has happened to the field of English literature over the past twenty-five years. As Stephen Greenblatt wrote in 2001, 'English literary history . . . has ceased to be principally about the fate of the nation; it is a global phenomenon'.[1] Similarly, American literature should be seen as no longer bound to the inner workings of any particular country or imagined organic community but instead as interwoven systematically with traversals between national territory and intercontinental space. Indeed, as Edward Said has suggested, the cultural identity of nations in this era of increasing globalization should be conceived in terms of space rather than time.[2] This spatial turn poses a particular challenge to an established tradition of American literature that, from the Puritans through the transcendentalists and beyond, was gripped by temporal perspectives: ideas of destiny, promise, rhetorical prophecy, the realization of millennial visions in future time. By contrast, remapping United States culture in global terms involves an estrangement of these native discourses of the sublime*, an unraveling not only of the exceptionalist model of manifest destiny* but also of the Emersonian rhetoric of idealism that has worked consistently to underpin and institutionalize it. For instance, to reimagine the

From *PMLA: Publications of the Modern Language Association of America* 118.1 (2003): 62–77.

American Pacific outside the 'historical project of Manifest Destiny', as Rob Wilson has suggested,[3] is to dissociate the American West from projections of utopian desire and to see it instead as a switching point between the mobile discourses of migration from Asia and the Americas where, according to perspective, east can become west and vice versa. To demystify and historicize the sublime in this way is to render it contingent and thus to emphasize that the subliminal imaginings of the United States, along with this mythical geography that has conventionally supported them, are reversible constructions whose arbitrary quality has been suppressed to sanctify the idea of 'nature's nation'.

This might seem nothing more than a standard deconstruction of American cultural identity, betokening nothing surprising. My point is, though, that this spatial turn in United States literary studies carries uncomfortable implications for some of the most cherished ideas and beliefs that have framed the construction of this field, beliefs that helped advance the cause of American literature through the twentieth century. To problematize the geographical integrity of the United States is, inevitably, also to problematize the 'natural' affiliation of certain values with a territory that can no longer be regarded as organically complete or self-contained. The formal methods of American studies in its midtwentieth-century heyday were predicated on what Vicente L. Rafael calls an 'integrationist logic',[4] which mirrored the accommodationist ideals of United States society: to integrate parallel academic discourses into an interdisciplinary whole was seen implicitly as a correlative to the assimilation of immigrant and regional differences in the consensual bosom of mainstream liberal culture, so that American studies in the 1950s became a patriotic subject in methodology as well as in thematic content. This tradition finds an echo in the work of [Annette] Kolodny, where progressive approaches to 'the complicating intersections of race, class, and gender' are linked to specific sites of struggle;[5] the frontier is described as a locus of 'cultural contact' and 'change';[6] and the academy is made to stand synecdochically for the possibilities of transformation in United States society. The issue here is not Kolodny's ethical or political commitments but rather the status of this kind of synecdochic gesture in a situation where all local boundaries have become multivalent and porous. In a world of transnational mobility and spatial dislocation, no enclosed community – neither university nor region nor nation – can define itself in a separatist manner, as did John Winthrop's providential 'City upon a Hill'. This means that Winthrop's values of 'liberality' and 'mutual Love' in a setting 'without dissimulation', values traditionally associated with the pastoral* forms of retreat and regeneration that have provided a powerful impetus throughout the course of American literature, begin to have less purchase on the interlocking, multifaceted global culture of today. To lose the sense of the United States as a privileged and protected space is to lose the sense of it harboring exemplary or exceptionalist qualities of any kind.

This erosion of American exceptionalism does not in itself signify the elimination or irrelevance of United States national identity. Ulf Hannerz has written of how 'there is a certain irony in the tendency of the term "transnational" to draw attention to what it negates – that is, to the continued significance of the national';[7] however, such irony should be understood not merely as a rhetorical accident but as endemic to that structural duplicity through which, at the beginning of the twenty-first century, the national and the transnational can be seen as uncomfortably interwoven. Taking a more futuristic position, Arjun Appadurai has argued that, because of the economics of multinational corporations and the decentered power of the new electronic media, 'the nation-state, as a complex modern political form, is on its last legs' and that the world is moving instead toward 'post-national social forms'.[8] Appadurai is right to point out the gradual erosion of 'isomorphism' in localized territories,[9] the ways in which entities like ethnicity, media, and finance can no longer be said to be commensurate with the boundaries of the nation-state, but to infer from such frictions and disjunctions a simple elision of the nation-state's authority seems less plausible. On occasion, we see a nation responding to its threatened loss of autonomy through a reactive, coercive nationalism that creates points of tension between bounded legislative areas and potentially unbounded spaces of cultural or economic exchange. At other times, we find this discourse of globalization working as an extrapolation and sublimation of United States interests; in typical idealist fashion, this globalizing rhetoric attempts simply to mask its material provenance.

An egregious example of the second kind of displacement occurs in Michael Hardt and Antonio Negri's *Empire* (2000), whose argument seems to recapitulate an imperial mentality in its description of empire as 'a *decentered* and *deterritorializing* apparatus of rule that progressively incorporates the entire global realm within its open, expanding frontiers'.[10] For Hardt and Negri, the power of global capitalism resides in the way it avoids becoming attributed to any specific locality, so that its empire 'presents a superficial world, the virtual center of which can be accessed immediately from any point across the surface'.[11] The spatial imaginary here is reminiscent of nothing so much as Ralph Waldo Emerson's essay 'Circles' (1841), which reworks Augustine's description of (in Emerson's words) 'the nature of God as a circle whose center was everywhere and its circumference nowhere'.[12] This analogy suggests how Hardt and Negri are implicitly imitating the traditional American geometry of transcendentalism and attempting, as Emerson did, to align the particular with the general and thus to render these refractory conceptions universal. As Fredric Jameson notes, what is now understood as globalization 'used to be called – when it was a far more limited phenomenon – Americanization', and there is an important sense in which this language of global empire conceals 'a fundamental dissymmetry in the relationship between the United States and every other country in the world'.[13] Nor, in fact, are radical anticapitalists and fundamentalist leaders in doubt about where this 'center of an imperialist project' lies, as the United States witnessed to its cost on 11 September 2001.[14]

My concern is not so much to interrogate the blind spots of United States culture as to challenge circular, self-fulfilling definitions of American literature by opening up the field as a site of perennial struggle and rupture. Although American literary history has become professionally consolidated as a tradition of self-reliance and self-expression, a culture constitutionally empowered to incorporate diversity in unity, it reveals within itself traces of innumerable savage, intractable conflicts – conflicts involving Native Americans, from the seventeenth century onward; Great Britain (over the question of political independence), from the late-eighteenth century; Mexico, in the 1840s; Spain, Cuba, and the Philippines, in the 1890s; Korea, Vietnam, Iraq, Afghanistan, and many other countries, in the twentieth and twenty-first centuries. The cradle of American literature, if one might be forgiven a Thoreauvian pun, is discord rather than Concord. Recognition of American literature as a discursive site for the explicit or implicit mediation of these kinds of ideological conflict provides a necessary ballast for academic discussions of transnationalism, which, with all their emollient talk around issues of hybridity and multiculturalism, can degenerate into flat, predictable exercises. Instead of being too easily dissolved into abstract formulations, transnationalism considered in relation to social or aesthetic practice can sharpen its focus on scenes where specific lines of tension are prevalent. A critical transnationalism can probe the significance of cultural jagged edges, structural paradoxes, or other forms of apparent incoherence and illuminate our understanding of where the culture of the United States is positioned within a framework of broader global affairs. Whereas the discourse of globalization can become vague and hypothetical, transnationalism seeks various points of intersection, whether actual border territories or other kinds of disputed domain, where cultural conflict is lived out experientially.

[. . .]

To offer an example of how these crosscurrents can modulate our reading of classic American literature, I want to look at how works by Emerson [. . .] in the middle of the nineteenth century manifest a particular concern with national boundaries, an anxiety that can be related to cultural memories of the War of 1812* and to the subsequent standoff between Britain and the United States in the 1840s over the Oregon Territory. While the works of Emerson and Thoreau are traditionally said to embody a new patriotic spirit in American literature, it is important to recognize how this sense of nationhood emerges from a negotiation with and partial suppression of transnational frictions and disturbances, so that the development of transcendentalism should be seen as interwoven systematically with the belligerent Anglophobia of this era.

47

[. . .]

In the light of these hostilities, Emerson's 1844 essay 'The Poet' showed an astute awareness of contemporary political disputes in its choice of regions where the American creative spirit might flourish:

> Our logrolling, our stumps and their politics, our fisheries, our Negroes, and Indians, our boats, and our repudiations, the wrath of rogues, and the pusillanimity of honest men, the northern trade, the southern planting, the western clearing, Oregon and Texas, are yet unsung. Yet America is a poem in our eyes; its ample geography dazzles the imagination, and it will not wait long for metres.[15]

The transcendentalists are often considered primarily in relation to the abstract, philosophical terms in which they chose to frame their discourse, with its emphasis on a rejection of Locke* and aspiration instead toward a recuperative Neoplatonism*. As we see from this passage from 'The Poet', however, Emerson's move in 1844 to nominate Oregon and Texas as fitting candidates for American poetic treatment can be seen as a critical correlative to contemporary expansionist movements in the political sphere. Tony Tanner suggests that the transcendentalists enjoyed an 'effortless confidence' in their intellectual conjunction of abstract and particular,[16] but while Emerson's equation of the circumference of the United States with the poetic imagination might seem effortless enough, it is based on a more severe sense of disjunction and antagonism. Emerson's stylistic genius involved eliding the contingent into the ideal so as to endow his idiosyncratic visions with an air of circular inevitability, but this rhetorical process cannot entirely suppress the embattled anti-English themes it embodies.

One of the difficulties in discussing Emerson's attitude toward national identity in general is that his conception of the nation-state tended to remain, characteristically, in flux. In *English Traits* (1856), he suggests at one point that the invention of new technology, such as steam trains and the telegraph, is rendering national communities obsolete: 'Nations have lost their old omnipotence [. . .][W]e go and live where we will'.[17] A deflection of the historical category of the nation into a more essentialized idiom of race, such as we see in *English Traits*, is one manifestation of this intellectual program; yet it would also be true to say that here, as in 'The American Scholar' and so many of his other works, Emerson chooses to focus on national characteristics and their implications. This implicit dialectic of nation and race might be understood as commensurate with the dialectic of politics and fate at which Emerson worries away throughout his work. Discussing the American seizure of Texas in 1845, for example, he remarks in *Journals* how 'it is quite necessary and true to our New England character that we should resist the annexation with tooth and nail', though he also goes on to observe, '[I]t is very certain that the strong British race which have now overrun so much of this continent, must also overrun that tract, and Mexico and Oregon also, and it will in the course of ages be of small import by what particular occasions and methods it was done'.[18] There is a certain irony in Emerson's attributing the overthrow of the British government's interests in the Oregon Country to the advance of a 'strong British race' in North America, and this attribution suggests how popular typological classifications of Anglo-Saxon racial characteristics in the mid-nineteenth century could not obviate the more immediate political antagonisms in this Anglo-American world. It also suggests how Emerson chose to justify manifest destiny by explaining it to himself as an inevitable phenomenon, a force of nature above the contingent values of political choice or historical circumstance. In his eulogy for Thoreau in 1862, Emerson testified to his late friend's patriotic credentials by recollecting how 'he wished to go to Oregon, not to London';[19] and this movement west becomes, for the transcendentalists, the guarantee of a symbolic rejection of England, a reformist gesture that they take to be their mythic destiny.

[. . .]

To reinscribe classic American literature in a transnational framework is to elucidate ways in which it necessarily enters into negotiation with questions of global power. 'Our American literature and spiritual history are, we confess, in the optative mood', declared Emerson in his 1842 lecture 'The Transcendentalist';[20] and, having internalized this progressive consciousness, the Americanist field has traditionally understood itself as more concerned with the production of different identities – national, regional, ethnic, individualist – than with what might seem more backward-looking representations of hostility. In *Culture and Imperialism*, though, Said writes about the need to involve students in understanding how the geographies associated with different cultural identities 'have always overlapped one another, through unhierarchical influence, crossing, incorporation, recollection, deliberate forgetfulness, and, of course, conflict';[21] and some restitution of this global milieu as a broad discursive matrix for American literature would help to move the subject out of that self-enclosed, exceptionalist circle whereby identities are valorized only with reference to themselves. As Singh and Schmidt point out, the inherent limitations of these old national narratives have often been recycled in more recent critical work indebted to the 'borders paradigm', with a concomitant 'erasure of questions of power'.[22] The issue is not just difference in itself but the harsh incommensurability of differences across nations and the ensuing struggles for articulation and mastery.

One consequence of a transnational approach to American literature, then, is to disturb any idea of it as a homogeneous or inclusive cultural field. The crucial point is precisely not to make United States perspectives synonymous with those of the wider world. The 'end of history' thesis outlined by Francis Fukuyama in 1992 suggested that 'a remarkable consensus concerning the legitimacy of liberal democracy as a system of government' had emerged throughout the world over the previous few years, as 'it conquered rival ideologies like hereditary monarchy, fascism, and most recently communism';[23] however, Fukuyama's conception of a 'worldwide Liberal Revolution' heralding a new species of 'Universal History' manifestly failed to take into account the sedimented infrastructures of power and their lingering impact on forms of the political and cultural unconscious.[24] The Fukuyama thesis bears a curious resemblance to classic American studies approaches of the 1950s, when, under the aegis of a resurgent cold-war nationalism, the attempt to disseminate United States values of 'freedom' around the world became widespread. Lionel Trilling's *The Liberal Imagination* (1950), with its advocacy of the creative imagination as an escape from dogmatic ideas, was perhaps the most famous explication of liberalism in relation to literature at the time. These understandings of the nation's supposedly free spirit were also analyzed in 1955 by Louis Hartz's *The Liberal Tradition in America*, which argued that the United States exemplified a state of 'moral unanimity' and 'liberal uniformity', so that alternative points of view – conservative, socialist, or otherwise – tended either to be incorporated in the national narrative of 'triumphant liberalism' or else forgotten.[25]

In this sense, Fukuyama's imagined world of universal liberal democracy, where all opposition is annealed, functions as a globalized version of Hartz's liberal America in the 1950s, where the absence of any 'comparative perspective' produced 'a silent quality in the national atmosphere, not so much blocking alien decisions as preventing them from ever being made'.[26] Hartz, like many other American cultural historians, pointed to the absence of 'a feudal tradition' in the United States as one of the country's defining characteristics:[27] yet it is not, perhaps, the simple chronological absence of a medieval tradition that has forced United States critical philosophy into this mold of liberal uniformity so much as an intellectual unwillingness to move laterally, to think of the possible relevance of medieval or Renaissance cosmologies to such an apparently anachronistic phenomenon as modern American literature. Partly because of the historical coincidence whereby American literature was first given definition in the 1780 and began to develop as a self-conscious enterprise in the early nineteenth century, when Romanticism was at its height, a massive institutional affiliation was established between American literature as an academic subject and a pedagogical ethic of interiority. This ethic led to the championing of writers such as Emerson and Thoreau for their expressions of self-reliance, their sacralization of their native country, and their projection of a natural affinity between an empathetic, subjective self and the wider circumference of their individual worlds. But what tends to be lacking here is the emphasis on spatial perspective that would resituate these subjectivist dynamics in relation to a broader epistemological and cultural matrix. This is the kind of play with spatial perspectives and trompe l'oeil effects that was popular in Renaissance art during the fifteenth and sixteenth centuries, at which time painters experimented with discrepancies between various ocular trajectories, between scholasticism and empiricism, between what one might have expected to find in a particular line of sight and what was actually there. The structural incompatibility of these aesthetic models – Renaissance perspective versus Romantic interiority – suggests one of the perennial conceptual difficulties facing students of American literature, which is that its deliberate foreshortening of textual and geographical perspectives can lead to an occlusion of the wider implications of what are, in writers like Emerson and Thoreau, complex international issues. Despite the overtly localized vistas of *A Week on the Concord and Merrimack Rivers* and *Walden*, the texts are elaborate, multifaceted works that need to be read in a more expansive transnational framework.

NOTES

1. Stephen Greenblatt, 'Racial Memory and Literary History', *PMLA* 116 (2001), p. 53.
2. See Edward Said, *Culture and Imperialism* (New York: Knopf, 1993), p. 16.
3. Rob Wilson, *Reimagining the American Pacific: From South Pacific to Bamboo Ridge and Beyond* (Durham: Duke University Press, 2000), p. 129.
4. Vicente L. Rafael, 'The Cultures of Area Studies in the United States', *Social Text* 41 (1994), p. 98.
5. Annette Kolodny, 'The Integrity of Memory: Creating a New Literary History of the United States', *American Literature* 57 (1985), p. 297.
6. Annette Kolodny, 'Letting Go Our Grand Obsessions: Notes toward a New Literary History of the American Frontiers', *American Literature* 64 (1992), p. 3.
7. Ulf Hannerz, *Transnational Connections: Culture, People, Places* (London: Routledge, 1996), p. 6.
8. Arjun Appadurai, *Modernity at Large: Cultural Dimensions of Globalization* (Minneapolis: University of Minnesota Press, 1996), pp. 19, 158.
9. Ibid., p. 46.
10. Michael Hardt and Antonio Negri, *Empire* (Cambridge, MA: Harvard University Press, 2000), p. xii.
11. Ibid., p. 58.
12. Ralph Waldo Emerson, *Essays: First Series*, ed. Alfred R. Ferguson and Jean Ferguson Carr (Cambridge, MA: Harvard University Press, 1979), p. 179.
13. Fredric Jameson, 'Notes on Globalization as a Philosophical Issue', in Jameson and Masao Miyoshi (eds), *The Cultures of Globalization* (Durham: Duke University Press, 1998), pp. 58–9.
14. Hart and Negri, *Empire*, p. xiv.
15. Ralph Waldo Emerson, *Essays: Second Series*, ed. Alfred R. Ferguson and Jean Ferguson Carr (Cambridge, MA: Harvard University Press, 1983), p. 22.
16. Tony Tanner, *The Reign of Wonder: Naivety and Reality in American Literature* (Cambridge: Cambridge University Press, 1965), p. 24.

17. Ralph Waldo Emerson, *English Traits*, ed. Douglas Emory (Cambridge, MA: Harvard University Press, 1994), p. 91.
18. Ralph Waldo Emerson, *The Journals and Miscellaneous Notebooks: 1845–1847*, ed. Ralph H. Orth and Alfred R. Ferguson (Cambridge, MA: Harvard University Press, 1971), p. 74.
19. Ralph Waldo Emerson, 'Thoreau', *Selected Essays*, ed. Larzer Ziff (New York: Viking Penguin, 1982), p. 399.
20. Ralph Waldo Emerson, 'The Transcendentalist', *Essays and Lectures*, ed. Joel Porte (New York: Library of America, 1983), p. 199.
21. Said, *Culture and Imperialism*, p. 331.
22. Amritjit Singh and Peter Schmidt, 'On the Borders between U.S. Studies and Postcolonial Theory', in Singh and Schmidt (eds), *Postcolonial Theory and the United States: Race, Ethnicity, and Literature* (Jackson: University Press of Mississippi, 2000), pp. 5, 43.
23. Francis Fukuyama, *The End of History and the Last Man* (London: Hamilton, 1992), p. xi.
24. Ibid., pp. 39, 55.
25. Louis Hartz, *The Liberal Tradition in America: An Interpretation of American Political Thought since the Revolution* (New York: Harcourt, 1955), pp. 10, 225, 176.
26. Ibid., pp. 81, 226.
27. Ibid., p. 6.

6

'THE LIMITS OF COSMOPOLITANISM AND THE CASE FOR TRANSLATION'

David Simpson

We seem to be rather urgently in need of something that might be called cosmopolitanism.

But what is it? The question is as obscure in the past of Romanticism as it is in the present of the globalization debate. Books and articles on cosmopolitanism in the contemporary world are numerous: most of them begin with some sort of disclaimer about being able to specify what exactly cosmopolitanism is. Many of the definitions are polemical. On the negative side, one can be a rootless cosmopolitan, a person without deep affiliations and habits, a wanderer; or, more positively, one can be a man of the world, knowing cabernet from carmignano – and which fork to drink it with. A whole range of almost cognate terms come to mind in describing cosmopolitanism, but none of them quite stand as synonyms: universalism and internationalism are too rationalistically strenuous, detachment too slight, disinterestedness too tangential and too philosophical. Transnationalism does not quite work, flexible citizenship (Aiwha Ong's term) is too negative and particular. Globalism is too, well, global. Metropolitanism comes close: cosmopolitan life is most visibly imaged in the city. But not all metropolitans are cosmopolitan. For liberal third-way sociologist David Held, cosmopolitanism is the ideal cement of the new global civil society, modeling 'dialogue with the traditions and discourses of others with the

From *European Romantic Review* 16.2 (2005): 141–52.

aim of expanding the horizon of one's own frame of meaning, and increasing the scope of mutual understanding'.[1] For Martha Nussbaum, similarly, it is the basis of an ethics.[2] Conversely, for Franz Fanon*, the cosmopolitanism of the new national middle class in the decolonizing states is part of the problem, the index of its detachment from a national culture and of its being deprived of a self-sufficient national economy, in contrast to the positive function of middle-class cosmopolitanism argued by Marx* and Engels in *The Communist Manifesto*'s account of a historically revolutionary middle class in the industrialized countries of nineteenth-century Europe.[3] For Timothy Brennan, cosmopolitanism denotes the 'comfortable culture of middle-class travelers' having nothing to do with the circumstances of those suffering the rigors of globalization.[4] The authors and editors of books and essays on cosmopolitanism have to take account of the bagginess and imprecision of the term even as they try to rein it in. Defining cosmopolitanism, says one set of editors, is after all a very uncosmopolitan thing to do.[5]

This rather acute little joke locates cosmopolitanism in the category of politeness, worldliness, good breeding: it takes one to know one, but you cannot quite specify how or why. And it exposes a gap at the heart of the concept – which is not a concept and has no heart – whereby the ethic of openness and curiosity useful to the liberals – cosmopolitanism as respect for and interest in the other, the unknown – runs against the sense that what marks the cosmopolitan person is *already knowing* what needs to be known, so that one is not ruffled or nonplussed by what the world throws up – a Byron, rather than a John Clare, in our dialect. Far from being curious about going there, wherever or whatever is on offer, the cosmopolitan has already been there, done that, and remembered as if by instinct how to respond. Thus we may even associate cosmopolitanism with the display of boredom, the sense of having already seen and done it all: Byronic melancholy. This is the other end of the social and emotional spectrum from the cosmopolitan conceived as the citizen of the world, the believer in the rights of man and the singleness of the human heart and mind. It is cosmopolitanism as lifestyle and quite different from that category of transnational experience Giorgio Agamben calls that of the refugee and sees as the coming condition of us all. Imposed transnationalism is not a matter of lifestyle – Agamben's image of the camp as the coming demise of all citizenship is not a pretty prospect – no choice of knives and forks there.

In our period, and above all in the years of the French Revolution, much of the prevailing social-historical dynamic devolved from the claim made by the other classes to what had been a specifically privileged, aristocratic demeanor. Speaking French in 1750 suggested the presence of a sophisticated and wealthy participant in the grand tour, or the halls of diplomacy. In the 1790s that same gesture, albeit briefly, invoked the badge of universal citizenship and the language of human rights, open to all. Thereafter, as we all know, came the reaction, when too evident an interest in the culture of the other – specifically that of France and of the emerging Germany – was pilloried as at best a failure of patriotism and national identity and at worst a sign of participation in an international revolutionary culture aiming at the destruction of thrones and altars across the whole of Europe and North America. Then again, with the defeat of Napoleon and the reconsolidation of the monarchies, a modest openness reappeared, whereby for example the obscure German metaphysics seen as so dangerous to the homeland in the 1790s was now repackaged as an entirely worthy spiritualism and commitment to the inner life. At the same time, as Marilyn Butler showed some time ago, the classical Mediterranean sphere became available to the liberals (the Shelleys and the Brownings) as an alternative to the gloomy nativist Christianity of the Gothic north and its victorious military coalition of the willing.[6]

Such, at least, are the main emphases of the historical sequence connecting up the middle years of the eighteenth century with the opening decades of the nineteenth. Closer inspection of course reveals a more consistent dialectic whereby each manifestation of one apparent extreme was being either challenged by other positions and factions or stressed from within. Kant's* cosmopolitanism, often produced as a definitional instance of Enlightenment at its purest, has thus been vigorously undercut by Kant's geography (as analyzed by David Harvey);[7] Pantisocracy's* alternative society can be found wanting in its sense of the role of women and its reliance upon a working (servant) class; abolitionism, with its egalitarian manifesto – 'am I not a man and a brother?' – critiqued for its alliance with received religion. The rights of man themselves rapidly turned after 1789 into the rights of some men, and no women. Freedom for France did not mean freedom for Haiti, and so on. Similarly, the high Enlightenment internationalism of the eighteenth century was always nagged by statements like David Hume's* about the propriety of preferring our own national culture to anyone else's, given its importance in the development of our habits and associations. Shaftesbury* himself, very much a man of the world, was concerned that we not get too involved in the excitement of exotic experience and information, to the point that we risk losing our hold on equanimity and common sense. The sense of national self-esteem and self-identity in Britain was building long before 1789, going back at least to the restoration of 1660 (if not before), and was intensified by the ideological need to legitimate the Hanoverian succession* and the union* with Scotland and to fund the vastly expensive wars that created an empire. The negatively capable adaptability of Chesterfield's* advice to his son was controversial for various reasons, but one of them must surely have been its willingness to abandon dogged local-national British identity in the interests of fitting in:

> By frequenting good company in every country, he [the gentleman] himself becomes of every country; he is no longer an Englishman, a

Frenchman, or an Italian; but he is an European: he adopts, respectively, the best manners of every country; and is a Frenchman at Paris, an Italian at Rome, an Englishman at London.[8]

Chesterfield is not of course in the business of recommending a complete openness to all kinds of otherness, just to the best salons of civilized and aristocratic Europe. This gentleman is no refugee, needing a Derridean* hospitality. He can afford to fit in because he knows where he belongs. But the posthumous publication of the *Letters* still occasioned a huge and largely critical debate about the propriety of not being authentically one's self, and one's national self. Cosmopolitan experience as the school of politeness was at odds with the integrity of the local and of loyalty to the domestic life. Shaftesbury, as I have said, had written of the need to go 'further abroad than the province we call home' to cultivate a civilized personality, but had also seen the dangers of going too far, of going native with the wrong sort of natives, either as a deranged virtuoso obsessed with the minutiae of exotic nature – insects and cockleshells – or as a reader captured by the melodrama of 'the monstrous birth, the horrid fact, or dire event' in faraway places.[9]

So the unstable demise of cosmopolitanism is there from the start, before Romanticism. Numerous eighteenth-century reflections upon the national characters of the nation states, European and beyond (though they tend to taper off into racial categories after leaving Europe – so we hear about the French, the Dutch, the Spanish, and then *negroes*), invoke relatively consolidated national cultures forming the personalities of the rank and file, with deviations into cosmopolitan flexibility open principally to the rich and mobile, those who can barouche around and learn French. But they must not go too far, or stay for too long. The myth of Robinson Crusoe, which shows a man able to preserve his culture and language in the face of both total isolation and contact with the heathen, was a giant wish-fulfillment, not an empirical projection. (Crusoe, significantly, is completely devoid of a sex drive.) Much of the urgency of setting limits to the cosmopolitan aspiration was derived from the debate about the commercial economy. Commerce opens us to the world, and to interact with it we have to learn to tolerate and even respect the values and habits of others. Truculent isolationism is bad for business (is it still, one wonders?). But to the degree that commerce enriches the nation it also threatens to establish a linguistic, cultural, and political fluidity that the nation cannot control (now called the multinational corporation).

[. . .]

Cosmopolitanism is neither local/national nor international, but both at once. The citizen of a town, a department, a country, is and is not a citizen of the world. Ideological pressure would continue to assert the priority of one or the other (usually the local/national, especially in Britain), but in the industrializing countries there could be no going back. Efforts to institutionalize anticosmopolitan practices and identities would not only persist but intensify in their violence and destructiveness (Fascism), even as the possibilities for a closed national economy would become more and more limited. Culture would be deployed to do the work that economic relations increasingly left behind. In the middle of the empire, there was Little England.

NOTES

1. David Held, Anthony McGrew, David Goldblatt and Jonathan Perraton, *Global Transformations: Politics, Economics and Culture* (Stanford: Stanford University Press, 1999), p. 449.
2. See Martha Nussbaum, 'Patriotism and Cosmopolitanism', in Joshua Cohen (ed.), *For Love of Country: Debating the Limits of Patriotism* (Boston: Beacon Press, 1996).
3. See Franz Fanon, *The Wretched of the Earth* (1961; New York: Grove Press, 1968), p. 148ff.
4. Timothy Brennan, 'Cosmopolitanism vs. International', *New Left Review* 7 (January–February 2001): 77.
5. Carol A. Breckenridge, Sheldon Pollock, Homi K. Bhabha and Dipesh Chakrabarty (eds), *Cosmopolitanism* (Durham: Duke University Press, 2002), p. 1.
6. See Marilyn Butler, *Romantics, Rebels, and Reactionaries: English Literature and its Background, 1760–1830* (New York: Oxford University Press, 1982), pp. 113–37.
7. See David Harvey, 'Cosmopolitanism and the Banality of Geographical Evils', in Jean Comaroff and John L. Comaroff (eds), *Millennial Capitalism and the Culture of Neoliberalism* (Durham: Duke University Press, 2001), pp. 271–309.
8. Anthony Ashley Cooper, 3rd Earl of Shaftesbury, *Characteristics of Men, Manners, Opinions, Times*, ed. John Robertson (Indianapolis: Bobbs-Merrill, 1964), vol. 3, p. 353.
9. Ibid., vol. 2, p. 252; vol. 1, p. 225.

7

'BETWEEN EMPIRES: FRANCES CALDERÓN DE LA BARCA'S *LIFE IN MEXICO*'

Amy Kaplan and Nina Gerassi-Navarro

The project of transatlantic studies has the potential to pry loose the tenacious grip of American exceptionalism by mapping the Atlantic as a space of multiple crossings and cultural exchanges. More than a geographic site, the Atlantic as 'the Great Divide' offers a conceptual framework that overrides the boundaries of the nation as the primary unit of knowledge. For over two centuries exceptionalist discourse has mapped the Atlantic as an absolute barrier that separates Old world from New and distinguishes the United States from European. In the discourse of Manifest Destiny*, the Atlantic divided the open space of an unsettled continent from the cramped cities of Europe; the promise of individual freedom and democracy from the rein of tyranny and class conflict; and providential westward expansion from the brutality of imperial conquest. This spatial binary had a temporal dimension, as John O'Sullivan, who coined the term in 1845, dubbed the United States the 'nation of futurity', as opposed to those European cultures weighted down by the past.[1]

Studies such as Paul Gilroy's and Joseph Roach's have amply supplanted this binary division with the concepts of the Black Atlantic* and the Circum-Atlantic, spaces that chart the interconnectedness of Europe, Africa, the Caribbean and the Americas. Yet the Spanish empire and early Spanish American republics have not figured as centrally into these new transnational

From *Symbiosis: A Journal of Anglo-American Literary Relations* 9.1 (2005): 3–27.

configurations within this perspective. The Atlantic seems to end at the Caribbean – with Cuba at the farthest reach. Similarly, from a Latin American perspective, the emergence of transatlantic studies represents the effort to explore the interconnections as well as patterns and displacements that exist primarily between Spain and Spanish America, leaving the relationship between the United States and Latin America for a more continental outlook. This essay pushes the edges of that transatlantic crossing a little further to highlight its tri-angulation. We return to the well-worn paradigm of Manifest Destiny in order to explore how Latin America, and Mexico in particular, was central to the for-mation and unsettling of US American exceptionalism, and how it might com-plicate the binary opposition of the Atlantic divide. It may be startling to recall that in 1824, the United States of Mexico, as the former Spanish colony named itself at independence, and the United States of America were similar in size and population. It is well known that the slogan of Manifest Destiny was mustered to legitimate the secession of Texas in 1835, its annexation in 1845 and the United States invasion of Mexico in 1846, which ended in 1848 with the north-ern power acquiring more than half of Mexico's territory. Less well studied is how Mexico, and other Latin American nations, may have posed ideological threats against which the USA defined itself as much as it did against Europe. Wars for national independence in the southern nations challenged the ima-gined uniqueness of their northern neighbor as an avatar of freedom and repub-licanism, and the ongoing civil wars there held out the chimera of unfinished revolutions. The ruins of ancient civilizations of the Aztecs, Mayans and Incas and the perseverance of the Catholic Church, threw a wrench into the geo-graphic and temporal dichotomy of a new world cleanly divorced from the old. Both the intermixture of the Spanish and Indians, which US Americans stereo-typed as a mongrel race, and the abolition of slavery in the former Spanish colonies, offered an image that threatened to taint the imagined homogeneity of the white nation in the North. In the tumultuous period between Mexican independence and the US Mexican war, the national identities of the United States of Mexico and of America were in the process of formation and flux, a process that took place in unstable – if unequal – conflict and negotiation with one another.

[. . .]

This essay addresses the fraught relationship between Mexico and the USA through the writing of a woman who was neither Mexican nor American, but was born in Scotland, and made her home in both new world nations in the 1830s and 40s. In 1839, Frances Calderón de la Barca travelled from Staten Island, New York, to Vera Cruz, Mexico with her husband, Angel Calderón de la Barca, the first minister appointed by Spain to recognize the independence of its former colony. Their journey followed a route between empires, from New

York to Cuba, the last colony of Spain in the Americas. As Frances Calderón left Cuba, she noted that the 'sudden transition from Yankee land to this military Spanish-Negro land is *dreamy*'.[2] When she arrived in the independent Mexico, she encountered it through the lenses of this transition between empires and through the fantasies and realities of their different racial and temporal grids. The Calderóns had planned to settle in Mexico for an indefinite time, but political turmoil in the Spanish Court limited their stay to two and a half years. When they returned to the United States, Frances Calderón collected and edited her letters and journal entries and published the two-volume *Life in Mexico*, which was sponsored by her friend William Hickling Prescott, the well known historian, whose immensely popular *History of the Conquest* of Mexico was to appear the same year as Calderón's book, 1843.

In *Life in Mexico*, Calderón de la Barca brings multiple perspectives to bear on her encounter with Mexico from the British, American and Spanish empires, at a time when Mexicans were struggling to define their own national project in relation to these competing imperial interests. She travelled to Mexico and wrote about the country under the aegis of two male representatives of empire, the Spanish ambassador and the US historian. Her relationship to each provided gendered political frameworks, which both enabled and constrained her writing, and through which she redefined her own mobility in Mexico beyond the conventions of 'woman's sphere'. In her writing, Frances Calderón de la Barca emerges as a migrating subject between these multiple and often conflicting frames. At the same time she represents Mexico as a nation between empires, struggling to define a national project in relation to the Aztec and Spanish empires of the past, in relation to Spain's reluctant acknowledgment of its former colony's independence, Great Britain's desire to enhance its investments, and a United States eager to expand westward and southward.

Calderón's connection to these imperial frameworks begins with her life history, for Mexico was not her first dramatic move, nor was it her first experience of empire. Frances Erskine Inglis, called Fanny throughout her life, was born in Edinburgh in 1804 to a well-to-do landowning family with ten children. Her father William Inglis went bankrupt in 1828 and moved to Normandy where he soon after died. Her mother then moved to Boston, with four of her daughters and several grandchildren, where they started a school for the daughters of the elite. After a social scandal forced its closure, the family opened a new school in Staten Island, a farming area that also served as fashionable summer retreat from the sweltering heat in Washington DC. In 1836–37 Calderón met her soon-to-be husband, Angel Calderón de la Barca, a Castilian born in Buenos Aires and educated in England, who was serving as the Spanish Minister to the US.

When the Calderóns moved to Mexico in 1839, her family had already spread to the outposts of the British Empire. She had a brother who died in

Madras, a brother-in-law who was a sea captain, and another who migrated to Jamaica. We might see Calderón's journey to Mexico as having parallels to her brother's journey to India. In the same way that joining the colonial army and administration offered an avenue for Scottish men to achieve a footing in the British Empire, Calderón's relocation, as the wife of the Spanish ambassador, followed a well worn imperial route, where she could regain a lost élite status, unachievable at home. In Mexico she could refashion herself as more European and aristocratic, by leaving behind the less prestigious position of immigrant school teacher in the United States, and by looking down at what she considered the provincial parvenus of the newly constituted Mexican élite. Yet the Calderóns' tenuous hold on status and power as they manoeuvred between empires could also mirror anxiety about her own deracinated state. In her two and a half year residence in Mexico, she did not simply keep a distance that would replicate her privileged position as a member of the Scottish élite. Her immersion in a new culture profoundly changed her, and she converted to Catholicism in the United States four years after the publication of *Life in Mexico*.

The title *Life in Mexico* has a double reference that indicates Calderón's own double relation to her subject matter. On the one hand, it implies distance, the gaze of an outsider looking in and reporting on what she sees throughout the country. On the other, it refers to her own life, to the experience of making a home for herself in Mexico. If there is an overarching narrative, it is one that proudly charts her journey from stranger to sojourner, from outsider to insider. Fluent in Spanish, she presents herself as someone eager to enter Mexican society and to see and learn as much as possible, even as she oscillates between attraction and repulsion, and establishes a sense of both intimacy and distance. In composing her text, she drew directly from her letters and journals and structured it in an epistolary form, divided into fifty-four letters, as though she was simply recording day-to-day events. The letters record Calderón's daily encounters with many aspects of life and customs in the city, journeys through the countryside, historical anecdotes and lively accounts of two revolutions. Scenes often seem loosely connected, as she jumps from present to past, nature to culture, upper class dress and interiors of homes and to the ubiquitous circulation of street beggars, 'léperos'. She prides herself on getting special access to exclusive spheres: convents and secret religious rituals, government leaders, intellectuals, and upper class families. She writes as vividly about street scenes, with their hawkers, working classes, Indian funerals, and church services, which make up the social life of the new elite classes. She pays special attention to the role of women in this class, to their dress, social activities, education and subtle racial and class divisions among them. In contrast to these scenes of domestic confinement, she recounts adventurous journeys to haciendas and mines, where she encounters the threats of being accosted by bandits, who overrun the countryside. Her descriptions range from the sublime*, in painting the greatly varied landscape, to the picturesque*, in encountering Indian villages, to the melancholic, in contemplating the ruins of Aztec civilization and the colonial reign. In the city and the countryside, she narrates the histories and legends inscribed in the landscape. She shows a direct engagement with the urgent project of Mexican intellectuals coming to terms with their multi-layered and contested past.

While *Life in Mexico* received positive views on both sides of the Atlantic for its lively writing and vivid portrayal of Mexico, reviewers appeared less comfortable with Calderón's lack of a distinct national identity and equal lack of conformity to the role of 'lady traveller'. The *Edinburgh Review* called her a 'Scottish lady, bred in New England, and married to a Spaniard, with whom she was domiciled for two years as Ambassadress in Mexico – a curious combination of personal accidents'. This combination, the reviewer conceded, made her uniquely qualified to penetrate 'that secluded part of the world', but it also made her behave in an excessively unladylike fashion, going to balls all night, riding horseback and mule-back 'Mexican style' accompanied by robbers, 'joining in every sort of dissipation which a Mexican season will furnish', including cock fights, gambling, bull fights and attending 'grotesque religious farces'.[3] Her own mixed background seemed to make the boundaries around her gender and nationality more porous and thus susceptible to her Mexican surroundings. A long review of 'Lady Travellers' in the *Quarterly Review*, published in London, even more explicitly condemned what the *Edinburgh Review* gingerly admired: 'We feel that it is not only tropical life we are leading, but, with the exception of an occasional trait of Scotch shrewdness, and, we must say it, of Yankee vulgarity, a tropical mind which is addressing us'. This view of Calderón as a discomfiting mixture echoed the common Anglo-American stereotype of Mexico as mongrel or motley, a degenerate hybrid of old and new world cultures. This melding of her subjectivity into her subject matter also bespoke of her violating the proprieties of gender, as the reviewer equated her crossing of national boundaries with her transgression of gender boundaries. Her writing is not only 'very un-English' but 'we may save ourselves the trouble of looking for anything *domestic* in it'.[4] According to this review, the strength of British women's travel writing lies in the way they never quite leave home.

In William Prescott's long laudatory review in the *North American Review*, he sees this attachment to home as precisely the problem with the English traveller, who carries 'castle, park, equipage, establishment' and in changing places 'changes nothing else' and thus cannot acknowledge the newness of his or her surroundings.[5] In this review, Prescott detaches Calderón from the British Empire, and makes her more of a North American with empathy for Mexican independence, which he compares to the United States' early need for recognition from Britain. Yet when he wrote to Charles Dickens seeking a British publisher for her text he stated: 'The English and Americans who visit these countries are so little assimilated to the Spaniards that they have had few opportunities of getting into the interior of their social life. Madame Calderón has improved her opportunities well, and her letters are those of a Spaniard writing in English'.[6] While Calderón's capacity to 'assimilate' produces anxiety among most reviewers for destabilizing the lines between genders and nations, for Prescott it enhances her female perspective, giving her access to the 'interior mechanism of society, its secret sympathies and familiar tone of thinking'.[7] By underscoring her perspective as a woman, ensconced in a domestic sphere, rather than violating it, Prescott gives Calderón credit for an intimate know-ledge that surpasses that of a famous list of male travel writers from different nations, including the most celebrated, Alexander von Humboldt*.

In contrast to both the British and US reviews, Mexican reviewers expressed outrage at what they saw as Calderón's violation of intimacy, which Prescott saw as the source of her authority. They focused on her parodic and condes-cending tone toward the rising criollo elite, and her satirical portraits of their national leaders, which they related to her imperious Spanish or more broadly European perspective, that of an aristocrat, who depicted their own class and national formation as imitative, provincial and second rate. Shortly after its release in Boston, the Mexican newspaper *El siglo diez y nueve* announced its plan to publish the translation of *Life in Mexico* in serialized form. A few English copies that were already circulating in Mexico had stirred strong criti-cism among many Mexicans who found their portraits vilified. In the hope of calming public anxiety, *El siglo diez y nueve* also announced it would welcome any comments from individuals who considered themselves unfairly portrayed. The government-sponsored newspaper, *Diario del gobierno de la republica mexicana*, criticized *El siglo diez y nueve* for wanting to publish such 'unjust, passionate, virulent diatribes'.[8] Furthermore, it stated that Calderón had clearly 'betrayed' the warmth of her Mexican hosts as well as her diplomatic obliga-tions. A frenzied exchange took place between the two newspapers regarding the author and the value of her letters, which concluded with the suspension of its projected serialized publication. These reviews also linked her misrepresen-tation of national identity to her transgression of gendered roles. They criticized her text as unladylike, as an abuse of hospitality that welcomed her into Mexican homes, and several critics blamed her husband for not exerting enough manly and diplomatic control over his wayward wife.

This blurring of domestic and national boundaries that so disturbed nine-teenth-century reviewers has made this remarkable book elusive to contempor-ary literary critics, even as historians have recognized the wealth of information it offers about nineteenth-century Mexico. The few critical essays about *Life in Mexico* treat Calderón as a Victorian woman traveller, but this designation does not do justice to the way she was multiply positioned as a déclassé Scotswoman, an immigrant schoolteacher in the US, an emissary from the Spanish monarchy, married to a man who himself circulated across the Spanish Atlantic. Is this text British, Scottish, North American, Mexican, or Spanish, or as Prescott wrote to Dickens, a text by a Spaniard writing in English? The category of national literature is not adequate to analyzing this text, nor is the dyadic relation between colonizer and colonized, as Calderón constructs herself as a subject migrating between empires and writing about a newly independent nation struggling to consolidate its national project between the competing claims of multiple empires. The text, furthermore, does not fit neatly into discussions of women travellers as either resistant to male forms of imperial power or asserting their female agency through their participation in the imperial project. Yet to focus on the fluidity of Calderón's text and her own migrating subjectivity is not to read her as a free floating subject, but to consider the ways in which her encounters with Mexico were structured by competing and overlapping imperial formations.

NOTES

1. John L. O'Sullivan, 'The Great Nation of Futurity', in Thomas Paterson (ed.), *Major Problems in American Foreign Policy* (Lexington: Heath, 1989), vol. 1, p. 241.
2. Frances Calderón de la Barca, *Life in Mexico* (1843; reprinted Berkeley: University of California Press, 1982), p. 24.
3. 'Madame Calderón's Life in Mexico', *The Edinburgh Review* (July 1843): 157.
4. 'Lady Travellers', *Quarterly Review* (June and September 1845): 116.
5. William H. Prescott, 'Madame Calderón's Life in Mexico', *North American Review* (January 1843): 141.
6. The *Correspondence of William Hickling Prescott, 1833–1847*, ed. Roger Wolcott, (Boston: Houghton Mifflin, 1925), pp. 315–16.
7. Ibid., p. 316.
8. See Michael Costeloe, 'Prescott's *History of the Conquest* and Calderón de la Barca's *Life in Mexico*: Mexican Reaction, 1843–44', *The Americas* 47.3 (1991): 337–48.

8

'PRINCIPLES OF A HISTORY OF WORLD LITERATURE'

Pascale Casanova

International literary space was formed in the sixteenth century at the very moment when literature began to figure as a source of contention in Europe, and it has not ceased to enlarge and extend itself since. Literary authority and recognition – and, as a result, national rivalries – came into existence with the formation and development of the first European states. Previously confined to regional areas that were sealed off from each other, literature now emerged as a common battleground. Renaissance Italy, fortified by its Latin heritage, was the first recognized literary power. Next came France, with the rise of the Pléiade* in the mid-sixteenth century, which in challenging both the hegemony of Latin and the advance of Italian produced a first tentative sketch of transnational literary space. Then Spain and England, followed by the rest of the countries of Europe, gradually entered into competition on the strength of their own literary 'assets' and traditions. The nationalist movements that appeared in central Europe during the nineteenth century – a century that also saw the arrival of North America and Latin America on the international literary scene – generated new claims to literary existence. Finally, with decolonization, countries in Africa, the Indian subcontinent, and Asia demanded access to literary legitimacy and existence as well.

From Pascale Casanova (2004) *The World Republic of Letters*. Cambridge, MA: Harvard University Press.

This world republic of letters has its own mode of operation: its own economy, which produces hierarchies and various forms of violence; and, above all, its own history, which, long obscured by the quasi-systematic national (and therefore political) appropriation of literary stature, has never really been chronicled. Its geography is based on the opposition between a capital, on the one hand, and peripheral dependencies whose relationship to this center is defined by their aesthetic distance from it. It is equipped, finally, with its own consecrating authorities, charged with responsibility for legislating on literary matters, which function as the sole legitimate arbiters with regard to questions of recognition. Over time, owing to the work of a number of pioneering figures remarkable for their freedom from nationalist prejudice, an international literary law came to be created, a specific form of recognition that owes nothing to political fiat, interest, or prejudice.

But this immense realm, a hundred times surveyed yet always ignored, has remained invisible because it rests on a fiction accepted by all who take part in the game: the fable of an enchanted world, a kingdom of pure creation, the best of all possible worlds where universality reigns through liberty and equality. It is this fiction, proclaimed throughout the world, that has obscured its real nature until the present day. In thrall to the notion of literature as something pure, free, and universal, the contestants of literary space refuse to acknowledge the actual functioning of its peculiar economy, the 'unequal trade' (to quote [Ferdinand] Braudel once more) that takes place within it.[1] In fact, the books produced by the least literarily endowed countries are also the most improbable; that they yet manage to emerge and make themselves known at all verges on the miraculous. The world of letters is in fact something quite different from the received view of literature as a peaceful domain. Its history is one of incessant struggle and competition over the very nature of literature itself – an endless succession of literary manifestos, movements, assaults, and revolutions. These rivalries are what have created world literature.

[. . .]

The link between the state and literature depends on the fact that, through language, the one serves to establish and reinforce the other. Historians have demonstrated a direct connection between the emergence of the first European states and the formation of 'common languages' (which then later became 'national languages'). Benedict Anderson, for example, sees the expansion of vernaculars, which supplied administrative, diplomatic, and intellectual support for the emerging European states of the late fifteenth and early sixteenth centuries, as the central phenomenon underlying the appearance of these states. From the existence of an organic bond, or interdependence, between the appearance of national states, the expansion of vernaculars into common languages, and the corresponding development of new literatures written in these vernaculars, it follows that the accumulation of literary resources is necessarily rooted in the political history of states.

More precisely, both the formation of states and the emergence of literatures in new languages derive from a single principle of differentiation. For it was in distinguishing themselves from each other, which is to say in asserting their differences through successive rivalries and struggles, that states in Europe gradually took shape from the sixteenth century onward, thereby giving rise to the international political field in its earliest form. In this embryonic system, which may be described as a system of differences (in the same sense in which phoneticists speak of language as a system of differences), language evidently played a central role as a 'marker' of difference. But it also represented what was at stake in the contests that took place at the intersection of this nascent political space and the literary space that was coming into existence at the same time, with the paradoxical result that the birth of literature grew out of the early political history of nation-states.

The specifically literary defense of vernaculars by the great figures of the world of letters during the Renaissance, which very quickly assumed the form of a rivalry among these 'new' languages (new in the literary market), was to be advanced equally by literary and political means. In this sense the various intellectual rivalries that grew up during the Renaissance in Europe may be said to have been founded and legitimized through political struggles. Similarly, with the spread of nationalist ideas in the nineteenth century and the creation of new nations, political authority served as a foundation for emerging literary spaces. Owing to the structural dependence of these new spaces, the construction of world literary space proceeded once more through national rivalries that were inseparably literary and political.

From the earliest stages of the unification of this space, national literary wealth, far from being the private possession of nations whose natural 'genius' it was supposed to express, became the weapon and the prize that both permitted and encouraged new claimants to enter international literary competition. In order to compete more effectively, countries in the center sought to define literature in relation to 'national character' in ways that in large measure were themselves the result of structural opposition and differentiation. Their dominant traits can quite often be understood – as in the cases of Germany and England, rising powers seeking to challenge French hegemony – in deliberate contrast with the recognized characteristics of the predominant nation. Literatures are therefore not a pure emanation of national identity; they are constructed through literary rivalries, which are always denied, and struggles, which are always international.

Given, then, that literary capital is national, and that there exists a relation of dependence with regard first to the state, then to the nation, it becomes possible to connect the idea of an economy peculiar to the literary world with the notion of a literary geopolitics. No national entity exists in and of itself. In a sense, nothing is more international than a national state: it is constructed solely in relation to other states, and often in opposition to them. In other words, no state – neither the ones that Charles Tilly calls 'segmented' (or embryonic) nor, after 1750, 'consolidated' (or national) states, which is to say the state in its modern sense – can be described as a separate and autonomous entity, the source of its own existence and coherence.[2] To the contrary, each state is constituted by its relations with other states, by its rivalry and competition with them. Just as the state is a relational entity, so the nation is international.

The construction (and reconstruction) of national identity and the political definition of the nation that developed later, notably during the course of the nineteenth century, were not the product of isolated experience, of private events unfolding behind the ramparts of an incomparable and incommensurate history. What nationalist mythologies attempt to reconstitute (after the fact, in the case of the oldest nations) as autarkic singularities arise in reality only from contact between neighboring peoples. Thus Michael Jeismann has been able to demonstrate that Franco-German antagonism – a veritable 'dialogue des ennemis' – permitted nationalism to flourish in each country in reaction against a perceived 'natural' enemy.[3] Similarly, Linda Colley has shown that the English nation was constructed through and through in opposition to France.[4]

The analysis of the emergence of nationalism needs to go beyond the assumption of a binary and belligerent relation between nations to take into account a much more complex space of rivalries that proceed both for and through a variety of forms of capital, which may be literary, political, or economic. The totality of world political space is the product of a vast range of national competition, where the clash between two historical enemies – such as the one described by Danilo Kiš between Serbs and Croats – represents only the simplest and most archaic form.[5]

[. . .]

The original dependence of literature on the nation is at the heart of the inequality that structures the literary world. Rivalry among nations arises from the fact that their political, economic, military, diplomatic, and geographical histories are not only different but also unequal. Literary resources, which are always stamped with the seal of the nation, are therefore unequal as well, and unequally distributed among nations. Because the effects of this structure weigh on all national literatures and on all writers, the practices and traditions, the forms and aesthetics that have currency in a given national literary space can be properly understood only if they are related to the precise position of this space in the world system. It is the hierarchy of the literary world, then, that gives literature its very form. This curious edifice, which joins together writers from different spaces whose mutual rivalry is very often the only thing they have in common – a rivalry whose existence, as I say, is always denied – was constructed over time by a succession of national conflicts and challenges to formal and critical authority. Unification of the literary world therefore depends on the entry of new contestants intent upon adding to their stock of literary capital, which is both the instrument and the prize of their competition: each new player, in bringing to bear the weight of his national heritage – the only weapon considered legitimate in this type of struggle – helps to unify international literary space, which is to say to extend the domain of literary rivalry. In order to take part in the competition in the first place, it is necessary to believe in the value of what is at stake, to know and to recognize it. It is this belief that creates literary space and allows it to operate, despite (and also by virtue of) the hierarchies on which it tacitly rests.

The internationalization that I propose to describe here therefore signifies more or less the opposite of what is ordinarily understood by the neutralizing term 'globalization', which suggests that the world political and economic system can be conceived as the generalization of a single and universally applicable model. In the literary world, by contrast, it is the competition among its members that defines and unifies the system while at the same time marking its limits. Not every writer proceeds in the same way, but all writers attempt to enter the same race, and all of them struggle, albeit with unequal advantages, to attain the same goal: literary legitimacy.

It is not surprising, then, that Goethe* elaborated the notion of *Weltliteratur** precisely at the moment of Germany's entry into the international literary space. As a member of a nation that was a newcomer to the game, challenging French literary and intellectual hegemony, Goethe had a vital interest in understanding the reality of the situation in which his nation now found itself. Displaying the perceptiveness commonly found among newcomers from dominated communities, not only did he grasp the international character of literature, which is to say its deployment outside national limits; he also understood at once its competitive nature and the paradoxical unity that results from it.

[. . .]

These resources – at once concrete and abstract, national and international, collective and subjective, political, linguistic, and literary – make up the specific heritage that is shared by all the writers of the world. Each writer enters into international competition armed (or unarmed) with his entire literary 'past': by virtue solely of his membership in a linguistic area and a national grouping, he embodies and reactivates a whole literary history, carrying this 'literary time' with him without even being fully conscious of it. He is therefore heir to the entire national and international history that has 'made' him what he is. The cardinal importance of this heritage, which amounts to a kind of 'destiny' or 'fate', explains why even the most international authors, such as the Spaniard Juan Benet or the Serb Danilo Kiš, conceive of themselves, if only by way of reaction against it, in terms of the national space from which they have come. And the same thing must be said of Samuel Beckett, despite the fact that few writers seem further removed from the reach of history, for the course of his career, which led him from Dublin to Paris, can be understood only in terms of the history of Irish literary space.

None of this amounts to invoking the 'influence' of national culture on the development of a literary work, or to reviving national literary history in its traditional form. Quite the contrary: understanding the way in which writers invent their own freedom – which is to say perpetuate, or alter, or reject, or add to, or deny, or forget, or betray their national literary (and linguistic) heritage – makes it possible to chart the course of their work and discover its very purpose. National literary and linguistic patrimony supplies a sort of a priori definition of the writer, one that he will transform (if need be, by rejecting it or, as in the case of Beckett, by conceiving himself in opposition to it) throughout his career. In other words, the writer stands in a particular relation to world literary space by virtue of the place occupied in it by the national space into which he has been born. But his position also depends on the way in which he deals with this unavoidable inheritance; on the aesthetic, linguistic, and formal choices he is led to make, which determine his position in this larger space. He may reject his national heritage, forsaking his homeland for a country that is more richly endowed in literary resources than his own, as Beckett and Michaux* did; he may acknowledge his patrimony while trying at the same time to transform it and, in this way, to give it greater autonomy, like Joyce (who, though he left his native land and rejected its literary practices and aesthetic norms, sought to found an Irish literature freed from nationalist constraints); or he may affirm the difference and importance of a national literature, like Kafka, [. . .] but also like Yeats and Kateb Yacine*. All these examples show that, in trying to characterize a writer's work, one must situate it with respect to two things: the place occupied by his native literary space within world literature and his own position within this space.

Determining the position of a writer in this way has nothing to do with the usual sort of national contextualization favored by literary critics. On the one hand, national (and linguistic) origin is now related to the hierarchical structure of world literature as a whole; and, on the other hand, it is recognized that no two writers inherit their literary past in exactly the same fashion. Most critics, however, are led by a belief in the singularity and originality of individual writers to privilege some aspect of their biography that hides this structural relation. Thus, for example, the feminist critic who studies the case of Gertrude Stein concentrates on one of its aspects – the fact that she was a woman and a lesbian – while forgetting, as though it were something obvious not needing to be examined, that she was American. Yet the United States in the 1920s was literarily a dominated country that looked to Paris in order to try to accumulate resources it lacked. Any analysis that fails to take into account the world literary structure of the period and of the place occupied in this structure by Paris and the United States, respectively, will be incapable of explaining Stein's permanent concern to develop a modern American national literature (through the creation of an avant-garde) and her interest in both American history and the literary representation of the American people (of which her gigantic enterprise *The Making of Americans* is no doubt the most outstanding proof). The fact that she was a woman in the community of American intellectuals in exile in Paris is, of course, of crucial importance for understanding her subversive impulses and the nature of her aesthetic ambitions. But the deeper structural relationship, obscured by critical tradition, remains paramount. Generally speaking, one can point to some feature of every writer's career – important, to be sure, but nonetheless secondary – that conceals the structural pattern of literary domination.

The dual historicization proposed here makes it possible not only to find a way out from the inevitable impasse of literary history, which finds itself relegated to a subordinate role and accused of being powerless to grasp the essence of literature; it also allows us to describe the hierarchical structure of the literary world and the constraints that operate within it. The inequality of the transactions that take place in this world goes unperceived, or is otherwise denied or euphemistically referred to, because the ecumenical picture it presents of itself as a peaceful world, untroubled by rivalry or struggle, strengthens received beliefs and assures the continued existence of a quite different reality that is never admitted. The simple idea that dominates the literary world still today, of literature as something pure and harmonious, works to eliminate all traces of the invisible violence that reigns over it and denies the power relations that are specific to this world and the battles that are fought in it. According to the standard view, the world of letters is one of peaceful internationalism, a world of free and equal access in which literary recognition is available to all writers, an enchanted world that exists outside time and space and so escapes the mundane conflicts of human history. This fiction, of a literature emancipated from all historical and political attachments, was invented in the most autonomous countries of world literary space. It is in these countries, which for the most part have managed to free themselves from political constraints, that the belief in a pure definition of literature is strongest, of literature as something entirely cut off from history, from the world of nations, political and military competition, economic dependence, linguistic domination – the idea of a universal literature that is nonnational, nonpartisan, and unmarked by political or linguistic divisions.

NOTES

1. See Ferdinand Braudel, *The Perspective of the World* (Berkeley: University of California Press, 1992), pp. 21–88.
2. See Charles Tilly, *European Revolutions, 1492–1992* (Oxford: Blackwell, 1993), pp. 29–36.
3. See Michael Jeismann, *Das Vaterland der Feinde: Studien zum nationalen Feindbegriff und Selbsverständnis in Deutschland und Frankreich, 1792–1918* (Stuttgart: Klett-Cotta, 1992).
4. See Linda Colley, *Britons: Forging the Nation, 1707–1837* (New Haven: Yale University Press, 1992).
5. Danilo Kiš, *La leçon d'anatomie*, tr. Pascale Delpech (Paris: Fayard, 1993), pp. 29–31.

PART II
THEORIES AND PRACTICE OF COMPARATIVE LITERATURE

THEORIES AND PRACTICE OF COMPARATIVE LITERATURE: INTRODUCTION

If Transatlantic Studies acknowledges the shifting position and value of the nation-state within global networks of flow and exchange (see Part I), it also needs to develop forms of literary criticism that respond to the relational, comparative frameworks in which intellectual enquiry takes place. This section samples some theories and examples of comparative criticism to suggest the importance of reading texts as part of a matrix of influence and response. In 1857 Matthew Arnold regarded such practice as inevitable, declaring that 'everywhere there is connexion, everywhere there is illustration: no single event, no single literature, is adequately comprehended except in its relation to other events, to other literatures' (59). Once we begin to read with this awareness, literature is no longer bound by artificially narrow parameters of nation, genre or ideology, but instead participates in what Goethe called *Weltliteratur**, where texts circulate and are encountered in a global space (see Hoesel-Uhlig).

As the excerpt by Pascale Casanova from the previous section attests, comparative criticism raises important questions of literary worth, of cultural capital, and of critical procedure. Canons that reflect national traditions are firmly established (and often politically expedient), but what might a canon of *Weltliteratur* look like? What would its principles of inclusion be? What kind of reader is able to practise comparative criticism most effectively? And, in the context of Transatlantic Studies, how does a comparative methodology advance understanding of this literary paradigm? For René Wellek and Austin Warren, writing in 1949, the comparativist project was invested with high political ideals that, they hoped, would transcend narrow nationalisms. Rather than restricting themselves to 'the external problems of source and influences, reputation and fame', Wellek and Warren advocated 'the study of literature in its totality' through the discovery of general patterns of style and language to be found in the aesthetic fabric of texts. Comparative criticism of this kind renounced the parameters of the nation by uncovering what David Damrosch has called 'the bedrock of universal brotherhood' (136). Wellek and Warren's universalism ('it is important to think of literature as a totality and to trace the growth and development of literature without regard to linguistic discussions') was a response to the global antagonisms of the Second World War. Their essay articulates a desire to suspend national categories as organising markers of interpretation, replacing them instead with a transnational textual field in which literatures are mined for their unifying elements.

Two essays reprinted here – by Tony Tanner and J. Hillis Miller – explore the division within comparative criticism between national distinctiveness and a transnational literary space. Tanner's piece on American and European Romanticism (first published as an essay in 1968) is a richly detailed taxonomy of image and metaphor that sets out to distinguish the key tropes belonging to either tradition. For example, 'Among American Romantics there is an unusual stress on a visual relationship with nature. "I become a transparent eyeball; I am nothing; I see all" – Emerson's famous formulation is relevant for much subsequent American writing'. In England, Tanner argues, the 'response was also auditory', suggesting a more developed sense of 'at least the possibility of communication, of significant relationship' with the environment. The role of Romantic writer is different too: most European Romantics, Tanner judges, 'were very politically minded and concerned with the development of society'; Americans, by contrast, 'did not have this revolutionary social dimension'. The essay as a whole works around such antiphonies, and of course runs the risk of insisting on difference where a reader might perceive similarity or affinity instead. Tanner's strength is in the localised detail of his examples, where he is able to make connections between, say, Jonathan Edwards, Emily Dickinson and Henry James. Transatlantic comparativism is deployed here to assert national uniqueness and a literary tradition that reflects such.

Arriving at very different interpretative conclusions, J. Hillis Miller's essay gestures towards Wellek and Warren with a great deal of sympathy, evidenced by its suspicion of national literary exceptionalism of all kinds. Contra Tanner, Miller sees the assertion of a proudly autonomous American romanticism as politically motivated:

> At a time when the role of Britain on the stage of world history is getting
> smaller and smaller, while the United States is a super-power with the

fate of the world in its hands, it seems ridiculous to have a literature here [i.e. the United States] which is a mere branch and twig of the Royal Oak.

However, he finds no grounds for supporting this 'notion of an American difference'; instead, Miller widens and extends the space of interpretation by reminding the reader that 'both English and American romanticism are permutations of linguistic materials at least two and a half millennia old'. Any responsible comparative criticism must therefore be aware of 'the larger recurrent linguistic paradigms going back to the Greeks and the Bible'. Like Wellek and Warren, Miller refutes the narrowness of our customary interpretative range, but, unlike them, he does not advocate a synthesising universalism as the endpoint of an expanded perspective. His essay finishes with an evocative image (to which we will return) to describe this wider critical focus. Each text 'is a node or intersection in an overdetermined network of associations, influences, constraints, and connections, often connections leaping far over chronological or geographical contiguity'. There is no hint here of the kind of coherent Western tradition that Wellek and Warren seek: instead the geometry of an 'overdetermined network' prevents the marshalling of transatlantic binary oppositions.

Both Robert Weisbuch and Richard Gravil also focus on the mid-nineteenth century to explore transatlantic comparative possibilities. Weisbuch's reading is determined by the theory of influence famously articulated by Harold Bloom in *The Anxiety of Influence* (1973), in which authors must creatively fend off their forebears to achieve literary autonomy. Weisbuch offers a series of comparative readings that play out such a relationship: Melville and Dickens; Whitman and Arnold; Thoreau and Wordsworth; Emerson and Carlyle. American authors work against and in response to powerful British modes of writing, and in so doing they create a new literature. In the extract reprinted here, Weisbuch maps different conceptions of time, where an Old World cultural lateness and enervation is pitted against a paradoxical New World youthfulness and apocalyptic regeneration. Weisbuch is concerned to think through the mythologies of national location, both geographical and temporal, that inform the transatlantic relationship. As in Tanner's piece, Weisbuch's sophisticated readings work to enforce national distinction; comparative criticism here plots a map of American resistance and invention. Richard Gravil is less inclined to advance such a thesis. The title of his book, *Romantic Dialogues*, indicates the extent to which a model of exchange and reciprocity dominates his comparative readings. The excerpt selected here is a detailed and nuanced account of Thoreau's textual engagement with William Wordsworth that argues for a sustained encounter of sympathy and resistance, appropriation and modification. Thoreau, Gravil writes, 'has the confidence to post his debts, or his challenges, up front', treating his relationship with the English poet as dynamic and productive, and never settling into the security of an exceptionalist position.

As Miller suggests here (and as the Paul Giles passage in Part I also explores), the act of comparison tests the imagined coherence of a text, making it vulnerable to alternative modes of discourse or, at least, more aware of its own internal tensions. As we discuss more fully in Part V, the fiction of an autonomous stylistic or ideological unity is exposed by the migration of competing narrative forms; in transatlantic comparative criticism, a textual relationality is established that counters the impulse to homogenise or purify literature according to ideas of national self-definition. Instead of reading Herman Melville, for example, as a model of American literary exceptionalism and non-conformity, it might be more instructive to place his work alongside that of British novelists such as Charles Dickens and Laurence Sterne to explore that border where New World autonomy and Old World inter-textuality meet. Expanding vistas of interpretation through acts of comparative reading works to demystify the assumptions of, for example, 'Americanness', 'Englishness', or 'Britishness' that have dominated the interpretative strategies of 'Area Studies' disciplines. In an important essay advocating a fundamental reorientation of academic subjects to take into account perspectives that extend beyond 'the container of the nation', Thomas Bender warns that 'the scholarly naturalization of the nation as the exclusive form of significant human solidarity has obscured the multi-scaled experience of history that is clearer to us today' (271). Comparative transatlanticism has the potential to liberate texts from the discursive spaces in which they have been read, such that the encounter facilitates what Wai Chee Dimock calls 'a new semantic template, a new form of the legible' (177). This 'new form of the legible' suggests that we interpret literature differently in the knowledge that it participates in a complex and diffuse series of inter-textual contacts.

The two final extracts in this section propose a vocabulary and metaphorical shape to this reading experience. Jeremy Boissevain, writing from a social anthropological perspective, details 'network theory' as a methodology for 'analyzing tension and asymmetry in social relations', asking 'questions about who is linked to whom, the nature of that linkage, and how the nature of the linkage affects behaviour'. Like Miller's image of 'an overdetermined network', Boissevain provides a pattern in which the discipline of comparative literary analysis might take place. Margaret McFadden uses the first transatlantic telegraph cable of 1866 as the inspiration for her study of the international nature of literary feminism by showing how 'this structure generated its own world of metaphors' – of matrix, network and web. Our extract from her book explores the historical and figurative resonances of these shapes, cited here as productive ways of imagining the transatlantic literary relationship.

FURTHER READING

Arnold, Matthew (1987) 'On the Modern Element in Literature', *Selected Prose*. Harmondsworth: Penguin Books, pp. 57–75.

Bassnett, Susan (1993) *Comparative Literature: A Critical Introduction*. Oxford: Blackwell.

Bender, Thomas (2006) 'The Boundaries and Constituencies of History', *American Literary History* 18.2: 267–82.

Bernheimer, Charles (ed.) (1995) *Comparative Literature in the Age of Multiculturalism*. Baltimore: Johns Hopkins University Press.

Chow, Rey (2004) 'The Old/New Question of Comparison in Literary Studies: A Post-European Perspective', *ELH* 71: 289–311.

Damrosch, David (2003) *What is World Literature?* Princeton: Princeton University Press.

Dimock, Wai Chee (2001) 'Literature for the Planet', *PMLA* 116.1: 173–88.

Hoesel-Uhlig, Stefan (2004) 'Changing Fields: The Directions of Goethe's *Weltliteratur*', in Christopher Prendergast (ed.) *Debating World Literature*. London: Verso, pp. 26–53.

I

'GENERAL, COMPARATIVE, AND NATIONAL LITERATURE'

René Wellek and Austin Warren

Comparisons between literatures, if isolated from concern with the total national literatures, tend to restrict themselves to external problems of sources and influences, reputation and fame. Such studies do not permit us to analyse and judge an individual work of art, or even to consider the complicated whole of its genesis; instead, they are mainly devoted either to such echoes of a masterpiece as translations and imitations, frequently by second-rate authors, or to the prehistory of a masterpiece, the migrations and the spread of its themes and forms. The emphasis of 'comparative literature' thus conceived is on externals; and the decline of this type of 'comparative literature' in recent decades reflects the general turning away from stress on mere 'facts', on sources and influences.

[. . .]

[One conception of the term 'comparative literature' identifies it] with the study of literature in its totality, with 'world literature', with 'general' or 'universal' literature. There are certain difficulties with these suggested equations. The term 'world literature', a translation of Goethe's* *Weltliteratur**, is perhaps needlessly grandiose, implying that literature should be studied on all five continents, from New Zealand to Iceland. Goethe, actually, had no such thing in mind. 'World literature' was used by him to indicate a time when all

From René Wellek and Austin Warren (1976). *Theory of Literature* (1949) Harmondsworth: Penguin.

literatures would become one. It is the ideal of the unification of all literatures into one great synthesis, where each nation would play its part in a universal concert. But Goethe himself saw that this is a very distant ideal, that no single nation is willing to give up its individuality. Today we are possibly even further removed from such a state of amalgamation, and we would argue that we cannot even seriously wish that the diversities of national literatures should be obliterated. 'World literature' is frequently used in a third sense. It may mean the great treasure-house of the classics, such as Homer, Dante, Cervantes, Shakespeare, and Goethe, whose reputation has spread all over the world and has lasted a considerable time. It thus has become a synonym for 'masterpieces', for a selection from literature which has its critical and pedagogic justification but can hardly satisfy the scholar who cannot confine himself to the great peaks if he is to understand the whole mountain ranges or, to drop the figure, all history and change.

The possibly preferable term 'general literature' has other disadvantages. Originally it was used to mean poetics or theory and principles of literature, and in recent decades Paul Van Tieghem[1] has tried to capture it for a special conception in contrast to 'comparative literature'. According to him, 'general literature' studies those movements and fashions of literature which transcend national lines, while 'comparative literature' studies the interrelationships between two or more literatures. But how can we determine whether, e.g. Ossianism* is a topic of 'general' or 'comparative literature'? One cannot make a valid distinction between the influence of Walter Scott abroad and the international vogue of the historical novel. 'Comparative' and 'general' literature merge inevitably. Possibly, it would be best to speak simply of 'literature'.

Whatever the difficulties into which a conception of universal literary history may run, it is important to think of literature as a totality and to trace the growth and development of literature without regard to linguistic distinctions. The great argument for 'comparative' or 'general' literature or just 'literature' is the obvious falsity of the idea of a self-enclosed national literature.

NOTE

1. Paul Van Tieghem, 'La synthèse en histoire littéraire: littérature comparée et littérature générale', *Revue de synthèse historique* 31 (1921): 1–27.

2

'NOTES TOWARDS A COMPARISON BETWEEN EUROPEAN AND AMERICAN ROMANTICISM'

Tony Tanner

One of the formative experiences of all those early American writers was of a sense of *space*, of vast unpeopled solitudes such as no European Romantic could have imagined. As the hero of Chateaubriand's* *René* says to his American auditors: 'Europeans constantly in a turmoil are forced to build their own solitudes'. The reverse was true for the American Romantic. Solitude was all but imposed on him. Nothing seemed easier for him than to take a few steps to find himself confronting and caught up in those measureless oceans of space where Whitman found his soul both surrounded and detached. This gravitation towards empty space is a constant in American literature, even if it appears only in glimpses, as for instance when the narrator of [Henry James's] *The Sacred Fount* turns away from the crowded house of Newmarch and staring up at the sky finds the night air 'a sudden corrective to the grossness of our lustres and the thickness of our medium'; or when the narrator of [F. Scott Fitzgerald's] *The Last Tycoon* says 'It's startling to you sometimes – just air, unobstructed, uncomplicated air'. Charles Olson is justified in starting his book on Melville (*Call me Ishmael*) with the emphatic announcement: 'I take SPACE to be the central fact to man born in America, from Folsom cave to now. I spell it large because it comes large here. Large, and without mercy'. But like those spiders who came under Jonathan Edwards's formidable scrutiny, the American artist, once he found himself at sea in space, had to do something to maintain himself,

From Tony Tanner (1989) *Scenes of Nature, Signs of Men*. Cambridge: Cambridge University Press.

and one instinctive response was to expand into the surrounding space. William Cullen Bryant* writes of 'The Prairies': 'I behold them from the first, / And my heart swells, while the dilated sight / Takes in the encircling vastness'; Whitman claims 'I chant the chant of dilation'; Emerson records how 'the heart refuses to be imprisoned; in its first and narrowest pulses it already tends outward with a vast force and to immense and innumerable expansions . . . there is no outside, no inclosing wall, no circumference to us'. Emerson's eye, and his mind after it, was continually drawn to the remotest horizons; the only true encirclement to a man obsessed with circles was earth's vanishing point, the very perimeter of the visible world where sight lost itself in space. When he writes about 'The Poet' and his attraction to narcotics of all kinds Emerson says: 'These are auxiliaries to the centrifugal tendency of a man, to his passage out into free space, and they help him to escape the custody of that body in which he is pent up, and of that jail-yard of individual relations in which he is enclosed'. Near the end of *Walden* Thoreau has some marvellous lines about the 'ethereal flight' of a hawk which sported alone 'in the fields of air'. 'It appeared to have no companion in the universe . . . and to need none but the morning and the ether with which it played'. Thoreau ends the book, appropriately enough, with the parable of the bug which hatches out in an old table and breaks free into 'beautiful and winged life', and Whitman at the end of *Song of Myself* literally feels himself diffused back into the elements: 'I depart as air . . .' In these three seminal American Romantics we find a similar 'centrifugal tendency', a dilation of self, which can become an abandoning of self, into the surrounding vastness. But of course if this were all we would have had no record of the movement since words are not carefully strung together by a man in the process of being metamorphosed into the circumambient air, as Emerson seems to recognize in a letter to Samuel Gray Ward: 'Can you not save me, dip me into ice water, find me some girding belt, that I glide not away into a stream or a gas, and decease in infinite diffusion?' Like those spiders swimming in the air, the American writer throws out filament, filament, filament, and weaves a web to sustain himself in the vastness. Paradoxically these webs are often notable for being composed of many very concrete particulars and empirically perceived facts (thus Thoreau is also one of the earthiest of writers); it is as though these solid details offered some anchoring attachment. When [Robert] Frost described a poem as a stay against confusion, he might have more accurately phrased it, for the American writer, as a stay against diffusion.

The web is the writer's style: the concrete details are the nourishing particles which the web ensnares and transforms. And what extraordinary webs the American Romantics (and indeed post-Romantics) have spun: Emerson's essays for instance, which often seem to tremble and blur with the very vertigo they were written to counteract, or *Walden* and *Moby-Dick* which, although they seem to repeat stock Romantic themes – the return to nature, the voyage – are of a stylistic idiosyncrasy which can scarcely be paralleled in European writing. And much of that style is not being used to explore self or environment so much as to fill in the spaces between self and environment. Again, *Song of Myself* might at first glance appear to have much in common with *The Prelude*, and the phrase 'egotistical sublime' which Keats applied to Wordsworth could certainly be extended to Whitman. And yet the sense of harmonious reciprocities between mind and landscape, that 'intimate communion' which, says Wordsworth, 'our hearts / Maintain with the minuter properties / Of objects which already are belov'd', is absent from Whitman's more desperate and sometimes hysterical ecstasies. 'My voice goes after what my eyes cannot reach, / With the twirl of my tongue I encompass worlds and volumes of worlds'. This verbal and visual pursuit of objects and worlds to fill up his void is somewhat different from the serene stealth with which, for Wordsworth, 'the visible scene / Would enter unawares into his mind / With all its solemn imagery'.

Among American Romantics there is an unusual stress on a visual relationship with nature. 'I become a transparent eyeball; I am nothing; I see all' – Emerson's famous formulation is relevant for much subsequent American writing. Thoreau, whose other senses were active enough, puts the emphasis on sight: 'We are as much as we see'. Whitman asks himself 'What do you see Walt Whitman?' in 'Salut au Monde' and answers literally and copiously, using the phrase 'I see' eighty-three times. Obviously new habits of attention, recovered visual intimacies with nature, were crucial for European Romantics as well (and Ruskin was to make of sight an instrument arguably more sensitive than anything to be found in American writing). But more often than in America, the English Romantics' response was also auditory. Keats listening darkling to his nightingale is only one of the many English Romantic poets whose ears were highly receptive to any vibrations or music that reached them. 'With what strange utterance did the loud dry wind / Blow through my ears', 'I heard among the solitary hills / . . . sounds / of undistinguishable motion', 'Then sometime, in that silence, while he hung / Listening, a gentle shock of mild surprise / Has carried far into the heart the voice / Of mountain torrents' – these examples from Wordsworth of the voice and utterances of landscape may be readily multiplied, perhaps the most famous being 'The Solitary Reaper', where the sound of the woman's song provides lasting nourishment for the poet:

> The music in my heart I bore,
> Long after it was heard no more.

The American Romantics do not give the impression of valuing auditory responses in quite this way. More to the point, for the English Romantics a purely visual relationship to the outside world betokened a state of deprivation, a loss of intimacy, a failure of poetic vision. Coleridge's 'Dejection: an Ode' hinges on this severance between self and surrounding things: 'I see them all so excellently fair, / I see, not feel, how beautiful they are!' And Shelley's 'Stanzas Written in Dejection', by lamenting the absence of some other 'heart' to 'share in my emotion' as he looks at the scene in front of him, is also asserting the insufficiency of mere sight. A purely or predominantly visual relationship with nature in fact can indicate a state of alienation or detachment from it. An auditory response suggests that the sounds of the environment mean something to the hearer, something within becomes alert to something without which seems to speak a comprehensible language. This suggests at least the possibility of communication, of significant relationship, perhaps even of a kind of dialogue. To be linked to a thing only by sight is at the same time to be severed from it, if only because the act of purely visual appropriation implies a definite space between the eye and the object. And American writers have been predominantly watchers. Thoreau, supposedly so immersed in his environment, can still use this strange image: 'I enter some glade in the woods . . . and it is as if I had come to an open window. I see out and around myself'. Having left man-made dwellings behind him, he reintroduces part of their architecture to describe his feelings. To be in the midst of nature and yet to see it as through an open window is surely in some way also to feel cut off from it. Emerson often refers to the world as 'spectacle' and is extremely sensitive to all shades of visual experience, as when he says it is enough to take a coach ride to have the surrounding world 'wholly detached from all relation to the observer'. He said of the soul: 'It is a watcher more than a doer, and it is a doer, only that it may the better watch'. This in turn anticipates James, whose central figures are all great watchers, thereby excluded from participation in the world they survey – like James himself, leaning intently out of one of the many windows in his house of fiction. Again, in Hemingway's characters their visual alertness and acuity is in part a symptom of their alienation.

Those American writers we associate with the New England Renaissance* (and many subsequently) most typically felt themselves to be swimming in space; not, certainly, tied fast into any society, nor really attached very firmly to the vast natural environment. In many ways this state was cherished and preferred; to sport in fields of air could be the ultimate ecstasy. On the other hand there was the danger of, as it were, vanishing or diffusing altogether. The emergent strategy, variously developed by different writers, was to spin out a web which could hold them in place, which would occupy the space around them, and from which they could look out into the world. But even when they scrutinized their environment with extreme care, and took over many of its details to weave into their webs of art, they were seldom in any genuine communion with nature. European Romantics, on the other hand, do seem to have enjoyed moments of reciprocal relationship with nature and could speak truly of what they 'half perceive and half create'. With Wordsworth they could consider 'man and nature as essentially adapted to each other'. In discovering nature they were at the same time discovering themselves; in internalizing what was around them they were at the same time externalizing what was within, as Coleridge often described. 'The forms / Of Nature have a passion in themselves / That intermingles with those works of man / To which she summons him'. That is Wordsworth, and it is just that sort of fruitful *intermingling* of Nature's and Man's creative potencies that is absent from American Romantic writing, which tends, rather, to testify that Nature holds off from man's approaches. Nature is indeed seen, seen with intense clarity through the intervening air, but it leaves precisely that intervening space to be filled by the writer's own filament. That marriage between subject and object, mind and nature, which is an abiding Romantic dream, is seldom consummated in the work of the American Romantics. When Emerson speaks of 'the cool disengaged air of natural objects' he is pointing to a perceptual experience which makes for important differences in American Romanticism.

Of course it would be an unacceptable simplification of Emerson's strangely fluid writing to fix on any one of his descriptions of nature as his definitive attitude. But in his first famous essay on 'Nature' we find a conception of nature markedly different from any to be found in any comparable European documents. Above all it is the fluidity, the insubstantiality, the transparency of nature which is stressed. Emerson may sound like Wordsworth when he talks of 'that wonderful congruity which subsists between man and the world' – so much was a stock Romantic piety, or hope. But what a strange congruity Emerson's is. To the poet, he says, 'the refractory world is ductile and flexible'. When a poetic mind contemplates nature, matter is 'dissolved by a thought'. The Transcendentalist*, says Emerson (and Transcendentalism was pertinently described as 'that outbreak of Romanticism on Puritan ground' by James Elliot Cabot)[1] has only to ask certain questions 'to find his solid universe growing dim and impalpable'. The 'poet turns the world to glass'; when he looks at nature he sees 'the flowing or the Metamorphosis'. 'The Universe is fluid and volatile': 'this surface on which we now stand is not fixed, but sliding'. If there is any 'fixture or stability' in all this sliding, dissolving, melting world, it is 'in the soul'. 'We are not built like a ship to be tossed, but like a house to stand', says Emerson. Since his Nature is distinctly watery, and the 'ethereal tides' seem at times almost to inundate him as he opens himself to them, we may wonder what will be the origin of this stable house of self which can stand firm in the flowing flux of Existence.

Although Emerson is sometimes very specific about individual facts and perceptions, the nature he refers to has no autonomy and very little local identity. It is a mental fabrication. We look in vain for the specificity of all those place-names which are so common in European Romanticism, whether it is Tintern Abbey or Mont Blanc or 'Lines Composed while Climbing the Left Ascent of Brockley Coome, Somersetshire, May 1795' (Coleridge). Emerson says that America's 'ample geography, dazzles the imagination' and a dazzled imagination may respond in unusual ways. His own response, more often than not, is to treat nature as a flimsy, flowing tissue of appearances. He is concerned either to see through it, or withdraw from it. It is indeed a source of emblems, but he tends only to assert this emblematical quality. Perhaps the difference between an emblem and a metaphor is that an emblem is a sign existing at a definite remove from what it signifies and composed of different material; while a metaphor merges the sign and the thing signified. For Emerson Nature was more a matter of emblems than metaphors; it provided no final resting place, no home, for the mind. Here, perhaps, we can detect vestiges of the old Puritan suspicion of matter as fallen, flawed, and misleading – despite Emerson's programmatic optimism about the essential benevolence of all creation. However it is, Emerson's Nature lacks the substantiality, the local external reality, to be found in many European Romantic writers. In Emerson Nature may be a symbol for the mind, or a manifestation of the invisible Over-Soul. What it tends not to be is its own solid self. Children, said Emerson, 'believe in the external world'. When we grow older we realize that it 'appears only'. Perhaps Emerson found no more dramatic phrase for his concept of Nature than when he suggested it might be 'the apocalypse of the mind'.

What Emerson has done is to interpose his version of a ductile, transparent, fluid, apparitional nature between himself and the hard, opaque, refractory (and dazzling) otherness of the real American landscape. This way he makes Nature amenable to himself and his purposes. It is notable how often he talks of playing with Nature as if it were a collection of baubles and toys. The genius, he writes in his journal, 'can upheave and balance and toss every object in Nature for his metaphor', we must be like Shakespeare, he says, who 'tosses the creation like a bauble from hand to hand'. Anything less tossable from hand to hand, less bauble-like, than the American landscape in the mid-nineteenth century would be hard to think of. But Emerson is swimming in air; and this Nature, this flowing stream of soft transparent playthings, is the web he has created to keep himself afloat. By contrast Wordsworth's or Keats's poetic Nature is, if not the apocalypse of reality, at least its consecration. More recent American writers have not found themselves in exactly the same vast otherness as the mid-nineteenth-century writers. If anything they have to deal with a congestion which would squash them rather than an emptiness which might swallow them, though of course there is a kind of crowdedness which feels like a vacancy. But when Wallace Stevens says that 'resistance to the pressure of ominous and destructive circumstance consists of its conversion, so far as possible, into a different, an explicable, an amenable circumstance', he seems to be placing the emphasis in a way which is typical of the American Romantic attitude, which has so often 'converted' the given environment into something amenable, not necessarily benevolent if we think of Poe, Hawthorne, Melville, but amenable – ductile to the weavings of their art.

NOTE

1. Quoted by Henry James, 'Emerson', *The American Essays*, ed. Leon Edel (Princeton: Princeton University Press, 1956), p. 70.

3

'ENGLISH ROMANTICISM, AMERICAN ROMANTICISM: WHAT'S THE DIFFERENCE?'

J. Hillis Miller

The claim that there is a distinct species of literature in America, as the American robin differs from the English robin, has a long tradition. The notion that American romanticism differs essentially from English romanticism is vigorously present in Emerson and in Whitman, as well as in multitudes of lesser writers, critics, and orators in mid-nineteenth-century America, for example in those speech-makers Dickens parodies in the splendid rhetoric of the Honourable Elijah Pogram in *Martin Chuzzlewit*:

> 'Our fellow-countryman is a model of a man, quite fresh from Natur's mould!' said Pogram, with enthusiasm. [Pogram is speaking of a certain unsavory Mr Chollop.] 'He is a true-born child of this free hemisphere! Verdant as the mountains of our country; bright and flowing as our mineral Licks; unspiled by withering conventionalities as air our broad and boundless Perearers! Rough he may be. So air our Barrs. Wild he may be. So air our Buffalers. But he is a child of Natur', and a child of Freedom; and his boastful answer to the Despot and the Tyrant is, that his bright home is in the Settin Sun'. (*Martin Chuzzlewit*, ch. 34)

It is easy to understand the appeal of such a declaration of independence for the American ethos and for the literature which expresses it. This claim is heard on many sides today. The chorus is likely to get louder and more numerous.

From J. Hillis Miller (1991) *Theory, Now and Then*. New York and London: Harvester Wheatsheaf.

Authenticity in a work of literature derives from its originality, its freshness, its distinctiveness. A valid work must represent a fresh start. It must make it new and make it better than it has ever been made before. Elijah Pogram's great work, the Pogram Defiance, 'defied the world in general to compete with our country upon any hook; and devellop'd our internal resources for making war upon the universal airth' (ibid.). If American romanticism can be shown to be a derivative, a pale offshoot of English romanticism or of European romanticism generally, moon to its sun, its claims to force and validity are greatly weakened. American literature needs to show that it has followed the westering sun and the westering of civilization. It must be nearest the sun, or it must be the sun, shedding light and power everywhere. As Harold Bloom observes in *Agon*, 'Whitman could identify himself . . . with the sun, once even asserting . . . that he could send forth sunrise from himself'.[1]

This need to affirm uniqueness and an independent history for American romanticism is perhaps especially strong again today. The reasons for this are evident. It can be said without cynicism that departments of American studies and specialists in American literature need to justify their existence. At a time when the role of Britain on the stage of world history is getting smaller and smaller, while the United States is a super-power with the fate of the world in its hands, it seems ridiculous to have a literature here which is a mere branch or twig of the Royal Oak, especially of an oak so feeble and so superannuated. In the conservative political climate of this particular moment there is a great need to be able to believe in a special and separate form of romanticism in America in order either to support or to attack the reigning ideology. In either case the appeal is to what is essentially American as opposed to various forms of unAmerican activity. We need to be able to match Emily Dickinson or Whitman, Stevens or Faulkner, against Shakespeare, Wordsworth, Dickens, or Yeats, and we need to be able to say that our American authors have special qualities not found elsewhere.

Moreover, powerful methodologies imported from abroad threaten the integrity of our homegrown or homemade traditions of interpretation, for example American pragmatism. These foreign imports threaten our need to believe that we can go it alone. Why do we need Derrida*, Lacan*, or Adorno*, or even Marx* and Nietzsche*, when we have Emerson, William James, Dewey*, and Kenneth Burke*?

Which of us can say he does not respond to the appeal of this assertion and share the assumptions behind it? The current vogue of Richard Rorty's* powerful *Mirror of Nature* is an example of this appeal. Harold Bloom's recent *Agon* gives the most vigorous polemical expression to what his 'Coda' calls 'The American Difference in Poetry and Criticism'. The central purpose of this admirable book is to persuade the reader that the tradition of Whitman, Dickinson, Crane, Stevens, Ashbery, Merrill, and Ammons is essentially different both from British and from continental poetic traditions, just as the criticism or philosophy of Emerson, Peirce*, James, and Burke is different from anything in England or on the continent:

> We *do* have a national criticism [writes Bloom], as we have had a national poetry since Whitman and Dickinson. There is an American or non-Hegelian* Negative, and it is indebted to Emerson for having pioneered a diachronic rhetoric . . . . From Emerson himself through Kenneth Burke, the American tradition of criticism is highly dialectical, differing in this from the British empirical tradition that has prevailed from Dr Johnson to Empson. But this American tradition precisely resembles Whitmanian poetry, rather than the Continental dialectics that have surged from Hegel through Heidegger* on to the contemporary Deconstruction* of Jacques Derrida and Paul de Man* . . . The American critic, here and now, in my judgment, needs to keep faith both with American poetry and the American Negative, which means one must not yield either to the school of Deconstruction or to the perpetual British school of Common Sense*. Our best poets, from Whitman through Stevens to Ashbery, make impossible and self-contradictory demands upon both their readers and themselves. I myself urge an antithetical criticism in the American grain, affirming the self over language, while granting a priority to figurative language over meaning. The result is a mixed discourse, vatic perhaps, and at once esoteric and democratic, but that is the burden of American tradition.[2]

Bloom a little too much here wants to have the cake of his fun with what he calls, alluding to a certain T-shirt, the 'Deconstruction Road Company', while at the same time eating the cake in the form of assimilating the insights of deconstruction into the priority of figurative over literal language. In any case, the doctrine of his book is heady stuff, and it is hard to keep one's head when assessing it, particularly when one is oneself one of the objects of the polemic, and particularly when the localized reading of American literary history is so strongly reinforced by those broader ideological currents I mentioned earlier and by its appeal to our pragmatic American desire for mastery over language, our desire to ask of a text, as Bloom puts it, not 'Am I getting this poem right?' but 'What is it good for, what can I do with it, what can it do for me, what can I make it mean?'[3] 'You should just shrug', says Bloom, 'when they tell you finally that it is a right reading'.[4] This is tremendously attractive, and not just to untrained students. If all reading is misreading, and if the strongest reader is the one most expert in misprision, why should I not do as Bloom does, or says he does, and make the text mean what I like, in spite of the fact that, for example, Stanley Fish's* current work on interpretative communities argues persuasively for the difficulty or even impossibility of doing this. When I seem freest, most asserting the powers of the strong self over language, I may be most the unwitting spokesman for ideological currents drifting around in the circumambient air. Though it may be impossible not to speak, in the name of some interpretative community or other, one would wish to be as self-conscious about this as possible, and so I raise my head above the Bloomian rhetoric and ask: How would one go about testing the theory that American romanticism is different?

There are, it seems to me, four possible theoretical presuppositions supporting an argument for the uniqueness of American romanticism. Though they are hardly compatible with one another, they tend to appear together in a contradictory mix. All are present implicitly or explicitly in Bloom's *Agon*. All are present, though in different proportions, in my passage from *Martin Chuzzlewit*.

First possibility: It can be argued that poetry arises from nature, from climate. Our flora and fauna, our landscape, the names for all our birds, beasts, mountains, and rivers, are different, therefore the poems of our climate will be different. We have bears, buffaloes, the Rocky Mountains and the Great Plains, wild asters and Black-eyed Susans,

> Deer walk upon our mountains, and the quail
> Whistle about us their spontaneous cries;
> Sweet berries ripen in the wilderness . . .
> [Wallace Stevens, 'Sunday Morning', ll. 114–16]

How can our poetry be expected to be like that of Wordsworth or Tennyson?

Second possibility: We are children not only of nature but also of freedom. Our democratic social structures, not only on the large scale but also in the fine grain of day to day personal intercourse, differ from those of old Europe, land of the despot and the tyrant. Consequently our poetry will also differ. It will be at once democratic and esoteric or élitist, since it will be a democratic agon of warring élites, none able to master all the others. What we need in order to show the uniqueness of American romanticism and American criticism is a sociologically based interpretation of both.

Third possibility: It can be argued that though American romanticism is based on European sources, as Emerson's work, for example, is conspicuously derived from Swedenborg, Plato, English and German romanticism, and so on, nevertheless American romanticism represents a distinct *clinamen* [inclination, bias], a swerve from these sources. Like father, unlike son. The law of misprision or strong misreading would lead us to expect American romanticism to be different, though Bloom's claim for a relatively smooth continuity and homogeneity from Emerson to Whitman to Crane to Stevens and beyond seems to contradict his major insight into literary history. This insight is the notion that though literature is made of literature and not as a reflection of nature or of social conditions, the line from one work to another is twisted, oblique, angled.

The uniqueness of American romanticism, this third theory would argue, arises from this divergence.

The fourth possibility is one version or another of the doctrine of continued inspiration, a familiar part of our American Protestant tradition, but familiar in English romantic poetic theory too from Shelley to Yeats. As Yeats puts this: 'Solitary men receive, as I think, the creative impulse from the lowest of the Nine Hierarchies, and so make and unmake mankind, and even the world itself, for does not "the eye altering alter all"?'[5] The authenticity and authority of poetry, this argument would run, comes in one way or another from some direct access to transcendent sources. Each poet starts afresh and rejects all who have come before in the name of a new inspiration. Bloom's 'Gnosticism' is of course a version of this, and he correctly demonstrates its presence for example in Emerson. By Gnosticism, says Bloom, 'I mean a timeless knowing, as available now as it was then . . . Gnostic freedom is a freedom for knowledge, knowledge of what in the self, *not* in the psyche or soul, is Godlike, and knowledge of God beyond the cosmos'.[6] Bloom cites the Emerson of 'Self-Reliance' on this:

> Yet see what strong intellects dare not yet hear God himself unless he speak the phraseology of I know not what David, or Jeremiah, or Paul. We shall not always set so great a price on a few texts, on a few lives . . . When we have new perception, we shall gladly disburden the memory of its hoarded treasures as old rubbish. When a man lives with God, his voice shall be as sweet as the murmur of the brook and the rustle of the corn.

How can our American romanticism not be unique if it arises out of the direct voice of God speaking afresh within the self of each new poet?

These four theories may be reconciled, in spite of their incompatibility, but only by establishing a hierarchy putting one at the top as the arch-explanation governing the others. The freshness of nature, for example, may be seen as Emerson sees it, that is, as the model for the poet-prophet's openness to the divine inspiration of the present moment. The poet, like a flower, must be cut off from the past and its wornout scriptures in order to be open to the supernatural influxes of the present. The uniqueness of American political and social democracy in turn may be caused, according to a certain form of material determinism, by the special qualities of our climate, and though our poets may necessarily use materials from the old-world writers, their swerve from English or continental romanticism is determined by their independent inspiration. The notion of continued and continually unique inspiration tends to affirm itself implicitly or explicitly as the top of the hierarchy. Bloom is more and more openly a religious writer, as much as René Girard, for example, though his Gnosticism is of course very different from Girard's Roman Catholicism. There is of course nothing wrong with this, but the relation between literary criticism and religious belief still seems to me extremely problematic and complex. It can be said that there is an almost irresistible temptation for literary critics to talk about everything else under the sun except literature.

The fact that all four of these supports for the theory that American romanticism is unique tend to be appealed to at once, in spite of their incoherence with one another, should put interpreters on guard. It should perhaps send them back to the texts to see if in fact there is evidence that any one of the four or some combination, however contradictory, actually operate to make an 'American difference' in poetry and criticism. Let me take as example the almost universal image of the liminal margin of the shore, whether seashore, lakeshore, or riverbank. Almost any writer in both English and American romanticism would provide examples of this motif. Any knowing reader can immediately think of a superabundance of examples. Moreover, most readers would agree that the image is important in the work of the poets in question, and most would agree that its interpretation in each case would expand to include all that is deepest and most problematic in the work of the poet. The image of the shore tends to be associated in each case with images of lines, whether as edges or as paths leading from here to there, and with images of circles receding out to the horizon's bound.

Think, for example, of the dreamer in Book Five of *The Prelude*, 'seated in a rocky cave / By the sea-side' (ll. 58–9), or of the passage in the first 'Essay upon Epitaphs' beginning 'Never did a child stand by the side of a running stream';[7] or of Keats' 'Bright Star', with its 'moving waters at their priestlike task / Of pure ablution round earth's human shores' (ll. 5–6); or of the dreamer in Shelley's 'The Triumph of Life', 'beneath the hoary stem / Which an old chestnut flung athwart the steep / Of a green Apennine': 'before me fled / The night; behind me rose the day, the deep / Was at my feet, and Heaven above my head' (ll. 24–8); or of the poems of Matthew Arnold with their many (and not wholly consistent) uses of the image of the shore, for example 'Dover Beach', with its echoes of Sophocles, Senancour, and, surely, Keats' 'Bright Star': 'The Sea of Faith / Was once, too, at the full, and round earth's shore / Lay like the folds of a bright girdle furled. / But now I only hear / Its melancholy, long, withdrawing roar' (ll. 21–5); or, to turn to American writing, of the line that goes from the circling shore of Thoreau's Walden Pond to Emerson's poem, 'Seashore', to Whitman's 'Out of the Cradle Endlessly Rocking', to Stevens' 'The Idea of Order at Key West', to Ammons' 'Corson's Inlet'.

There is of course not time here to explore all these examples in detail. My claim is that if this were to be done, it could be demonstrated not only that the image of the shore is in each case an inextricable part of the whole system of thought and imagery in the writer in question but that in each case the use of the image is at once constrained by traditional linguistic patterns which are much larger than something so small and local as English or American romanticism, and at the same time to some degree idiosyncratic, different from the use of the image in any of its 'sources' or in any of the immediately adjacent writers in the same country. It is the task of criticism both to identify the relation of a given use of such an image to the larger recurrent linguistic paradigms going back to the Greeks and the Bible and at the same time to identify the specificity of a given use, its difference from all those immediately around it, even those alleged to be its immediate 'source'. A formulation by Jacques Derrida in 'White Mythology' is exemplary here:

> It goes without saying that it will not do here to suppose some homoge-neous continuum (tradition constantly referred back to itself, whether the tradition of metaphysics or that of rhetoric). However, we must pay atten-tion to the more lasting constraints of this kind (which have had their effect through the systematic links of a very long chain); we must take the trouble to delimit their general functioning and the limits of the effects: otherwise we should risk mistaking the most derivative effects for the original characteristic of a hastily identified configuration, an imaginary or marginal mutation. We should be prey to a precipitate and impres-sionistic empiricism, concentrating on alleged differences which would in fact be mainly linear and chronological breaks. So should we step from discovery to discovery, each step marking a break! . . . Here we are led back to the program, not yet spelled out at all, of a new problematic of signatures.[8]

The notion of an American difference in poetry or criticism is an example of the fallacy of misplaced concreteness. It is at once too general and too specific. It ascribes a unity and a reified existence to an entity (American romanticism) which is a fictitious creation of the critic, made by ignoring all sorts of differ-ences from one text to another. At the same time it is not general enough to recognize that all the texts in both English and American romanticism are per-mutations of linguistic materials at least two and a half millenia old. No doubt local conditions, including at least the first three of my hypothetical causes of uniqueness, contribute to the specific form the permutation takes in a given case. No doubt also there are many breaks in the fabric, rents in the continuity of the tradition, leaps forward which are at the same time leaps backward to a configuration not immediately antecedent but perhaps centuries old.

[. . .]

I conclude with the assertion that each poem, essay, or work of fiction in English and American romanticism, or each isolatable passage from any one of these, is a node or intersection in an overdetermined network of associations, influences, constraints, and connections, often connections leaping far over chronological or geographical contiguity, and stretching out in all directions, before, behind, on all sides. These nodes or intersections are both too specific and too impersonal, unsigned, to be incorporated into generalizations at the level of claims that there is an American difference in poetry and criticism. Each must be patiently untangled and interpreted for itself, and the interpreter must do his best to resist the almost irresistible lure of premature generalization.

Our own American Henry James (or is he England's Henry James?) has in a familiar passage in the Preface to *Roderick Hudson* given a splendid model for this complexity of any cultural form, for example of a literary text. James is writing about the novelist's art, but what he says may be taken also as a parable of the critic's double responsibility. His need is to be faithful to the specificity of the text he interprets while honoring also the fact that this specificity lies in the innumerable relations of that text to the immense web of its manifold contexts. The interpreter too is as much inextricably woven into this context as is the writer. He cannot by any effort extricate himself and survey the whole from without. He too is constrained in what he can see and say by his placement within the web:

> The very condition of interest [writes James] [is] . . . the related state, to each other, of certain figures and things. To exhibit these relations, once they have all been recognized, is to 'treat' his idea, which involves neglecting none of those that directly minister to interest; the degree of that directness remaining meanwhile a matter of highly difficult appreciation, and one on which felicity of form and composition, as a part of the total effect, mercilessly rests. Up to what point is such and such a development *indispensable* to the interest? What is the point beyond which it ceases to be rigorously so? Where, for the complete expression of one's subject, does a particular relation stop – giving way to some other not concerned in that expression?
>
> Really, universally, relations stop nowhere . . .[9]

NOTES

1. Harold Bloom, *Agon: Towards a Theory of Revisionism* (New York: Oxford University Press, 1982), p. 333.
2. Ibid., pp. 19, 335–6.
3. Ibid., p. 19.
4. Ibid., p. 20.
5. W. B. Yeats, 'The Symbolism of Poetry', *Essays and Introductions* (London: Macmillan & Co., 1961), pp. 158–9.
6. Bloom, *Agon*, p. 4.
7. William Wordsworth, *Poetical Works*, ed. T. Hutchinson and E. de Selincourt (London: Oxford University Press, 1966), p. 729.
8. Jacques Derrida, 'White Mythology', *New Literary History* 6.1 (Autumn 1974): 30.
9. Henry James, 'Preface', *Roderick Hudson*, Sentry Edition (Boston, 1877), pp. xiv–xv.

4

'CULTURAL TIME IN ENGLAND AND AMERICA'

Robert Weisbuch

The Anglo-American contest is a struggle between two distinct senses of cultural time, British lateness and American earliness. By cultural time, I mean the collective metaphor that expresses an age's view of itself in relation to all of history. But it is not only a reflection of an historical attitude; once established, it directs and helps to determine perceptions beyond a strictly historical field. As John Lynen writes, 'The kind of time one assumes determines the kind of experience one will have, because it establishes the horizon of consciousness and therefore locates the positions from which the mind perceives'.[1] Lynen's emphases are more immediately metaphysical and less historically minded than my own; but my point is that cultural time has just such ontological and epistemological consequences as Lynen claims.

There are any number of other ways by which a culture may evaluate itself, but cultural time predominates in the nineteenth century. In the first of a series of essays on *The Spirit of the Age*, published in 1831, John Stuart Mill* reflects on his title:

> The 'spirit of the age' is in some measure a novel expression. I do not believe that it is to be met with in any work exceeding fifty years in antiquity. The idea of comparing one's own age with former ages, or with our

From Robert Weisbuch (1986) *Atlantic Doublecross: American Literature and British Influence in the Age of Emerson*. Chicago: University of Chicago Press.

notion of those which are yet to come, had occurred to philosophers; but it never before was itself the dominant idea of any age.[2]

In his monumental work *History, Man, and Reason*, Maurice Mandelbaum follows Mill in nominating historicism, 'the belief that an adequate assessment of its [any historical phenomenon's] value is to be gained through considering it in terms of the place which it occupied and the role which it played within a process of development', as a prime feature of the nineteenth century. Both the doctrine of Progress, with its sense of culture as advancing toward something new, and the doctrine of Organicism, with its sense of culture as unfolding whatever is implicit within it on the model of the growth of living things, nudged this historical sensibility toward a visionary theory. They also enlarged the meaning of history. 'What came to be viewed as the true subject of history was the total way of life and of feeling of a people'.[3]

Despite the optimizing tendencies of Progress in particular (for Organicism may imply decay and death), cultural time in England after the Renaissance is predominantly and anxiously late. Walter Jackson Bate quotes Addison* in the *Spectator* as Addison himself paraphrases Boileau: 'It is impossible for us, who live in the latter ages of the world, to make observations . . . which have not been touched on by others'. He quotes Steele in the *Guardian*: 'Nature being still the same, it is impossible for any modern writer to paint her otherwise than the ancients have done'. He discusses the distress caused by the failure of the 'greater genres', tragic drama and epic; and he documents the saddened acceptance of 'refinement' and 'propriety' as substitutes for 'nature' and 'genius'. Bate's theme is the eighteenth-century origins of the problem that haunts the writer still: 'his naked embarrassment (with the inevitable temptations to paralysis or routine imitation, to retrenchment or mere fitful rebellion) before the amplitude of what two thousand years or more of an art had already been able to achieve'. Many writers, and [Samuel] Johnson most vigorously, condemned an assumption of decline, but such opposition acknowledged the assumption's prevalence. Solace was available only through the odd idea which developed through the century and was most succinctly stated in the next by Macaulay: 'As civilization advances, poetry almost necessarily declines'.[4]

Such solace, never fully efficacious in the eighteenth century, is less so in the nineteenth, as civilization is increasingly distrusted and the sacrifices demanded by its advance are increasingly resented. Equations between culture and literature become figured differently: the writer's anxiety of influence is not the necessary result of processes by which culture perfects itself; it is part and parcel of the culture's decrepitude.

Bate and Harold Bloom ignore the writer's less solipsistic anxiety for his culture. Bate sees the problem as the accumulation of cultural achievement epitomized by the Renaissance; Bloom wavers between this view and a startling reduction of the problem to the single figure of Milton. Bate sees the problem eased, though not at all eliminated, by the inventions of new forms in the romantic period; Bloom sees the problem as gaining full force only with the advent of romanticism. Neither, in their travels between specific periods and general human responses, stops long enough at the middle place of culture. But British poets and novelists did so and the evidence is everywhere.

[. . .]

In the fiction as in the poetry of the British nineteenth century, the struggle with an acknowledged cultural lateness figures mightily. We cannot linger to discuss every occurrence of this anxiety, but if we take the three British novels of the mid-century that arguably matter most – Bronte's *Wuthering Heights*, Dickens' *Bleak House*, and Eliot's *Middlemarch* – their concerns with cultural lateness may stand for the rest.

The struggle is most plain in that tome on civilization and its discontents, *Wuthering Heights*. The obvious contrast created by the descriptions of the two abodes, Wuthering Heights and Thrushcross Grange, is frequently and correctly interpreted as a contrast between unprotected, emotional tumult and valley mildness, outdoors-nature and indoors-civilization, id and superego. The physical features of the Heights – its rough beams, primitive furnishings, and stone defenses – also signify cultural earliness; and its 'deeply set' windows are mirrored by Heathcliff's 'deep-set' eyes. In this unity with natural forces and his amoral libidinal energy, Heathcliff is Emily Bronte's hero of extreme cultural earliness. His defeat and subsequent perversion by the forces of advanced, fatigued Christian civilization and Victorian gentility are dramatized in terms of his soulmate's choice for Edgar Linton and the indoor, mild, protected life of Thrushcross Grange. But that soulmate, Catherine Earnshaw, whose choices represent the choices that have been made by civilization, sickens and dies – partly because she cannot resolve the conflict in her character between the early and the late, the unreined vital and the sublimating human, and partly because cultural lateness, when it tyrannizes over and seeks to eliminate the earliness of nature, brings death.

The second half of the romance tends to valorize civilization, not by reversing the values of the first half but by stressing the natural human aspirations expressed in civilized values once civilization is distinguished from the lateness of over-civilization. For example, books are a function of over-civilization in the first half of the novel: Catherine, once she is attracted to the life of Thrushcross Grange, is repelled by Heathcliff's illiteracy, only to find herself placed with the Edgar who remains steadfastly ensconced in his library while she sickens with libidinal hunger. But Catherine's daughter, after ridiculing Hareton for his inability to read, finds her way out of a tragic repetition pattern by repenting and instructing him in the energy of written language. Books, as imaginative and passionate and yet rational artifacts, books like *Wuthering Heights*, harmonize the values that had seemed implacably in conflict; and as nature-terms and civ-ilization-terms merge in the figures of Hareton and the second Catherine, a new garden is (literally) planted, and cultural lateness is defeated.

Cultural lateness may result in part from the passage of time, but its effect is the clogging of time. In *Wuthering Heights*, the tale is told by the work's most repressed, over-civilized, culturally late and attenuated character, Lockwood. He recounts the recountings of Nelly Dean, who is much like him in these respects, and the very enwrapping of the fallible narration serves as another indicator of lateness. The narrative travels backwards from its present-tense beginning (in 1801, significantly – the work lays the basis of the nineteenth century and dra-matizes its alternative possibilities), but, upon Catherine's death, any sense of moving forward to the present is made merely statistical. As many critics have noted, Heathcliff comes to imitate his victimizers; his son by Isabella Linton is a living caricature of every Thrushcross-civilized attenuation of energy, the rela-tionship between the offspring, Catherine and Linton, parodies by an exagger-ated repetition of events the conflicts of the original Catherine and Edgar; and their dual scorn of Hareton recalls the original rejection of Heathcliff. The tale catches up to the time of the narrative's beginning and frees itself into the literal future only when the younger Catherine and Hareton begin to conspire the puri-fied combination of Heights and Grange values. The couple will marry on New Year's Day. That is, time can go forward once the cultural clock has been turned back to beginnings for a new attempt at historical living.

[. . .]

'The youth of America is their oldest tradition', Oscar Wilde has a character say in *A Woman of No Importance*. 'It has been going on now for three hundred years'.[5] That isn't quite fair. The settlement of the continent was con-tinuing during Wilde's lifetime, the United States was still a relatively new con-figuration, and, as we have shown to the point of redundancy, American culture awaited definition. But yes, cultural earliness became the tradition to substitute for the lack of more tangible traditions; and this in part because the Americans, glancing at the omnipresent comparative model of Britain, could have no hope of competing for the rewards of cultural maturity. [William Cullen] Bryant* in 1843 foresees an Anglo-American struggle for 'which power holds and governs the world' wherein 'the mind of England, old and knit by years and wisdom into strength' is ably combatted by an America 'roused to new duties in its youth, and in the van with opinions born of the hour'.[6] And Emerson more aggressively tells Carlyle that 'England, an old and exhausted island, must one day be contented, like other parents, to be strong only in her children'.[7]

Cultural earliness became synonymous with the national faith to the extent that when Melville became an apostate his first move was to deny the benefits of earliness. In *Benito Cereno*, the Spanish and American sea captains are characterized, seated across from each other over a long dinner table, as 'a childless couple': the future is made sterile for the American too, as his over-ripe innocence, his willed naïveté, serves to further the slave trade and, by implication, all of the ills of European history. And [. . .] the New York of 'Bartleby the Scrivener: A Tale of Wall Street' is as walled-in, as lifeless and heartless, as devoid of the personal and the possible as the London of *Bleak House*. Alternately, in such paired tales as 'The Paradise of Bachelors' and 'The Tartarus of Maids', the sterility of British lateness and the savagery of American earliness result in like dehumanizations.

In dissent from the national faith, then, American writers might see the nation not as a new start but as the final, fatal outpost of a decrepit Euro-American civilization. (One could cite here as well the wide variety of Bachelor figures in Hawthorne – Chillingworth, Judge Pynchon, Coverdale, all of the over-rational scientists of inhuman perfection – as representative of a disastrous lateness.) Or they might render both earliness and lateness irrelevant in comparison to a human propensity for evil that infiltrates either. But again, such dissents prove the centrality of the claims for earliness, as when Thoreau, in defense of 'this vast, savage, howling mother of ours, Nature', warns in 'Walking' against a socially centered culture 'which produces at most a merely English nobility, a civilization destined to have a speedy limit'.[8]

Cultural earliness is an organic metaphor and its joys are the joys of youth. R. W. B. Lewis in *The American Adam* describes these joys most generally as 'a sense of promise and possibility'. Specifically, cultural earliness promises 'a life determined by nature and enriched by a total awareness'.[9] Most simply, as Thomas Paine* writes, 'We have it in our power to begin the world again'. And momentarily in that spirit, Melville, in his encomium on Hawthorne, defends America against the assumption he later would apply with a vengeance, 'that the world is getting grey and grizzled now. Not so. The world is as young today as when it was created; and this Vermont morning dew is as wet to my feet, as Eden's dew to Adam's'.[10]

The Adamic quill would provide specifically literary joys. British writers who believed that literature in England had declined since the Renaissance advanced the idea, best put by the artist Constable, that 'In the early ages of the fine arts, the productions were most affecting and sublime*' because 'the artists, being without human exemplars, *were forced to have recourse to nature*'. The Scottish critic Hugh Blair popularized this idea for Americans, convincing them (and they were not averse to being so convinced) that, in Benjamin Spencer's words, 'for the highest species of poetry and the grandest reaches of the imagination the vigorous temper of a youthful people was a more likely soil than that of a polished nation'.[11] Thus Emerson in 'The Poet' awaited a 'genius in America with tyrannous eye, which knew the value of our incomparable materials, and saw, in the barbarism and materialism of the times, another carnival of the gods whose picture he so much admires in Homer'.[12] In Whitman, just such a genius arrived.

Emerson's hope for a classical revival utterly different from the British Augustan one, returning barbarism rather than polished wit to literature, should remind us that cultural earliness is an imaginative fact, not a historical one. Only by relation to England was there any historical basis for it. 'We are good', writes the senior Henry James at mid-century, 'by comparison, not by position. When compared with the politics of the Old World, we present the auroral beauty of the morning emerging from the thick night'.[13] Even so, it would have been difficult to have found a true barbarian in Emerson's Boston, or indeed in puritan Boston two centuries earlier.

This helps to answer Wilde's incredulity concerning the three-hundred-year-old youth of America: myth need not age. Leo Marx cites 'all the later fictional narrators who begin in the same way, impulsively dissociating themselves from the world of sophistication, Europe, ideas, learning, in a word, *the world*, and speaking in accents of rural ignorance'. As myth, then, cultural earliness could claim not only to precede decadent lateness and thus be closer to life's priorities; it could claim to succeed it, as a curative undoing, and thus could defend against the clear absence of those achievements available to cultural maturity. 'In its simplest, archetypal form', Marx writes, 'the myth affirms that Europeans experience a regeneration in the New World. They become new, better, happier men – they are reborn'.[14]

But perhaps one could be reborn with memory intact. If they were sufficiently ingenious, Americans could take Horatio Greenough's dour remark, 'the country was young, yet the people were old',[15] and make it seem cause for utmost celebration. Within its own new history, America could seem final without appearing withered and elderly. It could be seen as the repudiation, the erasure, of all the evils of European history, or as the ultimate achievement of Christian, European culture. David Humphreys, one of the Connecticut Wits, exemplifies the heady rhetoric that could result from this doctrine of first-and-last: 'We began our political career, in a great measure, free from the prejudice, and favored with the knowledge of former ages and other nations'.[16] Looking before and after at the unprecedented expanse of time granted America by this valuable ambiguity, Americans would be able, sometimes, to ignore the thinness of the cultural present.

Thus the American Puritan myth by which America was the land of apocalypse. In scripture, the apocalypse occurs only at the moment of utmost corruption, when history has degenerated to a waste. But Puritans could load that corruption onto Old World history and see their own historical time as the beginning of the apocalyptic promise, 'requiring', in Sacvan Bercovitch's characterization, 'one last great act, one more climactic pouring out of the spirit, in order to realize itself'. European Christians would look for an end to history, Bercovitch continues, while the Americans could valorize their history as 'a preparation, the planting that anticipates a harvest'. Theirs is 'an errand to the end of time'.[17]

Bercovitch errs, however, when he sees this future orientation as invalidating the nostalgic myth of Lewis's American Adam.[18] It is logically inconsistent to envision a return and an unprecedented arrival simultaneously, but cultural earliness, an opportunistic myth, is not strictly logical; and, for nineteenth-century writers suffering the recognition of emptiness, there would be no fussy discriminations between Old Eden and the New Jerusalem as long as each offered a rebuttal to British jibes. Thus Bercovitch is right to emphasize that, in America, the meaning of the term frontier is sometimes transformed from a secular barrier separating nations to 'a mythical threshold', 'a *figural* outpost, the outskirts of the advancing Kingdom of God'. But to that we must add Edwin Fussell's recognition of the significant synonymity of the terms 'frontiersman' and 'backwoodsman' as the spatial idea of the frontier takes on a temporal dimension. To Fussell, 'back' suggests an American fear of cultural regression, 'front' a progressive national optimism. But regression, as we saw in considering the myth of the West, may mean a return not to chaos but to paradise, and thus the paradox engendered by these synonyms might be figured all-optimistically. As Eric J. Sundquist writes, 'going *back* and going *forth* are the same: the primitive is Past, but it is also West, and West is Future'.[19]

At best the paradox triumphs over British cultural lateness and over the American anxiety of mere immaturity as well. The triumph occurs by a surround-and-conquer strategy in each case. This myth of a new beginning that promised as well, by a quickening of time, a millennial ending made English writers, who dealt with society as is and with history as merely secular time, appear narrow and unadventuresome. The Americans could turn back on the British the charge of provincialism.

[. . .]

Clearly, cultural earliness allowed Americans to capitalise upon the barrenness of their present scene by considering this barrenness a clearing of the ground for an unprecedented development. Nonetheless, cultural earliness just as easily might mean cultural emptiness. Youth, cultural as well as personal, can be callow. We earlier reviewed the varieties of despair Americans themselves experienced in viewing the present and immediate past of their literary attempts; and while I would not make of the myth of American time (which we have just considered) a merely defensive rationalization – that may have become one of its uses but it would be entirely too cynical to reduce a cultural faith to an excuse – it demanded a leap of faith that the most springy of the literary nationalists could not make at every moment.

Like the joys, the sorrows of cultural earliness as emptiness and cultural youthfulness as immaturity or a negative savagery are seen most clearly in attempts to refute them. All that we have said of the proposed joys of earliness constitutes, in one sense, the largest refutation of sorrows. But there occurred as well an attempt to disown earliness either by considering Euro-Americans as the inheritors of a storied Indian past or by foisting earliness upon the Indian and separating oneself from him and it. In its more benevolent form, as an adoption of the Indian as the ancestor of the white American, an instant history might be appropriated.

NOTES

1. John F. Lynen, *The Design of the Present: Essays on Time and Form in American Literature* (New Haven: Yale University Press, 1969), p. 21.
2. John Stuart Mill, *The Spirit of the Age* (Chicago: University of Chicago Press, 1942), p. 1.
3. Maurice Mandelbaum, *History, Man, and Reason: A Study in Nineteenth-Century Thought* (Baltimore: Johns Hopkins University Press, 1971), pp. 42, 44–5, 54.
4. Walter Jackson Bate, *The Burden of the Past and the English Poet* (New York: W. W. Norton, 1970), pp. 39–40, 42–4, 61–2, 64, 95.
5. Oscar Wilde, *Complete Works*, ed. Robert Ross, 10 vols (Boston: Wyman-Fogg, 1909), vol. 7, p. 20.
6. Bryant quoted in Benjamin T. Spencer, *The Quest for Nationality: An American Literary Campaign* (Syracuse: Syracuse University Press, 1957), p. 86.
7. Ralph Waldo Emerson, *The Complete Works of Ralph Waldo Emerson*, Centenary Edition, ed. Edward Waldo Emerson, 12 vols (Boston and New York: Houghton Mifflin, 1903–4), vol. 5, pp. 275–6.
8. Henry David Thoreau, 'Walking', *Atlantic Monthly* 10 (1862): 670.
9. R. W. B. Lewis, *The American Adam: Innocence, Tragedy, and Tradition in the Nineteenth Century* (Chicago: University of Chicago Press, 1958), pp. 1, 25.
10. Thomas Paine, *Common Sense* in *Complete Writings*, ed. Philip S. Foner, 2 vols (New York: Citadel, 1945), vol. 1, p. 45; Herman Melville, 'Hawthorne and his Mosses' (part 2), *Literary World* 7 (24 August 1850): 145.
11. Spencer, *The Quest for Nationality*, p. 10.
12. Ralph Waldo Emerson, *The Collected Works of Ralph Waldo Emerson*, vol. III: *Essays: First Series*, ed. Joseph Slater, Alfred R. Ferguson and Jean Ferguson Carr (Cambridge, MA: Harvard University Press, 1983), p. 21.
13. Henry James Sr, 'Democracy and its Issues' in *Lectures and Miscellanies* (New York: Redfield, 1852), pp. 5–6.
14. Leo Marx, *The Machine in the Garden: Technology and the Pastoral Ideal in America* (London: Oxford University Press, 1964), pp. 109, 228.
15. Quoted in Spencer, *The Quest for Nationality*, p. 128.
16. David Humphreys, 'Preface' to 'On the Happiness of America' in *Miscellaneous Works*, Facsimile Edition, intro. William K. Bottorff (Gainesville, FL: Scholars' Facsimiles and Reprints, 1968), p. 24.
17. Sacvan Bercovitch, *The American Jeremiad* (Madison: University of Wisconsin Press, 1978), pp. 71, 94, 96.
18. Ibid., p. 169.
19. Ibid., pp. 163–4; Edwin Fussell, *Frontier: American Literature and the American West* (Princeton: Princeton University Press, 1965), p. 15; Eric J. Sundquist, *Home as Found: Authority and Genealogy in the Nineteenth-Century American Literature* (Baltimore: Johns Hopkins University Press, 1979), p. 45.

5

'NATURE AND *WALDEN*'

Richard Gravil

There is considerable consensus that Thoreau's career as a writer reflects a prolonged engagement with Wordsworth, and that the writing and revision of *Walden* spanned years in which he moved from frank admiration, little short of hero-worship, to tentative distancing. De Quincey's acid *Reminiscences*, Christopher Wordsworth's construction in his *Memoirs* of a soundly Tory Wordsworth, and London gossip as reported by Emerson and other visitors, may well, as Joseph J. Moldenhauer suggests, have colored Thoreau's views by 1851–53 as he revises *Walden*.[1] Wordsworth's own mind, the evidence suggested, had decayed, and was now in a disconcertingly deep sleep. Yet critical efforts to present Thoreau as irritably concerned to distance himself from Wordsworthian influence on these grounds seem to me peculiarly ill-conceived. *Walden* manifests an astonishing openness to the living Wordsworth. Given the publication of *The Prelude* in 1850, the fact that Thoreau's major textual revisions took place between one journal entry (16 July 1851) lamenting that nothing in later life 'comes up to, or is comparable with, the experiences of my boyhood', when 'life was ecstasy', and another (28 March 1857) claiming that 'Often I can give the truest and most interesting account of any adventure I have had after years have elapsed, for . . . all that continues to interest me after such a lapse of time is sure to be pertinent', strikes one as more than coincidental.

From Richard Gravil (2000) *Romantic Dialogues: Anglo-American Continuities, 1776–1862*. Basingstoke: Palgrave Macmillan.

In the midst of revising and shaping *Walden*, or to be more precise, as he was embarking on its major period of expansion and giving it its chapter form, Thoreau wrote what could be taken as a review of the first four books of *The Prelude*:

> Ah these youthful days! Are they never to return? When the walker does not too curiously observe particulars, but sees, hears, scents, tastes, and feels only himself, – the phenomena that show themselves to him, – his expanding body, his intellect, and heart. No worm or insect, quadruped or bird confined his view, but the unbounded universe was his. (30 March 1853)[2]

The textual evidence for a profound identification greatly outweighs some five or six ambivalent signals of self-differentiation elsewhere in Thoreau's work. Thoreau's Wordsworthian criticism of American writers for using foreign rather than indigenous materials (singing of Keatsian nightingales and Shelleyan skylarks on English hedges, for instance, instead of homely robins on American fences) is bizarrely taken as a sign of a proper 'American chauvinism' rather than what it is: a call to emulate, not imitate, the 'Lakers' in whom such indigenousness is endemic.[3] His experience in 1848, on Mount Ktaadn, of a 'vast, Titanic inhuman Nature', anything but motherly – it inspired such vertiginous responses as 'I stand in awe of my body . . . rocks, trees, wind on our cheeks! The *solid* earth! The *actual* world! The *common sense*! Contact! Contact! *Who* are we? *Where* are we?' – constitutes, it has been argued, a recantation of the Romantic view of Nature expressed in *Walden* six years later.[4] One might argue, rather, that Thoreau's organicism survived the experience, just as Wordsworth's survived his birdsnesting vertigo and the terrors of Ullswater, Stonehenge, and the Simplon Pass – and as Shelley's holistic philosophy synthesized the sublime terrors of Mont Blanc.

Thoreau's endlessly quoted remark that Wordsworth 'is too tame for the Chippeway' occurs in a Journal entry of 1841 asking for a wilder literature, expressive of nature's 'primeval aspects, sterner, savager than *any* poet has sung'.[5] The remark certainly announces that there is more to be done in the way of wildness, but it also implies that Wordsworth is, to date, rather surprisingly, the one Anglo-American poet one might even nominate as bard to an Indian nation. He expands the point into a broader argument in 'Walking' (1862): 'English Literature, from the days of the minstrels *to* the lake Poets, – Chaucer and Spenser and Milton, and even Shakespeare, included, – breathes no quite fresh and in this sense wild strain' (emphasis added). The desire in the same essay for a poet who could 'impress the winds and the streams into his service' and transplant his words to the page 'with earth adhering to their roots' so that they would 'bloom and bear fruit there for the faithful reader' established a model of the poet described, as Coleridge would say, 'in ideal perfection' and invites one to consider which poets have come closest to that ideal. The statement 'I do not know of *any* poetry to quote which adequately expresses this yearning for the Wild' is generally read as if it refers *not* to any failure by Paulding, or Shelley, or Bryant*, or Longfellow, or Emerson, or Thoreau, to do this, but *specifically* to Wordsworth's, yet the same 1862 essay borrows from Bishop Wordsworth's *Memoirs* an exemplary and explicit instance of the outdoor poet – 'When a traveller asked Wordsworth's servant to show him her master's study, she answered, "here is his library, but his study is out of doors"'.[6]

Given the pressure of Emerson's disenchantment, following his visit in 1848, the significance of this slender harvest of by no means adverse comment is surely the reverse of what might be expected. Thoreau's evident absorption of Wordsworth's poetry, and in the *Topographical Description*, constituted a bond that made his critique in *Walden* one of the most perceptive, and inward, that literature can show between two men who never met. The publication of *The Prelude* in 1850, along with De Quincey's and Christopher Wordsworth's disturbing versions of the later Wordsworth, seems to have sent Thoreau back to the *poetry*. Certainly he makes one disparaging remark in his Journal of 1851 on what he calls Wordsworth's 'coldness' in remarking of a beautiful scene that it gave him 'pleasure', and *Walden* makes a wry allusion to Wordsworth's sinecure as 'distributor of stamps': there was, he remarks in the opening chapter, little chance of the townsfolk of Concord offering *him* 'a sinecure with a moderate allowance'. What Thoreau made of the later Wordsworth and his lifestyle at Rydal Mount undoubtedly influences the strategy of *Walden*, whose subplot is, of course, recovery of precisely that visionary gleam that Wordsworth spends his career lamenting. But it would be as absurd to claim that criticism of this kind constitutes a rejection, as to suggest that his claim to have 'laboured' to read Chalmer's anthology of poetry 'without skipping' constitutes a rejection of the English lyrical tradition. In fact, Thoreau openly inscribes himself in that tradition, quoting liberally, alongside the much more conspicuously 'alien' infusions of Eastern writings, from Chaucer, Spenser, Shakespeare, Jonson, Chapman, Quarles, D'Avenant, Carew, Donne, Milton (several times), 'Ossian', and Cowper, along with Raleigh's Ovid and Pope's Homer.

Although stylistically *Walden* may appear to be a polar opposite to the major works of English Romantic poetry, in its affectation of prosaic woodnotes wild, its relation to that art is self-conscious. It openly celebrates an American Grasmere ('This is my lake country') and Thoreau imagines his hut as opening onto a mountain 'tarn'. His allusiveness to his immediate precursors is, given the pressures on American writers to repudiate recent English influence, pervasive, open, and genial. Unlike Emerson, Thoreau has the confidence to post his debts, or his challenges, up front, and unlike Emerson he recognizes and adapts the communicative strategies of the poets, their tonal shifts, their irony – in Thoreau's case a signally Wordsworthian trick of moving within the orbit of a single sentence from matter-of-factness to symbol and enigma – and their refusal of textual authority. Where Emerson merely claims to want an active reader, Thoreau adopts conspicuously Romantic strategies that make passivity untenable.

Along with many fainter echoes, *Walden* alludes conspicuously to Coleridge's 'The Eolian Harp', 'This Lime-Tree Bower', and 'Dejection: an Ode', and to Wordsworth's 'Goody Blake and Harry Gill', 'To my Sister', 'Tintern Abbey', the Arab Dream in *The Prelude*, 'There was a Boy', 'Influence of Natural Objects', 'Personal Talk', and *The Excursion*. Indeed the work opens with an allusion to Coleridge, situating his work in relation to the lyric dialogue of 1798–1802 – 'I do not propose to write an ode to dejection', Thoreau helpfully offers in his epigraph, 'but to brag as lustily as chanticleer in the morning, standing on his roost, if only to wake my neighbors up'[7] – and manifests throughout a revised Wordsworthian riposte to Coleridge's ode. Wordsworth's critique of Coleridge's defeatism occurs principally in three texts, 'Resolution and Independence', 'Intimations of Immortality', and *The Prelude*, all of which leave rhetorical footprints in *Walden*. But as Thoreau uses Wordsworth to critique Coleridge, he is also developing an equally intimate, and more self-defining, counter-critique of Wordsworth.

The opening reference to 'Dejection' is a more complex allusion than it looks: the chanticleer may be Chaucerian, but in *Christabel*, as Robert Weisbuch points out, Coleridge's owls awaken the crowing cock. *Christabel*'s 'Tu – whit! – Tu – whoo!' is not necessarily melancholy, any more than the owlet's cry in 'Frost at Midnight', but when he is serenaded Wordsworth-fashion by owls on the lake-side, Thoreau chooses to translate the owls' call as a cry of despair: 'O that I had never been bor-r-r-n!' ('Sounds'). These ostensibly Coleridgean owls are as suicidal as Wordsworth's (in 'The Boy of Winander') are jocund, and Thoreau may intend a playful reference to Wordsworth's attempts to cheer Coleridge up, while alluding wryly to Coleridge's own protestation – in 'The Nightingale' – against the alleged melancholy of literary nightingales. In a second compound allusion (also in 'Sounds'), Thoreau embeds, within a generally Wordsworthian approach to listening to the language of things, a peculiarly Coleridgean note, suggesting that 'All sound heard at the greatest possible distance produces one and the same effect, a vibration of the universal lyre'. Echoes, he affirms in the same chapter, partake of the nature of the reflecting element as well as of the thing echoed; it is a striking affirmation – influenced perhaps by Emerson's – of Wordsworth's insistence that the shouts of children make crags 'tinkle' and draw from the hills 'an alien sound of melancholy' (*Prelude* 1: 469–71). A third compounding of Wordsworth and Coleridge appears in Thoreau's Wordsworthian insistence, which he translates into Coleridgean metaphor, that the music of storms is Aeolian to a healthy ear ('Solitude'). The entire text of 'Sounds' and 'Solitude' creates a curious sense that Thoreau is participating in precisely the kind of intimately allusive dialogue that – as Lucy Newlyn has shown – Wordsworth and Coleridge practised between themselves, interjecting his own genial variations, and defining himself in sympathetic critiques. He uses Wordsworth and Coleridge as Shelley does in 'Mont Blanc': and, like Shelley, is most himself in that mode of self-definition.

In the body of *Walden*, after Thoreau's coincidentally Wordsworthian apology that it is a thing unprecedented that a man should talk so much about himself, and his equally Wordsworthian excuse that there is no one else he knows so well, a figure casting himself as a Solitary offers an account of the mind's ability to restore itself through intercourse with the wild. The text is famous among other things for its lengthy and Blakean diagnosis of 'marks of weakness, marks of woe' among his contemporaries, and for a portrait of a Canadian wood-chopper, whom Thoreau earnestly or playfully, but certainly inconclusively, probes for evidence of untutored genius or such spiritual strengths as are to be found in 'Michael' or the 'Leech-Gatherer'. The lure of the wild expresses itself more than once in dietary terms:

> I caught a glimpse of a woodchuck stealing across my path, and . . . was strongly tempted to seize and devour him raw; not that I was hungry then, except for that wildness which I felt he represented. ('Higher Laws');

or, in the same chapter, 'I could sometimes eat a fried rat with a good relish, if it were necessary'. But these aberrations of a most ascetic man need not be taken too literally (as that pun on 'relish' signifies). Rather, they point to Thoreau's need to out-savage the young Wordsworth (*Prelude* Book 1) poaching woodcocks on the Esthwaite fells or sporting in the thunder shower; an image of Wordsworth – it is hard to remember – that was not available to Thoreau when he first drafted *Walden*.

Thoreau's central theme is the nature of liberty, and its connection with imagination. His major symbol is the pond itself, the eye of the landscape, into which he gazes in acts of self-exploration: 'A lake', he says, 'is earth's eye; looking into which the beholder measures the depth of his own nature' ('The Ponds'). Not only is this pond one of 'the oldest scenes stamped upon my memory', first known when he was four, but he has drifted upon it in youthful reverie, and consults it now – as Wordsworth consults known landscapes in *Tintern Abbey* and *The Prelude* – both as a prism of his own development, against its own unchanging purity, and as a symbol of an identical self that still exists, and with which he can reconnect. The pond itself images such stability through change: when looking through its carapace of wintry ice, he sees a sandy bottom yet unchanged. It has not acquired 'one permanent wrinkle'. Its being seems permanent, yet it responds to the changing seasons, and to the minutest variation of surroundings or of atmosphere. Living 'reserved and austere, like a hermit in the woods' – the reference perhaps associates 'Tintern' and Grasmere – the pond 'is' the unfallen self: and in all kinds of ways, both Wordsworthian and more traditional, it serves to embody – as the Thoreauvian Yeats would put it – the generated soul.

NOTES

1. See Joseph J. Moldenhauer, '*Walden* and Wordsworth's *Guide to the English Lake District*', *Studies in the American Renaissance* (1990): 261–92.
2. Cited in J. Lyndon Shanley, *The Making of Walden: With the Text of the First Version* (Chicago: University of Chicago Press, 1957), pp. 7, 57.
3. Lorrie Smith, 'Walking from England to America', *New England Quarterly* 58: 2 (1985): 223–4.
4. Henry David Thoreau, *The Maine Woods, The Writings of Henry David Thoreau*, 20 vols (Boston: Houghton Mifflin, 1906), vol. 3, pp. 70, 78.
5. Henry David Thoreau, *The Journal of Henry David Thoreau*, ed. Bradford Torrey, in *The Writings of Henry David Thoreau*, vol. 1, p. 273.
6. Smith, 'Walking from England to America', p. 228.
7. Henry David Thoreau, *Walden and Civil Disobedience*, ed. Owen Thomas (New York: Norton, 1966), p. 1.

6

'ON BEGINNING TO TELL
A "BEST-KEPT SECRET"'

Margaret McFadden

By the century's end the 1866 cable had been supplemented by scores of others, webbing the Atlantic world into a grand structure of electrical communications [. . .] This structure generated its own world of metaphors, one of which Alli Trygg-Helenius drew upon in her Finnish-accented address to the International Council of Women in 1888. Underlying (in the most literal sense) the 'golden cable of sympathy' was a material system of copper and iron in the cold Atlantic. But also beneath – or, better, 'behind' – the system of sympathy lay something else: a very long pre-cable history of linkages between women in the Atlantic community, a history that attested to something Trygg-Helenius's very presence in Washington embodied: the movement of 'ladies' out of their 'appropriate places' to virtual and actual sites where intense woman-to-woman communication could take place.

One can, I believe, speak legitimately of a tradition of transatlantic female communication far older than either the cable or the steamer. Indeed, it is a tradition older even than many historians of women's international organizations and international feminism are aware; this is at least the central thesis of this book. Formal organizations grew up in the late nineteenth century, and the extensive scholarly attention directed to them has been more than justified. But what has not come clearly enough into view is the fact that such organizations

From Margaret McFadden (1999) *Golden Cables of Sympathy: The Transatlantic Sources of Nineteenth-Century Feminism*. Lexington: Kentucky University Press.

sprang out of ground that had been well prepared. The 'best-kept secret' noticed by Susan Bell and Karen Offen needs to begin to be told. Such is my aim here, although I believe something a good deal 'thicker' than 'intellectual ferment'[1] is involved.

[. . .]

THREE USEFULLY RELATED METAPHORS

The inherently international character of the nineteenth-century women's movement suggests one reason why it has not been much studied: it was both too obvious and too elusive. Cracking Bell and Offen's 'best-kept secret' necessitated envisioning by means of several organizing metaphors a process spreading out over time and space.

The central metaphors used here are 'matrix', 'network', and 'web'. An extremely rich word, 'matrix' is often encountered today in its mathematical sense of a rectangular grid or chart composed of vertical and horizontal lines that define cells or small fields. Geologists employ the term when speaking about the surrounding material from which one extricates fossils or crystals and to which one may look for an impression or mold of them. Printers have used the word to denote the mold in which the face of a piece of type is cast. But its original sense is *that from which a structure grows*. More precisely and interestingly for my purposes here, it means that in which something develops or takes shape or, in anatomy, the formative cells of a structure such as a fingernail. According to the *Oxford English Dictionary*, 'matrix' was used as late as 1896 with its figurative meaning of 'a place or point of origin and growth'. In Latin the word literally means 'womb' or 'breeding animal' and derives from *mater, matris*, mother. Thus, 'matrimony' and 'matron' come from the same root, as does 'matriculate', which originates in the medieval Latin *matricula*, diminutive of *matrix*, womb, origin, or public roll.

A mathematical matrix is, almost literally, a network. Indeed, in computer science, 'networks' and 'matrices' are closely allied concepts. While I often use the terms as near synonyms in this work, I am aware that they carry different metaphoric burdens. 'Net' and 'network' derive ultimately from the Indo-European root *ned*, to twist together. The fundamental activities pointed to are, thus, threadmaking and the production of open-weave fabrics to be used to hold, contain, or trap. Related are the Latin *nodus*, knot, and *nectere*, to bind – as well as the German word *netz*. The oldest sense of 'network' is that of a fabric of parallel threads or wires crossed at regular intervals by others, so as to form a mesh or lace pattern. Later, of course, a network became any interconnected physical system, such as of canals, tracks, or transmitting stations.

'Network' as a noun was defined in Samuel Johnson's 1755 *Dictionary of the English Language* as something with the form or construction of a net;

according to the *OED*, its figurative meaning as an interconnected chain or system was used in 1816 by Samuel Coleridge in his *Lay Sermons*. Its contemporary meaning as a group of 'interconnected or cooperating individuals' did not emerge until much later. According to *A Feminist Dictionary* (1985), 'network' as a verb is a word 'coined and used by women', meaning 'to establish good connections with other women and provide for each other information, concrete help, and personal or professional support'.[2] A networker would then be 'one who networks'. Note that this definition picks up the weblike connotations of a net.

Recent developments in linked-computer communication have served to fuse the meanings of 'net' and 'web'. Thus, 'Internet' is often synonymous with 'Worldwide Web'. Further complicating matters, a 1995 dictionary defines 'Internet' as 'a matrix of networks' connecting computers globally. I occasionally contribute to this confusion by referring to web construction and networking in the same context. Yet here again, a somewhat different etymological source furnishes similar meanings and connotations: since 'web' derives from the Indo-European word for 'weave', it is closely associated with 'net'.

One is also reminded of the structures made by spiders. Female spiders build webs by spinning out silk, beginning with a bridge thread, to which the first radius is fastened. This becomes the hub; all other radii are secured from there, and only after they are complete does the spider spin out the sticky spiral threads connecting them. Each web has only one hub, but radii are connected not only to the hub but to each other by means of the spiral threads. The example of spiders brings us back to the powerful interplay between 'matrix' and 'web'. In a classic text on spider webs, one reads: 'The spider catches its food in a silken web, swathes its prey in a silken bag, and wraps its eggs in a silken cocoon'.[3] Thus, the notion of a web or network being a site of new birth is far from an illogical mixing of metaphors.

The appeal of these etymological reverberations in a work such as this hardly needs pointing out. What I am exploring here are the modes of communicative action that came to exist for nineteenth-century women. Such actions and modes were generative, creating a point of origin and growth. They came to constitute a kind of womb, gestating and thus enabling the subsequent development of a more formal organizational structure.

A concluding note: it will have occurred to many by this time that these three metaphors are central to late modernity, with its dazzling revolutions in electronic communication, transport, and information storage and delivery. I hope that I have drawn upon them not because they are so profoundly up-to-date but because they are profoundly apt. In so doing, however, I have had to reckon with the significant fact that 'network analysis' is the province of not one but two different disciplines outside of history: computer science and 'structural' sociology. The former, as might be expected, offers few invitations to the interdisciplinary historian. The latter I have found interesting and occasionally suggestive.

Network theory has since its beginning become a complicated quantitative part of sociometry, using Boolean algebra; it has its own journal, called *Social Networks*, and its own section in the *Annual Review of Sociology*.[4] But it is the basic concept with which I am concerned: that is, understanding and mapping the connections between women – the meetings, the letters, the introductions – and finding the 'brokers', the nodes in the net, the mothers of the matrix, the beginnings of an 'old girls' network' in the nineteenth century. I am interested in how these connections became friendships, cliques, organizations, and also ultimately hierarchies and conflicts – resulting in either a glossing over of disagreements or actual splits on the basis of difference in politics, nationality, or language.

The basics of network analysis are very simple; in the words of Jeremy Boissevain, 'It asks questions about who is linked to whom, the nature of that linkage, and how the nature of the linkage affects behaviour'.[5] It is the transatlantic linkage among women in the nineteenth century that I am seeking to document.

NOTES

1. See Susan Groag Bell and Karen Offen, *Women, the Family, and Freedom: The Debate in Documents*, vol. II, 1880–1950 (Stanford: Stanford University Press, 1983).
2. Cheris Kramarae and Paula Treichler, *A Feminist Dictionary* (London: Pandora Press, 1985), p. 299.
3. Peter N. Witt, Charles F. Reed and David B. Peakall, *A Spider's Web: Problems in Regulatory Biology* (New York: Springer-Verlag, 1968), p. 5.
4. See, e.g., Ronald S. Burt, 'Models of Network Structure', *Annual Review of Sociology* 6 (1980): 79–141.
5. Jeremy Boissevain, 'Networks', in *The Social Science Encyclopedia*, ed. Adam Kuper and Jessica Kuper (London: Routledge & Kegan Paul, 1985), p. 557.

7

'NETWORK ANALYSIS: A REAPPRAISAL'

Jeremy Boissevain

WHAT NETWORK ANALYSIS CAN AND CANNOT DO

As an adjunct or complement to other research techniques, network analysis has at least ten important virtues:

1. Network analysis focuses systematic attention on interlinkages between units of analysis. These interlinkages may be outward links between individuals and between groups; they may also be inward links, setting out the interrelations between members of a group or other unit of analysis.
2. By focusing systematically on the relations between units of analysis, network analysis highlights their interdependency. In fact, this inter-dependency and its consequences for social action are assumptions underlying the network approach. The configurations of interlinked, and therefore interdependent, persons and groups are thus taken into account in trying to predict behaviour. By systematically tracing all interlinkages between units of analysis, one eliminates prior assumptions and therefore biases in favour of particular types of relations. Kinsmen, neighbours, and friends are not singled out and viewed in isolation from other relations.
3. The focus on interlinkage and interdependency provides a framework

From *Current Anthropology* 20.2 (June 1979): 392–4.

within which it is very difficult to separate micro- from macro-analytical levels and part from whole. Among other things, the network approach develops the view of a social field or of a society as a network of networks. While this is metaphorical – for a city or nation-state is obviously more than simply a network of networks – network analysis does force upon the social investigator pathways that lead away from micro- units of analysis. These last are therefore placed in a wider field of social relations. It is only through focusing on such outward links that Wolf,[1] for example, developed the concepts necessary to understand the relation between different levels of integration in the same society, thus breaking down the artificial boundaries between part and whole that had hitherto impeded social analysis in complex societies.

4. Network analysis focuses not only on interlinkage, but also on the content of the relations. In other words, the first plot of a network of relations provides a systematic blueprint for further investigation into their content.

5. Network analysis, by also focusing upon content, sensitizes the investigator to the inherent tension in social relations between persons who have differential access to resources which affect power chances. The way in which network analysis accents this inherent tension and asymmetry in social relations is an antidote to the structural-functional preoccupation with consensus, order, balanced opposition, and harmony.

6. Network analysis, thus, by providing a systematic framework for analyzing tension and asymmetry in social relations, sensitizes the investigator to the inherent dynamics in such relations. Since such relations are part of groups as well as institutional complexes, the social investigator is alerted to the dynamic nature of society and to the human dimension of such dynamism. Changes are thus perceived as inherent in personal relations and hence in society. This again is an antidote to the structural-functional assumption of equilibrium.

7. Network analysis also gets away from the piecemeal or institutional approach. By charting, for example, a person's network of intimates or the network activated by an action set or that of a politician mobilizing votes, network analysis moves beyond the tradition of limiting analysis to discrete institutional spheres such as economics, politics, or, especially for anthropologists, kinship. Network analysis cuts across the conceptual barriers of an institutional approach.

8. By its focus on interrelation, interdependency, and interaction, network analysis also makes it possible to deal with forms of social organization that emerge from interaction, such as patron-client chains, leader-follower coalitions, cliques, factions, cartels, and other

temporary alliances at various social levels. These forms of social organization in the recent past were generally ignored or relegated to interstitial, peripheral, or residual categories of social analysis. It will be obvious that there are forms of social organization the understanding of which is essential to the comprehension of many large and small events in the lives of persons and groups.

9. Network analysis provides a way of relating formal, abstract sociological analysis to everyday experience, for it links interpersonal relations to institutions. It thus humanizes social analysis by reintroducing 'people', as opposed to 'roles', and their choices and actions into the stream of events that constitutes history.

10. Finally, network analysis brings into sharp sociological focus the difficult analytical category of friends-of-friends, those persons who lie just beyond the researcher's horizon because they are not in direct contact with his informants.

These, then, are some of the things that network analysis can do. There are also things that it cannot do.

While network analysis can help plot the direction and concentration of immigrants and the location of industry, for example, used alone it cannot deal with the social processes that bring about immigration and industrialization. In other words, it cannot deal with the social forces underlying long-term processes. Nor can it deal adequately with the impact of educational reform, land distribution, more rights for women, etc., or with culture, cognition, or the social forces deriving from economic activity. These dimensions are essential for a complete understanding of social behaviour and developments. Network analysis alone cannot provide them. Used alongside other research methods and forms of conceptualization, however, it can provide important additional dimensions.

NOTE

1. Eric R. Wolf, 'Aspects of Group Relations in a Complex Society: Mexico', *American Anthropologist* 58 (1956): 1,065–78.

PART III
IMPERIALISM AND THE POSTCOLONIAL

IMPERIALISM AND THE POSTCOLONIAL: INTRODUCTION

The current interest in transatlantic scholarship has been encouraged and provoked by the intense attention paid to histories of slavery, colonialism and nationhood. Colonial expansion, and the slave trade upon which it was built, involved the transportation of material and intellectual goods; as a result, national identity was empowered to extend itself beyond the geographical borders of the nation state. The transatlantic paradigm is thus able to explore the complex relationship of colony to imperial centre by tracing the textual effects of New World discovery and settlement. Many of the central narratives of American colonisation – including Christopher Columbus's 'discovery' of the island of San Salvador in 1492, Vaz de Caminha's account of his 1500 exploration of what is now Brazil, Thomas Harriot's 1588 report of 'the new found land of Virginia', and William Bradford's 1630 history of puritan settlement in New England – characteristically incorporate a double focus. They look forward to the possibilities of a New World future of material or spiritual gain, and look back to the Old World with an awareness of the implications of colonial expansion for the distant European powers. The textual presence of imperial Europe in the Americas allows the transatlantic scholar to uncover the strategies of rhetorical and ideological dominance that drove the project of colonisation onwards. Indigenous voices of resistance, silenced for so long from the official narratives of New World discovery, have started to be recovered as an integral part of the history of the period (see, for example, Castillo and Schweitzer).

Colonial writing ignored what Elleke Boehmer has characterised as the 'agency, diversity, resistance, thinking, voices' of native peoples (23). The relationship between centre and periphery, as mediated through forms of discourse, is not, however, a simple opposition between the coloniser and colonised, nor does that relationship cease once national independence has been achieved. The discipline of Postcolonial Studies, which intersects so productively with our concern with the transatlantic, maps the process by which a colony becomes a nation; it describes the state of a national culture once the imperial structures have departed. That the break between a colonial identity and a postcolonial one is not absolute becomes an important element in configuring the networked and entangled geometry of the transatlantic space. Homi Bhabha's influential suggestion (114–15) that the voice of the colonised disrupts colonial discourse to produce a hybridised text, countering the coherencies of the imperial project, accords with the transatlantic model of estrangement outlined already in previous sections. In the context of the United States, the assertion of political independence in 1776 was not necessarily accompanied by the creation of an autonomous literature. In 1836 Emerson lamented his nation's ongoing reliance on imported literary models – 'Our age is retrospective' – that belied the achievements of national self-definition. As David Simpson has noted, 'It was to prove more difficult to declare independence from Samuel Johnson than it had been to reject George III' (33). Such difficulty in attaining a genuinely *post*colonial status results in a literature that invokes both the force of hegemonic imperial/national systems and the impulses of subversion that might undermine them. As many of the contributors in this section suggest, the effect of this kind of dialectic is a writing that reveals its location in networks of exchange – imperial, economic, intellectual, and rhetorical; it is a writing furthermore that questions the ideal of an autotelic, nationally-bordered discourse once the project of colonialism has been unleashed.

The excerpt from Peter Hulme's work on Shakespeare's *The Tempest* is part of his investigation into the tropes and metaphors that assisted the process of New World colonisation in the early modern period. Hulme details the twin frames of reference in the play – the Mediterranean and the American – to explore 'the links between Prospero's diminished but still imposing "authority", and the tropes of colonial discourse' that are his wider concern. Reading *The Tempest* as an early response to the narratives of empire, Hulme locates a number of New World terms (Caliban as an anagrammatical play on 'cannibal' being the most obvious) that have the effect of 'scrambling [the] traditional reference points within the supposedly familiar terms of the Mediterranean world'. The play's deployment of classical allusions, contributing to what Hulme calls its credentials 'as a fully European' drama, is matched by its broader range of reference (to Africa and to the Americas). Hulme seeks to demonstrate how Shakespeare, writing during the early years of global exploration and territorial expansion, opens up the geographical parameters of English Renaissance drama to present a compelling analysis of the colonialist impulse.

Stuart Hall's essay focuses explicitly on the complex diversity of cultures and traditions that constitute the colonial and postcolonial situation in the Caribbean. Rather than subscribing to an idea of coherence and unity in diasporic experience, he is sensitive to what he characterises as 'the ruptures and discontinuities' that constitute Caribbean identity. Such an identity, he argues, is a combination of different positionings, ones both self-located and externally imposed, that resist the fiction of a 'fixed essence . . ., lying unchanged outside history and culture'. Linking this conception of shifting cultural presence to Jacques Derrida's influential notion of linguistic *differance*, with its focus on deferred and continually unfolding meaning, Hall sets out to 'rethink the positioning and repositioning of Caribbean cultural identities' in relation to three inter-related and entangled ideological and discursive spaces: what he calls *Présence Africaine, Présence Européenne* and *Présence Americaine*. Each of these represents imagined and exerted forces of repression and resistance, played out in a New World diaspora of 'necessary heterogeneity and diversity'. Hall deliberately complicates the linked mythologies of national and racial purity by viewing the Caribbean as a 'juncture-point', from the beginning of the slave trade onwards, 'where the many cultural tributaries meet'.

Paul Gilroy's influential book *The Black Atlantic* (1993) is motivated by similar concerns in its reading of the history of colonial and postcolonial black identity within the spatial coordinates of the transatlantic. Against the 'overintegrated conceptions of culture' that assert the absolute difference of cultural nationalism, Gilroy examines how the nexus of imperialism and slavery created 'processes of cultural mutation and restless (dis)continuity' that constitute for him an idea of transnational modernity. He inextricably links the idea of being *rooted* with that of being *routed* within the 'rhizomorphic' mobility of the black Atlantic world. Central to Gilroy's work in this regard is the organising symbol of the ship; as physical object and as textual metaphor, it represents the space on and in which different cultural identities meet and are imbricated. Gilroy's work represents a paradigm shift in the fields of African-American and postcolonial studies, and it is not without its critics (see, for example, Chrisman and Sweeney). His reading of the contours of the black Atlantic, with its discrete and distant geographies linked and penetrated by the technologies and institutions of modernity, is nevertheless important in returning us to Bhabha's notion of the hybrid postcolonial space that disrupts the narrow nationalisms of both the dominant coloniser and the resistant colonisee. In his reading of the African-American author Ishmael Reed's 1972 novel *Mumbo-Jumbo*, James Snead exemplifies this idea by suggesting that those 'elements that insist on disrupting western culture's appetite for closed and secure progression' break through all attempts at national and racial cohesion. Instead of an imperialist impulse to 'collect', 'whereby things of differing values are lumped together under a single image', Snead prefers the metaphor of 'contagion' to describe 'the existence of recoverable *affinities* between disparate races of people'. Although 'affinity' might suggest a degree of harmonious confluence not necessarily present in the transatlantic space, the language of contagion provides a useful vocabulary for imagining the postcolonial obsolescence of those barriers of national and cultural purity that were central to the imperial undertaking.

The final two pieces excerpted here explore the postcolonial nature of the United States, especially as it is represented in some of its canonical nineteenth-century literature. The United States is perhaps unique among nations in being the world's first postcolonial *and* neo-colonial country, so any attempt to read it alongside the very different situations of, say, Ireland or India needs to be highly aware of this duality. Lawrence Buell's essay acknowledges this difficulty at the outset: a postcolonial reading of the United States could be seen as a hypocritical exercise serving to 'mystify modern America's increasingly interventionist role in world affairs'. Nevertheless, Buell is concerned here to counter what he regards as the parochialism of a US literary criticism that continues to think 'about how Whitman's prosodic experimentalism might have been encouraged by Emerson or Poe than by Keats or Tennyson'. He focuses on Whitman's self-conscious deployment of the European trope of colonial advance, the *translatio studii*, 'the transfer of art and learning from the Old World to the New'. Placing such an inherited figure into a poetry of American literary independence, Buell suggests, reveals 'America's ongoing struggle to extricate its forms of thought from old-world categories' of metaphoric and social figuration. Such a 'resistance-deference syndrome' represents a key strategy of postcolonial writing. Buell goes on to list some of the key elements of postcolonialism as they appear in the writing of the American Renaissance. These include: the semi-Americanisation of the English language; the presence of cultural hybridisation that registers the fault lines of an emerging nation; the central role of the author as an agent for national transformation; the difficulty of confronting a renewed neo-colonialism in the face of post-revolutionary failures; and the question of how, or if, to incorporate 'alien genres' into the national discourse (Snead's metaphor of contagion is again relevant here). The essay ends by pointing towards the ways in which the lingering marks of colonial domination might have authorised those 'new versions of cultural subordination' that characterise a neo-colonial United States.

The section closes with an excerpt from Wai Chee Dimock's radical reconceptualisation of 'deep time' literary history. Like Buell, Dimock finds the geographical parameters of 'American literature' too narrow to account for the globalised and multi-lingual channels in which it is placed. The force of the adjective 'American', she argues, works to shut down possibilities of spatial and temporal contact that, as we have seen, are intrinsic to the postcolonial paradigm. The colonialist impulse to order and unify is here redefined as a literary critical one to periodise. In both cases, the goal of control and stability proves to be illusory. As Dimock notes, 'The synchronic planes that come with periodization are no more integral and no more binding than the territorial borders that come with nations'. By expanding the geographical range and historical reach of literary analysis, Dimock presents an alternative mode of reading that is better equipped to take into account such transnational and transhistorical phenomena as slavery and colonialism. As she says, 'Deep time is denationalized space', a hybrid that 'is not fully describable under the stamp, the scope, and the chronology of European nations'. To illustrate this, she turns to the writing of American Transcendentalism, long regarded as an autonomously nativist canon, to identify its international scope. Her essay goes on to examine Emerson's English translations of Persian poetry (Emerson's source texts for these being already published German translations) to think through the effect of such radically alien writing on conventional interpretations of Emerson as a cultural nationalist. Viewed through the lens of 'deep time', 'Emerson is *American* only in caricature'.

FURTHER READING

Bhabha, Homi (1994) *The Location of Culture*. New York: Routledge.

Boehmer, Elleke (1995) *Colonial and Postcolonial Literature: Migrant Metaphors*. Oxford: Oxford University Press.

Castillo, Susan and Ivy Schweitzer (eds) (2001) *The Literatures of Colonial America: An Anthology*. Oxford: Blackwell.

Chrisman, Laura (2000) 'Rethinking Black Atlanticism', *The Black Scholar* 30.3–4: 12–17.

Kaplan, Amy (1993) 'Left Alone with America', in Donald Pease and Amy Kaplan (eds) *Cultures of United States Imperialism*. Durham: Duke University Press, pp. 3–21.

King, C. Richard (ed.) (2000) *Post-colonial America*. Urbana: University of Illinois Press.

Kutzinski, Vera M. (1992) 'American Literary History as Spatial Practice', *American Literary History* 4.3: 550–7.

Simpson, David (1986) *The Politics of American English, 1776–1850*. New York: Oxford University Press.

Singh, Amritjit and Peter Schmidt (eds) (2000) *Postcolonial Theory and the United States: Race, Ethnicity, and Literature*. Jackson: University Press of Mississippi.

Sweeney, Fionnghuala (2006) 'The Black Atlantic, American Studies and the Politics of the Postcolonial', *Comparative American Studies* 4.2: 115–33.

Szeman, Imre (2004) *Zones of Instability: Literature, Postcolonialism and the Nation*. Baltimore: Johns Hopkins University Press.

I

'PROSPERO AND CALIBAN'

Peter Hulme

The simplicity of the unified Mediterranean reading fractured with the demise of Prospero as its unquestioned transcendental guarantor. What has largely taken its place – especially since George Lamming's pioneering essay of 1960 [in his book *The Pleasures of Exile*] – is the reading that moves colonialism, and therefore the New World, Atlantic material, to the very centre of the play. [Here I] explore the links between Prospero's diminished but still imposing 'authority', and the tropes of colonial discourse that are the continuing focus of this volume. Under the pressure of some fine recent criticism and scholarship *The Tempest* has become a much more complex play than it used to be. What will be suggested here is that the key to this complexity lies in gauging the relationship between the Mediterranean and the Atlantic frames of reference within the play, a task made more difficult by the way in which that Atlantic discourse is itself often articulated through a re-inscription of Mediterranean terms.

The topography of the play can stand as an emblem of these complexities, particularly since it has been the subject of such long-standing debate. Predictably, there is a positivist tradition that tries to identify the island setting as Sicily or Malta or Lampedusa or Bermuda. And equally predictably there is an aestheticist tradition which says that the play takes place only in the rarefied latitudes of art and that any attempt to make sense of its geographical

From Peter Hulme (1986) *Colonial Encounters: Europe and the Native Caribbean, 1492–1797.* London: Methuen.

references is futile. Both traditions have a kernel of value. *The Tempest* is not a log-book, it need make no particular geographical sense; and to seek to identify the island is to misrecognize the project of the text, to mistake it for a different kind of text altogether. On the other hand, Shakespeare's plays have a wealth of geographical detail, some of it no doubt conventionally symbolic, but some of it not – as in the case, say, of *Othello* where the play's dramatic conflicts are very carefully mapped by the Mediterranean references. *The Tempest*'s complexity in this respect can be said to stem from its *dual* topography: the Mediterranean, certainly – Naples, Tunis and Algiers; but also the 'still-vexed Bermoothes'*. The latter has been dismissed as simply an exotic touch – distance being presumably immaterial to the immaterial Ariel – but it belongs to a larger pattern of New World terms, including Gonzalo's use of the colonial word 'plantation' – its only occurrence in Shakespeare; the Patagonian god called 'Setebos'; the Algonquian dance seemingly recalled in Ariel's first song; and of course Caliban*, metathesis of 'canibal', that first ethnic name noted by Europeans in the New World, and which serves to root those New World references in the Caribbean, that crucible of the early colonial ventures and ground of the historically archetypical meeting of cultures.

Caliban is, according to one recent critic, 'perhaps the most disputed character in the Shakespearean canon':[1] much admired, from Dryden onwards, for the originality of his creation, and yet almost impossible to put convincingly on stage. Morton Luce summed up the exasperation of many critics at 'this supreme puzzle' when he said that:

> if all the suggestions as to Caliban's form and feature and endowments that are thrown out in the play are collected, it will be found that the one half renders the other half impossible.[2]

Caliban is, to give a sample of these descriptions, 'a strange fish!' (II.ii.27); 'Legg'd like a man! and his fins like arms!' (II.ii.34); 'no fish' (II.ii.36); 'some monster of the isle with four legs' (II.ii.66); 'a plain fish' (V.i.266); and a 'misshapen knave' (V.i.268). He is also, at different times, a man and not a man according to Miranda's calculations.

Luce's exasperation over Caliban's resistance to visualization reminds him 'of the equally futile attempts to discover his enchanted island',[3] and the parallel is acute, though perhaps less of a dead-end than Luce imagines. The island is the meeting place of the play's topographical dualism, Mediterranean and Atlantic, ground of the mutually incompatible reference systems whose co-presence serves to frustrate any attempt to locate the island on a map. Caliban is similarly the ground of these two discourses. As 'wild man' or 'wodehouse', with an African mother whose pedigree leads back to the *Odyssey*, he is distinctly Mediterranean. And yet, at the same time, he is, as his name suggests, a 'cannibal' as that figure had taken shape in colonial discourse: ugly, devilish, ignorant, gullible and treacherous – according to the Europeans' descriptions of him. Cannibalism itself features only indirectly: Alonso, pondering the fate of his son, asks 'what strange fish / Hath made his meal on thee?' (II.i.108–9), 'a strange fish!' being Trinculo's first description of Caliban (II.ii.27). There is, however, a difference between the two processes. The topographical references are mutually contradictory, but Caliban's characteristics merely overburden him since Atlantic colonial discourse is itself based upon that Herodotean language discussed in the chapter on Columbus's log-book. [Hulme suggests that Herotodus's 'investigation' of Greece's 'barbarian' neighbours institutes a discourse of defining savage Otherness.] The play's title page catches this distinction nicely: the mutually con-tradictory topographies cancel each other out leaving the island 'uninhabited'; Caliban, on the other hand, bears his double inscription: Caliban, savage, deformed, slave – a multiple burden of Atlantic and Mediterranean descriptions. Discursively, it could be said, Caliban is the monster all the characters make him out to be. In a way Caliban, like Frankenstein's monster, carries the secret of his own guilty genesis; not however, like a bourgeois monster, in the pocket of his coat, but rather, like a savage, inscribed upon his body as his physical shape, whose overdetermination baffles the other characters as much as the play's direc-tors. The difficulty in visualizing Caliban cannot be put down to a failure of clarity in the text. Caliban, as a compromise formation, can exist only within dis-course: he is fundamentally and essentially beyond the bounds of representation.

Two emblems – one textual, the other geographical – can stand for the rela-tionship between the two frames of reference, Mediterranean and Atlantic. The first is a palimpsest on which there are two texts, an original Mediterranean text with, superimposed upon it, an Atlantic text written entirely in the spaces between the Mediterranean words, the exception being Caliban, who is thereby doubly inscribed, a discursive monster, a compromise formation bearing the imprint of the conflict that has produced him. The second emblem is Leslie Fiedler's when he adapts D. H. Lawrence's terms to talk about the discovery of America as a new magnetic pole compelling a reorientation of traditional axes: the conventional opposition between Europe and Africa, articulated within Mediterranean discourse, is disrupted by the third term of America, an 'other' so radically different that you can no longer bring yourself to respond to its threat by offering it your daughter, however much you imagine it wants you to.[4] So even before considering the fully Atlantic themes of the play – which must centre on the relationship between Prospero and Caliban – there is evi-dence of a scrambling of traditional reference points within the supposedly familiar terms of the Mediterranean world.

[. . .]

For Caliban the issue is simple: 'I am subject to a tyrant, a sorcerer, that by his cunning hath cheated me of the island' (III.ii.40–2): Prospero's power, his magic, has usurped Caliban of his rights. But the text inflects this usurpation in a particular direction: Prospero has taken control of Caliban, made him his slave, and yet 'We cannot miss him' (I.ii.313) – Caliban is indispensable to Prospero, the usurper depends upon the usurped. Why should this be if Prospero is so powerful a magician? Why should he have to depend upon a lowly slave like Caliban? We need to comprehend more clearly the precise nature of Prospero's magic.

This does not imply further investigation of Prospero as Renaissance magus on the way to enlightenment, or subtle distinctions between black and white magic. A simpler question needs answering: just how extensive is Prospero's power? In some ways this overlaps with the discussion of Prospero as playwright: he has the sort of power that can erect an invisible barrier, that can inflict physical punishment, and that can take human and animal form; but he does not have direct power over human thoughts, words and actions. But one can go beyond this, still on the basis of the play's own evidence: his magic is only effective within certain distances since he has depended on 'accident most strange' (I.ii.178) to bring the court party within his sphere of influence; it was not effective in Milan or else he could have defended himself against Antonio; or on the open seas since he and Miranda needed 'Providence divine' (I.ii.159) to come ashore; but *was* effective either immediately upon, or soon after, reaching the island since he freed Ariel from the cloven pine. If Prospero's extraordinary speech of abjuration is to be believed (V.i.33–57) his powers extend to plucking trees out of the ground, and even, as discussed earlier, to wakening the dead. But on the other hand he cannot, or will not, chop wood, make dams to catch fish or do the washing up, all tasks for which Caliban's services are required.

If such a listing seems open to the charge of excessive literalism, that is precisely the point. The text is not concerned with the exact configuration of Prospero's magical powers, but rather with two broad distinctions: Prospero's magic is at his disposal on the island but not off it; it can do anything at all except what is most necessary to survive. In other words there is a precise match with the situation of Europeans in America during the seventeenth century, whose technology (especially of firearms) suddenly *became* magical when introduced into a less technologically developed society, but who were incapable (for a variety of reasons) of feeding themselves. This is a topos that appears with remarkable frequency in the early English colonial narratives, as it had in the Spanish: a group of Europeans who were dependent, in some cases for many years, on food supplied by their native hosts, often willingly, sometimes under duress.

Possible verbal parallels with 'sources' such as Strachey's letter [a 1610 pamphlet, now known as *The True Reportory of the Wracke* and regarded as one of the sources for Shakespeare's play] tell us nothing about *The Tempest* as a

'Caribbean' play. But the topos of food is such a staple of Atlantic discourse that congeneric examples can significantly illuminate the materials that the play is here deploying.

NOTES

1. Sister Corona Sharp, 'Caliban: The Primitive Man's Evolution', *Shakespeare Studies* 14 (1981): 267.
2. Morton Luce, 'Introduction', *The Tempest* (London: n.p., 1938), pp. xxxii, xxxv.
3. Ibid., p. xxxv.
4. See Leslie Fiedler, 'The New World Savage as Stranger: or "Tis new to thee"', in Fiedler, *The Stranger in Shakespeare* (London: Croom Helm, 1973), p. 203.

2

'CULTURAL IDENTITY AND DIASPORA'

Stuart Hall

We cannot speak for very long, with any exactness, about 'one experience, one identity', without acknowledging its other side – the ruptures and discontinuities which constitute, precisely, the Caribbean's 'uniqueness'. Cultural identity, in this second sense, is a matter of 'becoming' as well as of 'being'. It belongs to the future as much as to the past. It is not something which already exists, transcending place, time, history and culture. Cultural identities come from somewhere, have histories. But, like everything which is historical, they undergo constant transformation. Far from being eternally fixed in some essentialised past, they are subject to the continuous 'play' of history, culture and power. Far from being grounded in mere 'recovery' of the past, which is waiting to be found, and which when found, will secure our sense of ourselves into eternity, identities are the names we give to the different ways we are positioned by, and position ourselves within, the narratives of the past.

It is only from this second position that we can properly understand the traumatic character of 'the colonial experience'. The ways in which black people, black experiences, were positioned and subject-ed in the dominant regimes of representation were the effects of a critical exercise of cultural power and normalisation. Not only, in Said's 'Orientalist' sense, were we constructed as different and other within the categories of knowledge of the West by those

From Jonathan Rutherford (ed.) (1990) *Identity: Community, Culture, Difference*. London: Lawrence & Wishart, pp. 222–37.

regimes. They had the power to make us see and experience *ourselves* as 'Other'. Every regime of representation is a regime of power formed, as Foucault* reminds us, by the fatal couplet 'power/knowledge'. But this kind of knowledge is internal, not external. It is one thing to position a subject or set of peoples as the Other of a dominant discourse. It is quite another thing to subject them to that 'knowledge', not only as a matter of imposed will and domination, by the power of inner compulsion and subjective con-formation to the norm. That is the lesson – the sombre majesty – of Fanon's* insight into the colonising experience in *Black Skin, White Masks*.

   This inner expropriation of cultural identity cripples and deforms. If its silences are not resisted, they produce, in Fanon's vivid phrase, 'individuals without an anchor, without horizon, colourless, stateless, rootless – a race of angels'.[1] Nevertheless, this idea of otherness as an inner compulsion changes our conception of 'cultural identity'. In this perspective, cultural identity is not a fixed essence at all, lying unchanged outside history and culture. It is not some universal and transcendental spirit inside us on which history has made no fundamental mark. It is not once-and-for-all. It is not a fixed origin to which we can make some final and absolute Return. Of course, it is not a mere phantasm either. It is *something* – not a mere trick of the imagination. It has its histories – and histories have their real, material and symbolic effects. The past continues to speak to us. But it no longer addresses us as a simple, factual 'past', since our relation to it, like the child's relation to the mother, is always-already 'after the break'. It is always constructed through memory, fantasy, narrative and myth. Cultural identities are the points of identification, the unstable points of identification or suture, which are made, within the discourses of history and culture. Not an essence but a *positioning*. Hence, there is always a politics of identity, a politics of position, which has no absolute guarantee in an unproblematic, transcendental 'law of origin'.

[. . .]

To capture this sense of difference which is not pure 'otherness', we need to deploy the play on words of a theorist like Jacques Derrida*. Derrida uses the anomalous 'a' in his way of writing 'difference' – *differance* – as a marker which sets up a disturbance in our settled understanding or translation of the word/concept. It sets the word in motion to new meanings without erasing the *trace* of its other meanings. His sense of *differance*, as Christopher Norris puts it, thus

> remains suspended between the two French verbs 'to differ' and 'to defer' (postpone), both of which contribute to its textual force but neither of which can fully capture its meaning. Language depends on difference, as Saussure* showed . . . the structure of distinctive propositions which

make up its basic economy. Where Derrida breaks new ground . . . is in the extent to which 'differ' shades into 'defer' . . . the idea that meaning is always deferred, perhaps to this point of an endless supplementarity, by the play of signification.[2]

This second sense of difference challenges the fixed binaries which stabilise meaning and representation and show how meaning is never finished or completed, but keeps on moving to encompass other, additional or supplementary meanings, which, as Norris puts it elsewhere, 'disturb the classical economy of language and representation'.[3] Without relations of difference, no representation could occur. But what is then constituted within representation is always open to being deferred, staggered, serialised.

Where, then, does identity come in to this infinite postponement of meaning? Derrida does not help us as much as he might here, though the notion of the 'trace' goes some way towards it. This is where it sometimes seems as if Derrida has permitted his profound theoretical insights to be reappropriated by his disciples into a celebration of formal 'playfulness', which evacuates them of their political meaning. For if signification depends upon the endless repositioning of its differential terms, meaning, in any specific instance, depends on the contingent and arbitrary stop – the necessary and temporary 'break' in the infinite semiosis of language. This does not detract from the original insight. It only threatens to do so if we mistake this 'cut' of identity – this *positioning*, which makes meaning possible – as a natural and permanent, rather than an arbitrary and contingent 'ending' – whereas I understand every such position as 'strategic' and arbitrary, in the sense that there is no permanent equivalence between the particular sentence we close, and its true meaning, as such. Meaning continues to unfold, so to speak, beyond the arbitrary closure which makes it, at any moment, possible. It is always either over- or under-determined, either an excess or a supplement. There is always something 'left over'.

It is possible, with this conception of 'difference', to rethink the positioning and repositioning of Caribbean cultural identities in relation to at least three 'presences', to borrow Aimé Césaire's* and Léopold Senghor's* metaphor: *Présence Africaine, Présence Européenne*, and the third, most ambiguous, presence of all – the sliding term, *Présence Americaine*. Of course, I am collapsing, for the moment, the many other cultural 'presences' which constitute the complexity of Caribbean identity (Indian, Chinese, Lebanese, etc.). I mean America, here, not in its 'first-world' sense – the big cousin to the North whose 'rim' we occupy, but in the second, broader sense: America, the 'New World', *Terra Incognita*.

Présence Africaine is the site of the repressed. Apparently silenced beyond memory by the power of the experience of slavery, Africa was, in fact, present everywhere: in the everyday life and customs of the slave quarters, in the languages and patois of the plantations, in names and words, often disconnected from their taxonomies, in the secret syntactical structures through which other languages were spoken, in the stories and tales told to children, in religious practices and beliefs in the spiritual life, the arts, crafts, musics and rhythms of slave and post-emancipation society. Africa, the signified which could not be represented directly in slavery, remained and remains the unspoken unspeakable 'presence' in Caribbean culture. It is 'hiding' behind every verbal inflection, every narrative twist of Caribbean cultural life. It is the secret code with which every Western text was 're-read'. It is the ground-bass of every rhythm and bodily movement. *This* was – is – the 'Africa' that 'is alive and well in the diaspora'.[4]

When I was growing up in the 1940s and 1950s as a child in Kingston*, I was surrounded by the signs, music and rhythms of this Africa of the diaspora, which only existed as a result of a long and discontinuous series of transformations. But, although almost everyone around me was some shade of brown or black (Africa 'speaks'!), I never once heard a single person refer to themselves or to others as, in some way, or as having been at some time in the past, 'African'. It was only in the 1970s that this Afro-Caribbean identity became historically available to the great majority of Jamaican people, at home and abroad. In this historic moment, Jamaicans discovered themselves to be 'black' – just as, in the same moment, they discovered themselves to be the sons and daughters of 'slavery'.

This profound cultural discovery, however, was not, and could not be, made directly, without 'mediation'. It could only be made *through* the impact on popular life of the postcolonial revolution, the civil rights struggles, the culture of Rastafarianism and the music of reggae – the metaphors, the figures or signifiers of a new construction of 'Jamaican-ness'. These signified a 'new' Africa of the New World, grounded in an 'old' Africa: a spiritual journey of discovery that led, in the Caribbean, to an indigenous cultural revolution; this is Africa, as we might say, necessarily 'deferred' – as a spiritual, cultural and political metaphor.

It is the presence/absence of Africa, in this form, which has made it the privileged signifier of new conceptions of Caribbean identity. Everyone in the Caribbean, of whatever ethnic background, must sooner or later come to terms with this African presence. Black, brown, mulatto, white – all must look *Présence Africaine* in the face, speak its name. But whether it is, in this sense, an *origin* of our identities, unchanged by four hundred years of displacement, dismemberment, transportation to which we could in any final or literal sense return, is more open to doubt. The original 'Africa' is no longer there. It too has been transformed. History is, in that sense, irreversible. We must not collude with the West which, precisely, normalises and appropriates Africa by freezing it into some timeless zone of the primitive, unchanging past. Africa must at last be reckoned with by Caribbean people, but it cannot in any simple sense be merely recovered.

It belongs irrevocably, for us, to what Edward Said once called an 'imaginative geography and history', which helps 'the mind to intensify its own sense of itself by dramatising the difference between what is close to it and what is far away'. It 'has acquired an imaginative or figurative value we can name and feel'.[5] Our belongingness to it constitutes what Benedict Anderson calls 'an imagined community'.[6] To *this* 'Africa', which is a necessary part of the Caribbean imaginary, we can't literally go home again.

The character of this displaced 'homeward' journey – its length and complexity – comes across vividly, in a variety of texts. Tony Sewell's documentary archival photographs, 'Garvey's Children: the Legacy of Marcus Garvey', tell the story of a 'return' to an African identity which went, necessarily, by the long route through London and the United States. It 'ends', not in Ethiopia but with Garvey's statue in front of the St Ann Parish Library in Jamaica: not with a traditional tribal chant but with the music of Burning Spear and Bob Marley's 'Redemption Song'. This is our 'long journey' home. Derek Bishton's courageous visual and written text, *Black Heart Man* – the story of the journey of a *white* photographer 'on the trail of the promised land' – starts in England, and goes, through Shashemene, the place in Ethiopia to which many Jamaican people have found their way on their search for the Promised Land, and slavery; but it ends in Pinnacle, Jamaica, where the first Rastafarian settlements were established, and 'beyond' – among the dispossessed of twentieth-century Kingston and the streets of Handsworth, where Bishton's voyage of discovery first began. These symbolic journeys are necessary for us all – and necessarily circular. This is the Africa we must return to – but 'by another route': what Africa has *become* in the New World, what we have made of 'Africa': 'Africa' – as we re-tell it through politics, memory and desire.

What of the second, troubling, term in the identity equation – the European presence? For many of us, this is a matter not of too little but of too much. Where Africa was a case of the unspoken, Europe was a case of that which is endlessly speaking – and endlessly speaking *us*. The European presence interrupts the innocence of the whole discourse of 'difference' in the Caribbean by introducing the question of power. 'Europe' belongs irrevocably to the 'play' of power, to the lines of force and consent, to the role of the *dominant*, in Caribbean culture. In terms of colonalism, underdevelopment, poverty and the racism of colour, the European presence is that which, in visual representation, has positioned the black subject within its dominant regimes of representation: the colonial discourse, the literatures of adventure and exploration, the romance of the exotic, the ethnographic and travelling eye, the tropical languages of tourism, travel brochure and Hollywood and the violent, pornographic languages of *ganja* and urban violence.

Because *Présence Européenne* is about exclusion, imposition and expropriation, we are often tempted to locate that power as wholly external to us – an
extrinsic force, whose influence can be thrown off like the serpent sheds its skin.
What Frantz Fanon reminds us, in *Black Skin, White Masks*, is how this power
has become a constitutive element in our own identities.

> The movements, the attitudes, the glances of the other fixed me there in
> the sense in which a chemical solution is fixed by a dye. I was indignant;
> I demanded an explanation. Nothing happened. I burst apart. Now the
> fragments have been put together again by another self.[7]

This 'look', from – so to speak – the place of the Other, fixes us, not only in its
violence, hostility and aggression, but in the ambivalence of its desire. This
brings us face to face with the dominating European presence not simply as the
site or 'scene' of integration where those other presences which it had actively
disaggregated were recomposed – re-framed, put together in a new way; but as
the site of a profound splitting and doubling – what Homi Bhabha has called
'this ambivalent identification of the racist world . . . the "Otherness" of the
Self inscribed in the perverse palimpsest of colonial identity'.[8]

The dialogue of power and resistance, of refusal and recognition, with and
against *Présence Européenne* is almost as complex as the 'dialogue' with Africa.
In terms of popular cultural life, it is nowhere to be found in its pure, pristine
state. It is always-already fused, syncretised, with other cultural elements. It is
always-already creolised – not lost beyond the Middle Passage*, but ever-
present: from the harmonics in our musics to the ground-bass of Africa, traversing and intersecting our lives at every point. How can we stage this dialogue
so that, finally, we can place it, without terror or violence, rather than being
forever placed by it? Can we ever recognise its irreversible influence, whilst
resisting its imperialising eye? The enigma is impossible, so far, to resolve. It
requires the most complex of cultural strategies. Think, for example, of the dialogue of every Caribbean filmmaker or writer, one way or another, with the
dominant cinemas and literature of the West – the complex relationship of
young black British filmmakers with the 'avant-gardes' of European and
American filmmaking. Who could describe this tense and tortured dialogue as
a 'one way trip'?

The Third, 'New World' presence, is not so much power, as ground, place,
territory. It is the juncture-point where the many cultural tributaries meet, the
'empty' land (the European colonisers emptied it) where strangers from every
other part of the globe collided. None of the people who now occupy the islands
– black, brown, white, African, European, American, Spanish, French, East
Indian, Chinese, Portuguese, Jew, Dutch – originally 'belonged' there. It is the
space where the creolisations and assimilations and syncretisms were negotiated. The New World is the third term – the primal scene – where the

fateful/fatal encounter was staged between Africa and the West. It also has to be understood as the place of many, continuous displacements: of the original pre-Columbian inhabitants, the Arawaks, Caribs and Amerindians, permanently displaced from their homelands and decimated; of other peoples displaced in different ways from Africa, Asia and Europe; the displacements of slavery, colonisation and conquest. It stands for the endless ways in which Caribbean people have been destined to 'migrate'; it is the signifier of migration itself – of travelling, voyaging and return as fate, as destiny; of the Antillean as the prototype of the modern or postmodern New World nomad, continually moving between centre and periphery. This preoccupation with movement and migration Caribbean cinema shares with many other 'Third Cinemas', but it is one of our defining themes, and it is destined to cross the narrative of every film script or cinematic image.

Présence Americaine continues to have its silences, its suppressions. Peter Hulme, in his essay on 'Islands of Enchantment'[9] reminds us that the word 'Jamaica' is the Hispanic form of the indigenous Arawak name – 'land of wood and water' – which Columbus's renaming ('Santiago') never replaced. The Arawak presence remains today a ghostly one, visible in the islands mainly in museums and archeological sites, part of the barely knowable or usable 'past'. Hulme notes that it is not represented in the emblem of the Jamaican National Heritage Trust, for example, which chose instead the figure of Diego Pimienta, 'an African who fought for his Spanish masters against the English invasion of the island in 1655' – a deferred, metonymic, sly and sliding representation of Jamaican identity if ever there was one! He recounts the story of how Prime Minister Edward Seaga tried to alter the Jamaican coat-of-arms, which consists of two Arawak figures holding a shield with five pineapples, surmounted by an alligator. 'Can the crushed and extinct Arawaks represent the dauntless character of Jamaicans. Does the low-slung, near extinct crocodile, a cold-blooded reptile, symbolise the warm, soaring spirit of Jamaicans?' Prime Minister Seaga asked rhetorically.[10] There can be few political statements which so eloquently testify to the complexities entailed in the process of trying to represent a diverse people with a diverse history through a single, hegemonic 'identity'. Fortunately, Mr Seaga's invitation to the Jamaican people, who are overwhelmingly of African descent, to start their 'remembering' by first 'forgetting' something else, got the comeuppance it so richly deserved.

The 'New World' presence – America, *Terra Incognita* – is therefore itself the beginning of diaspora, of diversity, of hybridity and difference, what makes Afro-Caribbean people already people of a diaspora. I use this term here metaphorically, not literally: diaspora does not refer us to those scattered tribes whose identity can only be secured in relation to some sacred homeland to which they must at all costs return, even if it means pushing other people into the sea. This is the old, the imperialising, the hegemonising, form of 'ethnicity'.

We have seen the fate of the people of Palestine at the hands of this backward-looking conception of diaspora – and the complicity of the West with it. The diaspora experience as I intend it here is defined, not by essence or purity, but by the recognition of a necessary heterogeneity and diversity; by a conception of 'identity' which lives with and through, not despite, difference; by *hybridity*. Diaspora identities are those which are constantly producing and reproducing themselves anew, through transformation and difference.

NOTES

1. Frantz Fanon, 'On National Culture', in *The Wretched of the Earth* (Harmondsworth: Penguin, 1963), p. 176.
2. Christopher Norris, *Deconstruction: Theory and Practice* (London: Methuen, 1982), p. 32.
3. Christopher Norris, *Derrida* (London: Fontana, 1987), p. 15.
4. See Stuart Hall, *Resistance Through Rituals: Youth Subcultures in Post-war Britain* (London: Hutchinson, 1976).
5. Edward Said, *Orientalism* (Harmondsworth: Penguin, 1985), p. 55.
6. See Benedict Anderson, *Imagined Communities: Reflections on the Origin and Rise of Nationalism* (London: Verso, 1983).
7. Frantz Fanon, *Black Skin, White Masks* (1952; London: Pluto Press, 1986), p. 109.
8. Homi Bhabha, 'Foreword' to Fanon, *Black Skin, White Masks*, pp. xiv–xv.
9. See Peter Hulme, 'Islands of Enchantment: Extracts from a Caribbean Travel Diary', *New Formations* 3 (Winter 1987): 81–95.
10. *Jamaica Hansard* 9 (1983–4): 363, quoted in Hulme, 'Islands of Enchantment'.

3

'THE BLACK ATLANTIC AS A COUNTERCULTURE OF MODERNITY'

Paul Gilroy

Striving to be both European and black requires some specific forms of double consciousness. By saying this I do not mean to suggest that taking on either or both of these unfinished identities necessarily exhausts the subjective resources of any particular individual. However, where racist, nationalist, or ethnically absolutist discourses orchestrate political relationships so that these identities appear to be mutually exclusive, occupying the space between them or trying to demonstrate their continuity has been viewed as a provocative and even oppositional act of political insubordination.

The contemporary black English, like the Anglo-Africans of earlier generations and perhaps, like all blacks in the West, stand between (at least) two great cultural assemblages, both of which have mutated through the course of the modern world that formed them and assumed new configurations. At present, they remain locked symbiotically in an antagonistic relationship marked out by the symbolism of colours which adds to the conspicuous cultural power of their central Manichean dynamic – black and white. These colours support a special rhetoric that has grown to be associated with a language of nationality and national belonging as well as the languages of 'race' and ethnic identity.

Though largely ignored by recent debates over modernity and its discontents, these ideas about nationality, ethnicity, authenticity, and cultural integrity are characteristically modern phenomena that have profound implications for

From Paul Gilroy (1993) *The Black Atlantic: Modernity and Double Consciousness*. London: Verso.

cultural criticism and cultural history. They crystallised with the revolutionary transformations of the West at the end of the eighteenth and the beginning of the nineteenth centuries and involved novel typologies and modes of identification. Any shift towards a postmodern condition should not, however, mean that the conspicuous power of these modern subjectivities and the movements they articulated has been left behind. Their power has, if anything, grown, and their ubiquity as a means to make political sense of the world is currently unparalleled by the languages of class and socialism by which they once appeared to have been surpassed. My concern here is less with explaining their longevity and enduring appeal than with exploring some of the special political problems that arise from the fatal junction of the concept of nationality with the concept of culture and the affinities and affiliations which link the blacks of the West to one of their adoptive, parental cultures: the intellectual heritage of the West since the Enlightenment. I have become fascinated with how successive generations of black intellectuals have understood this connection and how they have projected it in their writing and speaking in pursuit of freedom, citizenship, and social and political autonomy.

If this appears to be little more than a roundabout way of saying that the reflexive cultures and consciousness of the European settlers and those of the Africans they enslaved, the 'Indians' they slaughtered, and the Asians they indentured were not, even in situations of the most extreme brutality, sealed off hermetically from each other, then so be it. This seems as though it ought to be an obvious and self-evident observation, but its stark character has been systematically obscured by commentators from all sides of political opinion. Regardless of their affiliation to the right, left, or centre, groups have fallen back on the idea of cultural nationalism, on the overintegrated conceptions of culture which present immutable, ethnic differences as an absolute break in the histories and experiences of 'black' and 'white' people. Against this choice stands another, more difficult option: the theorisation of creolisation, métissage, mestizaje, and hybridity. From the viewpoint of ethnic absolutism, this would be a litany of pollution and impurity. These terms are rather unsatisfactory ways of naming the processes of cultural mutation and restless (dis)continuity that exceed racial discourse and avoid capture by its agents.

[The Black Atlantic] addresses one small area in the grand consequence of this historical conjunction – the stereophonic, bilingual, or bifocal cultural forms originated by, but no longer the exclusive property of, blacks dispersed within the structures of feeling, producing, communicating, and remembering that I have heuristically called the black Atlantic world. [It] is therefore rooted in and routed through the special stress that grows with the effort involved in trying to face (at least) two ways at once.

My concerns at this stage are primarily conceptual: I have tried to address the continuing lure of ethnic absolutisms in cultural criticism produced both by blacks and by whites. In particular, [I] explore the special relationships between 'race', culture, nationality, and ethnicity which have a bearing on the histories and political cultures of Britain's black citizens. I have argued elsewhere [in *'There ain't no black in the Union Jack': The Cultural Politics of Race and Nation* (1987)] that the cultures of this group have been produced in a syncretic pattern in which the styles and forms of the Caribbean, the United States, and Africa have been reworked and reinscribed in the novel context of modern Britain's own untidy ensemble of regional and class-oriented conflicts. Rather than make the invigorating flux of those mongrel cultural forms my focal concern here, I want instead to look at broader questions of ethnic identity that have contributed to the scholarship and the political strategies that Britain's black settlers have generated and to the underlying sense of England as a cohesive cultural community against which their self-conception has so often been defined. Here the ideas of nation, nationality, national belonging, and nationalism are paramount. They are extensively supported by a clutch of rhetorical strategies that can be named 'cultural insiderism'.[1] The essential trademark of cultural insiderism which also supplies the key to its popularity is an absolute sense of ethnic difference. This is maximised so that it distinguishes people from one another and at the same time acquires an incontestable priority over all other dimensions of their social and historical experience, cultures, and identities. Characteristically, these claims are associated with the idea of national belonging or the aspiration to nationality and other more local but equivalent forms of cultural kinship. The range and complexity of these ideas in English cultural life defies simple summary or exposition. However, the forms of cultural insiderism they sanction typically construct the nation as an ethnically homogeneous object and invoke ethnicity a second time in the hermeneutic procedures deployed to make sense of its distinctive cultural content.

The intellectual seam in which English cultural studies has positioned itself – through innovative work in the fields of social history and literary criticism – can be indicted here. The statist modalities of Marxist* analysis that view modes of material production and political domination as exclusively *national* entities are only one source of this problem. Another factor, more evasive but nonetheless potent for its intangible ubiquity, is a quiet cultural nationalism which pervades the work of some radical thinkers. This crypto-nationalism means that they are often disinclined to consider the cross catalytic or transverse dynamics of racial politics as a significant element in the formation and reproduction of English national identities. These formations are treated as if they spring, fully formed, from their own special viscera.

My search for resources with which to comprehend the doubleness and cultural intermixture that distinguish the experience of black Britons in contemporary Europe required me to seek inspiration from other sources and, in effect, to make an intellectual journey across the Atlantic. In black America's histories of cultural and political debate and organisation I found another, second perspective with which to orient my own position. Here too the lure of ethnic particularism and nationalism has provided an ever-present danger. But that narrowness of vision which is content with the merely national has also been challenged from within that black community by thinkers who were prepared to renounce the easy claims of African-American exceptionalism in favour of a global, coalitional politics in which anti-imperialism and anti-racism might be seen to interact if not to fuse.

[. . .]

Getting beyond these national and nationalistic perspectives has become essential for two additional reasons. The first arises from the urgent obligation to reevaluate the significance of the modern nation state as a political, economic, and cultural unit. Neither political nor economic structures of domination are still simply co-extensive with national borders. This has a special significance in contemporary Europe, where new political and economic relations are being created seemingly day by day, but it is a worldwide phenomenon with significant consequences for the relationship between the politics of information and the practices of capital accumulation. Its effects underpin more recognisably political changes like the growing centrality of transnational ecological movements which, through their insistence on the association of sustainability and justice, do so much to shift the moral and scientific precepts on which the modern separation of politics and ethics was built. The second reason relates to the tragic popularity of ideas about the integrity and purity of cultures. In particular, it concerns the relationship between nationality and ethnicity. This too currently has a special force in Europe, but it is also reflected directly in the post-colonial histories and complex, transcultural, political trajectories of Britain's black settlers.

What might be called the peculiarity of the black English requires attention to the intermixture of a variety of distinct cultural forms. Previously separated political and intellectual traditions converged and, in their coming together, overdetermined the process of black Britain's social and historical formation. This blending is misunderstood if it is conceived in simple ethnic terms, but right and left, racist and anti-racist, black and white tacitly share a view of it as little more than a collision between fully formed and mutually exclusive cultural communities. This has become the dominant view where black history and culture are perceived, like black settlers themselves, as an illegitimate intrusion into a vision of authentic British national life that, prior to their arrival, was as stable and as peaceful as it was ethnically undifferentiated. Considering this history points to issues of power and knowledge that are beyond the scope of this book. However, though it arises from present rather than past conditions, contemporary British racism bears the imprint of the past in many ways.

The especially crude and reductive notions of culture that form the substance of racial politics today are clearly associated with an older discourse of racial and ethnic difference which is everywhere entangled in the history of the idea of culture in the modern West. This history has itself become hotly contested since debates about multiculturalism, cultural pluralism, and the responses to them that are sometimes dismissively called 'political correctness' arrived to query the ease and speed with which European particularisms are still being translated into absolute, universal standards for human achievement, norms, and aspirations.

It is significant that prior to the consolidation of scientific racism in the nineteenth century, the term 'race' was used very much in the way that the word 'culture' is used today. But in the attempts to differentiate the true, the good, and the beautiful which characterise the junction point of capitalism, industrialisation, and political democracy and give substance to the discourse of western modernity, it is important to appreciate that scientists did not monopolise either the image of the black or the emergent concept of biologically based racial difference. As far as the future of cultural studies is concerned, it should be equally important that both were centrally employed in those European attempts to think through beauty, taste, and aesthetic judgement that are the precursors of contemporary cultural criticism.

Tracing the racial signs from which the discourse of cultural value was constructed and their conditions of existence in relation to European aesthetics and philosophy as well as European science can contribute much to an ethnohistorical reading of the aspirations of western modernity as a whole and to the critique of Enlightenment assumptions in particular. It is certainly the case that ideas about 'race', ethnicity, and nationality form an important seam of continuity linking English cultural studies with one of its sources of inspiration – the doctrines of modern European aesthetics that are consistently configured by the appeal to national and often racial particularity.

[. . .]

Notions of the primitive and the civilised which had been integral to premodern understanding of 'ethnic' differences became fundamental cognitive and aesthetic markers in the processes which generated a constellation of subject positions in which Englishness, Christianity, and other ethnic and racialised attributes would finally give way to the dislocating dazzle of 'whiteness'. A small but telling insight into this can be found in Edmund Burke's* discussion of the sublime*, which has achieved a certain currency lately. He makes elaborate use of the association of darkness with blackness, linking them to the skin of a real, live black woman. Seeing her produces a sublime feeling of terror in a boy whose sight has been restored to him by a surgical operation.

Perhaps it may appear on enquiry, that blackness and darkness are in some degree painful by their natural operation, independent of any associations whatsoever. I must observe that the ideas of blackness and darkness are much the same; and they differ only in this, that blackness is a more confined idea. Mr Cheselden has given us a very curious story of a boy, who had been born blind, and continued so until he was thirteen or fourteen years old; he was then couched for a cataract, by which operation he received his sight . . . Cheselden tells us, that the first time the boy saw a black object, it gave him great uneasiness; and that some time after, upon accidentally seeing a negro woman, he was struck with great horror at the sight.[2]

Burke, who opposed slavery and argued for its gradual abolition, stands at the doorway of the tradition of enquiry mapped by Raymond Williams* which is also the infrastructure on which much of English cultural studies came to be founded. This origin is part of the explanation of how some of the contemporary manifestations of this tradition lapse into what can only be called a morbid celebration of England and Englishness. These modes of subjectivity and identification acquire a renewed political charge in the post-imperial history that saw black settlers from Britain's colonies take up their citizenship rights as subjects in the United Kingdom. The entry of blacks into national life was itself a powerful factor contributing to the circumstances in which the formation of both cultural studies and New Left politics became possible. It indexes the profound transformations of British social and cultural life in the 1950s and stands, again usually unacknowledged, at the heart of laments for a more human scale of social living that seemed no longer practicable after the 1939–45 war.

[. . .]

[E]ven the laudable, radical varieties of English cultural sensibility examined by Williams and celebrated by Edward Thompson and others were not produced spontaneously from their own internal and intrinsic dynamics. The fact that some of the most potent conceptions of Englishness have been constructed by alien outsiders like Carlyle, Swift, Scott, or Eliot should augment the note of caution sounded here. The most heroic, subaltern English nationalisms and countercultural patriotisms are perhaps better understood as having been generated in a complex pattern of antagonistic relationships with the supranational and imperial world for which the ideas of 'race', nationality, and national culture provide the primary (though not the only) indices.

[. . .]

In opposition to [. . .] nationalist or ethnically absolute approaches, I want to develop the suggestion that cultural historians could take the Atlantic as one single, complex unit of analysis in their discussions of the modern world and use it to produce an explicity transnational and intercultural perspective. Apart from the confrontation with English historiography and literary history this entails a challenge to the ways in which black American cultural and political histories have so far been conceived. I want to suggest that much of the precious intellectual legacy claimed by African-American intellectuals as the substance of their particularity is in fact only partly their absolute ethnic property. No less than in the case of the English New Left, the idea of the black Atlantic can be used to show that there are other claims to it which can be based on the structure of the African diaspora into the western hemisphere. A concern with the Atlantic as a cultural and political system has been forced on black historiography and intellectual history by the economic and historical matrix in which plantation slavery – 'capitalism with its clothes off' – was one special moment. The fractal patterns of cultural and political exchange and transformation that we try and specify through manifestly inadequate theoretical terms like creolisation and syncretism indicate how both ethnicities and political cultures have been made anew in ways that are significant not simply for the peoples of the Caribbean but for Europe, for Africa, especially Liberia and Sierra Leone, and of course, for black America.

It bears repetition that Britain's black settler communities have forged a compound culture from disparate sources. Elements of political sensibility and cultural expression transmitted from black America over a long period of time have been reaccentuated in Britain. They are central, though no longer dominant, within the increasingly novel configurations that characterise another newer black vernacular culture. This is not content to be either dependent upon or simply imitative of the African diaspora cultures of America and the Caribbean. The rise and rise of Jazzie B and Soul II Soul at the turn of the last decade constituted one valuable sign of this new assertive mood. North London's Funki Dreds, whose name itself projects a newly hybridised identity, have projected the distinct culture and rhythm of life of black Britain outwards into the world. Their song 'Keep On Moving' was notable for having been produced in England by the children of Caribbean settlers and then re-mixed in a (Jamaican) dub format in the United States by Teddy Riley, an African-American. It included segments or samples of music taken from American and Jamaican records by the JBs and Mikey Dread respectively. This formal unity of diverse cultural elements was more than just a powerful symbol. It encapsulated the playful diasporic intimacy that has been a marked feature of transnational black Atlantic creativity. The record and its extraordinary popularity enacted the ties of affiliation and affect which articulated the discontinuous histories of black settlers in the new world. The fundamental injunction to 'Keep On Moving' also expressed the restlessness of spirit which makes that diaspora culture vital. The contemporary black arts movement in film, visual arts, and theatre as well as music, which provided the background to this musical release, have created a new topography of loyalty and identity in which the structures and presuppositions of the nation state have been left behind because they are seen to be outmoded. It is important to remember that these recent black Atlantic phenomena may not be as novel as their digital encoding via the transnational force of north London's Soul II Soul suggests. Columbus's pilot, Pedro Nino, was also an African. The history of the black Atlantic since then, continually crisscrossed by the movements of black people – not only as commodities but engaged in various struggles towards emancipation, autonomy, and citizenship – provides a means to reexamine the problems of nationality, location, identity, and historical memory. They all emerge from it with special clarity if we contrast the national, nationalistic, and ethnically absolute paradigms of cultural criticism to be found in England and America with those hidden expressions, both residual and emergent, that attempt to be global or outer-national in nature. These traditions have supported countercultures of modernity that touched the workers' movement but are not reducible to it. They supplied important foundations on which it could build.

Turner's extraordinary painting of the slave ship ['The Slave Ship' (1840)] remains a useful image not only for its self-conscious moral power and the striking way that it aims directly for the sublime in its invocation of racial terror, commerce, and England's ethico-political degeneration. It should be emphasised that ships were the living means by which the points within that Atlantic world were joined. They were mobile elements that stood for the shifting spaces in between the fixed places that they connected. Accordingly they need to be thought of as cultural and political units rather than abstract embodiments of the triangular trade. They were something more – a means to conduct political dissent and possibly a distinct mode of cultural production. The ship provides a chance to explore the articulations between the discontinuous histories of England's ports, its interfaces with the wider world. Ships also refer us back to the middle passage, to the half-remembered micro-politics of the slave trade and its relationship to both industrialisation and modernisation. As it were, getting on board promises a means to reconceptualise the orthodox relationship between modernity and what passes for its prehistory. It provides a different sense of where modernity might itself be thought to begin in the constitutive relationships with outsiders that both found and temper a self-conscious sense of western civilisation. For all these reasons, the ship is the first of the novel chronotopes* presupposed by my attempts to rethink modernity via the history of the black Atlantic and the African diaspora into the western hemisphere.

NOTES

1. See Werner Sollors, *Beyond Ethnicity* (New York: Oxford University Press, 1986).
2. Edmund Burke, *A Philosophical Enquiry into the Origin of Our Ideas of the Sublime and the Beautiful* (1757; Oxford: Oxford University Press, 1998), p. 131.

4

'AMERICAN LITERARY EMERGENCE AS A POSTCOLONIAL PHENOMENON'

Lawrence Buell

Americanists do not usually read American Renaissance* texts as if the implied reader were other than American; yet on reflection we know that is nonsense: actually, American writers keenly desired to be read abroad. Melville himself voyaged to England in order to market *White-Jacket* [a novel of 1850] and sometimes made (or consented to) substantive revisions in the interest of British readers. Indeed, the very first words of Melville's first book (the preface to *Typee*) were got up with British readership in mind, and that narrative is strategically sprinkled with familiarizing English place references (Cheltenham, Stonehenge, Westminster Abbey, etc.). In the passage from *White-Jacket*, the expository elaborateness and the obliquity with which it edges toward the narrator's outspoken antiauthoritarianism become more understandable if we take them as studiously devious in anticipation of being read by both patriotic insiders and Tory outsiders, whether literal foreigners or Yankee Anglophiles. We know from Melville's letters and criticism that he was acutely aware of the problem of negotiating between ideologically disparate readerships, but no one thinks much about the possibility that his doctrine that the great writer communicates to his ideal reader through double meanings which philistine readers are intended to miss might have been brought into focus partly by his position as a postcolonial writer.

The textual consequences of anticipating transcontinental readership are admittedly harder to establish than the impact of foreign literary influences.

From *American Literary History* 4.3 (1992): 411–42.

Open-and-shut cases like the diplomatically vacillating chapter on European travelers' accounts of America in [Washington] Irving's *The Sketch Book* are rare. Direct evidence is usually limited to textual variants for which the responsibility is unclear (Did the author devise? advise? consent? reluctantly agree to delegate?), or to ex cathedra statements (like Cooper's to a British publisher that *The Prairie* 'contains nothing to offend an English reader')[1] which do not in themselves prove that the work would have been written differently had the author designed it for an American readership alone. What we can assert more positively is this. First, that some of the most provincially embedded American Renaissance texts bear at least passing direct witness to anticipating foreign readers, like Thoreau's *Walden*, which (in keeping with its first 'publication' before the Concord lyceum) begins by addressing fellow townspeople but ends by musing as to whether 'John or Jonathan* will realize all this'.[2] And second, that the hypothesis of Americans imagining foreign as well as native opinion, whatever their conscious expectation of literal readership, makes luminous some otherwise puzzling moments in American Renaissance literature. One such moment is Whitman's abrupt reconception of his persona between 1855 and 1856 as coextensive not simply with America but with the world (e.g., in 'Salut au Monde!'). Another is the oddly extended sequence in *Moby-Dick* reporting the gam between the *Pequod* and the *Samuel Enderby*, and its aftermath (chs 100–1).

James Snead remarks that [Chinua] Achebe's novels 'provide an unexpectedly tricky reading experience for their western audience, using wily narrative stratagems to undermine national and racial illusions', such as 'the almost casual manner in which they present African norms' to international readers: glossary apparatus that seems deliberately incomplete, interjection of reminders of the Western reader's outsidership in the course of a cozily familiar-seeming, European-style realist narrative.[3] For example, the guidebook dimension of the passage quoted above creates a deceptive degree of transparency for the Western reader, inasmuch as its 'we have a saying' formula is a common introductory formula in Ibo proverbial statement not remarked upon as such; the passage, then, maintains a certain covertness despite, indeed because of, its forthrightness. Melville uses narrative geniality and cross-culturalism somewhat similarly in the sequence under view so as to sustain the young-America-style jauntiness with which *Moby-Dick* customarily treats old-world cultures, but without the kind of bluntness used against 'the Yarman', for instance.[4]

The gam with the *Samuel Enderby* reworks a cross-cultural comparison repeatedly made by British travelers to America: that Americans were grim workaholic zealots with no time for small talk. The chapter is obviously framed with national stereotypes in mind, Melville initially sketches the encounter between Ahab and Captain Boomer, or rather the interruptive byplay between

Boomer and the ship's surgeon, so as to make the Englishmen seem like patronizing boobies. Yet it is Ahab's truculence that finally comes off as more disturbing and that makes English joviality (itself an American stereotype) seem healthy by comparison. The last emotion to be expressed is the good-humored British captain's honest astonishment. In the ensuing chapter ('The Decanter') Ishmael aligns himself with that same spirit of comic banter (long since identified as an Ishmaelite trait) and pays a mockheroic homage to the whole firm of Enderby, which in fact turns out to have dispatched the first ships ever to hunt the sperm whale in the Pacific, the waters the *Pequod* is about to enter. Ishmael then proceeds, in what first looks like a complete digression, to report a later, more convivial and rousing gam with the *Samuel Enderby* in which he partook, a drunken feast 'at midnight somewhere off the Patagonian coast'.[5]

Ishmael's reinstitution of good fellowship with his English counterparts 'atones' ex post facto for Ahab's bad manners and 'validates' the English captain's good-humored bewilderment at Ahab's stormy departure. Yet through this dexterous maneuver, Melville is given license to laugh at the clichéd version of British thickheadedness not once but twice – first apropos Ahab's tragedy, then apropos the farce of sailorly roistering – thereby propitiating American cultural nationalism without offending British readers. It is testimony both to Melville's wiliness and to his deference that the vigorous in-house censorship upon which his British publishers insisted, of religiously and culturally offensive matter in the manuscript of *The Whale* (resulting in the deletion of chapter 25 on British coronation procedures, for instance), left chapters 100–1 untouched.[6]

[. . .]

The marks of postcolonialism in American Renaissance writing are far more numerous than a short article can hope to discuss. Here is a brief checklist of some of the most salient.

1. *The semi-Americanization of the English language.* What language shall we speak? American settlers did not face this question in its most radical form, as put by Ngugi wa Thiong'o in *Decolonizing the Mind*, which argues that African literature should be written in the indigenous languages. But the weaker version of the argument (namely how to creolize and neologize American English so that it spoke a voice of the culture distinct from the standardizing mother tongue) does certainly link Cooper and Emerson and Whitman and Twain with Amos Tutuola, Gabriel Okara, and Raja Rao, whose work sheds light on such subissues as the inextricability of 'naturalness' and 'artifice' in Whitman's diction and the inextricability of idealization and caricature in Cooper's vernacular heroes like Natty Bumppo. Bill Ashcroft, Gareth Griffiths, and Helen Tiffin remark that postcolonial

literatures are 'always written out of the tension between the abrogation of the received English which speaks from the center, and the act of appropriation which brings it under the influence of a vernacular tongue'.[7] That is a duality crucial to American literary emergence as well. In the early national period, we see it especially in texts that counterpoint characters who speak dialect (who are always comic) with characters who speak Standard English, for example, Colonel Manly versus his servant Jonathan in Royall Tyler's *The Contrast* and Captain Farrago versus his servant Teague O'Reagan in Hugh Henry Brackenridge's *Modern Chivalry*. At this stage, the vernacular is still clearly a national embarrassment to be indulged only obliquely, through satire. 'Vulgarity', as Bridgman puts it, 'had to be fenced in with quotation marks'.[8] This is the American equivalent of, say, the colloquial dramatic monologues of Indo-Anglian poet Nissim Ezekiel:

> I am standing for peace and non-violence
> Why world is fighting fighting
> Why all people of world
> Are not following Mahatma Gandhi
> I am simply not understanding.[9]

By the time of Thoreau and Whitman, the American inventiveness with language, through individual neologizing and provincial variant usages, that Tocqueville (and others) considered one of the most 'deplorable' consequences of democratization had become positive aesthetic values.[10] Thus without any hint of parody, in section 5 of 'Song of Myself', Whitman could allow the sublime* vision following from the persona's possession by his soul to come to rest on 'the mossy scabs of the worm-fence'[11] – the latter an American coinage never used in poetry before, referring to a characteristic motif of American agricultural construction that foreign visitors often singled out as particularly wasteful and ugly.[12] The 'mossy scabs' metaphor makes it absolutely clear, if further proof be needed, that Whitman seeks to fashion the sublime from the positively vulgar. Not that he was prepared to forgo literary English. His position – almost quintessentially postcolonial in this respect – was to justify an Americanization of English expression as the poetic way of the future on the ground that English itself was remarkable for its engraftment of other linguistic strains.

2. *The issue of cultural hybridization.* Another recurring motif in American Renaissance texts is their fondness for cross-cultural collages: Whitman's composite persona; Thoreau's balancing between the claims of post-Puritan, Greco-Roman, Native American, and Oriental mythographies in *A Week* and *Walden*; Melville's multimythic

elaboration of the whale symbol in tandem with the *Pequod* as a global village; Cooper's heteroglossic tapestry of six or seven different nationalities in *The Pioneers*. David Simpson argues, respecting Cooper, that Templeton's polyglot character, each resident speaking his or her own peculiar dialect (except for the Temple family, of course), registers the social fissures of still-experimental nationhood;[13] and I think we might further understand this phenomenon by thinking of it in reference to (for example) composite national-symbol characters like Salman Rushdie's Saleem Sinai (in *Midnight's Children*) and G. V. Desani's Mr Hatterr, or the syncretism of Wole Soyinka's interweave between Yoruba and Greek mythology. What Lewis Nkosi says of modern African Anglophone poetry's quest to define its path applies beautifully to the world of Cooper's *Pioneers*: '[T]he first requirement . . . was precisely to articulate the socio-cultural conditions in which the modern African writer had to function, the heterogeneity of cultural experiences among which the poet had to pick his or her way'.[14]

3. *The expectation that artists be responsible agents for achieving national liberation*, which in turn bespeaks a non-specialized conception of art and an ambivalence toward aestheticism that threatens to produce schizophrenia. Soyinka calls attention to the pressure upon the postcolonial African writer to 'postpone that unique reflection on experience and events which is what makes a writer – and constitute himself into a part of that machinery that will actually shape events'.[15] Emerson wrestles with a very similar looking public/private dilemma in 'The American Scholar' and later attempts at political interventions like the first Fugitive Slave Law* address. Anozie's statement that '[t]here seemed to exist a genetic struggle between a romantic pursuit of art for its own sake and a constantly intensive awareness of the social relevance of art'[16] could apply equally well to Soyinka and Emerson, though in fact it refers to Nigerian poet Christopher Okigbo, the closest approximation to a 'pure aesthete' among the major figures of the illustrious first contemporary generation of Nigeria's Anglophone literati but later killed as a soldier in the Biafran war.

4. *The problem of confronting neocolonialism*, the disillusionment of revolutionary hopes, which threatens to turn the artist against the audience that was prepared to celebrate him or her as symptomatic of cultural emergence. Postcolonial Africa, for instance, has inspired an oppositional literature that both helps to explain American Renaissance oppositionalism as a predictable postrevolutionary symptom and to define its limits. Thoreau as individualistic civil disobedient both is and is not the counterpart of Ngugi's revolutionary socialism.

5. *The problem of 'alien genres'*: Eurocentric genres that carry authority but seem not to be imitable without sacrifice of cultural authenticity. There is a striking semicorrespondence here between the critique of the protagonist-centered realist novel by third-world intellectuals and complaints by nineteenth-century American fictionists from Cooper to Hawthorne to James that the novel was not transplantable to American soil. Conversely, some genres have seemed not only transplantable with great ease but precisely tailored for American and other new-world contexts. A prime example is my next and last rubric, which I should like to unfold at somewhat greater length than the others.

6. *New-world pastoral*. 'Pastoralism' in the broadest sense of a recurring fascination with physical nature as subject, symbol, and theater in which to act out rituals of maturity and purification has long been seen as a distinctive American preoccupation, but without it being grasped how this can be generalized. Mutatis mutandis the same can be said of Canadian and Australian writing, although their versions of nature are (and for more complicated reasons than just geography) less benign than ours; and a version of the same can be said of third-world writing as well, despite manifest differences between white-settler pastoral and nonwhite indigene pastoral. Here the obvious analogue is negritude*, as well as other forms of cultural nationalism that hold up a precolonial ideal order as a salvific badge of distinctiveness. Retrospective pastoralization of ancient tribal structures occurs in the American Renaissance as well: particularly in the more sentimental treatments of Puritan heritage and the old plantation order, not to mention the even more vicarious sort of nostalgia represented by Anglo-American savagist fantasies like Longfellow's *Song of Hiawatha*. Perhaps this explains why Thoreau became simultaneously addicted to nature and to New England antiquities. *Walden* and *The Scarlet Letter* are predictable complements in their mutual preoccupation with cultural origins.

But to stay with pastoral at the level of physical nature, what Americanists tend to miss, and what recent postcolonial critiques have been helpful in pointing out (e.g., Amuta),[17] is the extent to which the conception of naturism as a mark of cultural independence needs to be countered by the conception of naturism as a neocolonial residue. Thomas Jefferson's *Notes on the State of Virginia*, which contains the classical statement of the American pastoral ideal, shows this clearly. Jefferson recommends that the new country follow the agrarian way in the explicit awareness that that will mean dependence on European manufactures. The preservation of national virtue, which he associates with rurality, he considers worth the cost. Some, even today, would argue that it is. But my point here is the lacuna in Jefferson's earlier thinking: his belief that moral self-sufficiency can coexist with economic dependence. Some years later, as Leo Marx shows in *The Machine in the Garden*, Jefferson changed his mind about America industrializing. What Marx does *not* diagnose is the status of Jefferson's original position as the intellectual artifact of a late-colonial intellectual. Marx shows, of course, that the conception of America as a pastoral utopia originates in Europe, but he ceases to think of European antecedence as important once pastoral thinking becomes naturalized in America by the mid-eighteenth century, and this in turn keeps him from beginning to approach figures like Jefferson and Thoreau in the light of being driven against their conscious intent by an ideological mechanism set in place to appropriate the New World in the interest of the Old – the antithesis of the state both men saw themselves as promoting.

Nothing could have been more natural than for the American Romantics to valorize physical nature as a central literary subject (whether benign, as in Transcendentalism, or ominous, as in *Moby-Dick* or the forest sequence in *The Scarlet Letter*), for this was an obvious way of turning what had often been deemed a cultural disadvantage into a cultural asset. But this same move, which capitalized upon an aesthetic value of international Romanticism as well as an established old-world image of the New World, was not without its risks. A text that illustrates these is the well-known sonnet addressed by William Cullen Bryant* in farewell to his friend the painter Thomas Cole, bound for Europe.

> Thine eyes shall see the light of distant skies:
> > Yet, Cole! thy heart shall bear to Europe's strand
> > A living image of thy native land,
> Such as on thy own glorious canvass lies;
> Lone lakes – savannahs where the bison roves –
> > Rocks rich with summer garlands – solemn streams –
> > Skies, where the desert eagle wheels and screams –
> Spring bloom and autumn blaze of boundless groves.
> Fair scenes shall greet thee where thou goest – fair,
> > But different – every where the trace of men,
> > Paths, homes, graves, ruins, from the lowest glen
> To where life shrinks from the fierce Alpine air.
> > Gaze on them, till the tears shall dim thy sight,
> > But keep that earlier, wilder image bright!

Bryant's valedictory tribute affirms a nationalist vision of America as nature's nation (lakes, savannahs, rocks, skies), over against a

European scene that everywhere bears 'the trace of men'. Bryant rightly credits Cole's American landscape paintings with having registered this sense of the American difference. Like Whitman, Bryant revises *translatio studii**, charging Cole to bear an American aesthetic gospel to Europe, but the poem's cautionary ending betrays a postcolonial anxiety as to whether Cole will keep the faith. That very significant and well-warranted anxiety is, however, a telling moment, the only moment that the poem begins to acknowledge the extent to which Bryant and Cole have in fact always already been affected by the European gravitational field whether consciously or not. Cole, like other self-consciously American landscape painters of his day, had been deeply influenced by the tropes of European Romantic landscape (and in his case also history) painting. As for Bryant, although his poem is replete with distinctively American references (such as bison, eagle, and the fall colors that regularly amazed European travelers), what strikes a modern reader much more strongly is its bondage to old-world language and form: 'savannahs' as a cosmopolitan synonym for 'prairies'; the placement of the eagle in a generic, symbolic 'desert'; 'Alpine' as a surrogate for the sublimity of American mountains; and above all, Bryant's unconsciously ironic choice of sonnet – a hypercivilized form if ever there was one – as the vehicle for enjoining his gospel of the 'wilder image'. In short, the authentic insider's view of America Bryant/Cole have to offer Europe as new-world cultural evangelists is at most a slightly nuanced version of the view that their position as Euro-American settlers has prepared them for.

In an excellent recent study of American landscape representation in the Revolutionary era, Robert Lawson-Peebles discusses this effect under the heading of 'the hallucination of the displaced terrain'. Lawson-Peebles points out that cultural nationalist visions of a pastoralized America pulled 'towards Europe and away from the facts of the American continent. Even the writers who attended closely to those facts shaped them so that they answered European criticisms, and in doing so they collaborated in a dream-world'.[18] Bryant is a clear case in point: it is almost as if 'the American Wordsworth' had set out with the intention of playing back to Coleridge an image of America just slightly (but not alarmingly) more feral than Coleridge had entertained 30 years before in *his* sonnet on 'Pantisocracy', which envisions a rural valley purified of nightmare and neurosis, where 'Virtue' dances 'to the moonlight roundelay' and 'the rising Sun' darts 'new rays of pleasaunce trembling to the heart'.[19]

In stressing the postcolonial basis of American pastoral visions like Bryant's, I do not mean to discredit them; on the contrary, I am convinced they potentially have great power even today as mimetic and ideological instruments. No doubt, for example, the American pastoral tradition helps account for the high degree of public environmental concern that now obtains in America, despite notorious slippages between doctrine and daily practice, between law and implementation. But in order to understand the potentially formidable continuing power of pastoral as a cultural instrument, we need also to understand the element of mimetic desire that has historically driven the pastoralizing impulse.

NOTES

1. James Fenimore Cooper, *Letters and Journals*, ed. James Franklin Beard, 6 vols (Cambridge, MA: Belknap-Harvard University Press, 1960–8), vol. 1, p. 166.
2. Henry David Thoreau, *Walden*, ed. J. Lyndon Shanley (Princeton: Princeton University Press, 1973), p. 333.
3. James Snead, 'European Pedigrees/African Contagions: Nationality, Narrative, and Communality in Tutuola, Achebe and Reed', in Homi K. Bhabha (ed.) *Nation and Narration* (London: Routledge, 1990), p. 241.
4. Herman Melville, *Moby-Dick*, ed. Harrison Hayford, Hershel Parker and G. Thomas Tanselle (Evanston: Northwestern University Press, 1988), pp. 351–60.
5. Ibid., p. 444.
6. Ibid., pp. 681–3.
7. Bill Ashcroft, Gareth Griffiths and Helen Tiffin, *The Empire Writes Back: Theory and Practice in Post-Colonial Literatures* (London: Routledge, 1989), p. 39.
8. Richard Bridgman, *The Colloquial Style in America* (New York: Oxford University Press, 1966), p. 7.
9. Nissim Ezekiel, *Latter-Day Psalms* (Delhi: Oxford University Press, 1982), p. 22.
10. Alexis de Tocqueville, *Democracy in America*, tr. Henry Reeve, ed. Phillips Bradley, 2 vols (New York: Vintage, 1945), vol. 2, p. 71.
11. Walt Whitman, *Leaves of Grass*, ed. Harold W. Blodgett and Sculley Bradley (New York: New York University Press, 1965), p. 33.
12. See Jane Louise Mesick, *The English Traveler in America, 1836–1860* (New York: Columbia University Press, 1922), pp. 161–2.
13. See David Simpson, *The Politics of American English, 1776–1850* (New York: Oxford University Press, 1986), pp. 149–201.
14. Lewis Nkosi, *Tasks and Masks: Themes and Styles of African Literature* (Harlow: Longman, 1981), p. 151.
15. Wole Soyinka, *Art, Dialogue and Outrage: Essays on Literature and Culture*, ed. Biodun Jeyifo (Ibadan: New Horn, 1988), p. 16.
16. Sunday Anozie, *Christopher Okigbo: Creative Rhetoric* (London: Evans, 1972), p. 175.
17. See Chidi Amuta, *The Theory of African Literature* (London: Zed, 1989), p. 49.
18. Robert Lawson-Peebles, *Landscape and Written Expression in Revolutionary America: The World Turned Upside Down* (Cambridge: Cambridge University Press, 1988), p. 57.
19. Samuel Taylor Coleridge, *The Poems of Samuel Taylor Coleridge*, ed. Ernest Hartley Coleridge (London: Oxford University Press, 1931), pp. 68–9.

5

'EUROPEAN PEDIGREES/AFRICAN CONTAGIONS: NATIONALITY, NARRATIVE, AND COMMUNITY IN TUTUOLA, ACHEBE, AND REED'

James Snead

By taking 'nation' as a form of spatial coherence, one inadequately addresses the problem of defining 'people'. Leopold Bloom [in James Joyce's novel *Ulysses*], displaced Jew, has good reason to define his 'Irishness' by place instead of race. Yet he quickly encounters an objection to his words 'same people'. For, as Joyce's Ned Lambert wittily shows, the term 'nation' itself embodies a paradox: a 'nation' is coherent, specific, and local; yet a person, the atomic essence of a nation ('I'm a nation'), does not constitute a *population*. Nations require plurality, yet plurality dilutes all strict standards of differentiation: 'Civilization is a re-agent, and eats away the old traits'.[1] There seems a principle of necessary dilution whereby the 'nation' must apply increasingly more general rubrics to its population, while at the same time continuing to include an ever widening spectrum of people.

Imperialism – the accumulation of diverse 'nations' under a single flag – may be seen an almost semantic imperative; 'force' replaces 'nature' in forging alliances; selective assimilation, rather than aggressive exclusion, allows the national concept to survive, despite the relative distance between concept and reality. For instance, the more successful the British Empire became, the less it was racially and linguistically pure 'British'. Indeed, from almost any starting point, national definitions include more than they exclude, precisely because of

From Homi K. Bhabha (ed.) (1990) *Nation and Narration*. London: Routledge, pp. 231–49.

the internal contradictions of the term 'nation' itself, which [. . .] can sustain an almost self-annulling level of generality [. . .].

As a result, the concept of 'nation' finds its meaning on the broadest, rather than on the most detailed, levels, even as it pretends to furnish us with the most specific segregations. It might be predicted, then, that the study of national literatures would involve similar contradictions. The temptation to regard 'language' or 'literature' as the guarantor of a nation's 'pedigree' (remember that *natio* has in Latin an almost eugenic connotation) recalls the similar (and frequently more destructive) employment of the concept of 'color'. In both cases an apparently exclusionary process is meant somehow to isolate the pure 'pedigree' of a race, a language, or a literature, even as that process ends up in a compensating search for some emblem of universality. Johnson's remark [the epigraph to the essay cites Samuel Johnson's 'languages are the pedigree of nations'] is perhaps more understandable against this background, though his linguistic definition of 'nation' raises as many problems as Leopold Bloom's topographical one.

[. . .]

It should be clear by now, though, that we are dealing with two versions of the 'universal', best differentiated by a term used in Ishmael Reed's *Mumbo Jumbo* (1972). Here, the Afro-American writer Reed accurately dissects what could be called the 'white' and the 'black' approaches to universality and communality. *Mumbo Jumbo* traces an imaginary history of western and non-western culture, wherein non-historical and non-material (hence 'primitive') elements insist on disrupting western culture's appetite for closed and secure progression. These disruptions of closed systems – which Reed typifies as 'eruptions of Jes Grew' – in fact renew rather than ravage what might have become stagnant ('They are calling it a plague when in fact it is an anti-plague').[2] Established institutions consistently view them as threats, however. Hence, in Reed's conception, western history becomes a series of failed and misguided attempts to ignore gaps in systems of national, cultural, or racial cohesion (what I have elsewhere called *cuts*) or to prevent them altogether: 'You must use something up-to-date to curb Jes Grew. To knock it dock it co-opt it swing it or bop it'.[3]

The European notion of 'universality' often takes on, as we have seen, the aspect of *collection*: it seems a drive to accumulate as many texts, artifacts, nations, peoples as possible, all under one roof, one rubric, or one ruler. *Mumbo Jumbo* somewhat cheekily suggests that the European notion of 'universality' is a mammoth power play, 'universal being a word co-opted by the Catholic Church when the Atonists took over Rome, as a way of measuring every 1 by their ideals'.[4] The twin imperatives 'exclude and accumulate' seem fitting under a kind of Hegelian* linearism that wants to incorporate within one

Spirit or mind ever greater areas of knowledge and material. 'Realm' becomes 'nation' becomes 'empire' becomes 'western' or 'European' civilization, but stays *white*. Accumulation, then, is an almost metaphorical movement, whereby things of differing values are lumped together under a single image or signifier for purposes of potential exchange, marketability, or common defense. Efforts both literary and political to include non-whites in this scheme have centered around white perspectives and maintained the dominance of the white narrative and white nations (at least until very recently).

[. . .]

Opposed to this critical stance of a 'universality' that encompasses – yet also confines and dominates – well-defined national distinctions, we have what might be called an African approach to universality: not *collection*, but a benevolent *contagion*, not of disease, but a shared awareness of shared energy. The transcendence of segregationist barriers that much African writing – and Reed's *Mumbo Jumbo* – exemplifies is exactly 'the indefinable quality that James Weldon Johnson called "Jes Grew" . . . "It belonged to nobody," Johnson said. "It's words were unprintable but its tune irresistible"'.[5] The dominant metaphor for 'Jes Grew' in Reed's text is 'contagion': all cultures, colors, and nationalities are subject to the ubiquity of its 'pandemic'.[6] 'Jes Grew' (in a sense, the main 'character' of *Mumbo Jumbo*) is the elusive force that certain repressive people (whom Reed names the 'Atonists') are trying to co-opt, confine, or destroy. But what might be the determinants of contagion? Perhaps the most important aspect of cultural contagion is that by the time one is aware of it, it has *already happened*. Contagion, being metonymic (*con* + *tangere* = 'touching together'), involves – most appropriately for an African tribal context – an actual process of contacts between people, rather than a quantitative setting of metaphorical value. If *collection* exists as a guarantor of *pro*spective value, then *contagion* is a *retro*spective attempt to assess a propinquity that seems to have always been present in latent form and has already erupted without cause or warning. Opposed to Dr Johnson's 'pedigree' that sought to discover lost, but recoverable *differences*, contagion represents the existence of recoverable *affinities* between disparate races of people. It is perhaps a tiny inkling of contagion that Achebe shows when we see the presumably austere Winterbottom in *Arrow of God* 'mystifying other Europeans with words from the Ibo language which he claimed to speak fluently'.[7] His fate was not uncommon in the chronicle of imperialism: even as they tried to collect ever newer local cultures and races, dominant powers found themselves caught up in the contagion they tried to put down. The sequence of contagion, collection (or repression) and new contagion furnishes the basic rhythm of Reed's various plots. Even as collection domesticates and organizes barriers and distances, contagion seems to have already made obsolete the barriers to its own spread.

Reed's narrative – together with Tutuola's and Achebe's novels – provides a well-targeted analysis of cultural cohesion as Europe and America have practiced it throughout 'written history' against the 'unwritten' strains of blackness that repeatedly threaten to spread. *Mumbo Jumbo* deals with the temptation of western culture to fasten a sense of superiority or national cohesion to particular texts, tropes, or routines. Inexplicably to the western mind, these texts, tropes, and routines soon (for the sake of convenience, let us say at around 1900) come to seem unstable, tainted, as if they have all along belonged not to the west, but to a distinct and mocking oppositional sensibility.

NOTES

1. Ralph Waldo Emerson, 'Race', in *The Portable Emerson*, ed. Carl Bode and Malcolm Cowley (New York: Penguin, 1981), p. 407.
2. Ishmael Reed, *Mumbo Jumbo* (New York: Doubleday, 1972), p. 27.
3. Ibid., p. 73.
4. Ibid., p. 153.
5. Ibid., p. 239.
6. Ibid., p. 27.
7. Chinua Achebe, *Arrow of God* (London: Heinemann, 1964), p. 184.

6

'DEEP TIME: AMERICAN LITERATURE AND WORLD HISTORY'

Wai Chee Dimock

In what follows, I invoke this historical depth to redraw the map of American literature. To take this depth seriously is to challenge the short, sharp, executive thrust of dates: 1776, or 1620, when the Mayflower arrived. Such dates (and the periodization based upon them) assume that there can be a discrete, bounded unit of time coinciding with a discrete, bounded unit of space: a chronology coinciding with a territory. Such a coincidence is surely a fiction. Rather than taking it for granted – rather than taking our measure of time from the stipulated beginning of a territorial entity – I propose a more extended duration for American literary studies, planetary in scope. I call this *deep time*. This produces a map that, thanks to its receding horizons, its backward extension into far-flung temporal and spatial coordinates, must depart significantly from a map predicated on the short life of the US. For the force of historical depth is such as to suggest a world that predates the adjective *American*. If we go far enough back in time, and it is not very far, there was no such thing as the US. This nation was not yet on the map, but the world was already fully in existence. The cumulative history of that existence, serving as a time frame both antecedent and ongoing, takes American literature easily outside the nation's borders. A diachronic axis has geographical consequences. Deep time is denationalized space.

What would American literature look like then? Can we transpose some familiar figures onto this broadened and deepened landscape? I would like to

From *American Literary History* 13.4 (2001): 755–75.

test that possibility. Using Islam as the temporal and spatial coordinates, non-binding but also nontrivial, I trace a thread of continuity spun out of its migration, dissemination, and hybridization. Running through the terrain usually called *American*, this thread will knot together kinships no doubt surprising to many. Such kinships would not have been recognized in a nation-centered paradigm. They owe their legibility to the deep field of a large-scale phenomenon: its scope, its tangled antecedents, its translations and permutations. World history, as instanced by this unusually extended, durable, and contested phenomenon, yields both the evidential domain and the analytic method, both the time frame and the spatial latitude to render salient a set of relationships, not strictly *American* because not strictly national. Scale enlargement, I argue, enlarges our sense of complex kinship.

My paradigm, in this sense, is the obverse of Edward Said's in *Orientalism* (1979), his account of images of the East (primarily Islam) in post-Enlightenment Europe. 'Taking the late eighteenth century as a very roughly defined starting point', Said argues, 'Orientalism can be discussed and analyzed as the corporate institution for dealing with the Orient – dealing with it by making statements about it, authorizing views of it, describing it, by teaching it, settling it, ruling over it'.[1] This corporate institution was clearly of European vintage: 'To speak of Orientalism therefore is to speak mainly, although not exclusively, of a British and French cultural enterprise'.[2] Started in England and France, and never leaving these nations far behind, Orientalism was less an homage to an alien world than a symptom of Western domination. As a regime of expert knowledge, it helped forge 'the idea of European identity as a superior one in comparison with all the non-European peoples and cultures'.[3] For Said, Orientalism is ideological through and through, and Eurocentric through and through. This is what he unmasks. And yet, in scaling the problem as he does – scaling it to put Eurocentrism at its front and center – he ends up reproducing the very map he sets out to critique. On this map, the West is once again the principal actor, the seat of agency. The Orient is no more than a figment of its ideological projection, brought 'home' to serve the needs of imperial rule. As Said himself says, his study is 'based more or less exclusively upon a sovereign Western consciousness out of whose unchallenged centrality an Oriental world emerged'.[4] His analytic domain is strictly 'within the umbrella of Western hegemony over the Orient'.[5]

That umbrella gives rise to an odd paradigm, oddly hierarchical and segregated: West versus East, the dominating versus the dominated. The latter exists only as clay molded by Western hands. The Orient is a fabrication, an artifact. As such, it has no agency of its own, no life apart from the ideological constructions foisted upon it, no ability to put its stamp at the head of any significant or durable genealogy. The historical sequence that Said narrates is a sequence that begins in the West and sticks always to that genetic locale. This is not so much a history of the world as a history of a gigantic ideological factory, a Western factory. Not surprisingly, Islam can show up here only as a product, not the maker but the made. To put agency and causality all on one side, as Said does, is to reaffirm an all-too-familiar map, a map scaled to fit the outlines of Western nations, scaled to highlight their input as dominant.

Can we draw a different input map of the world? A sequence that begins at an earlier point in history, that goes back to other parts of the globe? The concept of deep time is especially helpful here. Extending much further back than the late eighteenth century that is Said's starting point, deep time also pre-dates the 'umbrella of Western hegemony' materializing during that period. What this *longue durée* allows us to see is an Afro-Eurasian civilization, an Afro-Eurasian *hybrid*, much more interesting and consequential than it would appear when the taxonomic period is no more than a couple of hundred years. This hybrid is not fully describable under the stamp, the scope, and the chronology of European nations. Its long life demands a different time frame. Given that, it will in turn yield a genealogy more surprising and certainly more militant: one that challenges the jurisdiction of nations, of periods, and of taxonomic categories such as *East* and *West*.

For one thing, that genealogy goes beyond Europe, to a part of the globe Said mentions only briefly: the US. Black Muslims in America are not usually called 'Orientalists'. But that is what they are: a new twist on that word, the latest and most controversial variant.

[. . .]

It would be a mistake, however, to see this as a strictly twentieth-century phenomenon, affecting only African-American authors. Indeed, the importance of Islamic deep time lies precisely in its ability to break down some of the standard dividing lines, turning them into unexpected lines of kinship. For the longevity of this world religion weaves it not only into black history but also into the history of a very different segment of the American population. [James] Baldwin and Malcolm X [two twentieth-century figures whose response to Islam Dimock discusses in the essay] have company. They are the unlikely extensions, unlikely heirs, to a group of people rarely mentioned in the same breath: the Transcendentalists*.

The Transcendentalists were avid readers. Comparative philology and comparative religion – two newly minted disciplines of the nineteenth century – were high on their reading lists. The relative claims of various civilizations were hot topics for them. Henry David Thoreau, immersing himself in a translation of Manu's Sanskrit text, the *Institutes of Hindu Law* (1825), was as elated as Malcolm X would be by ancient Islam: 'I cannot read a sentence in the book of the Hindoos without being elevated as upon the table-land of the Ghauts. It has such a rhythm as the winds of the desert, such a tide as the Ganges, and seems as superior to criticism as the Himmaleh Mounts. Even at this late hour, unworn by time, with a native and inherent dignity it wears the English dress as indifferently as the Sanscrit'.[6] The Ganges and the Himalayas easily dwarf the landscape around Concord; they put America in perspective. Mindful of that, Thoreau's friend, Bronson Alcott, tried to borrow these books from the Boston Athenaeum on 24 March 1849: 'Collier's Four Books of Confucius, History of China (by the Jesuit), The Kings of Confucius, The Vedas, The Saama Vedas, Vishnu Parana, Saadi, Firdusi, The Zendavesta, The Koran'.[7]

Nor was this only a masculine pursuit. Margaret Fuller was an early and enthusiastic reader of Persian poetry, and was rueful about her lack of competence in the Asian languages: 'Gentle Sanscrit I cannot write. My Persian and Arabic you love not'.[8] Meanwhile, linguistic competence or not, Lydia Maria Child* was able to write a three-volume treatise called *The Progress of Religious Ideas through Successive Ages* (1855), beginning with 'Hindostan', followed by 'Egypt', 'China', 'Thibet and Tartary', 'Chaldea', and 'Persia', and ending with a 68-page chapter on 'Mohammedanism'. The Transcendentalists were internationalists to a fault. And none more so than Ralph Waldo Emerson.

[. . .]

Hybridity, indeed, was the condition not only of the texts that came to Emerson but of his own making as a reader. Monolingualism was alien to him; he was the offspring of five or six languages. Emerson learned the classical languages as part of his nineteenth-century education, and seemed to read Latin with ease. His borrowed books from the Boston Athenaeum and the Harvard College Library included many texts in French. On his own, Emerson also taught himself two other languages: German and Italian. The former was urged upon him by his brother. William Emerson was in Göttingen during 1824–5, attending the lectures of Jacob Eichhorn, full of the *Higher Criticism*, and writing home effusive in his praise of the German language. Emerson wrote back on 20 November 1824: 'If you think it every way advisable, indisputably, absolutely important that I shd do as you have done and go to G– & you can easily decide – why say it distinctly & I will make the sacrifice of time & take the risk of expense, immediately. So of studying German'.[9] By 1828 he apparently knew enough of the language to check out from the Harvard College Library volume 3 of Goethe's* *Werke* (1828–33), the beginning of a lifelong attachment to that author, carried on, from the very first, partly in German. Emerson clearly became fluent in the next few years. In 1834, he borrowed Wieland's *Sämmtliche Werke* (1824–6) from the Boston Athenaeum; in 1835, Schlegel's* *Sämmtliche Werke* (1822); in 1836, Grimm's *Kinder- und Haus-Märchen* (1819–22), Musaeus's *Volksmärchen der Deutschen* (1826), and Hardenberg's *Novalis Schriften* (1826). These readings would continue for the rest of his life.

NOTES

1. Edward Said, *Orientalism* (New York: Vintage, 1979), p. 3.
2. Ibid., p. 4.
3. Ibid., p. 7.
4. Ibid., p. 8.
5. Ibid., p. 7.
6. Henry David Thoreau, *The Journal of Henry David Thoreau*, ed. Bradford Torrey and Francis H. Allen (Boston: Houghton, 1949), pp. 266–7.
7. Quoted in Arthur Christy, *The Orient in American Transcendentalism* (New York: Columbia University Press, 1932), p. 243.
8. Margaret Fuller, *The Letters of Margaret* Fuller, ed. Robert N. Hudspeth, 5 vols (Ithaca: Cornell University Press, 1983–8), vol. 2, p. 122.
9. Ralph Waldo Emerson, *Letters of Ralph Waldo Emerson*, ed. Ralph L. Rusk, 6 vols (New York: Columbia University Press, 1939), vol. 1, p. 154.

PART IV
TRANSLATION

TRANSLATION: INTRODUCTION

In a world where multi-lingual populations share the same nation-state, and where nationality frequently exceeds geographical borders to create diasporic groups, translation plays an increasingly central role in communication. As we have seen in previous sections, the transatlantic exhibits the entanglements of diverse cultures and constituencies, in which language both constructs the nation as a discursive space and works to disrupt its imagined consistency. As translation theorists no longer speak of 'source' and 'target' languages, but rather of complex interactions between two or more idioms of equal status, Transatlantic Studies aims to move away from a hierarchical structure of origins and influence, decoupling itself from the centripetally-inclined ideology and rhetoric of national exceptionalism, to consider actively the dynamics of cultural and linguistic relationships. So although the technical aspects of translation studies may not have direct application for transatlantic criticism which is not also working across different linguistic domains, both its theoretical inquiries and metaphoric potential offer promising starting points even for monolingual discussions in this area.

For example, the relationship between the political power of language and the ethical questions that inhere in the very act of translation has become a key preoccupation for recent theorists. Indeed the Latin American critic Ilan Stavans has asserted that 'modernity . . . is not lived through nationality but . . . through translationality' (Sokol, 554). The etymology of the word 'translation' is comprised of two elements – *trans* (across) and *latus* (the past participle of *ferre*, to carry). This suggests a physical transportation, a 'carrying across' of meaning from one discursive space to another. Transference of ideas and cultural forms may be essential to their survival – but in new contexts, they will look different, and signify differently, from their 'originals'. Attempting to raise money to found a college in Bermuda in the 1720s, the British philosopher George Berkeley wrote, in famous verses 'On the Prospect of Planting Arts and Learning in America', of the impending translation of culture from Europe to the Americas:

> The Muse, disgusted at an age and clime
>> Barren of every glorious theme,
> In distant lands now waits a better time,
>> Producing subjects worthy fame . . .

> Westward the course of empire takes its way;
>> The first four acts already past,
> A fifth shall close the drama with the day;
>> Time's noblest offspring is the last.

But Stavans's idea of 'translationality' seeks to complicate any sense we might have of translation effecting a straightforward (and, as in the case of Berkeley's lines, teleological) transferral of semantic content. Critics such as Stavans, Lawrence Venuti and Susan Bassnett explore how linguistic (and therefore cultural) difference is often brought under the domesticating rubric of the host language. As Venuti has noted, language 'transparency results in a concealment . . . of the conditions of production' (Venuti, 61). In a colonial and postcolonial context, such linguistic 'concealment' evolves alongside those ideas of white, Eurocentric superiority deemed essential to the maintenance of empire itself. Caliban's resentment that Prospero, his coloniser, has imposed a strange language upon him, that he has in effect orchestrated an enforced translation, is memorably expressed: 'You taught me language, and my profit on't / Is I know how to curse' (*The Tempest*, I, ii). By erasing the possibility of a multilingual space, Prospero creates a situation in which resistance to colonisation is 'concealed' within the language of oppression itself.

The study of translation, then, has an important bearing on our concerns about the nexus of the local and the global, the national and the diasporic, the domestic and the foreign. To engage in an act of translation is to participate in a series of ethical choices that might have profound political implications; decisions over how much of the 'foreignness' of a text to suppress or to highlight have significance in ways that extend beyond the narrowly linguistic. Those acts of inclusion and exclusion that are marshalled under the rubrics of 'American exceptionalism', 'Manifest Destiny'* or 'the melting pot', for example, determine the potential for translatability of whole cultures, races and ethnicities:

they are linguistic acts that have tangible material consequences. The extract by Lori Chamberlain included here makes these consequences central to its argument, for the essay links translation with gender politics. Chamberlain examines the connections between patriarchal authority/authorship and the translated text (historically regarded as feminine and unfaithful), where translation is figured in terms both of its fidelity to an originating male authority and of its relationship to a 'mother tongue'. She reminds us that that this metaphor of the family is itself translatable into reflections on the body politic: 'the struggle for authorial rights takes place both in the realm of the family . . . and in the state, for translation has also been figured as the literary equivalent of colonisation, a means of enriching both the language and the literature appropriate to the political needs of expanding nations'. What she calls 'the metaphorics of translation' encompasses acts of violence carried out in the service of maintaining and expanding textual/national authority.

Translation need not, of course, be regarded solely as an act of colonialism. Venuti has pointed out the subversive work done by translators who refuse to domesticate the 'foreign', leaving visible, and potent, those expressions or ideas from parts of the world regarded as unfamiliar or dangerous. Walter Benjamin's influential essay 'The Task of the Translator', which is reprinted here, goes so far as to claim for translation the responsibility for allowing an 'original' text to live on: without translation, or, rather, without what Benjamin calls the 'translatability' of a text, he argues, the text itself will die. The importance that Benjamin attaches to translation points to a belief in the renewed possibilities *for* meaning that might reside in the translated text, as well as in the never fully-containable nature *of* that meaning. Translation, then, enables ways of signification that move away from the autonomous and the bordered, to expose instead a diverse and generative structure of syntactic and semantic expression. The short piece extracted here from Roman Jakobson's essay 'On Linguistic Aspects of Translation' (1959) treats this diversity as intrinsic to the operation of language itself, where meaning is approached via a potentially endless trail of signification. Translation operates between different languages, between 'verbal signs' and 'nonverbal sign systems', and within the same linguistic register (what Jakobson calls 'intralingual translation'). That 'there is ordinarily no full equivalence between code units' suggests the interpretative nature of translation, something which George Steiner makes central in his important book *After Babel*. For Steiner, interpretation as violence *and* as potential transformation constitutes the four-part process of translation he maps. It involves a progression from 'initiative trust' – a translator's willingness to 'venture a leap' when encountering the 'foreign text' – to the more aggressive step of 'appropriative penetration' where 'the text in the other [i.e. original] language has become almost materially thinner'. Such an act of possession is not without its own consequences for the 'native semantic field' however, and the third step in Steiner's scheme, incorporation, acknowledges that 'the act of importation can potentially dislocate or relocate the whole native structure'. The language of penetration gives way to that of 'infection' and 'contagion' (as in the excerpt by James Snead in Part III, above, 'Imperialism and the Postcolonial'): to domesticate the 'foreign' runs the risk of disrupting the 'native'. The final stage entails the re-establishment of balance, the restoration of significance to the original text through the diversity of its 'translations, imitations, thematic variants, even parodies'.

Steiner's teleological model, aiming for this restitution of equilibrium, perhaps underestimates the disruptive and distorting power of translation; yet his awareness of the dual nature of the act – that both the source and the host languages are transformed – is central to the transatlantic space, and informs Douglas Robinson's reading of what he calls 'hyperbolic translation'. Here the translator sets out to exaggerate or improve on the 'SL' (source language) by giving to the 'TL' (target language) the kind of 'fullness' that the original author was unable to supply. In the writing of the American Renaissance, Robinson suggests, such a strategy 'was perfectly suited to the kind of literary self-engenderment' that so preoccupied authors like Emerson and Whitman in their striving to establish a national tradition. Paradoxically the translation and interpretation of foreign texts became a key element in the invention of an American literature; but rather than regarding the direction of the influence as one-way, Robinson reminds us that translation of this kind establishes patterns of circulation that have reciprocal effects: 'if Baudelaire's and Mallarmé's strong readings of Poe generated French symbolism, Eliot's and Stevens's strong readings of the French Symbolists helped shape American modernism'. By focusing on the trope of the 'metaphor' (a word which comes from the Greek to 'carry over', as 'translation' comes from the same in Latin), Robinson argues that translation works by presenting us 'with a way of perspectivizing' texts, 'seeing them in interrelation' in a manner that does not (and, for Robinson, cannot) imply complete equivalence. The transatlantic, then, is the location for multiple forms of translation, for the 'carrying over' of materials that disrupt the clear horizon of the nation-state by introducing different vantage points from which it might be regarded.

The final two passages in this section provide examples of literary criticism that are concerned with the implications of transatlantic translation. Daniel Katz reads the poet Jack Spicer's book *After Lorca* (1957), a diffuse collection that includes translations of Lorca, original writing by Spicer that claims to be by Lorca, and letters from Spicer to 'Lorca'. The text is a complex meditation on the legitimacies of authorship that engages not only with the Spanish writer, but also with Whitman (a poet central to Lorca) and Ezra Pound (whose own work translates its source texts freely). No longer an autonomously-contained textual unit, the poem becomes for Spicer 'a preferably endless multilingual network of continual textual appropriation, reappropriation and misappropriation'. Katz argues that translation is the mode by which communication occurs across the borders of language, nation-state, and historical moment; it is also a form of haunting, of transubstantiation, where the dead and the living commingle in a 'bidirectional dialogue'. Anna Brickhouse, as part of her wider project to explore the multi-lingual practices and implications of American writing, focuses on an 1837 French translation of Phillis Wheatley's poetry that appeared in the Paris-based *Revue*, a journal produced by a number of Caribbean 'hommes de couleur'. Wheatley, a slave and the first major African-American poet, had had her work published in London in 1773: Brickhouse argues that her translation into French locates her 'political engagement in an international colonial arena'. Like Robinson's 'hyperbolic translation', the French text creates the 'wider political possibilities' that are only hinted at in Wheatley's original, so that the translated version of her poem 'On the death of JC, an infant' becomes 'a pointed response' to the quietism of the source text. This is still linguistic colonialism, but of a kind that works to articulate an anti-colonial politics; a dialogue is enacted between and across different historical circumstances to allow Wheatley's text, following Benjamin, an afterlife of significance in a multi-dimensional context that involves space and race as well as time.

FURTHER READING

Apter, Emily S. (2006) *The Translation Zone: A New Comparative Literature.* Princeton: Princeton University Press.

Bassnett, Susan and Harsih Trivedi (eds) (1999) *Post-colonial Translation: Theory and Practice.* New York: Routledge.

Derrida, Jacques (2001) 'What is a "Relevant" Translation?', *Critical Inquiry* 27.2: 174–200.

Gruesz, Kirsten Silva (2004) 'Translation: A Key(word) into the Language of America(nists)', *American Literary History* 16.1: 85–92.

Mulhern, Francis (1998) 'Translation, Re-writing Degree Zero', in *The Present Lasts a Long Time: Essays in Cultural Politics.* Cork: Cork University Press, pp. 164–70.

Sokol, Neal (2002) 'Translation and its Discontents: A Conversation with Ilan Stavans', *The Literary Review* 45.3: 554–71.

Venuti, Lawrence (1995) *The Translator's Invisibility: A History of Translation.* New York: Routledge.

I

'THE TASK OF THE TRANSLATOR'

Walter Benjamin

In the appreciation of a work of art or an art form, consideration of the receiver never proves fruitful. Not only is any reference to a certain public or its representatives misleading, but even the concept of an 'ideal' receiver is detrimental in the theoretical consideration of art, since all it posits is the existence and nature of man as such. Art, in the same way, posits man's physical and spiritual existence, but in none of its works is it concerned with his response. No poem is intended for the reader, no picture for the beholder, no symphony for the listener.

Is a translation meant for readers who do not understand the original? This would seem to explain adequately the divergence of their standing in the realm of art. Moreover, it seems to be the only conceivable reason for saying 'the same thing' repeatedly. For what does a literary work 'say'? What does it communicate? It 'tells' very little to those who understand it. Its essential quality is not statement or the imparting of information. Yet any translation which intends to perform a transmitting function cannot transmit anything but information – hence, something inessential. This is the hallmark of bad translations. But do we not generally regard as the essential substance of a literary work what it contains in addition to information – as even a poor translator will admit – the unfathomable, the mysterious, the 'poetic', something that a translator can reproduce only if he is also a poet? This, actually, is the cause of another

From Walter Benjamin (1955, trans. 1968; 1999) *Illuminations*. London: Pimlico.

characteristic of inferior translation, which consequently we may define as the inaccurate transmission of an inessential content. This will be true whenever a translation undertakes to serve the reader. However, if it were intended for the reader, the same would have to apply to the original. If the original does not exist for the reader's sake, how could the translation be understood on the basis of this premise?

Translation is a mode. To comprehend it as mode one must go back to the original, for that contains the law governing the translation: its translatability. The question of whether a work is translatable has a dual meaning. Either: Will an adequate translator ever be found among the totality of its readers? Or, more pertinently: Does its nature lend itself to translation and, therefore, in view of the significance of the mode, call for it? In principle, the first question can be decided only contingently; the second, however, apodictically. Only superficial thinking will deny the independent meaning of the latter and declare both questions to be of equal significance . . . It should be pointed out that certain correlative concepts retain their meaning, and possibly their foremost significance, if they are referred exclusively to man. One might, for example, speak of an unforgettable life or moment even if all men had forgotten it. If the nature of such a life or moment required that it be unforgotten, that predicate would not imply a falsehood but merely a claim not fulfilled by men, and probably also a reference to a realm in which it *is* fulfilled: God's remembrance. Analogously, the translatability of linguistic creations ought to be considered even if men should prove unable to translate them. Given a strict concept of translation, would they not really be translatable to some degree? The question as to whether the translation of certain linguistic creations is called for ought to be posed in this sense. For this thought is valid here: If translation is a mode, translatability must be an essential feature of certain works.

Translatability is an essential quality of certain works, which is not to say that it is essential that they be translated; it means rather that a specific significance inherent in the original manifests itself in its translatability. It is plausible that no translation, however good it may be, can have any significance as regards the original. Yet, by virtue of its translatability the original is closely connected with the translation; in fact, this connection is all the closer since it is no longer of importance to the original. We may call this connection a natural one, or, more specifically, a vital connection. Just as the manifestations of life are intimately connected with the phenomenon of life without being of importance to it, a translation issues from the original – not so much from its life as from its afterlife. For a translation comes later than the original, and since the important works of world literature never find their chosen translators at the time of their origin, their translation marks their stage of continued life. The idea of life and afterlife in works of art should be regarded with an entirely unmetaphorical objectivity. Even in times of narrowly prejudiced thought there was an inkling that life was not limited to organic corporeality. But it cannot be a matter of extending its dominion under the feeble sceptre of the soul, as Fechner* tried to do, or, conversely, of basing its definition on the even less conclusive factors of animality, such as sensation, which characterize life only occasionally. The concept of life is given its due only if everything that has a history of its own, and is not merely the setting for history, is credited with life. In the final analysis, the range of life must be determined by history rather than by nature, least of all by such tenuous factors as sensation and soul. The philosopher's task consists in comprehending all of natural life through the more encompassing life of history. And indeed, is not the continued life of works of art far easier to recognize than the continual life of animal species? The history of the great works of art tells us about their antecedents, their realization in the age of the artist, their potentially eternal afterlife in succeeding generations. Where this last manifests itself, it is called fame. Translations that are more than transmissions of subject matter come into being when in the course of its survival a work has reached the age of its fame. Contrary, therefore, to the claims of bad translators, such translations do not so much serve the work as owe their existence to it. The life of the originals attains in them to its ever-renewed latest and most abundant flowering.

Being a special and high form of life, this flowering is governed by a special, high purposiveness. The relationship between life and purposefulness, seemingly obvious yet almost beyond the grasp of the intellect, reveals itself only if the ultimate purpose toward which all single functions tend is sought not in its own sphere but in a higher one. All purposeful manifestations of life, including their very purposiveness, in the final analysis have their end not in life, but in the expression of its nature, in the representation of its significance. Translation thus ultimately serves the purpose of expressing the central reciprocal relationship between languages. It cannot possibly reveal or establish this hidden relationship itself; but it can represent it by realizing it in embryonic or intensive form. This representation of hidden significance through an embryonic attempt at making it visible is of so singular a nature that it is rarely met with in the sphere of nonlinguistic life. This, in its analogies and symbols, can draw on other ways of suggesting meaning than intensive – that is, anticipative, intimating – realization. As for the posited central kinship of languages, it is marked by a distinctive convergence. Languages are not strangers to one another, but are, a priori and apart from all historical relationships, interrelated in what they want to express.

With this attempt at an explication our study appears to rejoin, after futile detours, the traditional theory of translation. If the kinship of languages is to be demonstrated by translations, how else can this be done but by conveying the form and meaning of the original as accurately as possible? To be sure, that theory would be hard put to define the nature of this accuracy and therefore could shed no light on what is important in a translation. Actually, however, the kinship of languages is brought out by a translation far more profoundly and clearly than in the superficial and indefinable similarity of two works of literature. To grasp the genuine relationship between an original and a translation requires an investigation analogous to the argumentation by which a critique of cognition would have to prove the impossibility of an image theory. There it is a matter of showing that in cognition there could be no objectivity, not even a claim to it, if it dealt with images of reality; here it can be demonstrated that no translation would be possible if in its ultimate essence it strove for likeness to the original. For in its afterlife – which could not be called that if it were not a transformation and a renewal of something living – the original undergoes a change. Even words with fixed meaning can undergo a maturing process. The obvious tendency of a writer's literary style may in time wither away, only to give rise to immanent tendencies in the literary creation. What sounded fresh once may sound hackneyed later; what was once current may someday sound quaint. To seek the essence of such changes, as well as the equally constant changes in meaning, in the subjectivity of posterity rather than in the very life of language and its works, would mean – even allowing for the crudest psychologism – to confuse the root cause of a thing with its essence. More pertinently, it would mean denying, by an impotence of thought, one of the most powerful and fruitful historical processes. And even if one tried to turn an author's last stroke of the pen into the *coup de grâce* of his work, this still would not save that dead theory of translation. For just as the tenor and the significance of the great works of literature undergo a complete transformation over the centuries, the mother tongue of the translator is transformed as well. While a poet's words endure in his own language, even the greatest translation is destined to become part of the growth of its own language and eventually to be absorbed by its renewal. Translation is so far removed from being the sterile equation of two dead languages that of all literary forms it is the one charged with the special mission of watching over the maturing process of the original language and the birth pangs of its own.

If the kinship of languages manifests itself in translations, this is not accomplished through a vague alikeness between adaptation and original. It stands to reason that kinship does not necessarily involve likeness. The concept of kinship as used here is in accord with its more restricted common usage: in both cases, it cannot be defined adequately by identity of origin, although in defining the more restricted usage the concept of origin remains indispensable. Wherein resides the relatedness of two languages, apart from historical considerations? Certainly not in the similarity between works of literature or words. Rather, all suprahistorical kinship of languages rests in the intention underlying each language as a whole – an intention, however, which no single language can attain by itself but which is realized only by the totality of their intentions supplementing each other: pure language. While all individual elements of foreign languages – words, sentences, structure – are mutually exclusive, these languages supplement one another in their intentions. Without distinguishing the intended object from the mode of intention, no firm grasp of this basic law of a philosophy of language can be achieved. The words *Brot* and *pain* 'intend' the same object, but the modes of this intention are not the same. It is owing to these modes that the word *Brot* means something different to a German than the word *pain* to a Frenchman, that these words are not interchangeable for them, that, in fact, they strive to exclude each other. As to the intended object, however, the two words mean the very same thing. While the modes of intention in these two words are in conflict, intention and object of intention complement each of the two languages from which they are derived; there the object is complementary to the intention. In the individual, unsupplemented languages, meaning is never found in relative independence, as in individual words or sentences; rather, it is in a constant state of flux – until it is able to emerge as pure language from the harmony of all the various modes of intention. Until then, it remains hidden in the languages. If, however, these languages continue to grow in this manner until the end of their time, it is translation which catches fire on the eternal life of the works and the perpetual renewal of language. Translation keeps putting the hallowed growth of languages to the test: How far removed is their hidden meaning from revelation, how close can it be brought by the knowledge of this remoteness?

This, to be sure, is to admit that all translation is only a somewhat provisional way of coming to terms with the foreignness of languages. An instant and final rather than a temporary and provisional solution of this foreignness remains out of the reach of mankind; at any rate, it eludes any direct attempt. Indirectly, however, the growth of religions ripens the hidden seed into a higher development of language. Although translation, unlike art, cannot claim permanence for its products, its goal is undeniably a final, conclusive, decisive stage of all linguistic creation. In translation the original rises into a higher and purer linguistic air, as it were. It cannot live there permanently, to be sure, and it certainly does not reach it in its entirety. Yet, in a singularly impressive manner, at least it points the way to this region: the predestined, hitherto inaccessible realm of reconciliation and fulfilment of languages. The transfer can never be total, but what reaches this region is that element in a translation which goes beyond transmittal of subject matter. This nucleus is best defined as the element that does not lend itself to translation. Even when all the surface content has been extracted and transmitted, the primary concern of the genuine translator remains elusive. Unlike the words of the original, it is not translatable, because the relationship between content and language is quite different in the original and the translation. While content and language form a certain unity in the original, like a fruit and its skin, the language of the translation envelops its content like a royal robe with ample folds. For it signifies a more exalted language than its own and thus remains unsuited to its content, over-powering and alien. This disjunction prevents translation and at the same time makes it superfluous. For any translation of a work originating in a specific stage of linguistic history represents, in regard to a specific aspect of its content, translation into all other languages. Thus translation, ironically, transplants the original into a more definitive linguistic realm since it can no longer be dis-placed by a secondary rendering. The original can only be raised there anew and at other points of time. It is no mere coincidence that the word 'ironic' here brings the Romanticists* to mind. They, more than any others, were gifted with an insight into the life of literary works which has its highest testimony in trans-lation. To be sure, they hardly recognized translation in this sense, but devoted their entire attention to criticism, another, if a lesser, factor in the continued life of literary works. But even though the Romanticists virtually ignored transla-tion in their theoretical writings, their own great translations testify to their sense of the essential nature and the dignity of this literary mode. There is abun-dant evidence that this sense is not necessarily most pronounced in a poet; in fact, he may be least open to it. Not even literary history suggests the traditional notion that great poets have been eminent translators and lesser poets have been indifferent translators. A number of the most eminent ones, such as Luther*, Voss*, and Schlegel*, are incomparably more important as translators than as creative writers; some of the great among them, such as Hölderlin and Stefan George*, cannot be simply subsumed as poets, and quite particularly not if we consider them as translators. As translation is a mode of its own, the task of the translator, too, may be regarded as distinct and clearly differentiated from the task of the poet.

The task of the translator consists in finding that intended effect [*Intention*] upon the language into which he is translating which produces in it the echo of the original. This is a feature of translation which basically differentiates it from the poet's work, because the effort of the latter is never directed at the language as such, at its totality, but solely and immediately at specific linguistic contex-tual aspects. Unlike a work of literature, translation does not find itself in the centre of the language forest but on the outside facing the wooded ridge; it calls into it without entering, aiming at that single spot where the echo is able to give, in its own language, the reverberation of the work in the alien one. Not only does the aim of translation differ from that of a literary work – it intends lan-guage as a whole, taking an individual work in an alien language as a point of departure – but it is a different effort altogether. The intention of the poet is spontaneous, primary, graphic; that of the translator is derivative, ultimate, ideational. For the great motif of integrating many tongues into one true lan-guage is at work. This language is one in which the independent sentences, works of literature, critical judgments, will never communicate – for they remain dependent on translation; but in it the languages themselves, supplemented and reconciled in their mode of signification, harmonize. If there is such a thing as a language of truth, the tensionless and even silent depository of the ultimate truth which all thought strives for, then this language of truth is – the true language. And this very language, whose divination and description is the only perfection a philosopher can hope for, is concealed in concentrated fashion in translations. There is no muse of philosophy, nor is there one of translation. But despite the claims of sentimental artists, these two are not banausic. For there is a philosophical genius that is characterized by a yearning for that language which manifests itself in translations. '*Les langues imparfaites en cela que plusieurs, manque la suprême: penser étant écrire sans accessoires, ni chuchotement mais tacite encore l'immortelle parole, la diversité, sur terre, des idiomes empêche personne de proférer les mots qui, sinon se trouveraient, par une frappe unique, elle-même matériellement la vérité*'. ['The imperfection of languages consists in their plurality, the supreme one is lacking: thinking is writing without accessories or even whispering, the immortal word still remains silent; the diversity of idioms on earth prevents everybody from uttering the words which otherwise, at one single stroke, would materialize as truth'.] If what Mallarmé* evokes here is fully fathomable to a philosopher, translation, with its rudiments of such a language, is midway between poetry and doctrine. Its products are less sharply defined, but it leaves no less of a mark on history.

If the task of the translator is viewed in this light, the roads toward a solution seem to be all the more obscure and impenetrable. Indeed, the problem of ripening the seed of pure language in a translation seems to be insoluble, determinable in no solution. For is not the ground cut from under such a solution if the reproduction of the sense ceases to be decisive? Viewed negatively, this is actually the meaning of all the foregoing. The traditional concepts in any discussion of translations are fidelity and licence – the freedom of faithful reproduction and, in its service, fidelity to the word. These ideas seem to be no longer serviceable to a theory that looks for other things in a translation than reproduction of meaning. To be sure, traditional usage makes these terms appear as if in constant conflict with each other. What can fidelity really do for the rendering of meaning? Fidelity in the translation of individual words can almost never fully reproduce the meaning they have in the original. For sense in its poetic significance is not limited to meaning, but derives from the connotations conveyed by the word chosen to express it. We say of words that they have emotional connotations. A literal rendering of the syntax completely demolishes the theory of reproduction of meaning and is a direct threat to comprehensibility. The nineteenth century considered Hölderlin's translations of Sophocles as monstrous examples of such literalness. Finally, it is self-evident how greatly fidelity in reproducing the form impedes the rendering of the sense. Thus no case for literalness can be based on a desire to retain the meaning. Meaning is served far better – and literature and language far worse – by the unrestrained licence of bad translators. Of necessity, therefore, the demand for literalness, whose justification is obvious, whose legitimate ground is quite obscure, must be understood in a more meaningful context. Fragments of a vessel which are to be glued together must match one another in the smallest details, although they need not be like one another. In the same way a translation, instead of resembling the meaning of the original, must lovingly and in detail incorporate the original's mode of signification, thus making both the original and the translation recognizable as fragments of a greater language, just as fragments are part of a vessel. For this very reason translation must in large measure refrain from wanting to communicate something, from rendering the sense, and in this the original is important to it only insofar as it has already relieved the translator and his translation of the effort of assembling and expressing what is to be conveyed. In the realm of translation, too, the words εν αρχη ην ο χόγος [in the beginning was the word] apply. On the other hand, as regards the meaning, the language of a translation can – in fact, must – let itself go, so that it gives voice to the *intentio* of the original not as reproduction but as harmony, as a supplement to the language in which it expresses itself, as its own kind of *intentio*. Therefore it is not the highest praise of a translation, particularly in the age of its origin, to say that it reads as if it had originally been written in that language. Rather, the significance of fidelity as ensured by literalness is that the work reflects the great longing for linguistic complementation. A real translation is transparent; it does not cover the original, does not block its light, but allows the pure language, as though reinforced by its own medium, to shine upon the original all the more fully. This may be achieved, above all, by a literal rendering of the syntax which proves words rather than sentences to be the primary element of the translator. For if the sentence is the wall before the language of the original, literalness is the arcade.

Fidelity and freedom in translation have traditionally been regarded as conflicting tendencies. This deeper interpretation of the one apparently does not serve to reconcile the two; in fact, it seems to deny the other all justification. For what is meant by freedom but that the rendering of the sense is no longer to be regarded as all-important? Only if the sense of a linguistic creation may be equated with the information it conveys does some ultimate, decisive element remain beyond all communication – quite close and yet infinitely remote, concealed or distinguishable, fragmented or powerful. In all language and linguistic creations there remains in addition to what can be conveyed something that cannot be communicated; depending on the context in which it appears, it is something that symbolizes or something symbolized. It is the former only in the finite products of language, the latter in the evolving of the languages themselves. And that which seeks to represent, to produce itself in the evolving of languages, is that very nucleus of pure language. Though concealed and fragmentary, it is an active force in life as the symbolized thing itself, whereas it inhabits linguistic creations only in symbolized form. While that ultimate essence, pure language, in the various tongues is tied only to linguistic elements and their changes, in linguistic creations it is weighted with a heavy, alien meaning. To relieve it of this, to turn the symbolizing into the symbolized, to regain pure language fully formed in the linguistic flux, is the tremendous and only capacity of translation. In this pure language – which no longer means or expresses anything but is, as expressionless and creative Word, that which is meant in all languages – all information, all sense, and all intention finally encounter a stratum in which they are destined to be extinguished. This very stratum furnishes a new and higher justification for free translation; this justification does not derive from the sense of what is to be conveyed, for the emancipation from this sense is the task of fidelity. Rather, for the sake of pure language, a free translation bases the test on its own language. It is the task of the translator to release in his own language that pure language which is under the spell of another, to liberate the language imprisoned in a work in his re-creation of that work. For the sake of pure language he breaks through decayed barriers of his own language. Luther, Voss, Hölderlin, and George have extended the boundaries of the German language. – And what of the sense in its importance for the relationship between translation and original? A simile may help here. Just as a tangent touches a circle lightly and at but one point, with this touch rather than with the point setting the law according to which it is to continue on its straight path to infinity, a translation touches the original lightly and only at the infinitely small point of the sense, thereupon pursuing its own course according to the laws of fidelity in the freedom of linguistic flux. Without explicitly naming or substantiating it, Rudolf Pannwitz* has characterized the true significance of this freedom. His observations are contained in *Die Krisis der europäischen Kultur* and rank with Goethe's* notes to the *Westöstlicher Divan* as the best comment on the theory of translation that has been published in Germany. Pannwitz writes: 'Our translations, even the best ones, proceed from a wrong premise. They want to turn Hindi, Greek, English into German instead of turning German into Hindi, Greek, English. Our translators have a far greater reverence for the usage of their own language than for the spirit of the foreign works . . . The basic error of the translator is that he preserves the state in which his own language happens to be instead of allowing his language to be powerfully affected by the foreign tongue. Particularly when translating from a language very remote from his own he must go back to the primal elements of language itself and penetrate to the point where work, image, and tone converge. He must expand and deepen his language by means of the foreign language. It is not generally realized to what extent this is possible, to what extent any language can be transformed, how language differs from language almost the way dialect differs from dialect; however, this last is true only if one takes language seriously enough, not if one takes it lightly'.

The extent to which a translation manages to be in keeping with the nature of this mode is determined objectively by the translatability of the original. The lower the quality and distinction of its language, the larger the extent to which it is information, the less fertile a field is it for translation, until the utter preponderance of content, far from being the lever for a translation of distinctive mode, renders it impossible. The higher the level of a work, the more does it remain translatable even if its meaning is touched upon only fleetingly. This, of course, applies to originals only. Translations, on the other hand, prove to be untranslatable not because of any inherent difficulty, but because of the looseness with which meaning attaches to them. Confirmation of this as well as of every other important aspect is supplied by Hölderlin's translations, particularly those of the two tragedies by Sophocles. In them the harmony of the languages is so profound that sense is touched by language only the way an aeolian harp is touched by the wind. Hölderlin's translations are prototypes of their kind; they are to even the most perfect renderings of their texts as a prototype is to a model. This can be demonstrated by comparing Hölderlin's and Rudolf Borchardt's translations of Pindar's* Third Pythian Ode. For this very reason Hölderlin's translations in particular are subject to the enormous danger inherent in all translations: the gates of a language thus expanded and modified may slam shut and enclose the translator with silence. Hölderlin's translations from Sophocles were his last work; in them meaning plunges from abyss to abyss until it threatens to become lost in the bottomless depths of language. There is, however, a stop. It is vouchsafed to Holy Writ alone, in which meaning has ceased to be the watershed for the flow of language and the flow of revelation. Where a text is identical with truth or dogma, where it is supposed to be 'the true language' in all its literalness and without the mediation of meaning, this text is unconditionally translatable. In such case translations are called for only because of the plurality of languages. Just as, in the original, language and revelation are one without any tension, so the translation must be one with the original in the form of the interlinear version, in which literalness and freedom are united. For to some degree all great texts contain their potential translation between the lines; this is true to the highest degree of sacred writings. The interlinear version of the Scriptures is the prototype or ideal of all translation.

2

'ON LINGUISTIC ASPECTS OF TRANSLATION'

Roman Jakobson

For us, both as linguists and as ordinary word users, the meaning of any linguistic sign is its translation into some further, alternative sign, especially a sign 'in which it is more fully developed', as Peirce*, the deepest inquirer into the essence of signs, insistently stated. The term 'bachelor' may be converted into a more explicit designation, 'unmarried man', whenever higher explicitness is required. We distinguish three ways of interpreting a verbal sign: it may be translated into other signs of the same language, into another language, or into another, nonverbal system of symbols. These three kinds of translation are to be differently labeled:

1. Intralingual translation or *rewording* is an interpretation of verbal signs by means of other signs of the same language.
2. Interlingual translation or *translation proper* is an interpretation of verbal signs by means of some other language.
3. Intersemiotic translation or *transmutation* is an interpretation of verbal signs by means of signs of nonverbal sign systems.

The intralingual translation of a word uses either another, more or less synonymous, word or resorts to a circumlocution. Yet synonymy, as a rule, is not complete equivalence: for example, 'every celibate is a bachelor, but not every

From Roman Jakobson (1987) *Language in Literature*, ed. Krystyna Pomorska and Stephen Rudy. Cambridge, MA: Belknap Press.

bachelor is a celibate'. A word or an idiomatic phrase word, briefly a code unit of the highest level, may be fully interpreted only by means of an equivalent combination of code units, that is, a message referring to this code unit: 'every bachelor is an unmarried man, and every unmarried man is a bachelor', or 'every celibate is bound not to marry, and everyone who is bound not to marry is a celibate'.

Likewise on the level of interlingual translation, there is ordinarily no full equivalence between code units, while messages may serve as adequate interpretations of alien code units or messages. The English word *cheese* cannot be completely identified with its standard Russian heteronym *syr* because cottage cheese is a cheese but not a *syr*. Russians say: *prinesi syru i tvorogu* (bring cheese and [*sic*] cottage cheese). In standard Russian, the food made of pressed curds is called *syr* only if ferment is used.

Most frequently, however, translation from one language into another substitutes messages in one language not for separate code units but for entire messages in some other language. Such a translation is a reported speech: the translator recodes and transmits a message received from another source. Thus translation involves two equivalent messages in two different codes.

3

'THE HERMENEUTIC MOTION'

George Steiner

The hermeneutic motion, the act of elicitation and appropriative transfer of meaning, is fourfold. There is initiative trust, an investment of belief, underwritten by previous experience but epistemologically exposed and psychologically hazardous, in the meaningfulness, in the 'seriousness' of the facing or, strictly speaking, adverse text. We venture a leap: we grant *ab initio* that there is 'something there' to be understood, that the transfer will not be void. All understanding, and the demonstrative statement of understanding which is translation, starts with an act of trust. This confiding will, ordinarily, be instantaneous and unexamined, but it has a complex base. It is an operative convention which derives from a sequence of phenomenological assumptions about the coherence of the world, about the presence of meaning in very different, perhaps formally antithetical semantic systems, about the validity of analogy and parallel. The radical generosity of the translator ('I grant beforehand that there must be something there'), his trust in the 'other', as yet untried, unmapped alternity of statement, concentrates to a philosophically dramatic degree the human bias towards seeing the world as symbolic, as constituted of relations in which 'this' can stand for 'that', and must in fact be able to do so if there are to be meanings and structures.

But the trust can never be final. It is betrayed, trivially, by nonsense, by the discovery that 'there is nothing there' to elicit and translate. Nonsense rhymes,

From George Steiner (1975) *After Babel: Aspects of Language and Translation*. New York: Oxford University Press.

*poésie concrète**, glossolalia* are untranslatable because they are lexically non-communicative or deliberately insignificant. The commitment of trust will, however, be tested, more or less severely, also in the common run and process of language acquisition and translation (the two being intimately connected). 'This means nothing' asserts the exasperated child in front of his Latin reader or the beginner at Berlitz. The sensation comes very close to being tactile, as of a blank, sloping surface which gives no purchase. Social incentive, the officious evidence of precedent – 'others have managed to translate this bit before you' – keeps one at the task. But the donation of trust remains ontologically spontaneous and anticipates proof, often by a long, arduous gap (there are texts, says Walter Benjamin which will be translated only 'after us'). As he sets out, the translator must gamble on the coherence, on the symbolic plenitude of the world. Concomitantly he leaves himself vulnerable, though only in extremity and at the theoretical edge, to two dialectically related, mutually determined metaphysical risks. He may find that 'anything' or 'almost anything' can mean 'everything'. This is the vertigo of self-sustaining metaphoric or analogic enchainment experienced by medieval exegetists. Or he may find that there is 'nothing there' which can be divorced from its formal autonomy, that every meaning worth expressing is monadic and will not enter into any alternative mould. There is Kabbalistic* speculation, to which I will return, about a day on which words will shake off 'the burden of having to mean' and will be only themselves, blank and replete as stone.

After trust comes aggression. The second move of the translator is incursive and extractive. The relevant analysis is that of Heidegger* when he focuses our attention on understanding as an act, on the access, inherently appropriative and therefore violent, of *Erkenntnis* to *Dasein*. *Da-sein*, the 'thing there', 'the thing that is because it is there', only comes into authentic being when it is comprehended, i.e. translated. The postulate that all cognition is aggressive, that every proposition is an inroad on the world, is, of course, Hegelian*. It is Heidegger's contribution to have shown that understanding, recognition, interpretation are a compacted, unavoidable mode of attack. We can modulate Heidegger's insistence that understanding is not a matter of method but of primary being, that 'being consists in the understanding of other being' into the more naïve, limited axiom that each act of comprehension must appropriate another entity (we translate *into*). Comprehension, as its etymology shows, 'comprehends' not only cognitively but by encirclement and ingestion. In the event of interlingual translation this manoeuvre of comprehension is explicitly invasive and exhaustive. Saint Jerome* uses his famous image of meaning brought home captive by the translator. We 'break' a code: decipherment is dissective, leaving the shell smashed and the vital layers stripped. Every schoolchild, but also the eminent translator, will note the shift in substantive presence which follows on a protracted or difficult exercise in translation: the text in the other language has become almost materially thinner, the light seems to pass unhindered through its loosened fibres. For a spell the density of hostile or seductive 'otherness' is dissipated. Ortega y Gasset* speaks of the sadness of the translator after failure. There is also a sadness after success, the Augustinian *tristitia* [monastic sorrow] which follows on the cognate acts of erotic and of intellectual possession.

The translator invades, extracts, and brings home. The simile is that of the open-cast mine left an empty scar in the landscape. As we shall see, this despoliation is illusory or is a mark of false translation. But again, as in the case of the translator's trust, there are genuine borderline cases. Certain texts or genres have been exhausted by translation. Far more interestingly, others have been negated by transfiguration, by an act of appropriative penetration and transfer in excess of the original, more ordered, more aesthetically pleasing. There are originals, we no longer turn to because the translation is of a higher magnitude (the sonnets of Louise Labé after Rilke's* *Umdichtung*). I will come back to this paradox of betrayal by augment.

The third movement is incorporative, in the strong sense of the word. The import, of meaning and of form, the embodiment, is not made in or into a vacuum. The native semantic field is already extant and crowded. There are innumerable shadings of assimilation and placement of the newly-acquired, ranging from a complete domestication, an at-homeness at the core of the kind which cultural history ascribes to, say, Luther's* Bible or North's Plutarch*, all the way to the permanent strangeness and marginality of an artifact such as Nabokov's* 'English-language' *Onegin*. But whatever the degree of 'naturalization', the act of importation can potentially dislocate or relocate the whole of the native structure. The Heideggerian 'we are what we understand to be' entails that our own being is modified by each occurrence of comprehensive appropriation. No language, no traditional symbolic set or cultural ensemble imports without risk of being transformed. Here two families of metaphor, probably related, offer themselves, that of sacramental intake or incarnation and that of infection. The incremental values of communion pivot on the moral, spiritual state of the recipient. Though all decipherment is aggressive and, at one level, destructive, there are differences in the motive of appropriation and in the context of 'the bringing back'. Where the native matrix is disoriented or immature, the importation will not enrich, it will not find a proper locale. It will generate not an integral response but a wash of mimicry (French neo-classicism in its north-European, German, and Russian versions). There can be contagions of facility triggered by the antique or foreign import. After a time, the native organism will react, endeavouring to neutralize or expel the foreign body. Much of European romanticism can be seen as a riposte to this sort of infection, as an attempt to put an embargo on a plethora of foreign, mainly French eighteenth-century goods. In every pidgin we see an attempt to preserve a zone of native speech and a failure of that attempt in the face of politically and economically enforced linguistic invasion. The dialectic of embodiment entails the possibility that we may be consumed.

[. . .]

This is only another way of saying that the hermeneutic motion is dangerously incomplete, that it is dangerous because it is incomplete, if it lacks its fourth stage, the piston-stroke, as it were, which completes the cycle. The a-prioristic movement of trust puts us off balance. We 'lean towards' the confronting text (every translator has experienced this palpable bending towards and launching at his target). We encircle and invade cognitively. We come home laden, thus again off-balance, having caused disequilibrium throughout the system by taking away from 'the other' and by adding, though possibly with ambiguous consequence, to our own. The system is now off-tilt. The hermeneutic act must compensate. If it is to be authentic, it must mediate into exchange and restored parity.

The enactment of reciprocity in order to restore balance is the crux of the métier and morals of translation. But it is very difficult to put abstractly. The appropriative 'rapture' of the translator – the word has in it, of course, the root and meaning of violent transport – leaves the original with a dialectically enigmatic residue. Unquestionably there is a dimension of loss, of breakage – hence, as we have seen, the fear of translation, the taboos on revelatory export which hedge sacred texts, ritual nominations, and formulas in many cultures. But the residue is also, and decisively, positive. The work translated is enhanced. This is so at a number of fairly obvious levels. Being methodical, penetrative, analytic, enumerative, the process of translation, like all modes of focused understanding, will detail, illumine, and generally body forth its object. The over-determination of the interpretative act is inherently inflationary: it proclaims that 'there is more here than meets the eye', that 'the accord between content and executive form is closer, more delicate than had been observed hitherto'. To class a source-text as worth translating is to dignify it immediately and to involve it in a dynamic of magnification (subject, naturally, to later review and even, perhaps, dismissal). The motion of transfer and paraphrase enlarges the stature of the original. Historically, in terms of cultural context, of the public it can reach, the latter is left more prestigious. But this increase has a more important, existential perspective. The relations of a text to its translations, imitations, thematic variants, even parodies, are too diverse to allow of any single theoretic, definitional scheme. They categorize the entire question of the meaning of meaning in time, of the existence and effects of the linguistic fact outside its specific, initial form. But there can be no doubt that echo enriches, that it is more than shadow and inert simulacrum. We are back at the problem of the mirror which not only reflects but also generates light. The original text gains from the orders of diverse relationship and distance established between itself and the translations. The reciprocity is dialectic: new 'formats' of significance are initiated by distance and by contiguity. Some translations edge us away from the canvas, others bring us up close.

[. . .]

This view of translation as a hermeneutic of trust (*élancement*), of penetration, of embodiment, and of restitution, will allow us to overcome the sterile triadic model which has dominated the history and theory of the subject. The perennial distinction between literalism, paraphrase and free imitation, turns out to be wholly contingent. It has no precision or philosophic basis. It overlooks the key fact that a fourfold *hermeneia*, Aristotle's term for discourse which signifies because it interprets, is conceptually and practically inherent in even the rudiments of translation.

4

'THE TROPICS OF TRANSLATION'

Douglas Robinson

Having lived so long in Finland, I pay particular attention to the hyperbolic crossovers between my native and my adoptive countries: the way that the contemporary Finnish novelist Veijo Meri 'discovered' the archetypal Finnish male in Hemingway, discovered in essence that Hemingway was the greatest Finnish writer of our century, and donated Hemingway to Finnish literature not by translating him but by making his own novels in the 50s and 60s out of his dialogical engagement with Hemingway's work. Going farther back, Longfellow read the Finnish national epic, the *Kalevala*, in German translation in the early 1850s and, inspired by the shot in the arm that Elias Lönnrot's collection/composition gave Finnish literature, decided to do the same for American literature. The result was *The Song of Hiawatha* in Kalevala meter (trochaic tetrameter), borrowing much of the oral-epic manner of the Germanized Finnish text. It did not quite work, of course: the poem was immensely popular (still is, in some circles), but it did not transform American literature that way that the *Kalevala* did Finnish literature when it appeared in the 1830s and 40s. Longfellow failed to do what he set out to do, partly because *Hiawatha* was not authentic native American oral poetry, as the *Kalevala* was authentic native Finnish oral poetry; partly because nineteenth-century Americans did not identify their 'lost origins' with the Indians; and partly because Longfellow did not have the poetic talent of

From Douglas Robinson (1991) *The Translator's Turn*. Baltimore: Johns Hopkins University Press.

a Whitman, say, who published the truly transformative American epic in the same year as *Hiawatha, Leaves of Grass*. Longfellow made the obvious mistake: he thought that Americans needed an illustrious past, a genesis, when what they really needed (as Whitman knew) was an illustrious future, democratic vistas, as Whitman put it, or prospects, as Emerson put it. Neither a new *Beowulf* nor a *Song of Hiawatha* would do: white male Americans had cut themselves off from the European tradition that looked back to *Beowulf*, and they had never assimilated themselves (as the Spaniards had in South America, by interbreeding) to the Native American tradition that might have looked back to a *Song of Hiawatha*. Only the future remained – that, and an expansive present, a geographical breadth whose expansion to date pointed forward to an engulfment of the entire world, of the entire kosmos (to give it Whitman's spelling), ever bigger and bigger hunks until America contained *everything*.

Still, Longfellow had the right idea – just the wrong country. Hyperbolic translation (and the hyperbolizing of 'translation' as an ever more inclusive kind of transfer that would embrace *Hiawatha* as well as any more obvious transfer) was perfectly suited to the kind of literary self-engenderment that American writers were attempting in that astonishing decade that has come to be called the American Renaissance*. And just as the European Renaissance was born out of the translation of classical texts that had been 'discovered' in the Moorish libraries conquered in the south of Spain in the thirteenth century, so too was the American Renaissance born out of hyperbolic translations of foreign literatures near and far. John Irwin [in his 1980 book *American Hieroglyphics*] has shown the importance of the Egyptian hieroglyphics for the American Renaissance – as Steiner argues, an alien tradition is easier to appropriate than a familiar one, since the cultural clutter of a familiar tradition can shackle the appropriator. Still, Emerson's strong readings of Coleridge and the German Idealists* and Poe's strong readings of Shelley and the German romantics were crucial for the American Renaissance. And if Baudelaire's* and Mallarmé's* strong readings of Poe generated French Symbolism*, Eliot's and Stevens's strong readings of the French Symbolists helped shape American modernism. That period was most decisively shaped, perhaps, by Ezra Pound, probably the greatest hyperbolic translator of our time: by creating 'modernism' out of Sappho in Greek, Sextus Propertius in Latin, Arnaut Daniel in Provençal, Guido Cavalcanti in Italian, Li Po in Chinese, and on and on – by finding in each writer that spark, that Poundian touch, that Paterian glow of isolated moments, and fanning it into a TL flame – Pound shaped his period into what Hugh Kenner calls the 'Pound Era'.

You may have noticed how close this trope is to synecdoche, which also rescues from the SL text only that part or quality (that 'spark') that fits the translator's needs (or conception of the TL receptor's needs) and sloughs off the rest. Both the synecdochic and the hyperbolic translator condescend to the SL writer, assuming that he or she did not quite know what he or she wanted to say or how to say it, and taking upon themselves the task of preserving what is most representative or lasting in the SL text. We could probably quibble over specific translations, in fact – over whether they were synecdochic or hyperbolic – till the cows came home. But let me remind you once again that the purpose of this chapter is not to set up a stable taxonomy by which the (stable, objective) products of translation can be accurately described; it is to explore the translator's tools, which can be used and abused every which way. (The translator who confuses two of my tropes is like the home-handyman who punches holes with a Phillips screwdriver or adjusts storm windows with a claw hammer or drives nails with a pipewrench: just doing his or her job with the tools at hand. Idealists deplore this sort of sloppiness, but then idealists deplore just about everything – everything that falls short of their ideal, which is to say, everything real.) As Kenneth Burke* says, all of the master tropes flow into one another; all troping is perspectivizing. All troping is reducing, representing, dialecticizing. These are just words we use to describe a complex field – not 'real' categories into which actual acts of translation must be fit.

But apart from all that, is there any good reason for distinguishing the condescending improvement that the hyperbolic translator makes in the SL from the condescending improvement that the synecdochic translator makes in the SL? The main difference historically is that the hyperbolic translator has typically been a romantic, a believer in creative genius and its transformative effect on all texts, on everything it touches, while the synecdochic translator has typically been a pragmatist, a believer in getting the job done in as effective a way as possible. A good indication of this difference is that when hyperbolic translators delude themselves (or are deluded by their ideosomatic programming) into believing that they are striving for equivalence, they tend to think of equivalence in metaphoric terms (perfect equivalence, the great romantic ideal), while when synecdochic translators delude themselves (or are deluded by *their* ideosomatic programming) into believing that they are striving for equivalence, they tend to think of equivalence in metonymic terms (working equivalence, the great pragmatic ideal).

Still, lest I defend my division too strenuously and make it seem like I am attached to it, believe in it, let me close this section with an open invitation (once again) to do with these tropes what you will, conflate them, splinter them, whatever. I do not always think they work myself. The only reason I offer them to you is that they seem to work better than anything else I have seen; but they are not perfect, and never will be, and never need to be. They are tools. Use them as you like, or throw them in a drawer and let them collect greasy dust.

[. . .]

I am not setting up a rigidly systematic taxonomy of translation here, so don't start complaining about this or that type being missing in my discussion of a specific trope, or this or that illustration not working the way I say it does. Or rather, complain all you like (that is what keeps the dialogue going), but don't reject this chapter because you are unhappy with some of my illustrations. You are welcome to do whatever you like with my tropes and their illustrations: modify them, replace them, supplement them, whatever. In earlier drafts I called TV subtitling and simultaneous signing metaleptic, and here they have become synecdochic. It is all a matter of perspective, of how you look at things. I am suggesting *ways of seeing* translation, ways of construing a translation task, and to flesh out the complexity in a fairly accessible way, I am using six tropes with several different illustrations in each one. But there are hundreds of tropes, each of them probably perfectly applicable to some translation task, if someone would just go to the trouble of making the connection. And my illustrations are just illustrations. [. . .] I realize the temptation you must feel to rigidify my tropes and illustrations into 'objective' categories of translation, and if you want to do it badly enough, I cannot stop you. But I do not mean that to happen. I want to liberate translators from objective categories, not create new straitjackets for them. (I can just imagine translation teachers ten years from now saying, 'No, that type of metonymy is not appropriate for that type of text'.)

Metaphor comes from the Greek verb *metapherein*, to carry over, whose Latin cognate *transferre* gives us translation. And, just as metaphor has been called the 'supertrope', the trope that contains or implies all the others, so too is metaphorical translation, the striving for perfect identity between SL and TL, often called the supreme ideal of all translation. Metaphor, at least ideally, equates things: this is that. He is a lion. She is a rose. Metaphorical translation ideally equates texts: the TL is the SL. The two are identical. 'Nicht anstatt des andern', as Goethe* says of this ideal, 'sondern an der Stelle des andern'.

It cannot happen, of course: this is an ideal, not reality. Metaphor claims to equate things, but as Kenneth Burke says, it really only perspectivizes them, encourages us to see this in terms of that, that in terms of this. Metaphorical translation, too, claims to equate texts but really only perspectivizes them, encourages us to read English Odysseys in terms of the Greek original and the Greek Odysseia in terms of its English translations. In fact, all tropical translation does this: the part-part substitution of metonymy, the part-whole substitution of synecdoche, the whole-whole substitution of metaphor in its strict sense, all are perspectivizings, ways of juxtaposing two texts, ways of seeing them in interrelation, ways of 'turning' in a meaningful way from SL to TL.

It was the romantics who elevated metaphor to primacy among tropes, to supertrope status, and romantic translation theorists from Goethe to Steiner have been the most fervent proponents of metaphorical translation. But because they approach metaphor as a quasireligious *reality*, an impossible ideal that must be possible if life and language are to have any meaning at all, they tend to stress its rarity or even its nonexistence. If we cheerfully admit that it is only a trope, nothing more mystical than that, just a way of seeing, a way of perspectivizing, then it becomes much more ordinary, the sort of translation model that just about anybody could expect to experiment with, and succeed at. (Success, remember, does not mean achieving perfect identity between SL and TL but using that ideal heuristically to create a TL text that works in the overall translation dialogue.) Thanks to the romantics, we tend to associate metaphor with great literature, and metaphoric translation with great literary translation; but, though I do want to take a look at some metaphoric literary translation later, let me demonstrate the ordinariness of metaphoric translation conceived tropically by starting elsewhere.

5

'GENDER AND THE METAPHORICS OF TRANSLATION'

Lori Chamberlain

'At best an echo', translation has been figured literally and metaphorically in secondary terms. Just as Clara Schumann's performance of a musical composition is seen as qualitatively different from the original act of composing that piece, so the act of translating is viewed as something qualitatively different from the original act of writing. Indeed, under current American copyright law, both translations and musical performances are treated under the same rubric of 'derivative works'. The cultural elaboration of this view suggests that in the original abides what is natural, truthful, and lawful, in the copy, what is artificial, false, and treasonous. Translations can be, for example, echoes (in musical terms), copies or portraits (in painterly terms), or borrowed or ill-fitting clothing (in sartorial terms).

The sexualization of translation appears perhaps most familiarly in the tag *les belles infidèles* – like women, the adage goes, translations should be either beautiful or faithful. The tag is made possible both by the rhyme in French and by the fact that the word *traduction* is a feminine one, thus making *les beaux infidèles* impossible. This tag owes its longevity – it was coined in the seventeenth century – to more than phonetic similarity: what gives it the appearance of truth is that it has captured a cultural complicity between the issues of fidelity in translation and in marriage. For *les belles infidèles*, fidelity is defined by an implicit contract between translation (as woman) and original (as husband, father, or

From *Signs* 13.3 (1988): 454–72.

author). However, the infamous 'double standard' operates here as it might have in traditional marriages: the 'unfaithful' wife/translation is publicly tried for crimes the husband/original is by law incapable of committing. This contract, in short, makes it impossible for the original to be guilty of infidelity. Such an attitude betrays real anxiety about the problem of paternity and translation; it mimics the patrilineal kinship system where paternity – not maternity – legitimizes an offspring.

It is the struggle for the right of paternity, regulating the fidelity of translation, which we see articulated by the earl of Roscommon in his seventeenth-century treatise on translation. In order to guarantee the originality of the translator's work, surely necessary in a paternity case, the translator must usurp the author's role. Roscommon begins benignly enough, advising the translator to 'Chuse an author as you chuse a friend', but this intimacy serves a potentially subversive purpose:

> United by this Sympathetick Bond,
> You grow Familiar, Intimate, and Fond;
> Your thoughts, your Words, your Stiles, your Souls agree,
> No longer his Interpreter, but He.[1]

It is an almost silent deposition: through familiarity (friendship), the translator becomes, as it were, part of the family and finally the father himself: whatever struggle there might be between author and translator is veiled by the language of friendship. While the translator is figured as a male, the text itself is figured as a female whose chastity must be protected:

> With how much ease is a young Muse Betray'd
> How nice the Reputation of the Maid!
> Your early, kind, paternal care appears,
> By chast Instruction of her Tender Years.
> The first Impression in her Infant Breast
> Will be the deepest and should be the best.
> Let no Austerity breed servile Fear
> No wanton Sound offend her Virgin Ear.[2]

As the translator becomes the author, he incurs certain paternal duties in relation to the text, to protect and instruct – or perhaps structure – it. The language used echoes the language of conduct books and reflects attitudes about the proper differences in educating males and females; 'chast Instruction' is proper for the female, whose virginity is an essential prerequisite to marriage. The text, that blank page bearing the author's imprint ('The first Impression . . . Will be the deepest'), is impossibly twice virgin – once for the original author, and again for the translator who has taken his place. It is this 'chastity' which resolves – or represses – the struggle for paternity.

The gendering of translation by this language of paternalism is made more explicit in the eighteenth-century treatise on translation by Thomas Francklin:

> Unless an author like a mistress warms,
> How shall we hide his faults or taste his charms,
> How all his modest latent beauties find,
> How trace each lovelier feature of the mind,
> Soften each blemish, and each grace improve,
> And treat him with the dignity of Love?[3]

Like the earl of Roscommon, Francklin represents the translator as a male who usurps the role of the author, a usurpation which takes place at the level of grammatical gender and is resolved through a sex change. The translator is figured as a male seducer; the author, conflated with the conventionally 'feminine' features of his text, is then the 'mistress', and the masculine pronoun is forced to refer to the feminine attributes of the text ('*his* modest latent beauties'). In confusing the gender of the author with the ascribed gender of the text, Francklin 'translates' the creative role of the author into the passive role of the text, rendering the author relatively powerless in relation to the translator. The author-text, now a mistress, is flattered and seduced by the translator's attentions, becoming a willing collaborator in the project to make herself beautiful – and, no doubt, unfaithful.

This *belle infidèle*, whose blemishes have been softened and whose beauties have therefore been improved, is depicted both as mistress and as a portrait model. In using the popular painting analogy, Francklin also reveals the gender coding of that mimetic convention: the translator/painter must seduce the text in order to 'trace' (translate) the features of his subject. We see a more elaborate version of this convention, though one arguing a different position on the subject of improvement through translation, in William Cowper's 'Preface' to Homer's *Iliad*: 'Should a painter, professing to draw the likeness of a beautiful woman, give her more or fewer features than belong to her, and a general cast of countenance of his own invention, he might be said to have produced a *jeu d'esprit*, a curiosity perhaps in its way, but by no means the lady in question'.[4] Cowper argues for fidelity to the beautiful model, lest the translation demean her, reducing her to a mere '*jeu d'esprit*', or, to follow the text yet further, make her monstrous ('give her more or fewer features'). Yet lurking behind the phrase 'the lady in question' is the suggestion that she is the *other* woman – the beautiful, and potentially unfaithful, mistress. In any case, like the earl of Roscommon and Francklin, Cowper feminizes the text and makes her reputation – that is, her fidelity – the responsibility of the male translator/author.

Just as texts are conventionally figured in feminine terms, so too is language: our 'mother tongue'. And when aesthetic debates shifted the focus in the late eighteenth century from problems of mimesis to those of expression – in

M. H. Abrams'* famous terms, from the mirror to the lamp – discussions of translation followed suit. The translator's relationship to this mother figure is outlined in some of the same terms that we have already seen – fidelity and chastity – and the fundamental problem remains the same: how to regulate legitimate sexual (authorial) relationships and their progeny.

A representative example depicting translation as a problem of fidelity to the 'mother tongue' occurs in the work of Schleiermacher*, whose twin interests in translation and hermeneutics have been influential in shaping translation theory in this century. In discussing the issue of maintaining the essential foreignness of a text in translation, Schleiermacher outlines what is at stake as follows:

> Who would not like to permit his mother tongue to stand forth everywhere in the most universally appealing beauty each genre is capable of? Who would not rather sire children who are their parents' pure effigy, and not bastards? . . . Who would suffer being accused, like those parents who abandon their children to acrobats, of bending his mother tongue to foreign and unnatural dislocations instead of skillfully exercising it in its own natural gymnastics?[5]

The translator, as father, must be true to the mother/language in order to produce legitimate offspring; if he attempts to sire children otherwise, he will produce bastards fit only for the circus. Because the mother tongue is conceived of as natural, any tampering with it – any infidelity – is seen as unnatural, impure, monstrous, and immoral. Thus, it is 'natural' law which requires monogamous relations in order to maintain the 'beauty' of the language and in order to insure that the works be genuine or original. Though his reference to bastard children makes clear that he is concerned over the purity of the mother tongue, he is also concerned with the paternity of the text. 'Legitimacy' has little to do with motherhood and more to do with the institutional acknowledgment of fatherhood. The question, 'Who is the real father of the text?' seems to motivate these concerns about both the fidelity of the translation and the purity of the language.

In the metaphorics of translation, the struggle for authorial rights takes place both in the realm of the family, as we have seen, and in the state, for translation has also been figured as the literary equivalent of colonization, a means of enriching both the language and the literature appropriate to the political needs of expanding nations. A typical translator's preface from the English eighteenth century makes this explicit:

> You, my Lord, know how the works of genius lift up the head of a nation above her neighbors, and give as much honor as success in arms; among these we must reckon our translations of the classics; by which when we

have naturalized all Greece and Rome, we shall be so much richer than they by so many original productions as we have of our own.[6]

Because literary success is equated with military success, translation can expand both literary and political borders. A similar attitude toward the enterprise of translation may be found in the German Romantics*, who used *übersetzen* (to translate) and *verdeutschen* (to Germanize) interchangeably: translation was literally a strategy of linguistic incorporation. The great model for this use of translation is, of course, the Roman Empire, which so dramatically incorporated Greek culture into its own. For the Romans, Nietzsche* asserts, 'translation was a form of conquest'.[7]

Then, too, the politics of colonialism overlap significantly with the politics of gender we have seen so far. Flora Amos shows, for example, that during the sixteenth century in England, translation is seen as 'public duty'. The most stunning example of what is construed as 'public duty' is articulated by a sixteenth-century English translator of Horace named Thomas Drant, who, in the preface to his translation of the Roman author, boldly announces,

> First I have now done as the people of God were commanded to do with their captive women that were handsome and beautiful: I have shaved off his hair and pared off his nails, that is, I have wiped away all his vanity and superfluity of matter . . . I have Englished things not according to the vein of the Latin propriety, but of his own vulgar tongue . . . I have pieced his reason, eked and mended his similitudes, mollified his hardness, prolonged his cortall kind of speeches, changed and much altered his words, but not his sentence, or at least (I dare say) not his purpose.[8]

Drant is free to take the liberties he here describes, for, as a clergyman translating a secular author, he must make Horace morally suitable: he must transform him from the foreign or alien into, significantly, a member of the family. For the passage from the Bible to which Drant alludes (Deut. 21: 12–14) concerns the proper way to make a captive woman a wife: 'Then you shall bring her home to your house; and she shall shave her head and pare her nails' (Deut. 21: 12, Revised Standard Version). After giving her a month in which to mourn, the captor can then take her as a wife; but if he finds in her no 'delight', the passage forbids him subsequently to sell her because he has already humiliated her. In making Horace suitable to become a wife, Drant must transform him into a woman, the uneasy effects of which remain in the tension of pronominal reference, where 'his' seems to refer to 'women'. In addition, Drant's paraphrase makes it the husband-translator's duty to shave and pare rather than the duty of the captive Horace. Unfortunately, captors often did much more than shave the heads of captive women (see Num. 31: 17–18); the sexual violence alluded to in this description of translation provides an analogue to the political and economic rapes implicit in a colonializing metaphor.

Clearly, the meaning of the word 'fidelity' in the context of translation changes according to the purpose translation is seen to serve in a larger aesthetic or cultural context. In its gendered version, fidelity sometimes defines the (female) translation's relation to the original, particularly to the original's author (male), deposed and replaced by the author (male) of the translation. In this case, the text, if it is a good and beautiful one, must be regulated against its propensity for infidelity in order to authorize the originality of this *production*. Or, fidelity might also define a (male) author-translator's relation to his (female) mother-tongue, the language into which something is being translated. In this case, the (female) language must be protected against vilification. It is, paradoxically, this sort of fidelity that can justify the rape and pillage of another language and text, as we have seen in Drant. But again, this sort of fidelity is designed to enrich the 'host' language by certifying the originality of translation; the conquests, made captive, are incorporated into the 'works of genius' of a particular language.

It should by now be obvious that this metaphorics of translation reveals both an anxiety about the myths of paternity (or authorship and authority) and a profound ambivalence about the role of maternity – ranging from the condemnation of *les belles infidèles* to the adulation accorded to the 'mother tongue'. In one of the few attempts to deal with both the practice and the metaphorics of translation, Serge Gavronsky argues that the source of this anxiety and ambivalence lies in the oedipal structure which informs the translator's options.[9] Gavronsky divides the world of translation metaphors into two camps. The first group he labels pietistic: metaphors based on the coincidence of courtly and Christian traditions, wherein the conventional knight pledges fidelity to the unravished lady, as the Christian to the Virgin. In this case, the translator (as knight or Christian) takes vows of humility, poverty – and chastity. In secular terms, this is called 'positional' translation, for it depends on a well-known hierarchization of the participants. The vertical relation (author/translator) has thus been overlaid with both metaphysical and ethical implications, and in this missionary position, submissiveness is next to godliness.

[. . .]

The metaphorics of translation, as the preceding discussion suggests, is a symptom of larger issues of western culture: of the power relations as they divide in terms of gender; of a persistent (though not always hegemonic) desire to equate language or language use with morality; of a quest for originality or unity, and a consequent intolerance of duplicity, of what cannot be decided. The fundamental question is, why have the two realms of translation and gender been metaphorically linked? What, in Eco's terms, is the metonymic code or narrative underlying these two realms?[10]

This survey of the metaphors of translation would suggest that the implied narrative concerns the relation between the value of production versus the value of reproduction. What proclaims itself to be an aesthetic problem is represented in terms of sex, family, and the state, and what is consistently at issue is power. We have already seen the way the concept of fidelity is used to regulate sex and/in the family, to guarantee that the child is the production of the father, reproduced by the mother. This regulation is a sign of the father's authority and power; it is a way of making visible the paternity of the child – otherwise a fiction of sorts – and thereby claiming the child as legitimate progeny. It is also, therefore, related to the owning and bequeathal of property. As in marriage, so in translation, there is a legal dimension to the concept of fidelity. It is not legal (shall I say, legitimate) to publish a translation of works not in the public domain, for example, without the author's (or appropriate proxy's) consent; one must, in short, enter the proper *contract* before announcing the birth of the translation, so that the parentage will be clear. The coding of production and reproduction marks the former as a more valuable activity by reference to the division of labor established for the marketplace, which privileges male activity and pays accordingly. The transformation of translation from a reproductive activity into a productive one, from a secondary work into an original work, indicates the coding of translation rights as property rights – signs of riches, signs of power.

Notes

1. Earl of Roscommon, 'An Essay on Translated Verse', in *English Translation Theory, 1650–1800*, ed. T. R. Steiner (Assen: Van Gorcum, 1975), p. 77.
2. Ibid., p. 78.
3. Thomas Francklin, 'Translation: A Poem', in *English Translation Theory*, pp. 113–14.
4. William Cowper, 'Preface' to *The Iliad of Homer*, in ibid., pp. 13–56.
5. Friedrich Schleiermacher, 'Über die verschiedenden Methoden des Übersetzen', tr. André Lefevere, in *Translating Literature: The German Tradition from Luther to Rosenzweig*, ed. André Lefevere (Assen: Van Gorcum, 1977), p. 79.
6. Cited in Flora Ross Amos, *Early Theories of Translation* (1920; New York: Octagon, 1973), pp. 138–9.
7. Friedrich Nietzsche, *The Gay Science*, tr. Walter Kaufmann (New York: Random House, 1974), p. 90.
8. Cited in Amos, *Early Theories of Translation*, pp. 112–13.
9. Serge Gavronsky, 'The Translation: From Piety to Cannibalism', *SubStance* 16 (1977): 53–62.
10. Umberto Eco, *The Role of the Reader: Explorations in the Semiotics of Texts* (Bloomington: Indiana University Press, 1979), p. 68.

6

'JACK SPICER'S *AFTER LORCA*: TRANSLATION AS DECOMPOSITION'

Daniel Katz

Spicer's sense of poetry as dictation and the poet as a 'receiver' of a voice which is Other needs to be emphasized, as it goes a long way towards illuminating a notable, and indeed noted, oddity: that *After Lorca*, the book through which Spicer himself felt he had reached his poetic maturity, was in its conception a book of translations. As we have seen, the contradiction is only apparent, since for Spicer poetry is less a question of *finding* one's voice than of letting it be *lost*, just as 'craft' consists less in polishing poetic objects than in wrenching language outside of a context which would allow it to be objectified, or reified, into the status of 'poem'. But Spicer's use of translation as a vector for the paradoxical 'dictation' he was increasingly to strive for has additional implications, since it allows him to inscribe himself into a complex network of modernist genealogies, while also interrogating the relationship between the specificity of a given language and subjective positioning. Spicer's *Lorca* evolves into a complex set of polemical negotiations – not only with Lorca and with a foreign language, but also with Lorca's own similar negotiation with another poet and a foreign language, as the centrepiece of Spicer's collection is Lorca's famous 'Ode to Walt Whitman'. At the same time, Spicer's procedure is quite consciously in and of itself a homage to Ezra Pound's *Homage to Sextus Propertius*, as Spicer, like Pound, takes wild and deliberate liberties with his source text. Spicer 'receives' Lorca voicing Whitman while doubling Pound, inevitably

From *Textual Practice* 18.1 (2004): 83–103.

raising the question of who is dictating to whom and who is translated by what. This question of heritage becomes all the more complex when one remembers Pound's 'A Pact', the famous poem addressed to none other than Walt Whitman, of which the thrust is precisely the difficulty of coming to terms with cumbersome heritages. Spicer's elaboration of his own belatedness with regard to these texts is the drama, to the extent that any exists, in *After Lorca*. Meanwhile, *After Lorca* and the subsequent *Admonitions* represent a key juncture of translation theory with poetics in post-war American poetry.

The book *After Lorca* consists of a 'ghost-written' prose introduction by 'Lorca' himself, six prose 'letters' to 'Lorca' from 'Jack' interspersed among the thirty-three 'translations', and a verse 'postscript' for Marianne Moore entitled 'Radar'. According to Clayton Eshelman, ten of the 'translations' can only be considered as Spicer originals.[1] Among the Lorca texts which Spicer translated, the 'Ode to Walt Whitman' is by far the most famous and the longest. As commentators have noted, this is clearly a key text for Spicer, as it is here that Lorca openly discusses the homosexuality which he and Spicer shared. But Pound too presides over the project as a tutelary spirit, as some of Spicer's letters make clear. He sounds Poundian indeed in a letter to Robin Blaser, when he claims: 'What I am trying to do is to establish a *tradition*. When I'm through (although I'm sure no one will ever publish them) I'd like someone as good as I am to translate these translations into French (or Pushtu) adding more. Do you understand? No. Nobody does'. Later in the same letter, Spicer writes, 'I can see why Pound got so angry at the reaction to his "Propertius"'.[2] Spicer, in fact, went beyond Pound in his treatment of Lorca, not only substantially altering words or lines in individual poems, but also quite simply including poems of his own in the book, at times Lorcaesque, at times not. 'Tradition' for Spicer then means a preferably endless multilingual network of continual textual appropriation, reappropriation and misappropriation, for which 'translation' provides one important model. However, as the 'letters' make clear, translation also becomes *transubstantiation*, as the passing of one spirit or even body into another echoes and is echoed by the passing of languages. Translation and haunting are explicitly linked in *After Lorca*, which once again shows just how prescient a reader of Pound Spicer was. If in terms of Spicer's work translation must be written into the greater chain of mediated discourses which came increasingly to define 'poetry' both as act and inspiration, what is largely at issue in *After Lorca*, then, is precisely the status of this 'receptive' subjectivity of the translator. Spicer, rather than simply becoming the vehicle for Lorca's ghostly and Americanized voice, will in fact 'talk back' to 'Lorca' in a series of letters signed 'Jack'. Translation, crucially, is refigured as dialogue, but just as crucially, as epistolary dialogue – a series of entirely mediated messages and transmissions passed back and forth across borders of language, death and the earth's cover. And for Spicer, the task of the translator consists not so much in bringing the dead poet 'to life' as in hauling the live translator, precisely, into death. Herein lies one of the true values of the act of translation for Spicer and also, perhaps, much of his fascination with the myth of Orpheus*. In his penultimate letter to Lorca, 'Jack' claims that poetry freezes the instant the poet 'ceases to be a dead man'.[3] The relationship between poetry and death, but also poetry and prose, obsesses the book.

DEAD LETTERS

The prose texts of *After Lorca* – 'Lorca''s introduction and Jack's six letters to him – are concerned largely with defining poetry and are seen rightly as cornerstones of Spicer's poetics. Two points regarding them, however, have not been sufficiently stressed. First, if these texts often valorize 'poetry' at the expense of 'prose', they are written in prose themselves and Spicer's subsequent books more often than not contained a significant portion of what is conventionally called 'prose poetry'. This forces us to ask to what extent these texts as performatives undo or at least ironize their constative claims. Second, little thought has been given to the extent to which these reflections on 'poetics' are also explicitly reflections on *translation*.

The first text in prose is the introduction to the volume, attributed to 'Lorca'. Here, the programme of the book is clearly laid out: 'It must be made clear at the start that these poems are not translations. In even the most literal of them Mr. Spicer seems to derive pleasure in inserting or substituting one or two words which completely change the mood and often the meaning of the poem as I had written it', and 'Lorca' goes on to explain that Spicer also includes poems which are half translation, half originals and others that are not by Lorca at all, without the reader being given any 'indication which of the poems belong to which category'. 'Lorca' will wryly close his discussion of this matter with a metaphorical equivalence which underwrites the entire project – that of the human body and the literary corpus: 'Even the most faithful student of my work will be hard put to decide what is and what is not Garcia Lorca as, indeed, he would if he were to look into my present resting place. The analogy is impolite, but I fear the impoliteness is deserved'.[4] This figure is extended in Lorca's concluding sentences, which again treat of the strange 'mixture' of Spicer and Lorca of which *After Lorca* consists. I quote in full:

> The dead are notoriously hard to satisfy. Mr Spicer's mixture may please his contemporary audience or may, and this is more probable, lead him to write better poetry of his own. But I am strongly reminded as I survey this curious amalgam of a cartoon published in an American magazine while I was visiting your country in New York. The cartoon showed a gravestone on which were inscribed the words: 'HERE LIES AN OFFICER AND A GENTLEMAN'. The caption below it read: 'I wonder how they happened to be buried in the same grave?'[5]

That the dead are 'notoriously hard to satisfy' points not only to the debt that the translator may be said to owe to the 'original' which he parasites and exploits – it also recalls the manner in which the dead most classically express this dissatisfaction, to wit, as truculent ghosts. But the question left open is whether this act of translation is the transgression for which appeasement must be made, or the act of appeasement itself, extending as it does the 'life' of the dead poet's text. In his work on Pound, Daniel Tiffany has stressed how translation may be seen as a sacrifice on the part of the translator, who would deliver himself over to the service of the alien 'voice'. In this way, translation appears as 'a process whereby the original author or text is brought to life, resurrected, through a depletion of the translator's vitality, or, more seriously, through a reification, a deadening, of his native language. There is a terrible risk, of course, in feeding the dead from the store of one's own vitality'.[6] Yet if the 'original' text may be seen as a 'succubus' or 'parasite' feeding off the vitality of the living translator, the reverse is equally true, for the translator is a consummate 'grave-robber', as Chamberlain has referred to Spicer in this context,[7] stealing an alien 'voice' through which to speak what is, after all, his own tongue. Thus the importance of the Introduction by 'Lorca': in this book, not only will Lorca 'speak' through the 'voice' of Spicer, but the blatant forgery of the Introduction reminds us that Spicer is also always speaking through the 'mask' of 'Lorca'. The mixing of original poems with translations, the injection of original lines and words within the boundaries of the translations, is crucial for creating this sort of bidirectional dialogue. The officer and the gentleman indeed share the same grave, in the form of the patrician aristocrat Lorca and the seedy bohemian Spicer, and one melds into the other just as Lorca's corpse commingles with its resting place.

[. . .]

Just as mimetic exactitude cannot generally be maintained in translation (one must replace the poet's words with others, yet the poetic object is in essence nothing but words) so on the level of the signified, for Spicer 'translation' is also necessary:

> That tree you saw in Spain is a tree I could never have seen in California, that lemon has a different smell and a different taste, BUT the answer is this – every place and every time has a real object to *correspond* with your real object – that lemon may become this lemon, or it may even become this piece of seaweed, or this particular color of gray in this ocean. One does not need to imagine that lemon; one needs to discover it.

As translation becomes the search for 'correspondences', on the level of both the signifier and the signified (as the example of 'seaweed' rendering 'lemon' indicates), it can be effected only through the sort of 'correspondence' or exchange of voicings Spicer punningly has in mind in these letters, as he makes clear in closing this one: 'Even these letters. They *correspond* with something (I don't know what) that you have written (perhaps as unapparently as that lemon corresponds to this piece of seaweed) and, in turn, some future poet will write something which *corresponds* to them. That is how we dead men write to each other. Love, Jack'.[8] Translation is literally letter-writing, as Spicer sees each of his renderings as at once a *response* addressed to Lorca, prompted by his work and also as a *correspondence*, re-placing that work in another time, language and context. Spicer sees himself as sending Lorca's work back to him as well as extending Lorca mediumistically. Ross Clarkson has pointed out that for Spicer, 'Translation, as a correspondence with the dead, is more than transcribing a poem into another language; rather, translation is an instance of poetic community through communication between the living and the dead'.[9] Clarkson is entirely right, but I would like to stress that the form this communication takes is figured not as dialogue but as epistolary exchange; for Spicer, the emphasis on mediation and remainder, the material inscription of the sign and the gap between sender and receiver, remains paramount. If this mediation finds its supplement in Spicer's fantasm, issued by 'Lorca', of the decomposing bodies melding seamlessly into each other, their materiality, like that of newspapers cut up and repasted in collage, is equally stressed.

TRANSLATING THE HINTS

Spicer's conceit would be that 'Lorca' and 'Jack' are translated into each other on every level, and in this way he attempts to rewrite translation as erotic exchange rather than as a complex bookkeeping of indebtedness. Of course, what is most erotic about this mediumistic, ghostly dialogue is that one is spoken *by* the other as much as one speaks *to* him, in a sort of echolalic *mise-en-abyme* which both invokes and defeats the narcissism that Spicer alludes to in his translations of the two poems which Lorca had titled 'Narcissus'. Crucially, in terms of these tropes, yet another figure enters the discussion, and thus the grave: Walt Whitman.

The term 'translation' emerges at several key points in *Leaves of Grass*, and is one of Whitman's favourite words for examining two related issues: the relationship between author and reader, and the relationship between the singularity of the individual subject, and the traces and remainders which it is capable of producing: writing, footprints, and the green grass itself which grows out of corpses above their graves. Whitman in fact focuses first on the idea of translation in his effort to decipher the mysterious writing of the 'grass', whose proffered communication has given the title for his entire writing project. Shortly after 'reading' what he calls the 'hieroglyphic' of the grass as 'the beautiful uncut hair of graves' early in 'Song of Myself', Whitman attempts to imagine the lives of the bodies which now 'live' on in the form of the grass they literally nourish in their decomposition: 'I wish I could translate the hints about the dead young men and women,/ And the hints about old men and mothers, and the offspring taken soon out of their laps'.[10] Given the figural economy established here and so heavily marked by the book's title, it could be suggested that *Leaves of Grass* is nothing other than a reflection on translation, 'grass' signifying nothing but signification and mediation, or the world as foreign text . . .

NOTES

1. Clayton Eshelman, 'The Lorca Working', *Boundary* 27.1 (1977): 31–49.
2. 'Jack Spicer: Letters to Robin Blaser', *Line* 9 (1987): 48.
3. Jack Spicer, *The Collected Books of Jack Spicer*, ed. Robin Blaser (Santa Barbara: Black Sparrow Press, 1980), p. 48.
4. Ibid., p. 11.
5. Ibid., p. 12.
6. Daniel Tiffany, *Radio Corpse: Imagism and the Cryptaesthetic of Ezra Pound* (Cambridge, MA: Harvard University Press, 1995), p. 191.
7. Lori Chamberlain, 'Ghostwriting the Text: Translation and the Poetics of Jack Spicer', *Contemporary Literature* 26.4 (1985): 427.
8. Spicer, *Collected Books*, p. 34 (Spicer's italics).
9. Ross Clarkson, 'Jack Spicer's Ghosts and the Immemorial Community', *Mosaic* 34.4 (2001): 201.
10. Walt Whitman, *Complete Poetry and Collected Prose* (New York: Library of America, 1982), p. 193.

7

'THE FRENCH CARIBBEANIZATION OF PHILLIS WHEATLEY: A POETICS OF ANTICOLONIALISM'

Anna Brickhouse

Wheatley's 'On the death of JC, an infant', as its title makes clear, marks the death of a local New England child known by name to the poet as James. Like many of the other works appearing in *Poems on Various Subjects* [Wheatley's collection of poetry, first published in London in 1773], the poem is an elegy addressed to specific Boston readers, in this case James C's grieving parents:

> No more the flow'ry scenes of pleasure rise,
> Nor charming prospects greet the mental eyes,
> No more with joy we view that lovely face
> Smiling, disportive, flush'd with ev'ry grace.
> The tear of sorrow flown from ev'ry eye,
> Groans answer groans, and sighs to sighs reply
> What sudden pangs shot thro' each aching heart,
> When, *Death*, thy messenger dispatch's his dart!
> Thy dread attendants, all destroying Pow'r,
> Hurried the infant to his mortal hour.
> Could'st thou unpitying close those radiant eyes?
> Or fail'd his artless beauties to surprise?
> Could not his innocence thy stroke control,

From Anna Brickhouse (2004) *Transamerican Literary Relations and the Nineteenth-Century Public Sphere*. Cambridge: Cambridge University Press.

Thy purpose shake and soften all thy soul?
The blooming babe, with shades of *Death* o'erspread,
No more shall smile, no more shall raise its head;
But like a branch that from the tree is torn,
Falls prostrate, wither'd, languid, and forlorn.
'Where flies my *James*?' tis thus I seem to hear
The parent ask, 'Some angel tell me where
He wings his passage thro' the yielding air?'
Methinks a cherub bending from the skies
Observes the question and serene replies,
'In heav'n's high palaces your babe appears:
Prepare to meet him and dismiss your tears.'
Shall not th' intelligence your griefs restrain,
And turn the mournful to the cheerful strain?
Cease your complaints, suspend each rising sigh,
Cease to accuse the Ruler of the sky.
Parents, no more indulge the falling tear:
Let *Faith* to heav'n's refulgent domes repair,
There see your infant like a seraph glow:
What charms celestial in his numbers flow.
Melodious, while the soul-enchanting strain
Dwells on his tongue, and fills th'ethereal plain?
Enough – forever cease your murm'ring breath;
Not as a foe, but friend, converse with *Death*,
Since to the port of happiness unknown
He brought that treasure which you call your own.
The gift of heav'n entrusted to your hand
Cheerful resign at the divine command;
Not at your bar must sov'reign *Wisdom* stand.[1]

Adopting a rhetorical stance common to Wheatley's other writings on the deaths of loved ones, the poem describes the departed infant, 'that lovely face / Smiling, disportive, flush'd with ev'ry grace', and the universal sorrow inspired by his death ('The tear of sorrow flown from ev'ry eye'), before proceeding to imagine the more specific scene of the bereft parents: Wheatley's speaker ventures, ' "Where flies my *James*?" tis thus I seem to hear / The parent ask, "Some angel tell me where / He wings his passage thro' the yielding air?"' The parent's question is immediately answered by 'a cherub bending from the skies [who] / Observes the question and serene replies, / "In heav'n's high palaces your babe appears: / Prepare to meet him and dismiss your tears."' The remainder of the poem engages in a standard Christian argument about the triumph of the celestial world over the sorrowful earthly one, urging that the 'Parents, no more indulge the falling tear: / Let *Faith* to heav'n's refulgent domes repair. / There see your infant like a seraph glow'.

In the *Revue*, however, even the title of the purported translation of 'On the death of JC, an infant' immediately reveals its deviation both from Wheatley's English-language original and Grégoire's* French translation, which omits the titular initials, rendering the poem's title as 'Sur la mort d'un enfant' ('On the death of a child'). The *Revue*'s version of Wheatley's poem is titled 'Sur la mort d'un enfant *noir*' – 'On the death of a *black* child' – and its addressees are no longer the presumably white parents of JC, only a few among the many prominent Bostonians for whom Wheatley composed poems while still a slave.

I.

Le plaisir couronné de fleurs ne vient plus embellir nos moments.

II.

L'espérance n'ouvre plus l'avenir pour nous caresser par des illusions enchanteresses

III.

Puisque la joie et le bonheur nous ont quittés, que la poésie descende des cieux.

IV.

La poésie, douce et tendre mère, qui berce sur ses genoux ceux qui souffrent.

V.

La poésie qui pose ses lèvres sur les yeux gonflés et douloureux de ceux qui souffrent.

VI.

La poésie qui rafraîchit, du vent de ses ailes, le front brûlant des malheureux.

VII.

Que la poésie vienne! Car nous ne verrons plus ce visage enfantin, noir comme l'ébène, gracieux comme les feuilles de cocotier.

VIII.

Que la poésie vienne! Car de tous les yeux s'échappent des larmes. Les gémissements sont l'écho des gémissements; les sanglots répondent aux sanglots.

IX.

Quoi! Sans être émue, la mort a posé sa main froide sur l'adorable enfant.

X.

Elle a éteint la vie sur son visage qui s'est terni comme se ternit un brin d'herbe lorsque disparaît, sous une nuée, le rayon du soleil qui le dorait.

XI.

Où s'est enfui mon bien-aimé James? s'écrie le pére. Quand son âme
voltige dans les airs, anges conducteurs, indiquez-moi le chemin de
son passage.

XII.

La mère, elle, tristement assíse sur ses talons, les bras pendants, la tête
penchée sur la poitrine, ne dit rien (288–9).[2]

(Pleasure crowned with flowers no longer adorns our moments.

Hope no longer opens the future to caress us with enchanting illusions.

Since joy and happiness have left us, let poetry descend from the
heavens.

Poetry, sweet and tender mother, who rocks upon her knees those who
suffer.

Poetry who puts her lips upon the swollen and grieving eyes of those
who suffer.

Poetry who refreshes, with the wind of her wings, the burning brow of
the wretched.

Let poetry come! For we will no longer see this childish face, black like
ebony, graceful like the leaves of the coconut palm.

Let poetry come! For from all eyes tears escape. Moans are the echo of
moans; sobs respond to sobs.

What! Completely unmoved, death has put her cold hand on the
adorable child.

She has extinguished the life upon his face which became tarnished as a
blade of grass becomes tarnished when, under a cloud, the ray of the
sun that gilded it disappears.

Where has my beloved James fled? cries the father. When his soul
flutters in the air, angel guides, show me the path it is taking.

The mother, for her part, sitting sadly upon her heels, arms hanging,
head leaned on her chest, says nothing.)

The *Revue*'s rendering of Wheatley's poem ritually invokes 'La poésie', personi-
fied as a 'sweet and tender' mother, called upon in the poem to minister not only
to the dead child's parents but more generally to 'ceux qui souffrent', 'les malheureux' – those who suffer, the wretched – a group given no specific name in the
text but whose potential racial and political identities are nevertheless made clear
by the poem's (mis)translated title and the wider subjects covered in the journal.

While the argument of Wheatley's original text depends on what some critics
have envisioned as a poetics of liberation crystallizing around depictions of the
celestial world, the *Revue*'s 'On the death of a black child' remains steadfastly
focused on this world, where poetry is summoned from the heavens to aid the
suffering rather than vice versa. As in Wheatley's original poem, the parent (this

time specifically a father) asks where his beloved James has flown and calls on the angels to reveal the passage of his son's soul through the air. But while Wheatley's parent receives the unambiguous answer of a cherub, the father in the *Revue*'s version goes without a response from either the poet or the heavens. The *Revue*'s translation refuses the reassuring closure of Wheatley's original, instead ending abruptly on a tableau of the child's mother and the bodily manifestation of her grief: 'sitting sadly upon her heels, arms hanging, head leaned on her chest, [she] says nothing'. The mother's silence seems almost to rebuke the confident celestial discourse articulated by Wheatley's cherub, suggesting that the *Revue*'s translation is not just a reinterpretation of Wheatley but a pointed response to the perceived inadequacy of her faith in the world beyond in lieu of explicit racial and political consciousness. Indeed, the image of the grieving mother, entirely absent from Wheatley's original, recalls the carnage documented in the article with which the January 1837 issue opens, a final installment in a series of stories on what was called 'l'affaire de la Grand'Anse' – 'one of the sinister events of which the history of the colonies offers more than one example'. The Grand'Anse affair ensued when the French government denounced the political demonstration of a group of *gens de couleur* in a number of public writings as an 'insurrection', a term that eventually became de facto evidence in a series of death penalty convictions as well as the catalyst for a powerful surge of white Creole mob violence involving vigilante killings. 'How many mothers cried for their children! How many families ruined, dispersed, annihilated!' explodes the opening of the report, demanding that readers envision the human costs of the affair as reported to them from the safety of a Paris-based journal – as well as the more general human costs invisible within the safety of Wheatley's poetic orientation.[3]

The *Revue*'s critique of Wheatley is registered simply but powerfully in the transformation of the titular James C into the more representative 'enfant noir', the black child mourned by a questioning father and a silent mother. If these parents receive none of Wheatley's original reassurances about the power of faith, the *Revue*'s translation demands that poetry come to commemorate the precious racial and cultural specificity of their child's face: the color of his skin, 'noir comme l'ébène'; and his beauty, 'gracieux comme les feuilles de cocotier'. The figuration of the child's grace as a tropical plant widens the scope of the translation beyond the northern parameters of Wheatley's original, gesturing toward the Caribbean origin of the *Revue*'s main contributors as well as a distinctly transnational conception of the meaning of a black child's death in the history of the colonies covered by the journal. At the same time, the simile deployed to represent the child's blackness ('like ebony') in these lines contrasts sharply with Wheatley's own famous racial simile from her poem 'On being brought from Africa': 'Remember, Christians, Negroes, black as Cain,/May be refin'd and join the angelic train'. Though Grégoire did not include this particular poem in his work on Wheatley, the first English translation of *De la littérature des Nègres* in the United States, published by David Warden in 1810, effectively altered Grégoire's anthology by conspicuously including these memorable lines as an epigraph to the section on Wheatley – a couplet reiterating the racialist Christian theory that Africans descended from Cain, marked by a dark color and forever enslaved to pay for the ancestral sin of Abel's murder. While Wheatley's attitude toward the theory of racial difference that she cites is highly ambiguous, the *Revue* provided an explicit fictional commentary on the theory articulated in an early Guadeloupean short story that also appears in the journal's pages. The story depicts a young slave named Zélie who goes to Mass and learns the supposed cause of her servitude from the story of Abel and Cain, as interpreted by the priest; the story caustically explains that Caribbean slaveowners 'trace back almost to the birth of the world the line that separates them' from their slaves, 'dar[ing] to alter what they believe to be the divine word'.[4]

The *Revue des Colonies* thus incorporates a version of Wheatley that revises and invents within its documentation of the literary past, imagines what could have been, allowing Bissette* to produce for his reading public a politicized relation between Wheatley's poetry and other early writers of the Americas with whom the poet had never otherwise been anthologized or associated. Other examples of the journal's revisionist recovery of an early comparative American literary history include its treatment of such figures as Ignatius Sancho, born on a slave ship en route to the Americas though his literary works were written and published in England; Olaudah Equiano, author of the first self-written account of slavery in the African American tradition, an autobiography that became the prototype for nineteenth-century African American slave narratives; and Francis Williams, an early Jamaican poet and Latinist whose work was originally published in Edward Long's proslavery *History of Jamaica* in an attempt to discredit the possibility of veritable literary production by a person of African origin. The *Revue*'s appropriation of Long's racist diatribe for its preservation rather than its denigration of an early Afro-Jamaican poem exemplifies the journal's ability to excavate the components of a literary tradition out of a text that sought precisely to deny its existence, as well as the editor's refusal to allow the erasures of early African American literary production committed in contemporaneous discourses of US literary history – exemplified in Grégoire's *De la littérature des Nègres* by Jefferson himself – to go unchallenged.

NOTES

1. Phillis Wheatley, *Poems on Various Subjects Religious and Moral* (London: A. Bell, 1773), n.p.
2. *Revue des Colonies* (January 1837): 288–9.
3. Ibid., p. 273.
4. *Revue des Colonies* (September 1835): 134.

PART V
STYLE AND GENRE

STYLE AND GENRE: INTRODUCTION

One question any student of transatlantic literary relations must consider is whether the endlessly transferable features of global culture may have rendered 'transatlantic comparison' redundant. Is 'style' not now simply another facet of an internationalist repertoire of gestures? The stylistics of transatlantic comparison cannot any longer draw on monolithic assumptions about national character and authorial identity, or the transparency of 'influence'. It remains the case, however, that for anglophone Americans since the seventeenth century, reading and writing have been inescapably transnational and transatlantic activities. In the mid-nineteenth century comparative cultural politics and discussions of style developed a compounded vocabulary of relations and departures, in which both British and American writers attempted to account for the way in which language translated into new contexts generated new effects primarily in stylistic terms. American literary Romanticism, like the foundational phase of Comparative Literature described in a previous section, was predicated on the condition articulated by Julia Kristeva's 'foreigner', who 'feels strengthened by the distance that detaches him from the others as it does from himself and gives him not so much the sense of holding the truth but of making it and himself relative' (7). Post-Revolutionary writers were urged to develop a national voice related to but distinct from that of the country whose language they shared but from which they were politically dedicated to differ. English writers were characterised, admiringly or ironically, by their employment of what Hawthorne called 'beef-and-ale' solidity of specification, while on the other side of the Atlantic Francis Jeffrey, writing in *The Edinburgh Review* in 1809, identified in American writing a 'curious intermixture . . . of extreme homeliness and flatness, with a sort of turbulent and bombastic elevation', and Thomas Carlyle famously described Emerson's style (to him, in a letter), as redolent of the thin atmosphere on a mountain-top or like 'a bag of duck-shot held together with canvas'. Yet, as Jahan Ramazani has noted, 'globe-traversing influences, energies, and instances', 'far from being minor deviations from nation-based fundamentals' (332), have shaped literary style in ways that pressurise mononational aesthetic or generic conventions. Ramazani's concern is with modernist poetry, where 'a poetics of bricolage and translocation, dissonance and defamiliarization' (333) announces the impossibility of reductive geographical containers; but his essay serves as a reminder more generally of the effects that migrating tropes, vocabularies and allusions have on singular affiliations. This section presents a selection of critical reflections on style and genre with particular promise for the practice of transatlantic comparison.

In a celebrated essay, Leo Marx dubbed *The Tempest* 'Shakespeare's American fable' not merely for its possible sources in histories of the early colonial venture in Jamestown, Virginia, but on account of an opposition between nature and culture that Marx read as inaugurating a distinctive tradition of American pastoral*. Although not directly represented in this *Reader*, Marx's influence is evident in many of the following extracts. Starting from Marx's suggestion that the play 'may be read as a prologue to American literature', Eric Cheyfitz offers a revisionary reading that replaces Marx's version of the play with an overtly rhetorical model: 'In *The Tempest* the garden is not a form of nature. The garden is the garden of eloquence'. Cheyfitz's rich blend of postcolonial ideology, historicist methodology and Renaissance rhetorical theory aligns *The Tempest* with Emerson's *Nature* (1836) as dialogues founded on the trope of metaphor. The English term comes from a Greek root, *metaphora* (*meta*: over, *phereia*: to carry); in Rhetoric (the study of the art of language use), the figure of metaphor traditionally embodied the 'handing across or over' of meaning. The Latin word for metaphor is *translatio*, to cross over. The classical Latin trope *translatio studii et imperii**, which decreed that virtues flee a decadent civilisation for a simpler, regenerate one, encapsulates a rationale for temporal or spatial translation of cultural and political legitimacy: it melded originality or newness, with authority, and (as Cheyfitz and others note) encompassed the etymological and ideological inseparability of metaphor and translation – the topic of the previous section. Through the common crossing root form 'trans-', a much older tradition of rhetorical analysis acquired new associations in the American form of Romanticism that became known as Transcendentalism.

Cheyfitz (and behind him, Marx), Gilles Deleuze and Félix Guattari all pursue the metaphor of texts as machines – tools for thinking with – 'plugged in' (in Deleuze and Guattari's words) to other devices of similar type. The connections thus established are described in their celebrated metaphor of the rhizome, an underground root system that works its way laterally across the soil rather than vertically down into it (as, to extend the metaphor, influence may be figured as working, historically 'downwards' through generations of writing). As a way of conceptualising transatlantic relations, the rhizome has obvious possibilities for the kind of transitive or lateral reading of literary texts proposed by many of the authors represented in this *Reader*. In a series of highly metaphorical moves, Deleuze and Guattari's critique – at once Romantic and counter-Romantic – deconstructs organic metaphors of growth and structural integrity of texts, insisting that we should not interrogate individual terms in the rhizomatic sequence (or 'grammar') for their 'meaning', but ask instead about how they function in the networks that sustain them. A grammar of transatlantic literary connection would, following the logic of the extract below, replace the singularities and verticalities of national literary history with multiple forms and points of connection, effecting a 'deterritorialisation' of language use.

The title of the book from which Cheyfitz's 'Foreign Policy of Metaphor' is taken, *The Poetics of Imperialism*, gestures towards the inevitable mutual implication, in a comparative context, of style and politics. Nineteenth-century British responses to American poetry and fiction frequently levelled criticisms based on these works' 'failure' to measure up to an idealised 'purity' of genre. Indictment of the indecorum of American publications litter reviews of American poetic epics; critical responses to Melville's *Moby-Dick* on both sides of the Atlantic struggled to come to terms with its stylistic 'extravagance' and wondered whether a fiction that took such extreme liberties with the genre could properly be designated a novel. 'English', by contrast, was characterised by its stylistic *normality*: Robert Southey declared magisterially in the *Quarterly Review* in 1809 that 'Dwight has failed because he imitated bad models, and Barlow because he formed a bad style for himself'. Culture wars are also style wars, and genre criticism is no exception. From the earliest Classical texts onwards, rhetorical theory has been fond of organising literary into kinds: Epic, History, Satire, Pastoral, and so on, within an implied or stated hierarchy of types. This taxonomising impulse has characteristically served the politics of literary criticism as much as its poetics.

Margaret Cohen draws attention to the historical importance of the novel in constituting the 'imagined community' of the nation (see the Introduction to Part I, 'The Nation and Cosmopolitanism', above). Departing from this, and taking the emerging sub-genre of sea fiction in the nineteenth-century imagined space of the Atlantic as her object, she asks instead 'how the novel travels as a genre'. In a classic chapter on the theory of genre, Alistair Fowler describes it as 'much less a pigeonhole than a pigeon' (37). Many critics have made the point that genre is transformed in every enactment, elasticity inherent in its very performance. Like metaphor, it has the capacity to exhibit likeness in difference, simultaneously to preserve and distort similitude. Genre is, as Wai Chee Dimock puts it, a

> self-obsoleting system, a provisional set that will always be bent and pulled and stretched by its many subsets. Such bending and pulling and stretching are unavoidable, for what genre is dealing with is a volatile body of material, still developing, still in transit, and always on the verge of taking flight in some unknown and unpredictable direction. (86)

Although it is not Dimock's intention in the essay referred to, the transatlantic potential of such a formulation should be apparent. Cohen's essay on 'Traveling Genre', excerpted in this section, is a case in point, as it offers a series of case studies in the evolution of a highly popular transnational literary form dedicated to addressing 'transportable questions' by giving narrative form to oceanic crossing.

The elasticity of (circumatlantic) performance is Joseph Roach's subject in an anthropologically inflected account of how cultural memory travels encoded in theatricality. Roach's powerful formulation of 'the process of surrogation' operating between cultures allows us to reimagine the crossing trope as enacted in a different genre, drama, and folds familiar Anglo-American paradigms into a far broader range of cultural reference. His resonant phrase 'performing [the] past in the presence of others' brings history, style and genre into dynamic conjunction. Perspectives from postcolonial and comparative literature hover in the wings of a circumatlantic analysis that represents the transactions of memory as a series of staged contrasts: the formation of 'national' memory rendered relational.

The extract from Michael Bell's influential *Development of American Romance*, on the other hand, describes the 'sacrifice of relation' as a defining characteristic of American literature vis-à-vis its British counterpart. Bell's argument is a sophisticated later version of a powerful strand in nineteenth- and twentieth-century Anglo-American comparative critique; as such, it represents in this *Reader* perhaps the most dominant precursor of transatlantic literary studies. Nation- and genre-based, this tradition stretches back to the essentialist comparativism of Romantic cultural nationalism. America's newness, so the argument ran, offered something like a blank canvas to would-be national writers. In a series of essays, prefaces and commentaries, American authors from Washington Irving and James Fenimore Cooper to Nathaniel Hawthorne and Henry James; to T. S. Eliot, Lionel Trilling and Richard Chase offered a litany of ingredients believed to be absent from American life and held, equally, to be essential to the 'mature' forms of imaginative creation. 'It takes a great deal of history to make a little literature', as James wrote provocatively in his study of Hawthorne. The paucity of complex social relations, historical density and cultural institutions in the new nation meant that the quotidian details and particularities of, for example, the English realist novel were both inappropriate for and closed to American writers; instead, they were forced (as the 'thinness trope' would have it) to develop an alternative genre, the 'American Romance', characterised by indirection, symbolism, myth and abstract, cosmic themes. Into this critical tradition, Bell brings a strongly historicised set of generic oppositions; in effect, he creates two opposing traditions of fiction emerging from (in the case of the 'English novel') empirical Lockean* observation, and (in the case of 'American romance') Scottish Enlightenment philosophy's 'radically dualistic . . . separation of fancy and reason'. Neither the binaristic philosophic analysis nor its fictional consequences seem tenable now, but Bell is included as representative of a strand of comparative genre criticism that retains currency in some quarters of contemporary Americanist and transatlantic study. The following extract, from Nicolaus Mills's 'anti-genre' comparative critique, energetically refutes this kind of comparison. Published before Bell's book, it offers a corrective view in refusing to countenance any form of comparative genre critique, and instead finds a 'uniqueness and complexity [in] nineteenth-century American fiction' visible only to 'broad, comparative analysis'.

Such strident expressions of exceptionalism (particularly when based on criteria as sweeping as Mills's) no longer carry critical conviction. More recently, American critics such as Eve Bannet and Leonard Tennenhouse have been combining stylistics and genre criticism in carefully historicised comparative readings of writings from the late eighteenth century, to chart emergent differences that in some cases anticipate the moment of America's political separation from Britain. Drawing attention to a neglected transatlantic genre, epistolary manuals, Bannet makes a case for them as powerful, but flexible, vehicles of cultural authority operating transatlantically through their capacity to establish norms of epistolary communication. Her subtle analysis of a text that flourished over multiple Atlantic crossings, David Fordyce's New and Complete British Letter-Writer, shows how its power resided in its fluidity, its capacity to adapt through new American and British editions to changing circumstances of reading, writing and expectation. Her analysis reveals how silence (as Melville's Bartleby would rediscover more than half a century later) may be as eloquent a rhetorical tool in the cultural politics of the circumatlantic space as the most elaborate of metaphors. Tennenhouse's account of the transatlantic fortunes of one of fiction's foundational texts, Samuel Richardson's Clarissa, closes this section. Taking issue with Jay Fliegelman's claim (in Prodigals and Pilgrims: the American Revolution Against Patriarchal Authority) that Clarissa's popularity in late colonial America was attributable to the heroine's virtuous rebellion against arbitrary patriarchal authority, Tennenhouse re-grounds his transatlantic comparison in the specifics of developing differences between the print cultures and reading practices of the two nations in the Revolutionary era. Asking 'what American fiction did to the European sentimental tradition', he evokes an 'American Richardson': abridged, plot-intensive, less 'literary' than the longer 'English' version preferred by colonial readers, and minimally expressive. This local version shared many features in common with another subgenre popular in America, the captivity narrative. Neither of these richly detailed essays can be adequately represented in summary; for that, they must be read in full. Both, however, even in the excerpts we have been able to include here, make clear how attention to style and genre in a comparative context can deliver substantiated accounts of transatlantic literary transformation.

Further Reading

Chase, Richard (1957) *The American Novel and Its Tradition*. New York: Doubleday.

Derrida, Jacques (1980) 'The Law of Genre', *Critical Inquiry* 7: 55–81.

Dimock, Wai Chee (2006) 'Genre as World System', *Narrative* 14.1: 85–101.

Fowler, Alistair (1992) *Kinds of Literature: An Introduction to the Theory of Genres and Modes*. Cambridge, MA: Harvard University Press.

Kristeva, Julia (1991) *Strangers to Ourselves*, trans. Leon S. Roudiez. New York: Columbia University Press.

Manning, Susan (2002) *Fragments of Union: Making Connections in Scottish and American Writing*. Basingstoke: Palgrave.

Manning, Susan (2004) ' "Grounds for Comparison": The Place of Style in Transatlantic Romanticism', in Joel Pace and Matthew Scott (eds) *Wordsworth in American Literary Culture*. Basingstoke: Palgrave, pp. 19–42.

Marx, Leo (1964) *The Machine in the Garden: Technology and the Pastoral Idea in America*. New York: Oxford University Press.

Poirier, Richard (1967) *A World Elsewhere: The Place of Style in American Literature*. London: Chatto and Windus.

Ramazani, Jahan (2006) 'A Transnational Poetics', *American Literary History* 18.2: 332–59.

I

'ELOQUENCE AND TRANSLATION'

Eric Cheyfitz

Figurative language, of which metaphor, or translation, is the model, is the driving force of interpretation, that is, of language itself. For this language within language that is the force of language opens up a space between signified and signifier, a rupture of identity, where the conflictive play of dialogue takes place that constitutes the speakers (writers/readers) for and significantly through each other. Historically in the West, eloquence developed in Greece and retained both a dialogic, or 'democratic', component (democratic within the upper class) and an imperial component. That is, eloquence is conceived of both as what makes the *polis* the free marketplace of ideas, the place of open debate in the law courts and in councils, and, contradictorily enough, as what can mesmerize the other into silent assent. In *De Oratore* Cicero evokes these two aspects of eloquence, though not apparently with any irony, when he describes the orator's art as both 'kingly [*regium*]' and 'worthy of the free [*liberale*]'.[1] Emerson's entire oeuvre can be read within this dual figure of eloquence.

[. . .]

The significance of eloquence to English during the period of its national formation is a particularly crucial one; and it is one that is mediated by

From Eric Cheyfitz (1995) 'The Foreign Policy of Metaphor' and 'The Frontier of Decorum', in *Poetics of Imperialism: Translation and Colonization from the Tempest to Tarzan*. Oxford: Oxford University Press.

translation, by the dynamics of the domestic and the foreign [. . .] In the first three quarters of the sixteenth century, according to the generally accepted account given us by Richard Foster Jones,

> Eloquence inhered not in the native elements in the language but only in the words introduced into it from the classics. That the English language per se was considered uneloquent may be easily deduced from the adjectives most frequently used to describe it: rude, gross, barbarous, base, vile.[2]

Eloquence, then, and proper speech, as we have been defining it, are synonymous. Eloquent speech is speech that is native, not foreign, or 'barbarous' (and the Renaissance was well aware of the Greek derivation of the term); it is speech that is of the city or manor, not of the country or surrounding villages ('rude' and 'vile' would have been associated with the peasantry at the time); it is the speech of mind or spirit, not the body (it is not, that is, 'gross' speech); and it is the speech of the upper, not the lower classes (the classes to which all these adjectives would apply). Projected, during the period of its national development, onto the international scene, both temporally (in relation to classical languages, principally Latin) and spatially (in relation to the prestigious contemporary languages, principally Italian and French), English was regarded by the privileged, or highly literate, who have left us the written record, as profoundly alienated from, or beneath, itself.

The problem, then, for English at this juncture, or rather, for the sixteenth-century English men whose writings represent the language for us, was how it could be domesticated, or civilized. It was the problem of how the language could colonize itself, or be colonized by its most powerful users. To use the figure of colonization here is not far-fetched, first because, as we have read, English colonization at the time was not simply a process of settling a territorial exterior, but of settling an interior as well, or, rather, one in which the frontier between exterior and interior was blurred, just as Caliban's New-World island appears to float in an Old-World sea; and, secondly and centrally, because the tool of colonization, whether we are discussing New World colonization or colonization 'within' Britain, was translation.

Without connecting the force of translation in colonizing America with the force of translation in colonizing, or civilizing, English itself, scholars have certainly recognized the connection between conquest abroad and translation at home. 'A study of Elizabethan translations', F. O. Matthiessen* tells us,

> is a study of the means by which the Renaissance came to England. The nation had grown conscious of its cultural inferiority to the Continent, and suddenly burned with the desire to excel its rivals in letters, as well as in ships and gold. The translator's work was an act of patriotism. He,

too, as well as the voyager and merchant, could do some good for his country: he believed that foreign books were just as important for England's destiny as the discoveries of her seamen, and he brought them into his native speech with all the enthusiasm of a conquest.[3]

In linking, not incidentally, the voyager and the translator – two figures of transportation – Matthiessen's statement also points to the fact that the 'conquest' of foreign books, their translation into English, was also the means of the conquest of English itself, its translation from barbarity into civility.

Translators, Julia G. Ebel tells us, 'exemplify that quest for cultural and national identity which lies at the heart of Elizabethan literary activity'.[4] This quest for national identity played in the prefaces of translations, like Florio's of Montaigne*, and in some of the most popular English rhetorics, like those of Peacham* and Puttenham*. And translation was the central figure in the play. For consistently, as these texts testify, the test of the vernacular's identity was seen in its ability (or lack thereof) to adequately translate not only prestigious modern languages like French and Italian, but the great classical languages of Latin, Greek, and Hebrew. And this test, if passed, was continually figured as proof of the English language's (and hence the English nation's) civilized status, of the vernacular's emergence from barbarism, in the same way that Cicero in *De Optimo Genere Oratorum* implicitly understands Latin's ability to translate Greek (over and against those who doubted that ability) as a proof of its civility. In his dedicatory introduction to his translation of Pliny's *Natural History* (1601), Philemon Holland, linking this Roman past of translation to the English present, both remembers the period of England's barbarism and celebrates its civilized emergence when he writes of the translation of Latin texts into English as a 'requitall' for Rome's conquest of Britain.[5]

But if English translations of classical texts marked a moment of triumph in England's conquest to civilize what it saw as its own savage past, these translations simultaneously posed a threat to this emerging, civilized identity. It was not that the translations were seen as failures (they weren't, except by an opposed group of scholastics who saw their professional identity, their control of the classics, threatened), nor simply because of the perceived danger, which Holland's introduction also shows, that the pagan religious ideas of the classical authors might subvert the Christian purity of English (for translation was also a means of Christianizing the classics), but because of a fear in certain vocal intellectual circles that the vernacular's contact with foreign languages in the translation process would alienate it through a 'borrowing of other tunges', as Sir John Cheek put it in a prefatory letter included in Thomas Hoby's translation of *The Courtier* (1561). Cheek, along with others like Puttenham and Roger Ascham, wanted the language written 'cleane and pure, unmixt [with] and unmangeled [by]' foreign idiom.[6]

A crucial point should be stressed here. These scholars were not opposed to translation, quite the contrary, as their activities on behalf of it insist. Rather, we might say, they were for a certain kind of translation, one that assimilated the other completely to native ways, 'arraied', as Holland says of his Pliny, 'in the . . . habit' of 'English weed'. If Tudor England was not obsessed with racial purity (at least not as it would be, along with the rest of the West, after, as we have noted, a notion of the *biological* began to emerge in the late eighteenth century), it appears to have been obsessed with linguistic purity; and, indeed, whether implicit or explicit, there appears to have been a close connection between language and racial, or cultural, identity. Arrayed in his English weed, Pliny writes about this connection in the seventh book of his *Natural History*, just after noticing in passing what he finds to be the extravagant blackness of Ethiopians:

> Let us come to one only point, which to speake of seemeth but small, but being deeply weighed and considered, is a matter of exceeding great regard, and that is, the varietie of men's speech; so many tongues and divers languages are amongst them in the world, that one straunger to another seemeth well-neere to be no man at all.[7]

The notion of what is human, this passage suggests, is intimately tied to the perception of linguistic difference. Translation, then, its possibility, we might suppose, is conceived of in early modern Europe as being, quite literally, a humanizing activity, a passport or transport into the fully human of the native speaker's tongue, a tongue that has already been humanized itself by proving its equivalency, or even superiority, to the classical languages.

We must emphasize here that in understanding this 'quest for cultural and national identity' we are dealing not simply with one group of translators, those working in the domestic sphere, but with two groups, one at home and one far abroad, both, nevertheless, engaged in the activity of translating something designated as 'savagery' into something designated as 'civility'. Indeed, it is the figure of translation, in all of its political specificity, that constitutes these two categories; they do not exist prior to or outside of this figure, in some absolute, or natural, or neutral state. We must remember that the activity of intercultural communication, the realm of foreign policy, cannot be separated from the realm of intracultural communication, the realm of domestic policy.

NOTES

1. Cicero, *De Oratore*, trans. E. W. Sutton, The Loeb Classical Library (1942; reprinted Cambridge, MA: Harvard University Press, 1967), I. viii. 32.
2. Richard Foster Jones, *The Triumph of the English Language: A Survey of Opinions Concerning the Vernacular from the Introduction of Printing to the Restoration* (1953; reprinted Stanford: Stanford University Press, 1966), p. 5.
3. F. O. Matthiessen, *Translation, An Elizabethan Art* (Cambridge, MA: Harvard University Press, 1931), p. 3.

4. Julia G. Ebel, 'Translation and Cultural Nationalism in the Reign of Elizabeth', *Journal of the History of Ideas* 30 (1969): 595.
5. *The Historie of the World, Commonly Called, the Natural Historie of C. Plinus Secundus, Translated into English by Philemon Holland, Doctor in Physicke* (London, n.p., 1601).
6. John Cheek, 'A LETTER OF SYR J. CHEEKES to his Loving Frind Mayster THOMAS HOBY', in *The Book of the Courtier from the Italian of Count Baldassare Castiglione: Done into English by Sir Thomas Hoby* (1561; New York: AMS Press, Inc., 1967), p. 12.
7. *Historie of the World*, Book VII, p. 153.

2

'INTRODUCTION: RHIZOME'

Gilles Deleuze and Félix Guattari

Principle of multiplicity: it is only when the multiple is effectively treated as a substantive, 'multiplicity', that it ceases to have any relation to the One as subject or object, natural or spiritual reality, image and world. Multiplicities are rhizomatic, and expose arborescent pseudomultiplicities for what they are. There is no unity to serve as a pivot in the object, or to divide in the subject. There is not even the unity to abort in the object or 'return' in the subject. A multiplicity has neither subject nor object, only determinations, magnitudes, and dimensions that cannot increase in number without the multiplicity changing in nature (the laws of combination therefore increase in number as the multiplicity grows). Puppet strings, as a rhizome or multiplicity, are tied not to the supposed will of an artist or puppeteer but to a multiplicity of nerve fibers, which form another puppet in other dimensions connected to the first:

> Call the strings or rods that move the puppet the weave. It might be objected that *its multiplicity* resides in the person of the actor, who projects it into the text. Granted; but the actor's nerve fibers in turn form a weave. And they fall through the gray matter, the grid, into the undifferentiated . . . The interplay approximates the pure activity of weavers attributed in myth to the Fates or Norns.[1]

From Gilles Deleuze and Félix Guattari (1988) *A Thousand Plateaus: Capitalism and Schizophrenia*, tr. Brian Massumi. London: Athlone Press.

An assemblage is precisely this increase in the dimensions of a multiplicity that necessarily changes in nature as it expands its connections. There are no points or positions in a rhizome, such as those found in a structure, tree, or root. There are only lines. When Glenn Gould* speeds up the performance of a piece, he is not just displaying virtuosity, he is transforming the musical points into lines, he is making the whole piece proliferate. The number is no longer a universal concept measuring elements according to their emplacement in a given dimension, but has itself become a multiplicity that varies according to the dimensions considered (the primacy of the domain over a complex of numbers attached to that domain). We do not have units (*unités*) of measure, only multiplicities or varieties of measurement. The notion of unity (*unité*) appears only when there is a power takeover in the multiplicity by the signifier or a corresponding subjectification proceeding: This is the case for a pivot-unity forming the basis for a set of biunivocal relationships between objective elements or points, or for the One that divides following the law of a binary logic of differentiation in the subject. Unity always operates in an empty dimension supplementary to that of the system considered (overcoding). The point is that a rhizome or multiplicity never allows itself to be overcoded, never has available a supplementary dimension over and above its number of lines, that is, over and above the multiplicity of numbers attached to those lines. All multiplicities are flat, in the sense that they fill or occupy all of their dimensions: we will therefore speak of a *plane of consistency* of multiplicities, even though the dimensions of this 'plane' increase with the number of connections that are made on it. Multiplicities are defined by the outside: by the abstract line, the line of flight or deterritorialization according to which they change in nature and connect with other multiplicities. The plane of consistency (grid) is the outside of all multiplicities. The line of flight marks: the reality of a finite number of dimensions that the multiplicity effectively fills; the impossibility of a supplementary dimension, unless the multiplicity is transformed by the line of flight; the possibility and necessity of flattening all of the multiplicities on a single plane of consistency or exteriority, regardless of their number of dimensions. The ideal for a book would be to lay everything out on a plane of exteriority of this kind, on a single page, the same sheet: lived events, historical determinations, concepts, individuals, groups, social formations. Kleist* invented a writing of this type, a broken chain of affects and variable speeds, with accelerations and transformations, always in a relation with the outside. Open rings. His texts, therefore, are opposed in every way to the classical or romantic book constituted by the interiority of a substance or subject. The war machine-book against the State apparatus-book. *Flat multiplicities of n dimensions* are asignifying and asubjective. They are designated by indefinite articles, or rather by partitives (*some* couchgrass, *some* of a rhizome . . .).

Principle of asignifying rupture: against the oversignifying breaks separating structures or cutting across a single structure. A rhizome may be broken, shattered at a given spot, but it will start up again on one of its old lines, or on new lines. You can never get rid of ants because they form an animal rhizome that can rebound time and again after most of it has been destroyed. Every rhizome contains lines of segmentarity according to which it is stratified, territorialized, organized, signified, attributed, etc., as well as lines of deterritorialization down which it constantly flees. There is a rupture in the rhizome whenever segmentary lines explode into a line of flight, but the line of flight is part of the rhizome. These lines always tie back to one another. That is why one can never posit a dualism or a dichotomy, even in the rudimentary form of the good and the bad. You may make a rupture, draw a line of flight, yet there is still a danger that you will reencounter organizations that restratify everything, formations that restore power to a signifier, attributions that reconstitute a subject – anything you like, from Oedipal resurgences to fascist concretions. Groups and individuals contain microfascisms just waiting to crystallize. Yes, couchgrass is also a rhizome. Good and bad are only the products of an active and temporary selection, which must be renewed.

How could movements of deterritorialization and processes of reterritorialization not be relative, always connected, caught up in one another? The orchid deterritorializes by forming an image, a tracing of a wasp; but the wasp reterritorializes on that image. The wasp is nevertheless deterritorialized, becoming a piece in the orchid's reproductive apparatus. But it reterritorializes the orchid by transporting its pollen. Wasp and orchid, as heterogeneous elements, form a rhizome. It could be said that the orchid imitates the wasp, reproducing its image in a signifying fashion (mimesis, mimicry, lure, etc.). But this is true only on the level of the strata – a parallelism between two strata such that a plant organization on one imitates an animal organization on the other. At the same time, something else entirely is going on: not imitation at all but a capture of code, surplus value of code, an increase in valence, a veritable becoming, a becoming-wasp of the orchid and a becoming-orchid of the wasp. Each of these becomings brings about the deterritorialization of one term and the reterritorialization of the other; the two becomings interlink and form relays in a circulation of intensities pushing the deterritorialization ever further. There is neither imitation nor resemblance, only an exploding of two heterogeneous series on the line of flight composed by a common rhizome that can no longer be attributed to or subjugated by anything signifying. Rémy Chauvin expresses it well: 'the *aparallel evolution* of two beings that have absolutely nothing to do with each other'.[2] More generally, evolutionary schemas may be forced to abandon the old model of the tree and descent. Under certain conditions, a virus can connect to germ cells and transmit itself as the cellular gene of a complex species; moreover, it can take flight, move into the cells of an entirely different species, but not without bringing with it 'genetic information' from the first host (for example, Benveniste and Todaro's current research on a type C virus, with its double connection to baboon DNA and the DNA of certain kinds of domestic cats). Evolutionary schemas would no longer follow models of arborescent descent going from the least to the most differentiated, but instead a rhizome operating immediately in the heterogeneous and jumping from one already differentiated line to another. Once again, there is *aparallel evolution*, of the baboon and the cat; it is obvious that they are not models or copies of each other (a becoming-baboon in the cat does not mean that the cat 'plays' baboon). We form a rhizome with our viruses, or rather our viruses cause us to form a rhizome with other animals. As François Jacob says, transfers of genetic material by viruses or through other procedures, fusions of cells originating in different species, have results analogous to those of 'the abominable couplings dear to antiquity and the Middle Ages'.[3] Transversal communications between different lines scramble the genealogical trees. Always look for the molecular, or even submolecular, particle with which we are allied. We evolve and die more from our polymorphous and rhizomatic flus than from hereditary diseases, or diseases that have their own line of descent. The rhizome is an anti-genealogy.

[. . .]

Principle of cartography and decalcomania: a rhizome is not amenable to any structural or generative model. It is a stranger to any idea of genetic axis or deep structure. A genetic axis is like an objective pivotal unity upon which successive stages are organized; a deep structure is more like a base sequence that can be broken down into immediate constituents, while the unity of the product passes into another, transformational and subjective, dimension. This does not constitute a departure from the representative model of the tree, or root – pivotal taproot or fascicles (for example, Chomsky's* 'tree' is associated with a base sequence and represents the process of its own generation in terms of binary logic). A variation on the oldest form of thought. It is our view that genetic axis and profound structure are above all infinitely reproducible principles of *tracing*. All of tree logic is a logic of tracing and reproduction. In linguistics as in psychoanalysis, its object is an unconscious that is itself representative, crystallized into codified complexes, laid out along a genetic axis and distributed within a syntagmatic structure. Its goal is to describe a de facto state, to maintain balance in intersubjective relations, or to explore an unconscious that is already there from the start, lurking in the dark recesses of memory and language. It consists of tracing, on the basis of an overcoding structure or supporting axis, something that comes ready-made. The tree articulates and hierarchizes tracings; tracings are like the leaves of a tree.

The rhizome is altogether different, a *map and not a tracing*. Make a map, not a tracing. The orchid does not reproduce the tracing of the wasp; it forms a map with the wasp, in a rhizome. What distinguishes the map from the tracing is that it is entirely oriented toward an experimentation in contact with the real.

The map does not reproduce an unconscious closed in upon itself; it constructs the unconscious. It fosters connections between fields, the removal of blockages on bodies without organs, the maximum opening of bodies without organs onto a plane of consistency. It is itself a part of the rhizome. The map is open and connectable in all of its dimensions; it is detachable, reversible, susceptible to constant modification. It can be torn, reversed, adapted to any kind of mounting, reworked by an individual, group, or social formation. It can be drawn on a wall, conceived of as a work of art, constructed as a political action or as a meditation. Perhaps one of the most important characteristics of the rhizome is that it always has multiple entryways; in this sense, the burrow is an animal rhizome, and sometimes maintains a clear distinction between the line of flight as passageway and storage or living strata (cf. the muskrat). A map has multiple entryways, as opposed to the tracing, which always comes back 'to the same'. The map has to do with performance, whereas the tracing always involves an alleged 'competence'. Unlike psychoanalysis, psychoanalytic competence (which confines every desire and statement to a genetic axis or over-coding structure, and makes infinite, monotonous tracings of the stages on that axis or the constituents of that structure), schizoanalysis rejects any idea of pre-traced destiny, whatever name is given to it – divine, anagogic, historical, economic, structural, hereditary, or syntagmatic. (It is obvious that Melanie Klein has no understanding of the cartography of one of her child patients, Little Richard, and is content to make ready-made tracings – Oedipus, the good daddy and the bad daddy, the bad mommy and the good mommy – while the child makes a desperate attempt to carry out a performance that the psycho-analyst totally misconstrues.) Drives and part-objects are neither stages on a genetic axis nor positions in a deep structure; they are political options for problems, they are entryways and exits, impasses the child lives out politically, in other words, with all the force of his or her desire.

[. . .]

History is always written from the sedentary point of view and in the name of a unitary State apparatus, at least a possible one, even when the topic is nomads. What is lacking is a Nomadology, the opposite of a history. There are rare successes in this also, for example, on the subject of the Children's Crusades: Marcel Schwob's book multiplies narratives like so many plateaus with variable numbers of dimensions. Then there is Andrzejewski's book, *Les portes du paradis* (The gates of paradise), composed of a single uninterrupted sentence; a flow of children; a flow of walking with pauses, straggling, and forward rushes; the semiotic flow of the confessions of all the children who go up to the old monk at the head of the procession to make their declarations; a flow of desire and sexuality, each child having left out of love and more or less directly led by the dark posthumous pederastic desire of the count of Vendôme;

all this with circles of convergence. What is important is not whether the flows are 'One or multiple' – we're past that point: there is a collective assemblage of enunciation, a machinic assemblage of desire, one inside the other and both plugged into an immense outside that is a multiplicity in any case.

NOTES

1. Ernst Jünger, *Approches; drogues et ivresse* (Paris: Table Ronde, 1974), p. 304, s. 218.
2. Rémy Chauvin in *Entretiens sur la sexualité*, ed. Max Aron, Robert Courrier and Etienne Wolff (Paris: Plon, 1969), p. 205.
3. François Jacob, *The Logic of Life*, tr. Betty E. Spillman (New York: Pantheon, 1973), pp. 291–2, 311.

3

'TRAVELING GENRES'

Margaret Cohen

Throughout the history of criticism, the institutional organization of literary studies has resulted in a powerful tradition subsuming the novel to the study of nationally based literary formations. In the 1980s and 90s one of the most productive expressions of this national focus was attention to the novel's role in constituting the nation as imagined community. Even at historical moments when images of the nation have been offered on the level of the novel's content, however, national identification was *never* true on the level of the novel's form. To take the case of the nineteenth century, the great era of modern cultural nationalism, writers used a single poetics, historical realism, to provide an image of the modern nation in the United Kingdom, France, Russia, Spain, and Germany. There are local variants of historical realism, certainly, but it is striking that those novels most closely associated with imagining the nation are using an 'international' literary currency, much as modernism was to become the 'international style' in the domain of visual culture and the decorative arts in the following century.

With the recent focus on globalization, critics are now devoting increased attention to this cosmopolitan dimension to the novel's literary history. Their inquiry resumes a long-standing strain of Europeanist comparative work on the novel's travels (see, for example, Bakhtin* and Lukács*), even as it explores non- and supranational literary geographies such as the novel's

From *New Literary History* 34.3 (2003): 481–96.

transatlantic development absent from the earlier historiography of the novel which was focused on the geography of Europe. I hope to contribute to the discussion by asking how the novel travels as a genre. What does it mean to speak of travel and transit in the case of poetic patterns? How do literary codes circulate and translate across distinct yet interrelated cultural and literary fields?

To answer these questions, we run immediately into the long-standing question of what is meant by the notion of genre. For many years, it was a much invoked yet also discredited term, weakly theorized, if theorized at all, sometimes used, as Jameson explains, to characterize a recurring poetic pattern, and sometimes used to describe texts joined by a way of viewing the world. Most recently, the disrepute of genre has only intensified. For poststructuralism, it exemplifies the kind of inert classification that reduces the textuality of literature to static clichés. For readers interested in discourse and broad cultural motifs, genre is 'mere' convention, the bread and butter of traditional literary critics devoid of broad cultural resonance.

The materialist lineage has done the most to preserve genre as an analytic category, because the concept enables discussion of the social dimension of poetics. Generic features of a text are features that extend beyond the text, that are recognized by readers and appropriated by writers. If genres appeal to an audience, so the materialist view runs, it must be because they can do something for this audience, that they offer a compelling solution to some of the unresolved questions that structure its horizons. These unresolved questions can have to do with the state of the literary field and they can have to do with the ideological and social contradictions shaping society as a whole. The genres that are successful find an integrated way of addressing questions of literature and society simultaneously. The materialist approach to genre is a good starting point for distinguishing the multiple levels at which a genre must be working for it to travel. Genres that travel across space, like genres that endure across time, must be able to address social and/or literary questions that are transportable, that can speak to divergent publics or a public defined in its diversity, dispersion, and heterogeneity.

Let us consider the features that distinguish a traveling genre by looking at one of the most important and underdiscussed novelistic forms that appealed to a transatlantic public of the nineteenth century. The genre is maritime fiction, also called nautical fiction, 'naval novels', and 'le roman maritime'. It was invented by James Fenimore Cooper with *The Pilot*, published in 1823. In this novel, Cooper took the codes of historical fiction, pioneered by Walter Scott, to map the boundaries and identity of the nation, and translated them to the supranational space of the open sea. Critics today are often imbued with the Romantic vision of the sea and imagine it as a limit space where history, representation, and social experience break down. From Cooper's first pages,

233

however, he makes clear that the theater of his adventures is a deeply social supranatural realm. *The Pilot* opens:

> A single glance at the map will make the reader acquainted with the position of the eastern coast of the island of Great Britain, as connected with the shores of the opposite continent. Together they form the boundaries of the small sea that has for ages been known to the world as the scene of maritime exploits.[1]

Gesturing towards the national boundaries that historical and realist fiction were concerned to secure, Cooper reverses the relation of foreground to background so the 'boundaries' of the nation now define the edges of the Atlantic that Cooper terms not only the 'small sea', but subsequently 'the disputed ocean', 'the great avenue through which commerce and war have conducted the fleets of . . . Europe'.[2] When Cooper imagines the unity of the Atlantic as the interactions of competing imperial projects, he suggests it as precisely the kind of heterogeneous space that has recently led to its renewed prominence in cross-cultural studies, where the Atlantic is seen to constitute, in Paul Gilroy's formulation, 'one single, complex unit of analysis' defining 'the modern world'.[3] Why should sea fiction travel so fast and so well? The answer to the question is multilayered and complex. One layer is the history of a broader narrative field: overseas voyage narratives were in fact *the* most popular literary works in an international literary field during the rise of the novel and sea fiction is in continuation with this form. The international appeal of overseas-voyage narrative certainly derives from the cross-culture relevance of seafaring during this wave of global expansion and the specifically international world such narrative depicts.

Another layer of the popularity of sea fiction in the nineteenth century is its transportable significance. The history of sentimental fiction amply demonstrates that international thematics are not necessary for a form's portability; that forms with a circumscribed focus can travel well if they perform cultural work that is meaningful across diverse social contexts. Think, for example, of the enthusiastic international reception of Richardson's *Pamela* and *Clarissa*, though both novels depict homespun domestic English heroines. The ability of their sufferings to travel derives from the transportable relevance of the social questions they engage. Sentimental fiction appealed to societies where liberal ideals were taking shape but had not fully emerged, and we can understand it as negotiating one question both central and problematic to the liberal project, which is how to have a society founded on both equality and freedom. Sentimental fiction offers as solution an idealized aesthetic and ethical sphere of sociability, founded on the bonds of sympathy.

A similar transportability characterizes the cultural work of sea fiction, too. We return here to the contextualizing frame of labor and its urgency for the nineteenth century. In depicting a heroism of labor in the form of know-how, sea fiction compensates for the degradation of the labor process. This heroism also offers an explicitly international and potentially universal democratic quality that could be the common denominator of a new association. Sea fiction's international of know-how finds its counterpoint in the international of workers imagined by vanguard political theorists of the 1820s, 30s, and 40s.

Another level at issue in the international success of sea fiction is the transportability of its literary techniques. Adventure fiction has always been one of the most translatable and well traveled among novelistic genres (with an afterlife in the transportability of adventure film today), for its dramatic energy depends on action, not on the specific details or mode of linguistic representation, though of course the interest of those actions may be culturally specific. Nonetheless, the deed has a powerful imaginative existence beyond its linguistic representation and thus is relatively independent of a specific language. To put this another way, seafaring is itself characterized by a precise technical language that is strongly denotative and easily translatable, as is evident from the translatability of practical manuals of seafaring across the conquest of open ocean seafaring. This is precisely the technical vocabulary that features so prominently in active description.

Genres that travel must not only contain elements that can pass from national literary context to national literary context, they also have flexibility and play, offering a way to negotiate cultural differences.

NOTES

1. James Fenimore Cooper, *The Pilot; A Tale of the Sea* (1823), ed. Kay Seymour House (Albany: State University of New York Press, 1986), p. 12.
2. Ibid.
3. Paul Gilroy, *The Black Atlantic* (Cambridge, MA: Harvard University Press, 1993), p. 15.

4

'INTRODUCTION: HISTORY, MEMORY, AND PERFORMANCE'

Joseph Roach

Circum-Atlantic Memory

Both intercultural and internally self-referential occasions of performance mark the connected places and times that constitute what I am calling, as the geo-historical locale for my thesis about memory as substitution, the circum-Atlantic world. As it emerged from the revolutionized economies of the late seventeenth century, this world resembled a vortex in which commodities and cultural practices changed hands many times. The most revolutionary commodity in this economy was human flesh, and not only because slave labor produced huge quantities of the addictive substances (sugar, coffee, tobacco, and – most insidiously – sugar and chocolate in combination) that transformed the world economy and financed the industrial revolution. The concept of a circum-Atlantic world (as opposed to a transatlantic one) insists on the centrality of the diasporic and genocidal histories of Africa and the Americas, North and South, in the creation of the culture of modernity. In this sense, a New World was not discovered in the Caribbean, but one was truly invented there. Newness enacts a kind of surrogation – in the invention of a new England or a new France out of the memories of the old – but it also conceptually erases indigenous populations, contributing to a mentality conducive to the practical implementation of the American Holocaust. While a great deal of the

From Joseph Roach (1996) *Cities of the Dead: Circum-Atlantic Performance*. New York: Columbia University Press.

unspeakable violence instrumental to this creation may have been officially for-gotten, circum-Atlantic memory retains its consequences, one of which is that the unspeakable cannot be rendered forever inexpressible: the most persistent mode of forgetting is memory imperfectly deferred.

For this region-centered conception, which locates the peoples of the Caribbean rim at the heart of an oceanic interculture embodied through per-formance, I am indebted to Paul Gilroy's formulation of the 'Black Atlantic'. In three prescient books, *'There Ain't No Black in the Union Jack': The Cultural Politics of Race and Nation* (1987), *The Black Atlantic: Modernity and Double Consciousness* (1993), and *Small Acts: Thoughts on the Politics of Black Cultures* (1993), Gilroy expands the cultural horizons of modern history in a way that does not begin and end at national borders but charts its course along the dark currents of a world economy that slavery once propelled: 'A new struc-ture of cultural exchange', he writes, 'has been built up across the imperial net-works which once played host to the triangular trade of sugar, slaves and capital'.[1] The idea of circum-Atlantic cultural exchange does not deny Eurocolonial initiatives their place in this history – indeed, it must newly recon-sider and interrogate them – but it regards the results of those initiatives as the insufficiently acknowledged cocreations of an oceanic interculture. This inter-culture shares in the contributions of many peoples along the Atlantic rim – for example, Bambara, Iroquois, Spanish, English, Aztec, Yoruba, and French. I argue [. . .] that the scope of the circum-Atlantic interculture may be discerned most vividly by means of the performances, performance traditions, and the representations of performance that it engendered. This is true, I think, because performances so often carry within them the memory of otherwise forgotten substitutions – those that were rejected and, even more invisibly, those that have succeeded.

The key to understanding how performances worked *within* a culture, recog-nizing that a fixed and unified culture exists only as a convenient but danger-ous fiction, is to illuminate the process of surrogation as it operated *between* the participating cultures. The key, in other words, is to understand how circum-Atlantic societies, confronted with revolutionary circumstances for which few precedents existed, have invented themselves by performing their pasts in the presence of others. They could not perform themselves, however, unless they also performed what and who they thought they were not. By defin-ing themselves in opposition to others, they produced mutual representations from encomiums to caricatures, sometimes in each other's presence, at other times behind each other's backs. In the very form of minstrelsy, for example, as Eric Lott suggests in *Love and Theft: Blackface Minstrelsy and the American Working Class* (1993), there resides the deeply seated and potentially threaten-ing possibility of involuntary surrogation through the act of performance. 'Mimicry', writes Homi K. Bhabha, 'is at once resemblance and menace'.[2] This is so because, even as parody, performances propose possible candidates for succession. They raise the possibility of the replacement of the authors of the representations by those whom they imagined into existence as their definitive opposites.

A number of important consequences ensue from this custom of self-definition by staging contrasts with other races, cultures, and ethnicities. Identity and difference come into play (and into question) simultaneously and coextensively. The process of surrogation continues, but it does so in a climate of heightened anxiety that outsiders will somehow succeed in replacing the original peoples, or autochthons. This process is unstoppable because candidates for surrogation must be tested at the margins of a culture to bolster the fiction that it has a core. That is why the surrogated double so often appears as alien to the culture that reproduces it and that it reproduces. That is why the relentless search for the purity of origins is a voyage not of discovery but of erasure.

The anxiety generated by the process of substitution justifies the complicity of memory and forgetting. In the face of this anxiety – a momentary self-consciousness about surrogation that constitutes what might pass for reflexivity – the alien double may appear in memory only to disappear. That disappearance does not diminish its contributions to cultural definition and preservation; rather, it enables them. Without failures of memory to obscure the mixtures, blends, and provisional antitypes necessary to its production, for example, 'whiteness', one of the major scenic elements of several circum-Atlantic performance traditions, could not exist even as perjury, nor could there flourish more narrowly defined, subordinate designs such as 'Anglo-Saxon Liberty'. Even the immaculate 'guardian angels' who sing the chorus of divine origin in James Thomson's 'Rule Britannia'*, for example, must have recourse to a concept charged with high antithetical seriousness to rhyme with 'waves'. In *Playing in the Dark: Whiteness and the Literary Imagination* (1992), Toni Morrison interprets the angelic chorus exactly: 'The concept of freedom did not emerge in a vacuum. Nothing highlighted freedom – if it did not in fact create it – like slavery'.[3]

On the one hand, forgetting, like miscegenation, is an opportunistic tactic of whiteness. As a Yoruba proverb puts it: 'The white man who made the pencil also made the eraser'. On the other hand, the vast scale of the project of whiteness – and the scope of the contacts among cultures it required – limited the degree to which its foils could be eradicated from the memory of those who had the deepest motivation and the surest means to forget them. At the same time, however, it fostered complex and ingenious schemes to displace, refashion, and transfer those persistent memories into representations more amenable to those who most frequently wielded the pencil and the eraser. In that sense, circum-Atlantic performance is a monumental study in the pleasures and torments of incomplete forgetting. But more obdurate questions persist: Whose forgetting? Whose memory? Whose history?

LOCATIONS AND BEARINGS

Because anything like what might be called coverage of the possible inclusions under the rubric of circum-Atlantic performance would be beyond the imaginable scope of this [argument], I have settled here on the exploration of particular historical formations at specific times at two sites, London and New Orleans. Though remote from one another in obvious respects – antiquity, climate, and cuisine spring quickly to mind – these places are not arbitrarily selected. As river-sited ports of entry linking interior lines of communication to sea lanes, London and New Orleans have histories joined at a pivotal moment in the colonial rivalry of francophone and anglophone interests as they collided in the late seventeenth and eighteenth centuries in North America and the West Indies. Historians have stressed the importance of the conflict between Great Britain and France on sea and land – the 'whale' against the 'elephant' – in the forging of modern nation-states and 'Great Powers'.[4] These European interests, however, were intimately connected with Amerindian and African ones. A significant body of recent historical and ethnohistorical research has reexamined those latter interests as dynamic and inventive (rather than inert) in the face of Eurocolonial expansion. My selective history of circum-Atlantic performance draws heavily on this renovated scholarship of encounter and exchange.

The great Iroquois Confederacy, for instance – a creation of centuries of Forest Diplomacy – negotiated through brilliant intercultural performances the Covenant Chain of trade and military alliances that linked the fur-producing hinterlands of the vast Great Lakes region to the thinly held European enclaves of the eastern seaboard. In 'Culture Theory in Contemporary Ethnohistory' (1988), William S. Simmons describes these diplomatic and trade relations as 'an interaction and confrontation between autonomous social entities, rather than as a one-sided playing out of Eurocolonial myths of manifest destiny'*.[5] Iroquois played a significant and self-promoting role in the geometric proliferation of wealth centered in the triangular trade: carrying a different cargo along each leg of the Atlantic triangle comprising the Americas (raw materials), Europe (manufactured goods), and Africa (human beings), the holds of merchant ships never had to cross blue water empty. The consequences of the ensuing material productions are incalculable; the mother of hemispheric superstructural invention, they provide a common matrix for [. . .] diversified performance genres.

Even for the largest system, however, heuristic opportunity, like God or the Devil, is in the details. One site of circum-Atlantic memory that I propose to excavate is located in London in 1710, during the performance-rich state visit to Queen Anne's court by four Iroquois 'Kings'. Among other public exhibitions and entertainments, a staging of Sir William Davenant's operatic version of Shakespeare's *Macbeth* honored their embassy, a performance during which their hosts insisted that the Native Americans be placed in full view onstage. Such an imposition need not have been as alien or as intimidating as might be supposed. Experienced in staging Condolence Councils, those great intersocietal mourning and peace rituals that mediated among Dutch, French, English, and diverse Algonquian and Iroquoian interests, the Mohawks referred to themselves as *onckwe*, 'the Real People'. As such, they believed themselves descended from Deganawidah, the semidivine peacemaker who, with the aid of Hiawatha, overcame witchcraft and the cyclical violence of feuding clans to establish the Great League of Peace and Power. Thereafter the league existed to settle grievances, condole losses, and negotiate alliances through gift exchange and ritual performance of speeches, songs, and dances. The Kings came to London to promote the Anglo-Iroquois invasion of French Canada in the interests of the fur trade, and they arrived at a decisive moment during the War of the Spanish Succession*, when events were leading up to the Treaties of Utrecht in 1713–14.

According to *The New Cambridge Modern History*, the watershed Peace of Utrecht – whereby Great Britain acquired the coveted *Asiento*, the monopoly on the slave trade in the Spanish West Indies – 'marks the passing of the Mediterranean as the centre of world trade and power rivalries [when] attention shifted to the Atlantic'.[6] Alfred Thayer Mahan, summarizing the War of the Spanish Succession in *The Influence of Sea Power Upon History* (1890), the most materially influential work of academic theory written in the past century, describes its consequences: 'Before that war England was one of the sea powers; after it she was *the* sea power, without any second'.[7] In the festival panegyric *Windsor-Forest* (1713), a poetical celebration of the Peace of Utrecht, Alexander Pope imagined the glorious deforestation of rural England in the cause of maritime empire:

> Thy Trees, fair *Windsor*! now shall leave their Woods,
> And Half thy Forests rush into my Floods,
> Bear *Britain*'s Thunder, and her Cross display,
> To the bright Regions of the rising Day.[8]

[. . .] The geopolitical advantages won by Great Britain in this general peace and the supremacy that the Royal Navy had attained motivated the French to attempt to consolidate their position in North America, including strategic development of the territory bearing the name of Louis XIV. They did this in part by situating a fortified city in Louisiana near the mouth of the Mississippi River, roughly equidistant along water routes between Canada and their island possessions in the West Indies, demarcating a great arc of Gallic entitlement arrayed to contest further trans-Appalachian expansion by the Anglo-Americans and the Real People.

We now know that success did not ultimately crown the French grand strategy. But in the meantime, contemporaneously with the apogee of the North

American Covenant Chain, the French in colonial Louisiana relocated significant numbers of West Africans, principally Bambara, from one African regional interculture, Senegambia, into an area already possessing highly developed Amerindian performance cultures. Circumstances favored the reciprocal acculturation of Creoles of various lineages within a unique network of African, American, and European practices. These included mortuary rituals, carnival festivities, and a multitude of musical and dance forms that others would eventually describe (and appropriate) under the rubric of jazz. At the same time, the Africans brought with them vital necessities such as skilled agriculture: 'The survival of French Louisiana', writes Gwendolyn Midlo Hall in her magisterial *Africans in Colonial Louisiana: The Development of Afro-Creole Culture in the Eighteenth Century* (1992), 'was due not only to African labor but also to African technology'.[9] Under the superimpositions of slavery, as well as around its fringes beyond the margins of the *ciprière* (swamp), there flourished a powerful culture that reinvented Africa – and ultimately America – within the only apparently impermeable interstices of European forms. In that respect, Louisiana participated in the formation of the complex identities of the circum-Caribbean rim (Fiehrer), even as it negotiated its incremental assimilation into the hypothetical monoculture of Anglo North America.

The other main site that I explore, then, is located in the records of the long 'Americanization' (that is, Anglification and Africanization) of Latin New Orleans, a process that begins before the Louisiana Purchase in 1803 and continues to be reenacted in the streets of this performance-saturated city today. A principal public instrument of this reenactment remains Mardi Gras, nominally a French cultural residue, which long ago was appropriated by so many competing interests of ethnicity, nationality, class, race, religion, gender, and caste that its meaning can be assessed appropriately only in relationship to other genres of circum-Atlantic and Caribbean performance. Through its complex hierarchy of ritualized memory, Mardi Gras stages an annual spectacle of cultural surrogations, including the multilayered imbrication of carnivalesque license, symbolic freedom marches by descendants of Afro-Amerindian Maroons, and the discursive claims of 'Anglo-Saxon Liberty' as realized in float parades and debutante balls. The history of performance in New Orleans supports the wisdom of the exhortation that opens Hall's account of African Louisiana: ' "National history" must be transcended, and colonial history treated within a global context'.[10]

MATERIALS AND METHODS

The various contributors to *Questions of Evidence: Proof, Practice, and Persuasion Across the Disciplines* (1991), a compendium of essays originally published in *Critical Inquiry*, explore the interdisciplinary dimensions of the issues set forth in the editors' introduction: 'the configuration of the fact-evidence distinction in different disciplines and historical moments'.[11] By creating a category called 'circum-Atlantic performance' that intentionally cuts across disciplinary boundaries and the conventional subcategories and periodizations within them, I have incurred an obligation to be explicit about the materials and methods – the evidence – I have used to imagine what that category entails.

One important strategy of performance research today is to juxtapose living memory as restored behavior against a historical archive of scripted records. In the epigraph at the head of this chapter from his *History and Memory* (1992), Jacques Le Goff sets out the variety of mnemonic materials – speech, images, gestures – that supplement or contest the authority of 'documents' in the historiographic tradition of the French *annalists*.[12] Their vast projects – for instance, histories of private life, histories of death, or histories of memory itself – attend especially to those performative practices that maintain (and invent) human continuities, leaving their traces in diversified media, including the living bodies of the successive generations that sustain different social and cultural identities.

Summarizing the fruits of research into the transmission of culture in societies distinguished by different modalities of communication, Le Goff identifies 'three major interests' of those 'without writing': (1) myth, particularly myths of origin; (2) genealogies, particularly of leading families; and (3) practical formulas of daily living and special observances, particularly those 'deeply imbued with religious magic'.[13] While acknowledging the preliminary usefulness of such formulations, typically organized under the portmanteau concept of orality, performance studies goes on to question the assumption that the 'interests' Le Goff defines do not also manifest themselves in societies 'with writing' – and, for that matter, in those with print, electronic media, and mass communications. Performance studies complicates the familiar dichotomy between speech and writing with what Kenyan novelist and director Ngugi wa Thiong'o calls 'orature'. Orature comprises a range of forms, which, though they may invest themselves variously in gesture, song, dance, processions, storytelling, proverbs, gossip, customs, rites, and rituals, are nevertheless produced alongside or within mediated literacies of various kinds and degrees. In other words, orature goes beyond a schematized opposition of literacy and orality as transcendent categories; rather, it acknowledges that these modes of communication have produced one another interactively over time and that their historic operations may be usefully examined under the rubric of performance. Ngugi defines the power of orature in collective memory aphoristically: 'He is a sweet singer when everybody joins in. The sweet songs last longer, too'.[14]

The historical implications of the concept of orature, though not necessarily under that name, have engaged the attention of scholars in a number of disciplines. In a recent study of the role of theatricality in the early cultural history of the United States, for instance, *Declaring Independence: Jefferson, Natural*

Language, and the Culture of Performance (1993), Jay Fliegelman begins with the significant but long-neglected fact that the Declaration of Independence was just that – a script written to be spoken aloud as oratory. He goes on to document the elocutionary dimension of Anglo-American self-invention, which Thomas Jefferson himself defined in comparison to the expressive speech of Native Americans, on the one hand, and Africans, on the other.[15] Under the close scrutiny of circum-Atlantic memory, no material event, spoken or written, can remain 'pure', despite Jefferson's special pleading for the revival of Anglo-Saxon as the primal tongue of essential law and liberty.

That the chant of the Declaration of Independence calls on the spirits of Jefferson's Anglo-Saxon ancestors to authorize his claims – to inalienable rights, including the right to revolt against tyranny – recalls the ritual of freedom described by C. L. R. James in *The Black Jacobins: Toussaint L'Ouverture and the San Domingo Revolution* (1938):

> Carrying torches to light their way, the leaders of the revolt met in an open space in the thick forests of the Morne Rouge, a mountain overlooking Le Cap. There Boukman gave the last instructions and, after Voodoo incantations and the sucking of the blood of a stuck pig, he stimulated his followers by a prayer spoken in creole, which, like so much spoken on such occasions, has remained. 'The god who created the sun which gives us light . . . orders us to revenge our wrongs. He will direct our arms and aid us. Throw away the symbol of the god of the whites who has so often caused us to weep, and listen to the voice of liberty, which speaks in the hearts of us all'.[16]

Endowed by their Creator with liberty, whose voice spoke through them, the Haitians set about the task of altering and abolishing their government with spoken words, which they then took the trouble to write down.

Taking cognizance of the interdependence of orature and literature, the materials of the present study are thematized under categories of those restored behaviors that function as vehicles of cultural transmission. Each category pairs a form of collective memory with the enactments that embody it through performance: death and burials, violence and sacrifices, laws and (dis)obedience, commodification and auctions, origins and segregation. All of these may be written about, of course, but even the laws need not have been written down. They remain partially recorded in the literature, but they are actually remembered and put into practice through orature, a practice that may be prolonged, supplemented, or revised by printed and photographic representations of the performance events.

Although these thematic materials are broadly conceived in the amplitude of circum-Atlantic relations, my method is to study them at narrowly delimited sites. My observations of the street performances of Mardi Gras in New

Orleans, for instance, have been accumulating since 1991. That was the last year in which the most traditional of the old-line carnival 'krewes' paraded: the passage of a new civil rights ordinance by the New Orleans City Council in December of that year gave the century-and-a-half-old men's clubs the choice of desegregating their membership or staying home. The assertion of legal control over carnival by the City of New Orleans revived memories of the carnival krewes' central role in planning and executing the armed overthrow of the racially integrated government of William Pitt Kellogg in 1874. Known to historians as 'the Battle of Liberty Place', this was in fact a bloody riot incited by a race-baiting elite. The ordinance controversy, played out for three years in the council chambers and the media as well as in the streets and running concurrently with the sudden political rise of Klansman David Duke, burst open a deep, suppurating sore that festers in local memory more poisonously than history can write.

The method of observation that I employ takes its cue from 'Walking in the City', an essay included in the 'Spatial Practices' section of Michel de Certeau's *Practice of Everyday Life* (1984). 'To walk', de Certeau notes, 'is to lack a place'.[17] But to walk is also to gain an experience of the cityscape that is conducive to mapping the emphases and contradictions of its special memory. De Certeau looks for key points of articulation between human behavior and the built environment, noting the 'pedestrian speech acts' uttered by authors 'whose bodies follow the thicks and thins of an urban "text" they write without being able to read it'.[18] Quotidian 'speech acts' offer a rich assortment of year-round performances, particularly in a polyglot entrepot and tourist mecca like New Orleans, but festivals – 'time out of time' – intensify and enlarge them to Gargantuan proportions. As the Mardi Gras revelers take over the streets, canalized by police barricades and conditioned reflexes, their traditional gestures and masked excesses activate the spatial logic of a city built to make certain powers and privileges not only seasonally visible but perpetually reproducible. The crowded spaces become a performance machine for celebrating the occult origin of their exclusions. Walking in the city makes this visible.

Meanwhile, around the public housing projects and under the highway overpasses, the Mardi Gras Indians – 'gangs' of African-Americans who identify with Native American tribes and parade on unannounced routes costumed in heart-stoppingly beautiful hand-sewn 'suits' – proudly transform their neighborhoods into autonomous places of embodied memory. More intensely than any of the float parades or promiscuous masquerades of Mardi Gras, the Indians restage events of circum-Atlantic encounter and surrogation in which European experience remains only obliquely acknowledged, if at all. Their bodies document those doublings through musical speech, images, and gestures [. . .] As George Lipsitz points out in *Time Passages: Collective Memory and American Popular Culture* (1990), 'the Mardi Gras Indians of New Orleans offer an important illustration of the persistence of popular narratives in the modern world'[19] (see also Lipsitz, *Dangerous Crossroads*). Their spectacular appearances at Mardi Gras season (which nonetheless remain aloof from it) are only one genre of performance in the year-round cornucopia of Afrocentric forms, among them, the Second Line parades staged by numerous social aid and pleasure clubs and ritual celebrations of death 'with music', popularly known as jazz funerals.

The three-sided relationship of memory, performance, and substitution becomes most acutely visible in mortuary ritual. This study closely attends to those epiphanies. In any funeral, the body of the deceased performs the limits of the community called into being by the need to mark its passing. United around a corpse that is no longer inside but not yet outside of its boundaries, the members of a community may reflect on its symbolic embodiment of loss and renewal. In a jazz funeral, the deceased is generally accompanied at least part of the way to the cemetery by a brass band and a crowd of mourners who follow an elegant grand marshall (or 'Nelson').

After the body is 'cut loose' – sent on its way in the company of family members – a popular celebration commences, less like a forgetting than a replenishment. As Willie Pajaud, longtime trumpeter for the Eureka Brass Band, once put it: 'I'd rather play a funeral than eat a turkey dinner'. Animated by a 'joyful noise', supported in many instances by the testimony of deep, spirit-world faith, the dead seem to remain more closely present to the living in New Orleans than they do elsewhere – and not only because they are traditionally interred in tombs above ground. Walking in the city makes this audible.

Read in the context created by the sounds and sights of these restored behaviors, then, the documents concerning the London visit of the Iroquois Kings take on a new and different kind of life. In addition to the various performances they attended while in London – a puppet show, a cockfight, a military review, a concert, a Shakespearean tragedy – the Native Americans created other events by their spectacular passages through the streets (Altick). They swept up those walking through the city in impromptu festivals: 'When the four *Indian Kings* were in this Country about a Twelve-month ago', Joseph Addison* recalled, speaking through the persona of Mr Spectator, 'I often mix'd with the Rabble and followed them a whole Day together, being wonderfully struck with the Sight of every thing that is new or uncommon'.[20] Addison's ambiguous modifier – who is being struck with new sights here? The Kings? The Rabble? Mr Spectator? – stages what might be termed the 'ethnographic surrealism' of this circum-Atlantic event. One important reason why popular performance events entered into the records at this time in greater detail than is usual for such ephemera is that the Kings attended a number of them, while their invited presence at others was heavily advertised to boost attendance.

The daily repertoires of the two official theaters, Drury Lane and the Queen's Theatre, Haymarket, are particularly worthy of attention in this regard. In addition to the performance of *Macbeth* at which the Kings were present, two other revivals held pointed circum-Atlantic interest: John Dryden's *The Indian Emperour; or, The Conquest of Mexico by the Spaniards* (1665) and Thomas Southerne's *Oroonoko; or, The Royal Slave* (1694). At a time of institutional canonization of Shakespeare as the national poet, however, not all the relevant high-culture performances took place onstage. On the same day that the Native Americans departed from England, the great Shakespearean actor Thomas Betterton was buried in Westminster Abbey. His passing held an epoch-marking meaning for many, including Richard Steele*, who published a eulogy in *The Tatler*. Betterton's fifty-year career spanned the reigns of Charles II, James II, William and Mary, and Queen Anne; and Steele remarks on the edifying spectacle of attending this 'last Office'.[21] The breadth of the address of this eulogy, which begins with 'Men of Letters and Education' and then quickly enlarges to embrace all 'Free-born People',[22] highlights the powers Steele once attributed to Betterton's moving, speaking body in life but now invests in the stillness of his corpse. That is the power of summoning an imagined community into being. The hailing of the 'Free-born', in their role as enthusiasts for enactments of 'what is great and noble in Human Nature' by those who 'speak justly, and move gracefully',[23] is piquantly juxtaposed to the critique of social and musical cacophony in the immediately preceding number of *The Tatler*, which ends with an unfavorable allusion to 'the Stamping Dances of the *West Indians* or *Hottentots*'.[24]

Steele's account of Betterton's funeral demonstrates the importance of *The Tatler* and *Spectator* to the way in which I am trying to understand the role of performance in circum-Atlantic memory. In *Imagined Communities: Reflections on the Origin and Spread of Nationalism* (1983; rev. 1991), Benedict Anderson stresses the role of printed media in the vernacular, particularly the newspaper, in the formation of modern national consciousness out of dynastic, feudal, and sacred communities.[25] Like the obsequies performed at tombs of the Unknown Soldier, which Anderson also highlights,[26] the burial of an actor, a practitioner of a despised profession, in the cathedral of English dynastic memory suggests a cultural use of marginal identities to imagine a new kind of community. Attending such a ritual performance as a friend of the deceased, Steele the pioneering journalist grasped – or created – its significance as national news.

Steele and Addison characteristically turned local performances into print, for circulation among an expanding audience of readers, and then print into performances, for the edification of many more listeners who heard the papers read aloud in public places. The innovative effects of this form of orature have been convincingly demonstrated on one side of the Atlantic by Michael G. Ketcham in *Transparent Designs: Reading, Performance, and Form in the Spectator Papers* (1985) and on the other by Michael Warner in *The Letters of the Republic: Publication and the Public Sphere in Eighteenth-Century America* (1990). Reports of the authorial deaths of Addison and Steele would seem to have been exaggerated. Theatre historians, however, attempting to reconstruct the acting of Betterton and others from accounts in *The Tatler* and *The Spectator*, have excerpted and anthologized only the choice descriptive passages concerning the stage. To a historian who views theatre in the context of many kinds of performance, such passages take on a more robust life when they are returned to their original place among the wonderful peripatetic observations of the various restored behaviors of Augustan London.

NOTES

1. Paul Gilroy, *'There Ain't no Black in the Union Jack': The Cultural Politics of Race and Nation* (Chicago: University of Chicago Press, 1987), p. 157.
2. Homi K. Bhabha, *The Location of Culture* (London: Routledge, 1994), p. 86.
3. Toni Morrison, *Playing in the Dark: Whiteness and the Literary Imagination* (New York: Vintage, 1992), p. 38.
4. Linda Colley, *Britons: Forging the Nation, 1707–1837* (New Haven: Yale University Press, 1992), p. 1.
5. William S. Simmons, 'Culture Theory in Contemporary Ethnohistory', *Ethnohistory* 35 (1988): 6.
6. J. S. Bromley (ed.), *The New Cambridge Modern History*, vol. 6, *The Rise of Great Britain and Russia, 1688–1715/25* (Cambridge: Cambridge University Press, 1971), p. 571.
7. Alfred Thayer Mahan, *The Influence of Sea Power upon History, 1660–1783* (1890; reprinted. New York: Dover, 1987), p. 225.
8. Alexander Pope, *The Poems of Alexander Pope*, vol. 1, *Pastoral Poetry and An Essay on Criticism*, ed. E. Audra and Aubrey Williams (New Haven: Yale Unversity Press, 1961), vol. 1, p. 189.
9. Gwendolyn Midlo Hall, *Africans in Colonial Louisiana: The Development of Afro-Creole Culture in the Eighteenth Century* (Baton Rouge: Louisiana State University Press, 1992), p. 121.
10. Ibid., p. xii.
11. James Chandler, Arnold I. Davidson, and Harry Harootunian (eds), *Questions of Evidence: Proof, Practice, and Persuasion Across the Disciplines* (Chicago: Chicago University Press, 1991), p. 2.
12. Jacques Le Goff, *History and Memory*, tr. Steven Rendall and Elizabeth Claman (New York: Columbia University Press, 1992), p. xvii.
13. Ibid., p. 58.
14. Ngugi wa Thiong'o, interview with Bettye J. Parker, in G. D. Killam (ed.), *Critical Perspectives on Ngugi wa Thiong'o* (Washington, DC: Three Continents, 1984), p. 61.
15. Jay Fliegelman, *Declaring Independence: Jefferson, Natural Language, and the Culture of Performance* (Stanford: Stanford University Press, 1993), pp. 98, 192.
16. C. L. R. James, *The Black Jacobins: Toussaint L'Ouverture and the San Domingo Revolution* (1938; 2nd edn, New York: Random House, 1989), p. 87.
17. Michel de Certeau, *The Practice of Everyday Life*, tr. Steven Rendall (Berkeley: University of California, 1984), p. 103.
18. Ibid., p. 93.
19. George Lipsitz, *Time Passages: Collective Memory and American Popular Culture* (Minneapolis: University of Minnesota Press, 1990), p. 234.

20. *The Spectator*, ed. Donald F. Bond, 5 vols (Oxford: Clarendon, 1965), vol. 1, p. 211.
21. *The Tatler*, ed. Donald F. Bond, 3 vols (Oxford: Clarendon, 1987), vol. 2, p. 422.
22. Ibid., p. 423.
23. Ibid., pp. 422–3.
24. Ibid., p. 421.
25. Benedict Anderson, *Imagined Communities: Reflections on the Origin and Spread of Nationalism* (London: Verso, 1991), pp. 33–6.
26. Ibid., p. 9.

5

'ROMANCE AND RATIONAL ORTHODOXY'

Michael Davitt Bell

William Congreve* and Clara Reeve*, among others in England, gave currency to the 'generic' distinction between romance and novel, in terms similar to those Hawthorne used in the *Seven Gables* preface; but English writers generally defined romance in psychological or ethical rather than aesthetic terms, and they went far beyond the formal discrimination of genres to raise questions of intention and effect. As J. M. S. Tompkins describes prevailing British opinion at the end of the eighteenth century:

> 'Romance' implied a seductive delusion, pathetic or ludicrous, according to the quality of the victim and the angle of the commentator. . . . To be romantic [was] to prefer the satisfactions of imagination to those of reason.[1]

'Romance' was the term for *any* tale or novel that acknowledged itself to be a work of invention rather than imitation, of 'fancy' rather than 'reason'. 'We now use the term *romance*', wrote Sir Walter Scott in 1827, 'as synonymous with fictitious composition'.[2]

The same primary connotations obtained in contemporaneous American usage. In 1824, for instance, General William Sullivan declared the facts and scenes of the Revolution 'so strange and heroic that they resemble ingenious

From Michael Davitt Bell (1980) *The Development of American Romance: The Sacrifice of Relation*. Chicago: Chicago University Press, 1980.

fables, or the dreams of romance, rather than the realities of authentic history'.[3] Or there is the account of the persecution of his sect by the Mormon saint, Parley P. Pratt: 'would to God it were a dream – a novel, a romance that had no existence save in the wild regions of fancy'.[4] For Pratt, clearly, 'novel' and 'romance' are virtually synonymous; generic distinction is subordinate to a more basic discrimination between all fiction and actuality. In the same vein, in 1800, Charles Brockden Brown distinguished romance not from the novel but from history. Romance, for him, was not one kind of fiction as opposed to another but all fiction as opposed to fact.

This is the most prevalent distinction in nineteenth-century critical terminology. In an 1836 review of Bulwer's *Rienzi*, Poe discriminated carefully between the author's 'scrupulous fidelity to all the main events in the *public* life of his hero' and 'the relief afforded through the personages of pure romance which form the filling in of the picture'.[5] In 1857 Irving informed a correspondent who had inquired about the truth of the personal portions of *The Alhambra*: 'Everything in the work relating to myself, and to the actual inhabitants of the Alhambra, is unexaggerated fact. It was only in the legends that I indulged in *romancing*'.[6] Of his campaign biography of Franklin Pierce, Hawthorne wrote nervously in 1852: 'though the story is true, yet it took a romancer to do it'.[7] And in Melville's *Confidence-Man* the Cosmopolitan replies to Charlie Noble's question about whether the story of Charlemont is 'true':

> Of course not; it is a story which I told with the purpose of every story-teller – to amuse. Hence, if it seem strange to you, that strangeness is the romance; it is what contrasts it with real life; it is the invention, in brief, the fiction as opposed to the fact.[8]

The fundamental property of romance, then, was conceived to be its departure from 'truth', from 'fact', its cutting of the Jamesian cable tying imagination to 'reality'. To describe romance in this way was not, finally, to distinguish it from realism or mimesis, for the general run of nineteenth-century comments on romance distinguish it not from *realism* but from *reality* – and this point is crucial. Romance was not an abstract or symbolic representation of objective reality; as we shall see, it was involved with objective representation only when 'mingled' with history. Furthermore, even 'purely' aesthetic descriptions of romance, defining it in terms of liberated formal experiment, do not quite coincide with nineteenth-century discussions of the mode. American critics and commentators, at least before Poe, were far less concerned with form itself, with 'beauty', than with the sources of imaginative fictional utterance. For them the 'unreality' of romance was above all psychological. In Irving's *Tales of a Traveller*, following the burlesque 'Adventure of the Popkins Family', a skeptical Englishman condemns the tale as 'a mere piece of romance, originating in the heated brain of the narrator'.[9] What matters most, then, in nineteenth-century discussions of romance, is neither content nor form but psychological motive and effect.

At the heart of this theory of romance, radically dualistic in its separation of fancy and reason, imagination and actuality, was a profound concern with the origins of fictional (as opposed to historical) rhetoric – origins perhaps masked, 'for our illusion', by historical 'mingling', but origins nevertheless intensely there. 'My *instinct*', as Melville wrote to his British publisher, John Murray, in 1848, 'is to out with the Romance, & let me say that instincts are prophetic, & better than acquired wisdom'.[10] To 'out with the Romance' was first of all to substitute 'instinct' for 'acquired wisdom', fantasy for reason. This was the context in which Brown, Irving, Poe, Hawthorne, and Melville chose to become 'romancers'. To 'out with the Romance' was, to paraphrase James, to sacrifice the 'relation' between the car of imagination and the reality of earth. Romance emanated from, and appealed to, the unfettered imagination, the 'heated brain', of narrator or reader. It was therefore both deeply fascinating and deeply subversive.

It was inevitable that the theory of romance should turn, at least initially, on questions of psychology and morality. Well into the nineteenth century it was the consensus of American ministers, moralists, and critics that the writing or reading of imaginative fiction was at best frivolous and usually dangerous. As Thomas Jefferson wrote of what he called 'the inordinate passion prevalent for novels:

> When this poison infects the mind, it destroys its tone and revolts it against wholesome reading. Reason and fact, plain and unadorned, are rejected. Nothing can engage attention unless dressed in all the figments of fancy, and nothing so bedecked comes amiss. The result is a bloated imagination, sickly judgment, and disgust towards all the real businesses of life.[11]

Similarly, in a chapter on 'Romances and Novels' in his *Brief Retrospect of the Eighteenth Century* (1803), the Reverend Samuel Miller complained that fiction-reading has 'a tendency too much to engross the mind, to fill it with artificial views, and to diminish the taste for more solid reading'. 'To fill the mind with unreal and delusive pictures of life', he insisted, 'is, in the end, to beguile it from sober duty, and to cheat it of substantial enjoyment'. Fiction and imagination, according to received opinion, were antithetical to and subversive of a whole series of American values: 'reason and fact', 'the real businesses of life', 'sober duty'. They were thus regarded with open hostility.[12]

To be sure, this hostility was not uniquely American. Still, historical circumstance and intellectual tradition conspired to make it especially acute in the new nation. When British fiction emerged at the beginning of the eighteenth century, England already had a long and distinguished heritage of nonutilitarian literature, a heritage notably lacking in the colonies; and by the late 1780s, when Americans were beginning to write novels and romances in significant numbers, England boasted an achieved tradition in fiction in the works of Defoe, Richardson, Fielding, Smollett, Sterne, and their contemporaries. These writers were frequently attacked in England for immorality, although Richardson was largely protected by his alleged concern for promoting and rewarding virtue. But whatever the protests lodged against their works, these men had succeeded; they had established a precedent. Before Cooper and Irving, there were no such exemplary careers in America, with the brief and hardly encouraging exception of Charles Brockden Brown's.

Orthodox American opinion, religious or secular, confronted the aspiring romancer with a set of rationalist axioms – aesthetic, metaphysical, political, and ultimately psychological. Rhetoric was inferior to meaning, possibility to actuality, stimulation to stability, imagination to reason or judgment. Imagination, if not strictly controlled, posed a threat both to individual happiness and to social cohesion. These assumptions, generally pervasive in Colonial America, were particularly so in Puritan New England, and they were reinforced by the spread of Scottish Common Sense* philosophy in the late eighteenth and early nineteenth century.

Terence Martin has detailed the terms in which Scottish thought denounced fiction, but they are worth summarizing here, since they were also the terms used to discuss fiction in America before the Civil War. Imagination, the Scottish writers agreed, was 'naturally' subordinate to judgment or reason, but it was all too easy, as Dugald Stewart warned in 1792, 'by long habits of solitary reflection to reverse this order of things and to weaken the attention to sensible objects to so great a degree, as to leave the conduct almost wholly under the influence of imagination'. As an antidote, Stewart recommended – in terms consistently echoed by Irving, Hawthorne, and others – '*mingling* [my emphasis] gradually in the business and amusements of the world'. Imagination, Stewart admitted, was the source of sensibility, sympathy, and genius. Unchecked, however, it led the mind into melancholy and even insanity. 'To a man of an ill-regulated imagination', he wrote, 'external circumstances only serve as hints to excite his own thoughts, and the conduct he pursues has in general far less reference to his real situation, than to some imaginary one in which he conceives himself to be placed'. Given these dangerous tendencies, literary encouragement of fantasy was clearly folly. For 'those intellectual and moral habits, which ought to be formed by actual experience of the world, may be gradually so accommodated to the dreams of poetry and romance as to disqualify us for the scene in which we are destined to act'.[13]

A threat to individual happiness, imagination was also deeply dangerous to social order. 'The imagination', wrote Hugh Blair, whose *Lectures on Rhetoric and Belles Lettres* (1783) were widely influential in America, 'is most vigorous and predominant in youth; with advancing years, [it] cools, and the under-standing ripens'. More characteristic of youth than of stable maturity, imagin-ative literature was also more typical of primitive than of modern societies and partook, therefore, of the other salient quality of youth and barbarism: 'In the infancy of all societies', according to Blair, 'men are much under the dominion of imagination and passion'. 'Imagination and passion'. That this equation was by 1783 a commonplace does not diminish its importance. There was, as yet, no explicit identification of fantasy with sublimated eroticism, although the idea is implicit in most Scottish-influenced writing and would come very close to the surface in the works of American romancers. But the Scottish philoso-phers and their American pupils were mainly interested in effects and results, and these, to them, were perfectly clear. 'Poetry', in Blair's definition, was 'the language of passion, or of enlivened imagination'.[14] It was on 'understanding' that society had to rely for order and stability. Hence the hysterical fears of orthodox ministers and moralists in the aftermath of the French Revolution. The American Samuel Miller saw the corrupting tendencies of imaginative fiction thus:

> Every opportunity is taken to attack some principle of morality under the title of a 'prejudice'; to ridicule the duties of domestic life, as flowing from 'contracted' and 'slavish' views; to deny the sober pursuits of upright industry as 'dull' and 'spiritless'; and, in a word, to frame an apology for suicide, adultery, prostitution, and the indulgence of every propensity for which a corrupt heart can plead an inclination.[15]

It is significant that Blair and his contemporaries associated imagination with the very state of society to which Rousseau and his followers appealed for the sanction of their revolutionary doctrines.

One should be cautious in discussing the 'influence' of Scottish philosophy in America. It did not so much introduce new attitudes as provide a new and con-veniently secular means of supporting what were already firm convictions. For this very reason, the vocabulary it contributed took hold in the United States with extraordinary tenacity, and – what matters here – our writers of fiction were firmly locked in its grasp. Brown expressed his enthusiasm for Blair's *Rhetoric* as early as 1787. Poe, we are told, 'knew at first hand Hugh Blair's *Lectures on Rhetoric and Belles Lettres*, Lord Kames's *Elements of Criticism*, the critical writings of Archibald Alison, Thomas Reid, and especially Dugald Stewart'.[16] At Bowdoin, during Hawthorne's undergraduate years, freshmen studied Blair's *Rhetoric* in the third trimester; in the first two terms of the senior year they read through Stewart's *Philosophy*.

It is more difficult to discover the extent of Irving's and Melville's reading in Common Sense philosophy and aesthetics, but the influence of at least the atti-tudes conveyed by Scottish thought is clear in both. In 1824, for instance, Irving warned a nephew against entering 'the seductive but treacherous paths of literature' in thoroughly conventional terms:

> Do not meddle much with works of the imagination – Your imagination needs no feeding, indeed it is a mental quality that always takes care of itself; and is too apt to interfere with the others. Strengthen your judgment; cultivate habits of close thinking, and in all your reading let KNOWLEDGE be the great object.[17]

As for Melville, orthodox condemnation of fiction provided him with one of his major themes. In 1810 the Reverend James Gray, educated in Scotland and very much under the influence of Common Sense thought, warned a young Philadelphia audience against the dangers of fiction:

> Permit me to caution you against ever making the characters of romance a standard by which to judge of character in real life. For . . . perhaps it may be found that no persons are more apt to err and blunder, when introduced on the stage of real life than those whose imaginations have been deeply impressed with the characters of fictitious composition.[18]

Strikingly similar sentiments are expressed briefly by Melville in the guidebook episode in *Redburn* and at length in *Pierre*, in the hero's discovery, after trying to live his life according to literary models, that a work of art, 'though a thing of life, was, after all, but a thing of breath, evoked by the wanton magic of a creative hand'.[19] Especially close to Gray – although Melville had surely never read his address – is the narrator's question in *The Confidence-Man*, whether 'after poring over the best novels professing to portray human nature, the studious youth will still run the risk of being too often at fault upon actually entering the world'.[20] It matters not at all, in the final analysis, whether Melville read Gray, or Stewart, or any of the Scottish writers. Their ideas permeated his literary culture; they were inescapable. Romance, first of all, was 'fiction' opposed to 'fact'.

It seems clear, then, that Brown, Irving, Poe, Hawthorne, and Melville turned to 'romance' in a hostile climate, a climate in which the fictionality of fiction was accentuated and condemned. It is thus not surprising that the primary nineteenth-century meaning of 'romance', as pure and dangerous fantasy, played an important part in their thinking about their chosen mode. How, precisely, this climate affected them, how it influenced their choice of vocation and the works they produced, is a complicated matter.

NOTES

1. J. M. S. Tompkins, *The Popular Novel in England, 1770–1800* (London: Constable, 1932), p. 210.
2. Sir Walter Scott, 'On the Supernatural in Fictitious Composition', in Ioan Williams (ed.), *Sir Walter Scott on Novelists and Fiction* (London: Routledge & Kegan Paul, 1968), p. 314.

3. General William Sullivan, 'Address of the Bunker Hill Monument Association to the Selectmen of the Several Towns in Massachusetts', in George Washington Warren, *The History of the Bunker Hill Monument Association* (Boston: James R. Osgood, 1877), p. 85.

4. Parley P. Pratt, *Autobiography of Parley Parker Pratt* (Salt Lake City: Deseret Book Co., 1938), p. 227.

5. *The Complete Works of Edgar Allan Poe*, ed. James A. Harrison, 17 vols (New York: Thomas Y. Crowell, 1902), vol. 7, p. 236.

6. Washington Irving, in Pierre M. Irving, *The Life and Letters of Washington Irving*, 4 vols (New York: Putnam, 1864), vol. 4, p. 236.

7. Randall Stewart, *Nathaniel Hawthorne: A Biography* (New Haven: Yale University Press, 1948), p. 133.

8. Herman Melville, *The Confidence-Man: His Masquerade*, ed. Hershel Parker (New York: Norton, 1971), p. 160.

9. Washington Irving, *Tales of a Traveller* (New York: Putnam, 1865), p. 376.

10. Merrell R. Davis and William H. Gilman (eds), *The Letters of Herman Melville* (New Haven: Yale University Press, 1960), p. 70.

11. Paul Leicester Ford (ed.), *The Writings of Thomas Jefferson*, 10 vols (New York: Putnam, 1899), vol. 10, pp. 104–5.

12. Samuel Miller, *A Brief Retrospect of the Eighteenth Century*, 2 vols (New York: T. J. Swords, 1803), vol. 2, pp. 179, 176.

13. Dugald Stewart, *Elements of the Philosophy of the Human Mind*, 2 vols (Boston: Wells & Lilly, 1821), vol. 1, pp. 276–8.

14. Hugh Blair, *Lectures on Rhetoric and Belles Lettres* (1783; Philadelphia: James Kay, 1844), pp. 72, 66, 421.

15. Miller, *Retrospect*, vol. 2, p. 175.

16. Edd Winfield Parks, *Edgar Allan Poe as Literary Critic* (Athens: University of Georgia Press, 1964), p. 10.

17. Washington Irving, *Letters, Volume II, 1823–1838*, ed. Ralph M. Aderman, Herbert L. Kleinfield, and Jenifer S. Brooks (Boston: Twayne, 1979), p. 84.

18. Quoted in Terence Martin, *The Instructed Vision: Scottish Common Sense Philosophy and the Origins of American Fiction* (Bloomington: Indiana University Press, 1961), p. 67.

19. Herman Melville, *Pierre, or the Ambiguities*, in *The Writings of Herman Melville*, vol. 7 (Evanston and Chicago: Northwestern University Press and The Newberry Library, 1971), p. 169.

20. Melville, *The Confidence-Man*, p. 60.

6

'THE FAILURE OF GENRE CRITICISM'

Nicolaus Mills

The descriptive failings of genre criticism and its variants are not isolated phenomena [. . .] They are directly related to the historical theories genre criticism has used to explain the uniqueness of American fiction and to the modifications of these theories the variants of genre criticism have employed. At the root of both approaches is the belief that the explanation for the uniqueness of American fiction is to be found in the conditions out of which it grew rather than in the fiction itself. Overlooked is the distinction between writing history and writing a novel made by R. G. Collingwood in *The Idea of History*,

> Where they do differ is that the historian's picture is meant to be true. The novelist has a single task only: to construct a coherent picture, one that makes sense. The historian has a double task: he has both to do this, and to construct a picture of things . . . as they really happened.[1]

In contrast to Collingwood, the genre critics and those whom they have influenced assume a causal relationship between history and literature that borders on determinism.

The nineteenth-century version of this relationship appears most prominently in Tocqueville's *Democracy in America*,

From Nicolaus Mills (1973) *American and English Fiction in the Nineteenth Century: An Antigenre Critique and Comparison*. Bloomington and London: Indiana University Press.

I should say more than I mean if I were to assert that the literature of a nation is always subordinate to its social state and political constitution. I am aware that, independently of these causes, there are several others which confer certain characteristics on literary productions; but these appear to me to be the chief.[2]

The connection that Tocqueville draws between American history and American literature depends upon two observations. The first is the general observation that in democratic nations writers have a taste for 'abstract expressions' and a need to describe 'man himself taken aloof from his country and his age'.[3] The second is the specific observation that in America literary conditions are the product of two related forces: the dullness of a society without rank or tradition and the vitality of a national ethos. 'Nothing conceivable is so petty, so insipid, so crowded with paltry interests – in one word, so anti-poetic – as the life of a man in the United States', Tocqueville notes, and then adds, 'But among the thoughts which it suggests, there is always one that is full of poetry, and that is the hidden nerve which gives vigor to the whole frame'.[4] The thought 'full of poetry' that Tocqueville has in mind is the American march across the wilderness, a 'magnificent image' that continues to haunt every American 'in his least as well as in his most important actions'. Tocqueville's analysis does not become more detailed because he believed that 'properly speaking' America had 'no literature' – only 'journalists'.[5] But it is a short transition from his kind of theorizing about American literature to that which is still prevalent. How short a transition it is can be seen by examining four assertions that explicitly characterize genre criticism and implicitly (albeit less uniformly) characterize its variants.

1. *The English novel did not survive in America because the texture of American society was too thin to support such an art form:* This view has its origins in Lionel Trilling's assertion in *The Liberal Imagination*,

   In this country the real basis of the novel has never existed – that is, the tension between a middle class and an aristocracy which brings manners into observable relief as the living representation of ideals and the living comment on ideas'.[6]

   Trilling's views on what the absence of a traditional class structure means are amplified by Marius Bewley in *The Eccentric Design*:

   But the American novelist had only his *ideas* with which to begin: ideas which, for the most part, were grounded in the great American democratic abstractions. And he found that these abstractions were disembodied, that there was no social context in which they might acquire a rich human relevance. For the traditional novelist, the universal and the particular come together in the world of manners;

but for the American artist there was no social surface responsive to his touch.[7]

The assumption underlying these statements is that in only one kind of historical situation will a writer look closely at society and find enough value in it to produce 'traditional' novels. But what is confused is an attitude toward society and society itself. To assume that because he lacked a socially thick environment the American writer was forced to turn away from society and to abandon the English novel form is to ignore all the other reasons he had for writing the way he did. It is also to overlook the more obvious fact that a writer like Henry James was able to describe American society with the detail of an English novelist, and that Hawthorne, when he lived and worked in Europe, continued to describe European society as he did American society.

2. *The thinness of American society accounts not only for the absence of the English novel in America but provides a basic explanation for the form of American fiction:* To quote Marius Bewley again,

> The absence of a traditional social medium in America compelled the original American artist to confront starkly his own emotional and spiritual needs which his art then became the means of comprehending and analysing.[8]

In critical practice this statement means that social thinness sets into play forces that produce the American rather than the English novel. Yet it is impossible to apply this statement with any consistency or to find a good theoretical justification for it. Certainly it does not work out in terms of genre. The prose romance that Richard Chase finds so characteristic of American fiction did not flourish in the nineteenth century where life in the United States was thinnest. There the stark prose of Hamlin Garland and Edward Eggleston was dominant. Similarly, in Britain a socially active Sir Walter Scott was able to develop his romances out of a vivid sense of past and present tradition, and Emily Brontë had no difficulty in ignoring most of the literary and social conventions around her and extending the development of the gothic romance. The problem gets even worse if one tries to update such a view. For it is difficult to see how social thinness can account for the form of American fiction after World War One. Yet most of the thin-soil critics claim that the American fictional tradition continues beyond this period.

3. *The historical uniqueness of America accounts for the uniqueness of American fiction:* This view can occur as either a reversal or an extension of the negative historical explanations of American fiction, but when combined with a sense of English and American history, it has

none of their obvious failings. The following passage from *The Eccentric Design* provides a case in point:

> But the writers I have dealt with here suggest that 'life' for the serious American artist has a distinctive quality and set of interests of its own, and that these have traditionally been determined and conditioned by the deprivations and confinements of the American condition, and directed by a specific set of problems or tensions growing out of the historical circumstances of America's existence. Obviously no generalizations can be offered that will apply equally to all the novelists treated here, nor even to as many as two of them in the same way. But this much, at least, is worth hazarding: the novelists treated here are, as a group, extraordinarily non-sensuous . . . Because the American tradition provided its artists with abstractions and ideas rather than with manners, we have no great characters, but great symbolic personifications and mythic embodiments that go under the names of Natty Bumppo, Jay Gatsby, Huckleberry Finn, Ahab, Ishmael – all of whom are strangely unrelated to the world of ordinary passions and longings, for the democrat is at last the loneliest man in the universe.[9]

One can dispute various contentions in such a passage, but its ultimate weaknesses become apparent only when the whole conceptual value of historical explanations for the uniqueness of American fiction is questioned. To insist that such explanations are misleading when they take the kind of expansive form discussed here is not, of course, to maintain that American fiction in the nineteenth century was idiosyncratic or ahistorical. It is instead to argue that, although the form of American fiction often grew out of a response to American history, knowing the historical situation does not provide a causal explanation for the literary form. It provides an explanation only for one of several influences with which the form deals. In order to establish a direct connection between history and a literary form (or even the life within a literary form), it is necessary to remember that we are moving between two different realms and that the given conditions of the first are not automatically the imagined conditions of the second. Therefore, showing causality requires either knowledge that a particular set of historical circumstances inevitably leads to a particular literary result or relatively complete understanding of the point where a writer's imagination ends and his thought is imposed by his environment. Take away these conditions, as we must when analyzing nineteenth-century American fiction, and what remains to be said is important, but it reveals only cultural parallels and influences.

4. *The complaints of American writers against American society are evi-*

dence that the texture of American society forced them to write romances rather than novels: This line of reasoning is pursued by Lionel Trilling in *The Liberal Imagination*. After citing the passages in James's life of Hawthorne in which James enumerates all that is missing from American society, Trilling concludes:

> That is, no sufficiency of means . . . no opportunity for the novelist to do his job of searching out reality, not enough complication of appearance to make the job interesting. Another great American novelist of very different temperament had said much the same thing decades before: James Fenimore Cooper found that American manners were too simple and dull to nourish the novelist.[10]

The shortcomings of such an interpretation of Cooper or Hawthorne or James become apparent when one looks closely at their specific complaints about America, which do not yield the conclusion that in this country the novel was uniquely difficult to write. In Cooper's *Notions of the Americans* all forms of writing are judged difficult to accomplish in the United States:

> The second obstacle against which American literature has to contend is in the poverty of the materials . . . There are no annals for the historian; no follies (beyond the most vulgar and commonplace) for the satirist; no manners for the dramatist; no obscure fictions for the writer of romance; no gross and hardy offences against decorum for the moralist; nor any of the rich artificial auxiliaries of poetry.[11]

Similarly, in his preface to *The Marble Faun* Hawthorne is not maintaining, as Richard Chase claims he is, 'that romance, rather than the novel, was the predestined form of American narrative'.[12] To the contrary, what is especially revealing about Hawthorne's *Marble Faun* preface is his assertion of how difficult it is to write a romance in America,

> No author, without a trial, can conceive of the difficulty of writing a romance about a country where there is no shadow, no antiquity, no picturesque* and gloomy wrong . . . as is happily the case with my dear native land.[13]

Indeed, even Henry James in his study of Hawthorne is not arguing that Hawthorne or the American writer was forced to create romances rather than novels. Early in the biography James specifically observes that the uses a writer makes of a provincial environment are 'relative' and depend on his 'point of view', and on the same page as his list of complaints about all that is 'absent in the texture of American life', he comments that the feeling one gets on imagining Hawthorne's surroundings 'is that of compassion for a romancer looking for subjects in such a field'.[14]

Once we are beyond the limitations of genre criticism and its variants, what can be said about the uniqueness of nineteenth-century American fiction makes sense only if two conditions are met: American fiction is analyzed in comparison with rather than in isolation from English fiction, and the question of form in American fiction is treated in its full dimension.

The most obvious and important value of a comparative analysis of nineteenth-century American and English fiction is that it puts the two traditions in perspective, creating a situation in which what is said about the one can be tested against the other. Without this kind of critical possibility the question of uniqueness in nineteenth-century American fiction cannot be answered. It can merely be approached from a well-reasoned but isolated point of view. If properly used, a comparative analysis also guarantees that the differences between writers like Melville and Jane Austen will not serve as the basis for generalizations about American fiction. This is not to say a comparison of Melville and Austen may not be of value but that it raises further problems: Are not many of the differences between Melville and Austen, like many of those between Hardy and Austen, explicable by their relative positions within a literary tradition? Is this distinction not as important as the factor that they represent different traditions? Are not the conclusions that can be drawn about such disparate writers far too broad to include writers as similar as Scott and Cooper? These questions need to be asked, but they can be settled only when a comparison of American and English fiction analyzes the two traditions at the points at which they are closest, e.g., in the work of Scott and Cooper or Melville and Hardy. Any less tightly drawn comparison will not stand up as a generalization.

The same kinds of problems make it necessary to treat the question of form in American fiction in terms of its overall effect. Too often in the past the uniqueness of American fiction has been defined on the basis of only one aspect of form, for example symbolism; or else so-called distinguishing elements in American fiction, like myth and allegory, have been studied independently of the larger context in which they appear. Overlooked has been the fact that the novel cannot, as Philip Rahv observes in *The Myth and the Powerhouse*, 'accommodate a declaration of independence by the smaller unit' but must rely on the cumulative effect of a number of elements: style, plot, subject matter, inventiveness.[15]

The value of approaching form in this way can be seen with special clarity if we put the problem of defining the uniqueness of American fiction into architectural terms and substitute the idea of a building for that of a book. Knowing the location of the building, the materials from which it is constructed, and its intended purpose still leaves a vague picture of the structure. We may realize the building will be glass and steel and contain offices rather than apartments, but we do not know its actual shape or what peculiar significance it may acquire. In the case of a book of fiction, knowing plot, style, and subject matter (or a much broader range of elements) does not in itself provide an adequate picture of form or of meaning. We need to understand much more; at the very least, the relationship and cumulative effect of all the elements comprising the text in question.

The point to which this analogy returns is that a broad, comparative analysis has the capacity to reveal, as genre criticism and its variants do not, the uniqueness and the complexity of nineteenth-century American fiction. Stated as a general proposition, what this comes down to is:

1. Distinguishing American from English fiction requires analysis of the total process by which certain qualities common to both traditions are given unique emphasis in one or the other tradition.

2. The most accurate measure of the difference between the two traditions is reflected in two facts:

   (a) Nineteenth-century American fiction gives an ultimate importance (and textual dominance) to certain ideational or visionary concerns that finally makes these concerns superior to or situationally transcendent of the social context in which they appear.

   (b) Nineteenth-century English fiction gives a qualified importance (and textual limitation) to such concerns that finally makes them coextensive with or subordinate to the social context in which they appear.

NOTES

1. R. G. Collingwood, *The Idea of History* (New York: Oxford University Press, 1967), p. 246.
2. Alexis de Tocqueville, *Democracy in America*, ed. Phillips Bradley, 2 vols (New York: A. A. Knopf, 1958), vol. 2, p. 63.
3. Ibid., pp. 73, 81.
4. Ibid., pp. 78–9.
5. Ibid., pp. 78, 59.
6. Lionel Trilling, 'Art and Fortune', in *The Liberal Imagination* (1950; New York: Scribner, 1976), p. 260.
7. Marius Bewley, *The Eccentric Design* (London: Chatto and Windus, 1959), p. 15.
8. Ibid., p. 19.
9. Ibid., pp. 292–3.
10. Lionel Trilling, 'Manners, Morals and the Novel', in *Liberal Imagination*, p. 213.
11. James Fenimore Cooper, *The Travelling Bachelor or Notions of the Americans*, 2 vols (New York: Stringer and Townsend, 1852), vol. 2, p. 108.
12. Richard Chase, *The American Novel and its Tradition* (New York: Doubleday, 1957), p. 18.
13. Nathaniel Hawthorne, *The Marble Faun* (Columbus: Ohio State University Press, 1968), p. 3.
14. Henry James, *Hawthorne* (1880; Ithaca: Cornell University Press, 1956), pp. 10, 34.
15. Philip Rahv, *The Myth and the Powerhouse* (New York: Farrar, Straus and Giroux, 1966), p. 53.

7

'EMPIRE AND OCCASIONAL CONFORMITY: DAVID FORDYCE'S *COMPLETE BRITISH LETTER-WRITER*'

Eve Tavor Bannet

Despite growing interest in letter-writing practices and widespread agreement that letters were central to eighteenth-century culture, there is no modern study of eighteenth-century British or American epistolary manuals. Oblivious to the veil cast by the longstanding naturalization of letters and of the ability to write them, as well as to the fact that letters were the communications technology of the first British empire, colonial studies have overlooked epistolary manuals even when arguing that print made colonization possible. Cultural studies too have left epistolary manuals unread, unaware both that the content of their model letters and their outwork performed ideological work, and that they functioned as conduct books as well as guides to conversation and correspondence. J. H. Plumb once observed that 'ideas acquire dynamism when they become social attitudes'.[1] Epistolary manuals were conduct books in which ideas and practices were modeled, taught, and imitated as social attitudes in and for the everyday.

[. . .]

Eighteenth-century 'Complete Letter-Writers' were compendia of fragments: anthologies of diverse and largely discontinuous model letters, and of formulae for cards and for legal documents such as indentures, wills, bonds, and bills

From *Huntington Library Quarterly* 66.1–2 (2003): 55–79.

of exchange that were bound together in book form with a short grammar, instructions for punctuation, directions for addressing people of different ranks, a list of contractions, and a spelling dictionary for homonyms. They sometimes also included directions for making and preserving ink, for cutting the nibs on quill pens, and for folding and formatting missives, along with instructions in elementary mathematics and accounting. The grammatical and orthographical outwork in eighteenth-century Letter-Writers marks a significant shift in function from seventeenth-century manuals such as Thomas Blount's *Academy of Eloquence,* where model letters tailored to a courtly audience were sandwiched between instructions about tropes and pages of commonplaces. The new function of epistolary manuals heralded by the new grammatical and orthographical outwork was to promulgate correct written English and correct – otherwise known as 'polite' – epistolary norms.

[. . .]

Eighteenth-century Letter-Writers therefore raise issues of conformity, standardization, and normalization that have preoccupied historians of language as well as nationalist Scottish historians since the 1980s, when [French cultural theorists] [Etienne] Balibar and [Pierre] Macherey first argued that imposition of a national language and literature suppressed the traditional dialects or national languages – and the local or native cultures – of provincials, the working classes, and the colonized. Eighteenth-century Letter-Writers raise these issues all the more forcibly because orthographical, grammatical, stylistic, and formal uniformity in epistolary writing was the means of removing stultifying impediments to profitable 'commerce' among different regions of Britain and of the British Empire. In the eighteenth century, people in different counties of England still understood each other's speech almost as poorly as native Gaelic or Scots speakers understood the English. Mutual incomprehension was not just a problem of the Celtic fringe. At the beginning of the century, Defoe found the Devonshire dialect incomprehensible, and grammarian Hugh Jones observed that the speech of Yorkshire and that of Somerset were mutually unintelligible. At the end of the century, James Adams (a Scot) declared that Suffolk outdid all the counties in England in 'queer cant', and Noah Webster observed that 'the people of distant counties in England can hardly understand one another, so various are their dialects'.[2] 'Commerce' among the different counties and nations of Britain and of the first British empire – in all the eighteenth-century meanings of the word commerce: exchange, traffic, conversation, intercourse, and trade – depended on developing a single uniform written language, 'universal' letter-writing norms that would ensure clarity or 'perspicuity', and harmony or 'correspondence', in epistolary exchange. As Joseph Priestley pointed out, this was hardly a new thought, since it was through a written language that the Chinese empire had governed, and created the possibility of communication among, speakers of a hundred mutually incomprehensible Chinese dialects.

Eighteenth-century epistolary manuals indicate, however, that issues of conformity and uniformity across provinces were far less univocal and unambiguous than postmodern theorists and cultural critics have supposed. One factor that undermined epistolary standardization in the very act of its institution was that Letter-Writers were only occasionally identical even with themselves. Even successive reprints by the same printer with the same title were often different from one another. *The Complete Letter-Writer or Polite English Secretary,* for instance, is not the same book in its twelfth edition of 1768 as it had been in its sixth edition of 1759, much less in its third edition of 1756, even though all these editions were issued by the same printer, Stanley Crowder in London. Successive reprints of a manual by the same author on different sides of the Atlantic could likewise be substantially different. *The American Instructor; or Young Man's Best Companion,* first printed in America by Benjamin Franklin and David Hall in 1731, continued to bear the name of its English author 'George Fisher, Accomptant' on its title page, even though the preface to Franklin's edition – and to every successive American edition by printers in New York, Philadelphia, Boston, and Worcester to 1801 – pointed out that 'in the British Edition of this Book, there were many Things of little or no Use in these Parts of the World: In this Edition those Things are omitted, and in their Room many other Matters inserted, more immediately useful to us Americans'. These American editions also differed slightly, but significantly, from one another: what was 'useful to us Americans' was not identical in different states or provinces at different times. The compendium's composition from discontinuous fragments made it easy to create a new manual by mixing and matching from other manuals, or to change the composition and import of an extant manual by slipping letters – and other things – in and out of successive editions. The reader of the 1750 Boston reprint of John Hill's English classic, *The Young Secretary's Guide; or A Speedy Help to Learning,* will be puzzled as to why Boston printer Thomas Fleet claimed that his apparently accurate reprint had been 'made suitable to the People of New England' – until she notices that Fleet has omitted Hill's table of contents in order to slip in, almost unnoticed among the usual 'forms of Bills, Bonds etc', a short tract on 'The Advantage *Englishmen* enjoy by the Trial by Juries, above any other nation under Heaven', and another tract arguing – against Lord Mansfield and the English government at the time – 'That Juries are Judges of Law in some respect, as well as of Fact'. Fleet was covertly preparing users of his manual in New England for opposition, in redefinition as well as in defense of their rights as *Englishmen.* In the wake of the 1765 Stamp Act* fiasco, when Britain imposed Admiralty courts on the American colonies, an Englishman's right to trial by jury became one of the contested issues that led to revolution and independence.

Together with successive fashions in epistolary style and different 'brands' or series of epistolary manuals, the lack of fixity in epistolary models meant that the prestigious 'metropolitan' model was everywhere and nowhere present. Indeed, Noah Webster pointed to this slipperiness and indeterminacy of the genteel and supposedly 'metropolitan' model to argue the absurdity of provincials who tried to imitate the mother country, and to explain their inability ever to do so without difference. Like letters themselves, epistolary manuals were an 'occasional' genre: while displaying certain constant features, they were adapted and readapted to particular audiences at particular political and historical junctures. Localism and difference reasserted themselves in this occasional way, not only in the midst of a didactic, standardizing imperial discourse, but sometimes in subversive and fairly self-conscious dialogue with it.

In Fordyce's case, localism expressed itself in his commitment to a more 'world bred' form of higher education.

[. . .]

The *Letter-Writer*'s curious spin on [Scottish Enlightenment ideas of 'the moral sense, moral taste, and sympathy, and his incipient notions of the division of labor'] derived from Fordyce's conviction that our motive to virtue is some form of self-interest, and consequently that 'where there arises any appearance of opposition between our Duty and our Satisfaction or Interest', it 'will raise strong and often unsurmountable Prejudices against the Practice of Virtue'.[3] This meant that to promote virtue and 'reform the moral and political culture', educators and reformers had to harness men's self-interest and desire for gain for the higher purpose of 'training up good Citizens and useful members of the State in their respective Characters and Relations of Parents, Children, Magistrates, Subjects, Soldiers and Countrymen'.[4] These were, of course, precisely the sorts of characters whose social attitudes and moral dispositions could populate epistolary manuals, and Fordyce heralded the *Letter-Writer*'s reformist goals by opening with a correspondence between a father and the master of an academy who agree that the purpose of education is to promote the welfare both of the individual and of society.

But in the *Letter-Writer*, where the full argument was necessarily suppressed, Fordyce's conjunction of self-interest and virtue produced a curious moral philosophy, reminiscent of no one so much as Benjamin Franklin, in which gainful conduct is identified with virtue, and virtue figures as a means of gain. As a young man is told by a parental mentor: 'You know what is right, and what is wrong. The path of prosperity lies before you'.[5] Fordyce's model letters taught that to rise in and benefit from this new empire of gainful opportunity that 'Britishness' offered, a man must not only practice the so-called Protestant virtues of diligence, punctuality, industry, honesty, sobriety, and frugality. He must also demonstrate an equally Franklinian concern with the 'character' and 'credit' that his conduct, his appearance, and the company he kept would earn him because 'the character of a man of business in particular, is greatly benefitted or injured by the company he keeps'.[6] Young men were advised not only to avoid 'bad company' but also to conduct their conversations and select their friends with a view to 'the profit of the speakers',[7] privileging friendship with older men who could act as their guides and patrons over friendship with their peers. The same virtues that advanced a man in business (diligence, frugality, and the rest) would also gain him the useful friends he needed to advance himself:

> no consideration will gain you more esteem, or make you more noticed by those who may perhaps, hereafter, be valuable friends, than industry and business, and a decent and becoming behaviour, both to superiors and equals.[8]

And young men were advised to cultivate their minds and their hearts, secure in the knowledge that the union of a good head to a good heart would turn out to be profitable in the highest sense:

> A good head will form a proper judgement of what should be done in our respective stations of life, and a good heart will incline us to do it, to the utmost of our power. A man of this description seems best fitted, upon every principle of reason and religion, to answer the great ends of his creation, which consist in the fulfilment of his duty to God, his neighbour and himself.[9]

At the same time, as with other figures of the Scottish Enlightenment, Fordyce's attitude to Britain as a political unit was ambivalent, even subversive. He presented post-Union* Britain as the reality on the ground rather than as the ideal solution to Scotland's poverty: 'since we cannot pretend to alter the Course of Human Affairs, nor reform the Errors of Civil Government, a right Education of individuals seems to be the only Method left us to rectify, or supply the Defects of both'.[10] This less than whole-hearted endorsement of 'Britain' led Fordyce in two complementary directions. It led him to the teaching of a republican politics that, across the Atlantic thirty years later, would subvert imperial incorporation from within by affirming what Fordyce calls 'the ardent Love of Liberty, the Spirit of Independence on the Fortunes and Vices of Mankind, and the inexpiable Hatred of Tyranny and Tyrants, however dignified by Rank and Titles'.[11] And it led him to debate and qualify the rightness of conforming to those standard, 'polite' conversational and epistolary models that are marked as 'English' in a *British* Letter-Writer designed to teach 'Polite Modern Letter-Writing'.

In [Fordyce's] *Dialogues* [*Concerning Education*], Cleora criticizes the artifice, insincerity, and deceit of polite phrases, such as '[Your] humble Servant',

267

that were commonly used in letters and in conversation. These were, she says, 'once real Badges or Expressions of Servitude, by which Inferiors signified their Dependence on their Superior, in those times when *Vassalage* prevailed',[12] but should now be banned along with hierarchy. Cleora argues that 'the polite Forms of ordinary Conversation are only a more specious kind of Lies', and she calls for different, more natural, and sincere forms of language that import 'more of that Equality and Friendship which ought to reign in Society'.[13] Her mentor and conversational partner, Simplicitus, agrees that the 'ordinary Forms of Civility and Polite Phrases that are used by well bred people [are] no more than Counters which . . . may glitter and amuse the Eye as much as real Gold', without being what they seem; but he argues that 'their value is known'; that they are taken at face value by no one but 'Fools'; that we would be 'reckoned awkward, antiquated Creatures, and even somewhat unsociable, if we despise or transgress them'; and that it would be a 'Folly' to do so'.[14] The uncertainty of many Scots and provincials about their ability to speak and conduct themselves without betraying their lack of English, metropolitan breeding is certainly to be heard here. But the point Fordyce is making is that treating the forms of politeness in conduct, conversation, and letters as lying 'Counters' is useful. Although little more than what Derrida* calls a *passpartout* – an entrance ticket, passport, and guarantee of safe passage – in *foreign countries*, it would be folly not to present them. It should be remembered that the English language and culture were foreign to Scots, as Alexander Carlyle, among others, pointed out: 'to every man bred in Scotland, the English language was in some respects a foreign tongue, the precise value and force of whose words and phrases he did not understand'.[15] And in the *Letter-Writer*, it is to a young man who is 'going to a strange country, where you will find opinions, modes and customs, different from that which prevail in that of your nativity' that an uncle particularly recommends the 'obliging and complaisant' behavior in which politeness consists.[16]

Allied with just practices, the uncle explains, polite forms of conduct and of oral and written discourse will ensure a man's success in any foreign country in which he seeks to advance himself, not least by enabling him to avoid giving offense by concealing what he really thinks of the natives' religion, customs, and politics. A man should neither adopt nor prefer the ways of foreigners, Fordyce insisted in another letter 'To a Friend . . . on Traveling'. Instead, he should use manners and forms of speech that Fordyce carefully marks as *English*, only to ensure his safe passage among foreigners during the time he is obliged to spend among them:

> [Travelers] should in particular be cautioned against imbibing prejudices respecting the customs of his own country, and attaching themselves to those which they see abroad. I do not pretend to say an Englishman ought

not to conform himself to the manners of Italy while he remains there; but I affirm that it is preposterous in him to think of retaining those manners when he returns home; for surely it must be allowed, if it be right to affect the Italian in Italy, it is also right, on the same principle, to resume the Englishman in England.[17]

In England, not in Britain. Ian Duncan has observed that 'command of metropolitan discourse' enabled 'post-Union Scots to enter the imperial professions and pass as "British" (rather than Scottish) subjects'.[18] For Fordyce, however, the ability to 'pass' was more than a question of conformity for the purpose of acceptance in the society or polity; the polite and agreeable conduct that enabled a man to 'pass' had the instrumental character repeatedly stressed by Scottish factor James Robinson in Falmouth, Virginia, in his instructions to his shopkeeper agents in the Virginia hinterlands:

> in your Trade be generous, easy, affable, and free to your customers, pointed and exact in fulfilling your engagements on even your most trivial promises. By these methods you will engage their esteem, regard and confidence and on this plan alone a large and extensive trade can be acquired and carried on.[19]

Polite and affable manners were a useful means of gain. After all, as a father in Fordyce's *Letter-Writer* writes to a son just 'entering upon commercial life:' 'You are to remember that Friends are as necessary to promote the grand ends of Commercial as of Social life'.[20] Friendship too was an instrument and means.

Elsewhere in the *Letter-Writer*, Fordyce taught an equally strategic 'world-bred' kind of conformity, in which individuals deploy civil forms and virtues as a 'Counter' to purchase respectability and advancement while treating them – especially in others – as entirely suspect and fake. Fordyce's letters of advice repeatedly point out that despite the fact that in Enlightenment doctrine, friendship is the basis of society, in actuality 'the mask of friendship is too frequently assumed to perpetuate the most insidious purposes',[21] with the result that 'numbers have been induced not only to doubt the reality of friendship but to consider it a mere fiction'.[22] Presumably other men were faking a character of virtue and industry, and adopting the correct and artificial forms of politeness to obtain the 'credit', 'friendship', and patronage of those who could benefit and advance them too. In any case, the basis of society in friendship, and the unity of imperial 'Britain' through uniform conversational and epistolary forms devolves into a mere fiction. There is no genuine common basis in metropolitan *English* manners, or in friendships based upon them, in this *British* epistolary world. Fordyce insists that a man should therefore always be on his guard; he should be careful never to speak or write on any subject in an 'unguarded manner'.[23]

Fordyce's recommendation of strategic conformity to *English* forms of epistolary and conversational civility turns into its opposite here. For in Fordyce's manual, ambitious young men are advised to guard their speech by various forms of not speaking. They are advised to practice secrecy and reserve: 'This talent or quality of secrecy is of the highest importance to many of the concerns of human life, nor can intercourse, either friendly or commercial, be carried on without it';[24] 'a well-governed reserve in general argues wisdom, and promotes peace'.[25] They are advised to guard themselves in the midst of society by observing the conversation of others, while speaking as little as possible themselves: 'Be quick to hear, but slow and cautious in speaking; it being far more easy to betray our ignorance, and give undesigned offence, than to conciliate the esteem of strangers'.[26] But by this secrecy, silence, and reserve, a man could also stand outside the society of strangers and the system of language in which he seemed to be participating at the very moment of his participation. He could elude incorporation in the very midst of the foreign incorporating linguistic and social body.

This insistence on silence is all the more remarkable for its insertion in the midst of a Letter-Writer, which by definition had the function of promoting linguistic exchange by teaching what contemporaries commonly called 'written conversation'. As Fordyce put it: 'Letters are the copies of conversation'.[27] Yet one might say that this emphasis on silence represents the inverted mirror image of that merely occasional conformity which, in Fordyce's *Complete Letter-Writer*, has appropriated correspondence – and indeed, *Britishness* – to itself.

NOTES

1. Quoted in Donald J. Withrington, 'What Was Distinctive about the Scottish Enlightenment?' in Jennifer J. Carter and Joan H. Pittock (eds), *Aberdeen and the Enlightenment* (Aberdeen: Aberdeen University Press, 1987), p. 15.
2. Noah Webster, *Dissertations on the English Language* (1789; reprinted, Menston: Scolar Press, 1967); Gerald Knowles, *A Cultural History of the English Language* (London: Arnold, 1997), p. 134.
3. David Fordyce 'Elements of Moral Philosophy', in Robert Dodsley, *The Preceptor* (London, 1758), II, 354.
4. David Fordyce, *Dialogues Concerning Education*, 2 vols (London, 1745; 1747), vol. 2, p. 49.
5. David Fordyce, *New and Complete British Letter-Writer, or Young Secretary's Instructor in Polite Modern Letter-Writing*, (London, [1790?]), p. 133.
6. Ibid., p. 37.
7. Ibid., p. 120.
8. Ibid., p. 155.
9. Ibid., p. 136.
10. Fordyce, *Dialogues*, vol. 2, p. 16.
11. Ibid., p. 22.
12. Ibid., p. 46.
13. Ibid.
14. Ibid., p. 49.

15. Christopher J. Berry, *Social Theory of the Scottish Enlightenment* (Edinburgh: Edinburgh University Press, 1997), pp. 16–17.
16. Fordyce, *Letter-Writer*, p. 56.
17. Ibid., p. 163.
18. Ian Duncan, 'Adam Smith, Samuel Johnson, and the Institutions of English', in Robert Crawford (ed.), *The Scottish Invention of English Literature* (Cambridge: Cambridge University Press, 1998), p. 41.
19. T. M. Devine (ed.), *A Scottish Firm in Virginia, 1767–1777: W. Cuninghame and Co.* (Edinburgh: Scottish History Society, 1984), p. 48.
20. Fordyce, *Letter-Writer*, p. 150.
21. Ibid., p. 105.
22. Ibid., p. 101.
23. Ibid., p. 105.
24. Ibid., p. 104.
25. Ibid., p. 106.
26. Ibid., p. 120.
27. Ibid., p. 24.

8

'THE AMERICANIZATION OF CLARISSA'

Leonard Tennenhouse

Since Ian Watt's definitive study [*The Rise of the Novel* (1957)], criticism of the English novel tends to assume that Richardson either initiated or helped to establish the predominant form of the English novel. Whether one claims, as Watt did, that the form rose to hegemony because it addressed the interests of a middle class on the rise well before the novel came along and gave the emergent class moral support, or whether we argue, alternatively, that domestic fiction helped to bring that class into being, the fact remains that such novels as *Pamela* and *Clarissa* established the form of domestic fiction reproduced by the so-called great tradition of English fiction. From its inception, the mainstream novelistic tradition not only counted women among its readership, but also authorized women to articulate the beliefs and values of the readership as a whole. For literate classes composed of both men and women, Richardson made passive aggression into a sublime testament that any literate person had a self to withhold, a source of self-worth and cultural authority which would go unrecognized were it not for the fact it was written in English. It apparently meant a great deal to a polite English readership that he demonstrated at such elaborate length the necessity of casting one's interior life in written form, for the publishing history of his novels indicates that a certain kind of verbosity – what might be called a protracted display of personal literariness – was essential to the English Richardson's success. The putative author – though a woman –

From *The Yale Journal of Criticism* 11.1 (1998): 186–91.

was the model for 'the individual', and her discourse presumed that virtually anyone with sufficient literacy could emulate a brand of interiority that denoted a superior quality of Englishness. What happens to this assumption as the text that produced it came to be reproduced on the Western side of the Atlantic?

Beginning in the early seventeenth century and for almost two centuries thereafter, colonial British subjects confronted the dilemma of maintaining their English identity outside of England. Living in North America required members of the English community to formulate new courtship practices and marriage rules, in order for their offspring to remain English. Perhaps the first narrative form to deal with this problem, the captivity narrative, is a good place to look for formal precedents to the seduction novel. Produced in significant quantities and consumed before as well as after the American Revolution, this narrative characteristically used daughters both to pose the problem of maintaining English identity in British North America and to offer a resolution: either the captive daughter was returned undefiled to her family, or else she died in captivity. In either case, her blood remained pure. As Nancy Armstrong has written of Mary Rowlandson's* account of her captivity, '[t]he exclusive nature of the patriarchal prerogative' makes it possible for Englishness to descend from the father to the daughter and through her into the family of another Englishman, 'thereby preserving the Englishness of the colonial community'.[1] In the colonies, then, the daughter of a European serves as the special kind of fetish that Annette Weiner calls 'an inalienable possession', in that she can neither be seized nor traded without endangering the group's identity.[2] Daughters who acquire this iconic status have to die when they leave their father's family. Identifying this cultural logic in narratives of the late eighteenth century, Armstrong points out that daughters who do leave the community without their father's blessing can return to that community either through death, as Richardson's Clarissa did, or 'through their daughters, as in the case of Charlotte Temple*'.[3]

[. . .]

As I have already suggested, the American *Clarissa* may be distinguished from her English counterpart by her minimal expression of emotions, and she spends even less time writing personal letters. The narrator simply informs the reader that Clarissa 'wrote to Mr Lovelace that as she had no other means of escaping her brother's tyranny, she would meet him the next Monday at the garden gate and put herself under his protection'.[4] With this statement, letter writing ceases. What had merely provided an occasion for the English Clarissa to carry on highly nuanced emotional performances in prose – namely, the seduction plot – thus becomes the stock-in-trade of the American edition. It is entirely accurate to say that the abridged Richardson dispenses with all but the most necessary verbal performances in order to concentrate on the conduct of the female body. To explain what this shift from the body as the source of emotive language to the body as the source of sexual experience does to the concept and fate of individual identity, let me briefly compare a few key episodes from each of the two Richardsons on this basis.

In what is arguably the most erotic moment of the English version of *Pamela*, we find the heroine's letters quite literally assuming the position of her body as the object of Mr B's desire: 'Artful slut', he says as he gropes about her body in search of letters she has surreptitiously authored, 'I never undressed a girl in my life; but I will now begin to strip my pretty Pamela; and I hope I shall not go far before I find [her letters]'.[5] But when Mr B tries to undress his reluctant serving girl in the American edition, as he does on quite a few occasions, it is solely for purposes of taking possession of her body; he takes no interest in Pamela's letters. Here, within three sentences, we encounter two such attempts on her virtue:

> The squire was dressed in women's clothes, but no sooner did he come up to Pamela's bed, then he began to use such indecent freedom, that she soon discovered what he was. The distress in which Pamela was, made her use every expression to induce him to withdraw, upon which he uttered several bitter imprecations upon himself that he had never intended her the least injury. Another attempt was made on her, but she was so much overpowered, that she was obliged to be put to bed.[6]

That the American version has no interest in transferring value from Pamela's body to her writing makes most of the prose in the English edition unnecessary to the narrative preferred by American readers.

Like her English counterpart, the American Pamela insists on returning to her father the minute she figures out what lascivious designs her new master has in mind, and like his English counterpart, Mr B reneges on his promise to comply. He sends her to his remote country seat, the better to seduce her. Once squirreled away in his country house, however, the American pair neglect to carry on the full-fledged letter-writing war which preoccupied them in the English edition. Pamela simply rejects a bogus marriage offer and leaves her diary where Mr B is sure to discover that she does indeed mean what she says; her diary entry for that day confirms it. Writing is just as basic to this heroine's identity, I am suggesting, but basic in a more proto-juridical way. In that it verifies more primary practices of speech and conduct, thus her suitability for marriage as well as the sincerity with which she would enter into it, writing establishes the consensual basis for a successful relationship. To put it another way, Pamela must demonstrate she is capable of saying no before she can be trusted to say yes.

If the American Richardson deletes certain features from the English Richardson and modifies the role they play in determining the heroine's marriagability, then the American version expands other features out of all proportion to the importance they commanded in the English edition. The episode dealing with Mr B's illegitimate daughter, Sally Godfrey, is notable in this respect. The episode takes up a fraction of the longer English edition and seems to exist only for purposes of displaying Pamela's extraordinary kindness toward those less fortunate than she. Thus we must ask ourselves why this event, of all those comprising the tediously long description of Pamela's married life, looms so large in the American edition. A visit to the girl at boarding school in the abridged edition reveals that Miss Godfrey has acquired a quality of deportment and a degree of literacy capable of overriding the unfortunate circumstances of her birth, thus making her eligible for marriage into the respectable classes. Sally Godfrey resembles Charlotte Temple's illegitimate daughter in that she too has been raised in England by a surrogate family, while Sally's mother, more fortunate than Charlotte, is reported to be 'doing well' in Jamaica. In both cases, the woman, once ruined, achieves some measure of social redemption, in so far as she has observed the model of good conduct. That her redemption depends on her literacy as opposed to the purity of her lineage suggests that in the editions preferred in America following the Revolution, cultural reproduction was far more important to national identity than the continuation of a bloodline. Indeed, one American abridgment (Boston, 1793) even suggests a similarity between the heroine and Sally Godfrey in celebrating Pamela's accomplishments: 'Pamela Andrews was the daughter of John and Elizabeth Andrews, (or at least reputed so) who lived in a small village in the West of England, and who, by pinching themselves more than they were already by the narrowness of circumstances, got her taught to read and write'.[7]

Even though the abridgment's rejection of the epistolary mode in favor of third-person narration is the most obvious stylistic difference between the American and English editions, the quote clearly indicates that Pamela's literacy is the first and most important fact we must know, if we are to understand the events that lead to her fortunate marriage. What inferences may be drawn from this paradox? In England, as in the unabridged Richardson, the heroine's writing points back to a source residing in the body, a source linking her identity with a natural and unspoiled interiority; the American version gives us no reason to think her writing either originates in her body or locates value in her origins. Indeed, the opening line of the 1793 Boston edition suggests that just the reverse is true. Writing does not point back to qualities inherent in the body. As we quickly discover, everything depends on the female body conducting itself according to a written model. Since in both Richardsons, the heroine's status depends upon her relationship to writing, it behooves us to look more closely at the difference between the two in terms of what happens to writing at the moment of rape.

If Pamela's seduction provides the stuff of domestic comedy, Clarissa's rape can only be called a domestic tragedy. Far from overturning the logic of cultural reproduction spelled out in the abbreviated *Pamela*, however, the American *Clarissa* actually observes the same logic in a more exaggerated form. In marked contrast with what might be called the damaged writing with which the English novel registers the same act of violence, the absence of her personal record in the abridged *Clarissa* recasts the heroine's rape from an assault on her sensibility into a devastating physical experience, as the narrator explains:

> What followed was the most vile and inhuman acts of violence. The distressed lady, roused from the dreadful lethargy into which she was sinking, pleaded for mercy, and cried, I will be yours – , indeed, to obtain mercy, I will be yours! But no mercy could she find. Her strength, her intellects failed her. Fits upon fits followed, which procured her no compassion . . .[8]

More peculiar than this relatively explicit description of the rape is Clarissa's consent to the dirty deed – provided that Lovelace first agree to marry her. The option of consent in some form is what must be inferred from her pathetic statement of surrender, 'I will be yours'. Neither this description of the sexual encounter nor her capitulation to it appeared in the English version. Only the American narrative of seduction holds open the possibility of marriage under the duress of sexual assault.

Because sham marriages were far more common among people lower on the social scale, the kind of ceremony Lovelace proposes was particularly unacceptable to an English readership learning to think of an affective, companionate marriage as the only legitimate one. As the American version of the Sally Godfrey episode suggests, such unions came to be increasingly associated with a colonial culture where they apparently seemed more acceptable and even necessary. In the English novel, down is the only direction in which a woman can go once she has been sexually compromised. But a heroine could be both virtuous and fallen, embodying Pamela and Sally Godfrey at once, in the American version, where the two no longer represented contradictory types. Indeed, the Sally Godfrey episode demonstrated that a woman's sexual downfall was reversible in the seduction narrative preferred by an American readership; after the seduction she might even improve her social position, provided the conditions were right. If *Pamela* demonstrated under what conditions one can overcome a potential fall in status, then *Clarissa* worked in reverse, to demonstrate under what conditions one was destined to fall. In thus working in tandem, moreover, the two novels reveal the conditions under which a seduction story could itself become a model for cultural reproduction.

According to this model, the sexual purity of the daughter is much less important than her ability to form a household where the rules of good conduct – hence Englishness itself – can be reproduced in and by subsequent generations. This is not to say that the story of cultural reproduction according to Mary Jemison won out over the kind of captivity narrative exemplified by Mary

Rowlandson, much less that the American seduction novel could allow its heroine to go native. Not at all. I am simply suggesting that during the early Republic sexual impurity does not necessarily cancel out Englishness, for remain English one must. After political separation from England, the popularity of the seduction novel suggests, it was more important than ever to have the kind of cultural identity formerly acquired by being born of English parents. The conditions under which one could acquire and maintain such an identity had simply changed.

This, I believe, is the reason why Clarissa's Uncle Morden enters so intrusively into the abridged edition as a potential form of agency. The American Richardson assigns this absent relative a role resembling that played by Charlotte Temple's father. Her active apologist and would-be redeemer, her father arrives at Charlotte's side just in time to see Rowson's heroine expire. She begs his pardon, and he grants it. He then leaves America with her new-born daughter whom he plans to bring up back in England. Of the aftermath of this climactic episode, Rowson's narrator has this to say: 'After the first tumult of grief subsided, Mrs Temple gave up the chief of her time to her grand-child, and as she grew up and improved, began to fancy she again possessed Charlotte'.[9] Uncle Morden's interventions on Clarissa's behalf similarly increase in importance in the American edition, where they promise to cancel out the fact of her rape and excommunication from the Harlowe family. The American novel clearly empowers Morden as a father surrogate. Convinced of Clarissa's innocence, he pleads with the girl's family, we are told, to send a nurse to care for her. When brother James steps in to prevent his mother from offering any succor, Morden is reported to have declared, 'in me shall the dear creature have the father, uncle, and brother she has lost'.[10] In view of the American adaptation of the Sally Godfrey episode, I am inclined to take this statement literally to mean that had Morden arrived in time, he might have eventually given Clarissa in marriage to another English gentleman, as certain to be smitten as Morden himself by her tragic beauty and genteel deportment. Indeed, it is fair to say that all such departures from the longer version of *Clarissa* place value on the quality of the copy in contrast to the original. What counts for an American readership, we must conclude, is not so much the loss of purity as one's fidelity to the idea of a home one imagined to be English. Nor does the heroine's conduct have to meet the father's approval any more than she has to marry the man whom he selects for her. In all cases, substitutes will do. Morden can assume the position of the true father by behaving like one, and by behaving like one, he might well have legitimated the ravished Clarissa, had she lasted just a little longer. Pursuing the logic of this comparison to its conclusion, we reach a vantage point from which to understand why *Clarissa* might have been an even better story had the heroine been willing to endure a pregnancy and provide Morden with a substitute daughter before she died.

NOTES

1. Nancy Armstrong, 'Why Daughters Die: The Racial Logic of American Sentimentalism', *The Yale Journal of Criticism* 7.2 (1994): 10.
2. Annette Weiner, *Inalienable Possessions: The Paradox of Keeping-While-Giving* (Berkeley: University of California Press, 1992).
3. Armstrong, 'Why Daughters Die', p. 11.
4. Samuel Richardson, *Clarissa or the History of a Young Lady* (Boston: Samuel Hall, 1795), p. 28.
5. Samuel Richardson, *Pamela, or Virtue Rewarded* (New York: W. W. Norton, 1958), p. 245.
6. Samuel Richardson, *The Pleasing History of Pamela* (Boston: Samuel Hall, 1793), p. 20.
7. Ibid., p. 1.
8. Richardson, *Clarissa*, pp. 80–1.
9. Susanna Rowson, *Charlotte Temple* (New York: Oxford University Press, 1986), p. 118.
10. Richardson, *Clarissa*, p. 111.

PART VI
TRAVEL

TRAVEL: INTRODUCTION

In an extract in Part V, Deleuze and Guattari advocate 'nomadology' as a reading practice. Their development of this term from ethnography, transforming it into a metaphorical tool for a 'deterritorialised' critical comparatism, encourages a decentralised form of reading that may be particularly appropriate to a Transatlantic Studies conceived around a geometry of circulation, exchange, transitions and transformations. The appropriateness of travel theory for transatlanticism is, perhaps, self-evident. So many accounts, from at least the sixteenth century, of the Americas from a European standpoint have come from travellers, embedded in narratives of their travels. And, from the later eighteenth century, the flow of travellers across the Atlantic in the other direction increased, to produce a balancing body of work devoted to seeing Europe through American eyes. One part of Elizabeth Bishop's 1965 volume of poems *Questions of Travel* is called 'Elsewhere': the selections in this section suggest collectively how views from elsewhere might help to define transatlantic perspectives.

Travel accounts write distance, transience, departure and arrival into narratives of personal journeys that may be more or less typified; to travel is to be in motion, to see the world from a series of dynamic, shifting viewpoints. For the traveller, it has the effect that all knowledge, subsequently, is comparative and everything is perceived from (at least) two perspectives. Travel writing and travel theory are by no means the domain of the 'literary'; anthropology, geography, history, ethnography and linguistics all take an interest and have a stake in theorising travel. An enormous body of travel literature and a growing corpus of travel theory have had a substantial impact on all areas of reading: in different ways they have made inescapable an awareness of the 'situatedness' of all knowledge, the intrinsic relation between the location of the knower and what is 'known'. Nomadism, for example, allows European observers (in Mary Baine Campbell's terms, in her essay reprinted here) to loosen 'psychic borders' and become 'voluntarily indoctrinated into a different and more narrative form of spatial knowledge'.

Tourists, emigrants, ethnographers and exiles constitute large but discrete bodies of transatlantic travellers, each with a literature and a discourse. The literature of emigration is discussed by Stephen Fender in his book *Sea Changes*, excerpted below. Fender argues for a close relationship between the experience of emigration and the 'sense of being American', the connection being discursive rather than causal: both are described in terms of separations and departures, breaks with past constraints, and present or future possibilities of freedom. Focusing on Protestant emigrants to North America, he identifies 'paradisal and colonial' aspects to their account of travelling experience and its part in the development of a 'distinctively republican American voice' and subsequent adoption in the optative literature of American possibility, from Emerson to Whitman to Carlos Williams. This was an exceptionalist rhetoric, the journey as a rite of passage into new modes of perception. For these writers, and for the American ideology they voiced, the life left behind or discarded cast no shadow forwards into the future. It was not, of course, a universal adoption: Washington Irving, Nathaniel Hawthorne, Herman Melville, Margaret Fuller and Henry James all wrote complex travel narratives that suggest how the backdrop of emigration may have condemned all Americans to a displaced existence, a touristic mentality neither connected with the past nor at home in the present. William W. Stowe considers some of these works in *Going Abroad: European Travel in Nineteenth-Century American Culture*; the excerpt below looks at travellers' guidebooks as sacred texts articulating a 'liturgy' of travel. They evoke a virtual space incorporating information, practical advice and magical possibility – 'handbooks of devotion', they come to define the experience of travel and the encounter with otherness. They offer a stable point of view, promise knowledge and orientation, and minimise the dangers of alienation.

It is precisely this latter that focuses the work of the Palestinian-American intellectual Edward Said, a key figure in the West's development of comparative perspectives. His *Orientalism*, discussed earlier in the *Reader*, is a foundational text of postcolonial theory; another essay not included here, 'Traveling Theory', considers how ideas travel and mutate with new surroundings. The piece we have chosen to reprint here, 'Reflections on Exile', asserts an 'essential association' between nationalism and exile; they are 'opposites informing and constituting each other'. Distinguishing exiles from emigrants, refugees and tourists, Said considers them representatives not specifically of an American but of a modern condition. Exile is the shadow side of nationalism's triumphant assertion of belonging; both breed a sense of specialness or exceptionalism. He shows how new nationalisms emerge from solidarity amongst exiled groups, leading in their turn to further cycles of exile and group formation. Rootlessness is the defining feature of exile for Said; it is the modern form of tragedy. Exile bears on transatlantic theory and practice in several ways: historically, it was as exiles that many Europeans arrived and settled in the Americas; comparative literature was promulgated as a discipline in the American academy largely by displaced European intellectuals; exiles are by definition travellers, who bring past experience to bear on new encounters, for whom knowledge is always contapuntal; the experience of exiles questions the authority and the permanence of boundaries and frontiers. Scholars have also argued for a more direct literary connection, with Georg Lukács, for example, claiming that the genre of the novel is itself the product of 'transcendental homelessness', and Theodor Adorno* (in Said's paraphrase) asserting that 'the only home truly available now . . . is in writing'. And – not least – a compelling body of transatlantic literature takes exile as its overt or implicit subject: Melville's Wellingborough Redburn discovers his own transcendental homelessness as a result of his journey to rediscover his British roots; Pound's Cantos offer a dizzying kaleidoscope of exilic motions through time and place; the subject of Michel de Certeau's 'Ethno-Graphy', Jean de Léry, was a sixteenth-century French exile who fled first to Geneva and thence to Brazil, where he participated in the founding of a Calvinist community. The history of his journey, published in 1578 as *Histoire d'un voyage faict en la terre du Brésil*, addresses the problems of finding an adequate correlative in writing for an experience of radical otherness – the core issue, at its starkest, for every narrative of travel. De Certeau traces the movements of de Léry's account across the terrain of his encounter. Two barriers, linguistic (the problem of leakage of meaning in translation) and spatial (the extent and expanse of territory, flora, fauna and customs to be registered), become the structuring features of an ethnography – a scientific description of race and culture – that folds personal experience into the transmission of information. Language, he shows, is a point of departure every bit as much as place is, or the ethos of the dis-placed observer: translation, travel and the comparative perspective are mutually implicated in this writing.

In her influential book *Imperial Eyes: Travel Writing and Transculturation*, from which the brief extract below is taken, Mary Louise Pratt develops the ethnographic dimension of travel writing to include recognition of reciprocity, arguing that the periphery (the 'other') and the metropolis (the perspective of home) are mutually constitutive. Pratt's dialectical approach to travel writing establishes the useful concept of the 'contact zone': 'the space of colonial encounters, the space in which peoples geographically and historically [and, we might add, linguistically] separated come into contact with each other'. The term has had extended currency in postcolonial writing, and more recently in transatlantic criticism that concerns itself with encounters across borders and boundaries. Pratt's term for a figure who operates freely within a contact zone is 'transculturator'; her reading of Alexander von Humboldt's 1799–1804 exploration of Central and South America exemplifies the complexities and reciprocities of such a transcultural engagement. Akin to James Fenimore Cooper's Leatherstocking Natty Bumppo, or the Scottish-South American hero 'Don Roberto' (Robert Cunningham-Grahame), the transculturator is a go-between, like the *métis* who operated as translators and guides between the Indian and French or British camps in the Franco-British conflict in Canada in 1757–63. Like exiles, the *métis* were figured as cultural hybrids, needed by both sides but trusted by neither.

Mary Baine Campbell's essay moves away from thematised perspectives to conclude the section with a comprehensive overview of the field of contemporary travel theory and its embeddedness in a range of major theoretical discourses beyond the postcolonial and ethnographic studies mentioned above; her historical survey of twentieth-century feminist, Marxist*, historicist, poststructuralist, cultural materialist and psychoanalytic approaches to travel advances a catholic repertoire of possibilities for transatlantic criticism.

FURTHER READING

Adams, Percy (1962) *Travelers and Travel Liars, 1660–1800*. Berkeley: University of California Press.

Clifford, James (1997) *Routes: Travel and Translation in the Late Twentieth Century*. Cambridge, MA: Harvard University Press.

Cohen, Margaret, and Carolyn Dever (eds) (2002) *The Literary Channel: The International Invention of the Novel*. Princeton: Princeton University Press.

Franklin, Wayne (1979) *Discoverers, Explorers, Settlers: The Diligent Writers of Early America*. Chicago: University of Chicago Press.

Mazzeo, Tilar (2005) 'The Impossibility of Being Anglo-American: The Rhetoric of Emigration and Transatlanticism in British Culture, 1791–1833', *European Romantic Review* 16.1: 59–78.

Rojek, Chris and James Urry (eds) (1997) *Touring Cultures: Transformations of Travel and Theory*. London: Routledge.

Said, Edward (1983) 'Traveling Theory', in Edward Said, *The World, the Text, and the Critic*. Cambridge, MA: Harvard University Press.

Schmeller, Erik S. (2004) *Perceptions of Race and Nation in English and American Travel Writers, 1833–1914*. New York: Peter Lang.

Taylor, Andrew (2004) ' "Mixture is a secret of the English Island": Transatlantic Emerson and the Location of the Intellectual', *Atlantic Studies* 1.2: 158–77.

Youngs, Tim (2004) 'The Importance of Travel Writing', *European English Messenger* 13.2: 55–62.

I

'REFLECTIONS ON EXILE'

Edward Said

We come to nationalism and its essential association with exile. Nationalism is an assertion of belonging in and to a place, a people, a heritage. It affirms the home created by a community of language, culture and customs; and, by so doing, it fends off exile, fights to prevent its ravages. Indeed, the interplay between nationalism and exile is like Hegel's* dialectic of servant and master, opposites informing and constituting each other. All nationalisms in their early stages develop from a condition of estrangement. The struggles to win American independence, to unify Germany or Italy, to liberate Algeria were those of national groups separated – exiled – from what was construed to be their rightful way of life. Triumphant, achieved nationalism then justifies, retrospectively as well as prospectively, a history selectively strung together in a narrative form: thus all nationalisms have their founding fathers, their basic, quasi-religious texts, their rhetoric of belonging, their historical and geographical landmarks, their official enemies and heroes. This collective ethos forms what Pierre Bourdieu*, the French sociologist, calls the *habitus*, the coherent amalgam of practices linking habit with inhabitance. In time, successful nationalisms consign truth exclusively to themselves and relegate falsehood and inferiority to outsiders (as in the rhetoric of capitalist versus communist, or the European versus the Asiatic).

From Edward Said (2001) *Reflections on Exile and Other Literary and Cultural Essays*. London: Granta.

And just beyond the frontier between 'us' and the 'outsiders' is the perilous territory of not-belonging: this is to where in a primitive time peoples were banished, and where in the modern era immense aggregates of humanity loiter as refugees and displaced persons.

Nationalisms are about groups, but in a very acute sense exile is a solitude experienced outside the group: the deprivations felt at not being with others in the communal habitation. How, then, does one surmount the loneliness of exile without falling into the encompassing and thumping language of national pride, collective sentiments, group passions? What is there worth saving and holding on to between the extremes of exile on the one hand, and the often bloody-minded affirmations of nationalism on the other? Do nationalism and exile have any intrinsic attributes? Are they simply two conflicting varieties of paranoia?

These are questions that cannot ever be fully answered because each assumes that exile and nationalism can be discussed neutrally, without reference to each other. They cannot be. Because both terms include everything from the most collective of collective sentiments to the most private of private emotions, there is hardly language adequate for both. But there is certainly nothing about nationalism's public and all-inclusive ambitions that touches the core of the exile's predicament.

Because exile, unlike nationalism, is fundamentally a discontinuous state of being. Exiles are cut off from their roots, their land, their past. They generally do not have armies or states, although they are often in search of them. Exiles feel, therefore, an urgent need to reconstitute their broken lives, usually by choosing to see themselves as part of a triumphant ideology or a restored people. The crucial thing is that a state of exile free from this triumphant ideology – designed to reassemble an exile's broken history into a new whole – is virtually unbearable, and virtually impossible in today's world. Look at the fate of the Jews, the Palestinians and the Armenians.

[. . .]

Although it is true that anyone prevented from returning home is an exile, some distinctions can be made between exiles, refugees, expatriates and émigrés. Exile originated in the age-old practice of banishment. Once banished, the exile lives an anomalous and miserable life, with the stigma of being an outsider. Refugees, on the other hand, are a creation of the twentieth-century state. The word 'refugee' has become a political one, suggesting large herds of innocent and bewildered people requiring urgent international assistance, whereas 'exile' carries with it, I think, a touch of solitude and spirituality.

Expatriates voluntarily live in an alien country, usually for personal or social reasons. Hemingway and Fitzgerald were not forced to live in France. Expatriates may share in the solitude and estrangement of exile, but they do not suffer under its rigid proscriptions. Émigrés enjoy an ambiguous status. Technically, an émigré is anyone who emigrates to a new country. Choice in the matter is certainly a possibility. Colonial officials, missionaries, technical experts, mercenaries and military advisers on loan may in a sense live in exile, but they have not been banished. White settlers in Africa, parts of Asia and Australia may once have been exiles, but as pioneers and nation-builders the label 'exile' dropped away from them.

Much of the exile's life is taken up with compensating for disorienting loss by creating a new world to rule. It is not surprising that so many exiles seem to be novelists, chess players, political activists, and intellectuals. Each of these occupations requires a minimal investment in objects and places a great premium on mobility and skill. The exile's new world, logically enough, is unnatural and its unreality resembles fiction. Georg Lukács*, in *Theory of the Novel*, argued with compelling force that the novel, a literary form created out of the unreality of ambition and fantasy, is *the* form of 'transcendental home-lessness'. Classical epics, Lukács wrote, emanate from settled cultures in which values are clear, identities stable, life unchanging. The European novel is grounded in precisely the opposite experience, that of a changing society in which an itinerant and disinherited middle-class hero or heroine seeks to con-struct a new world that somewhat resembles an old one left behind for ever. In the epic there is no *other* world, only the finality of *this* one. Odysseus returns to Ithaca after years of wandering; Achilles will die because he cannot escape his fate. The novel, however, exists because other worlds *may* exist, alternatives for bourgeois speculators, wanderers, exiles.

No matter how well they may do, exiles are always eccentrics who *feel* their difference (even as they frequently exploit it) as a kind of orphanhood. Anyone who is really homeless regards the habit of seeing estrangement in everything modern as an affectation, a display of modish attitudes. Clutching difference like a weapon to be used with stiffened will, the exile jealously insists on his or her right to refuse to belong.

This usually translates into an intransigence that is not easily ignored. Wilfulness, exaggeration, overstatement: these are characteristic styles of being an exile, methods for compelling the world to accept your vision – which you make more unacceptable because you are in fact unwilling to have it accepted. It is yours, after all. Composure and serenity are the last things associated with the work of exiles. Artists in exile are decidedly unpleasant, and their stub-bornness insinuates itself into even their exalted works. Dante's vision in *The Divine Comedy* is tremendously powerful in its universality and detail, but even the beatific peace achieved in the *Paradiso* bears traces of the vindictive-ness and severity of judgement embodied in the *Inferno*. Who but an exile like Dante, banished from Florence, would use eternity as a place for settling old scores?

James Joyce *chose* to be in exile: to give force to his artistic vocation. In an uncannily effective way – as Richard Ellmann has shown in his biography – Joyce picked a quarrel with Ireland and kept it alive so as to sustain the strictest opposition to what was familiar. Ellmann says that 'whenever his relations with his native land were in danger of improving, [Joyce] was to find a new incident to solidify his intransigence and to reaffirm the rightness of his voluntary absence'. Joyce's fiction concerns what in a letter he once described as the state of being 'alone and friendless'. And although it is rare to pick banishment as a way of life, Joyce perfectly understood its trials.

But Joyce's success as an exile stresses the question lodged at its very heart: is exile so extreme and private that any instrumental use of it is ultimately a trivialization? How is it that the literature of exile has taken its place as a *topos* of human experience alongside the literature of adventure, education or discovery? Is this the *same* exile that quite literally kills Yanko Goorall [a character in Joseph Conrad's tale 'Amy Foster', discussed by Said earlier in the essay] and has bred the expensive, often dehumanizing relationship between twentieth-century exile and nationalism? Or is it some more benign variety?

Much of the contemporary interest in exile can be traced to the somewhat pallid notion that non-exiles can share in the benefits of exile as a redemptive motif. There is, admittedly, a certain plausibility and truth to this idea. Like medieval itinerant scholars or learned Greek slaves in the Roman Empire, exiles – the exceptional ones among them – do leaven their environments. And naturally 'we' concentrate on that enlightening aspect of 'their' presence among us, not on their misery or their demands. But looked at from the bleak political perspective of modern mass dislocations, individual exiles force us to recognize the tragic fate of homelessness in a necessarily heartless world.

A generation ago, Simone Weil posed the dilemma of exile as concisely as it has ever been expressed. 'To be rooted', she said, 'is perhaps the most important and least recognized need of the human soul'. Yet Weil also saw that most remedies for uprootedness in this era of world wars, deportations and mass exterminations are almost as dangerous as what they purportedly remedy. Of these, the state – or, more accurately, statism – is one of the most insidious, since worship of the state tends to supplant all other human bonds.

Weil exposes us anew to that whole complex of pressures and constraints that lie at the centre of the exile's predicament, which, as I have suggested, is as close as we come in the modern era to tragedy. There is the sheer fact of isolation and displacement, which produces the kind of narcissistic masochism that resists all efforts at amelioration, acculturation and community. At this extreme the exile can make a fetish of exile, a practice that distances him or her from all connections and commitments. To live as if everything around you were temporary and perhaps trivial is to fall prey to petulant cynicism as well as to querulous lovelessness. More common is the pressure on the exile to join – parties, national movements, the state. The exile is offered a new set of affiliations and develops new loyalties. But there is also a loss – of critical perspective, of intellectual reserve, of moral courage.

It must also be recognized that the defensive nationalism of exiles often fosters self-awareness as much as it does the less attractive forms of self-assertion. Such reconstitutive projects as assembling a nation out of exile (and this is true in this century for Jews and Palestinians) involve constructing a national history, reviving an ancient language, founding national institutions like libraries and universities. And these, while they sometimes promote strident ethnocentrism, also give rise to investigations of self that inevitably go far beyond such simple and positive facts as 'ethnicity'. For example, there is the self-consciousness of an individual trying to understand why the histories of the Palestinians and the Jews have certain patterns to them, why in spite of oppression and the threat of extinction a particular ethos remains alive in exile.

Necessarily, then, I speak of exile not as a privilege, but as an *alternative* to the mass institutions that dominate modern life. Exile is not, after all, a matter of choice: you are born into it, or it happens to you. But, provided that the exile refuses to sit on the sidelines nursing a wound, there are things to be learned: he or she must cultivate a scrupulous (not indulgent or sulky) subjectivity.

Perhaps the most rigorous example of such subjectivity is to be found in the writing of Theodor Adorno*, the German-Jewish philosopher and critic. Adorno's masterwork, *Minima Moralia*, is an autobiography written while in exile; it is subtitled *Reflexionen aus dem beschädigten Leben (Reflections from a Mutilated Life)*. Ruthlessly opposed to what he called the 'administered' world, Adorno saw all life as pressed into ready-made forms, prefabricated 'homes'. He argued that everything that one says or thinks, as well as every object one possesses, is ultimately a mere commodity. Language is jargon, objects are for sale. To refuse this state of affairs is the exile's intellectual mission.

Adorno's reflections are informed by the belief that the only home truly available now, though fragile and vulnerable, is in writing. Elsewhere, 'the house is past. The bombings of European cities, as well as the labour and concentration camps, merely precede as executors, with what the immanent development of technology had long decided was to be the fate of houses. These are now good only to be thrown away like old food cans'. In short, Adorno says with a grave irony, 'it is part of morality not to be at home in one's home'.

To follow Adorno is to stand away from 'home' in order to look at it with the exile's detachment. For there is considerable merit in the practice of noting the discrepancies between various concepts and ideas and what they actually produce. We take home and language for granted; they become nature, and their underlying assumptions recede into dogma and orthodoxy.

The exile knows that in a secular and contingent world, homes are always provisional. Borders and barriers, which enclose us within the safety of familiar territory, can also become prisons, and are often defended beyond reason or necessity. Exiles cross borders, break barriers of thought and experience.

[. . .]

For an exile, habits of life, expression or activity in the new environment inevitably occur against the memory of these things in another environment. Thus both the new and the old environments are vivid, actual, occurring together contrapuntally. There is a unique pleasure in this sort of apprehension, especially if the exile is conscious of other contrapuntal juxtapositions that diminish orthodox judgement and elevate appreciative sympathy. There is also a particular sense of achievement in acting as if one were at home wherever one happens to be.

This remains risky, however: the habit of dissimulation is both wearying and nerve-racking. Exile is never the state of being satisfied, placid, or secure. Exile, in the words of Wallace Stevens, is 'a mind of winter' in which the pathos of summer and autumn as much as the potential of spring are nearby but unobtainable. Perhaps this is another way of saying that a life of exile moves according to a different calendar, and is less seasonal and settled than life at home. Exile is life led outside habitual order. It is nomadic, decentred, contrapuntal; but no sooner does one get accustomed to it than its unsettling force erupts anew.

2

'ETHNO-GRAPHY: SPEECH, OR THE SPACE OF THE OTHER: JEAN DE LÉRY'

Michel de Certeau

Signified through a concept of writing, the work of redirecting the plurality of ways [of writing] toward the single productive center is precisely what Jean de Léry's* story attains. As his preface already indicates, the tale is fabricated from 'memoirs . . . written in Brazilian ink and in America itself', a raw material doubly drawn from the tropics, since the very characters that bring the primitive object into the textual web are made from a red ink extracted from the *paubrasil*, a wood that is one of the principal imports to sixteenth-century Europe.

Yet only through the effect of its organization does the *Histoire* 'yield profit'. To be sure, the literary *operation* that brings back to the producer the results of signs that were sent far away has a condition of possibility in a *structural* difference between an area 'over here' and another 'over there'. The narrative plays on the relation between the structure which establishes the separation and the operation which overcomes it, creating effects of meaning in this fashion. The break is what is taken for granted everywhere by the text, itself a labor of suturing.

THE BREAK

At the manifest level, in the distribution of masses, the separation (between 'over here' and 'over there') first appears as an occanic division: it is the Atlantic, a rift between the Old and the New World. In telling of tempests, sea

From Michel de Certeau (1988) *The Writing of History*. New York: Columbia University Press.

monsters, acts of piracy, 'marvels', or the ups and downs of transoceanic navigation, the chapters at the beginning and at the end (chapters 1–5 and 21–2) develop this structural rupture along the historical line of a chronicle of a crossing: each episode modulates uncanniness according to a particular element of the cosmological range (air, water, fish, bird, man, etc.), adding its proper effect to the series, in which difference is simultaneously the generative principle and the object to be made credible. The chapters that present Tupi society (7–19), bordered by the preceding, exhibit the same principle but now systematically, according to a scheme of dissimilarity that must affect every genre and every degree of being in order to situate the 'over there' within the cosmos: 'This American land where, as I shall be deducing, everything that is seen, whether in the customs of its inhabitants, the shapes of its animals, or in general in what the earth produces, is *dissimilar* in respect to what we have in Europe, Asia, and Africa, might well in our eyes be called a *new* world'.[1]

In this landscape the figure of dissimilarity is either a deviation from what can be seen 'over here' or, more often, the combination of Western forms that seem to have been cut off, and whose fragments seem to be associated in unexpected ways. Thus, among the four-footed animals (of which there exists 'not one . . . that in any or every aspect in any fashion can resemble our own'), the *tapiroussou* is 'half-cow and half-donkey', 'being both of the one and of the other'.[2] The primitives incorporate the splitting that divides the universe. Their picture of the world follows a traditional cosmological order whose scaffolding is exposed, but it is a picture covered with countless broken mirrors in which the same fracture is reflected (half this, half that).

THE WORK OF RETURNING

This structural difference, particularized in the accidents that happen along the way or in the portraits in the gallery of primitives, only forms the area where an operation of return is effected, in a mode drawn according to the literary zones that it crosses. The narrative as a whole belabors the division that is located everywhere in order to show that the *other returns to the same*. In this fashion it inserts itself within the general problem of *crusade* that still rules over the discovery of the world in the sixteenth century: 'conquest and conversion'.[3] But this narrative displaces that problem through an effect of distortion that is introduced structurally by the breakage of space into two worlds.

[. . .]

A part of the world which appeared to be entirely other is brought back to the same by a displacement that throws uncanniness out of skew in order to turn it into an exteriority behind which an interiority, the unique definition of man, can be recognized.

This operation will be repeated hundreds of times throughout ethnological works. In Léry's case we see it evinced in the staging of the primitive world, through a division between *Nature*, whose uncanniness is exteriority, and *civil* society, in which a truth of man is always legible. The break between over here and over there is transformed into a rift between nature and culture. Finally, nature is what is other, while man stays the same. By the way, we can observe that this metamorphosis, a product of the displacement generated by the text, makes of nature the area where *esthetic* or *religious* experience and admiration are expressed and where Léry's prayer is spoken, while the social space is the place where an *ethics* is developed through a constant parallel between festivity and work. In this already modern combination, social production, what reproduces sameness and marks an identity, posits nature, esthetics, and religiosity outside of itself.

We can follow in some detail the arc traced by the story. [...] In a first movement, it goes toward alterity: first the travel in the direction of the land over there (chapters 1–5), and then the overview of marvels and natural wonders (chapters 7–13). This movement has its final punctuation with the ecstatic song glorifying God (the end of chapter 13). The poem, Psalm 104, marks a vanishing point opening onto alterity, what is out of this world and unspeakable. At this point, with the analysis of Tupi society (chapters 14–19), a second movement begins: it goes from the most uncanny (war, chapter 14; anthropophagia, chapter 15) in order to progressively unveil a social model (laws and police, chapter 18; therapeutics, health, the cult of the dead, chapter 19). Then passing through the oceanic break, the narrative can bring this civilized primitive as far back as Geneva by way of return (chapters 21–2).

This work is indeed a *hermeneutics of the other*. Onto the shores of the New World it transports the Christian exegetical apparatus which, born of a necessary relation with Jewish alterity, has been applied in turn to the biblical tradition, to Greco-Latin antiquity, and to many more foreign totalities. On one more occasion it draws effects of meaning from its relation with the other. Ethnology will become a form of exegesis that has not ceased providing the modern West with what it needs in order to articulate its identity through a relation with the past or the future, with foreigners or with nature.

The functioning of this new hermeneutics of the other is already sketched in Léry's text in the shape of two problematic issues that transform its theological usage. These are the linguistic operation of translation, and the position of a subject in relation to an expanse of objects. In both cases the (oceanic) break that characterizes the difference is not suppressed; on the contrary, the text presupposes and thwarts this break in order to be grounded as a discourse of knowledge.

The bar between the Old and the New World is the line on which an *activity of translation* can be seen replacing a theological language. This discrete transformation is indicated by two chapters of which both – since one is devoted to departure and the other to return – constitute a navigational lock, a transit, between the travelogue and the picture of the Tupi world. The first, chapter 6, tells of theological debates at Fort Coligny in the Rio Bay and of the 'inconstancy and variation' of Villegagnon 'in matters of religion', the cause for the disembarkation of the Huguenot mission among the Tupis on the coast, 'who were incomparably more humane with us'.[4] The other, chapter 20, which Léry designates as the 'colloquy of the savage's language',[5] is a dictionary – or rather a French-Tupi Berlitz guide.

According to the first account, the Island of Coligny mediates between the Old and the New World and is a place where divisiveness and the confusion of languages reign supreme. It is a Babel* in the twilight of the universe. Yet confusion is no longer avowed here. It is hidden in a language of hypocrisy (that of Villegagnon), where what is said is not what is thought, much less what is done. At the end of the globe, at the threshold of the unknown Tupi world, deception proliferates beneath the veil of a literal reproduction of Calvinist* theology: such are the public prayers of the 'zealot' Villegagnon, whose 'inner side and heart it was discomfiting to get to know'.[6] Is this not tantamount to saying that at this point language no longer holds an anchor in reality, and that at the farthest borders of the West it floats detached from its truth and from any firm grounding, caught up into the indefinite turnings of a lure?

Chapter 20 comes at the end of the description of the Tupi lands. After the linguistic confusion surrounding the Island of Coligny, this vast picture of the primitive world is an epiphany of things, the *discourse of an effectivity*. Clearly the contents were first given as antinomic, but they were divided and elaborated in such a way as to become, in their human sector, a world which does justice to the truth of Geneva. Thus, a reality is already there, and it saturates Léry's statements. What separates the Western world from that world is no longer an array of things, but their appearance – essentially, a foreign language. From stated difference there only remains a *language to be translated*. Whence the chapter which provides the code for linguistic transformation. It allows unity to be restored by folding upon one another all the heterogenous peelings that cover an identity of substance.

The dictionary becomes a theological instrument. Just as religious language is perverted by a usage which is 'discomfiting to get to know' and which refers to unfathomable intentions or 'heart', now, situated on the very line that the rift of the universe demarcated, translation *lets* primitive reality pass into Western discourse. All that is needed is to have one language 'converted' into another. As Calvin already suggested, the operation of translation frees one from reducing language to a first tongue from which all others would be derived; it replaces the being-there of a beginning with a transformation which unravels on the surface of languages, which makes a single meaning pass from tongue to tongue, and which will soon provide linguistics, the science of these transformations, with a decisive role in all recapitulative strategies.

In the place where the *Histoire* locates it, foreign language already acquires the double function of being the way by which a substance (the effectivity of primitive life) happens to uphold the discourse of a European knowledge, and of being a fable, a speech which is unaware of what it expresses before decipherment can provide it with meaning and practical usage. The being which authenticates the discourse is no longer directly received from God; it is made to come from the foreign place itself, where it is the gold mine hidden under an exotic exteriority, the truth to be discerned beneath primitive babble.

For Léry this economy of translation entails, moreover, a general problematic. For example, it orders the analysis of living beings and therein becomes specific. In effect, plants and animals are classified according to the modulations of a constant distinction between what is seen (appearance) and what is eaten (edible substance). Exteriority captivates the eye, it astonishes or horrifies, but this theater is often a lie and a fiction in respect to edibility, which measures the utility, or the essence, of fruits and animals. The double diagnostic of taste corrects seductions or repulsions of the eye: is it healthy or not to eat, raw or cooked? The same holds for exotic fable, the enchanting but often deceptive voice: the interpreter discriminates in terms of utility when, first creating a distance between what it says and what it does not say, he translates what it does not say in forms of truth that are good to hear back in France. An intellectual edibility is the essence that has to be distinguished from ravishments of the ear.

From the baroque spectacle of flora and fauna to their edibility; from primitive festivals to their utopian and moral exemplariness; and finally from exotic language to its intelligibility, the same dynamic unfolds. It is that of *utility* – or, rather, that of *production*, at least insofar as this voyage which increases the initial investment is, analogically, a productive labor, 'a labor that produces capital'. From the moment of departure from Geneva a language sets out to find a world; at stake is a mission. Deprived of effectivity – without grounding – at the furthermost borders of the West (on the Island of Coligny, chapter 6), it finally appears as a language of pure conviction or subjectivity, a language that is incapable of defending its objective statements against deceptive use, leaving its speakers no recourse but to flee. This language is opposed, on the other side of things, to the world of total alterity, or of primitive nature. Here effectivity is at first uncanniness. But within the breadth of this alterity, analysis introduces a rift between exteriority (esthetics, etc.) and interiority (meaning that can be assimilated). It causes a slow reversion, beginning with the greatest exteriority (the general spectacle of nature, then the forests, etc.), and progresses toward the regions of greater interiority (sickness and death). It thus prepares primitive effectivity to become, by means of translation (chapter 20), *the world that is spoken by an initial language*. The point of departure was an over here (a 'we') relativized by an elsewhere (a 'they'), and a language deprived of 'substance'. This point of departure becomes a place for *truth*, since here the *discourse which comprehends the world* is in use. Such is the production for which the primitive is useful: it makes language move from the affirmation of a conviction into a position of knowledge. Yet if, from its point of departure, the language to be restored were theological, what is reinstated upon return is (in principle) either scientific or philosophical.

This position of knowledge is upheld by using the line between *over here and over there* in a way that also results from the transformation that is being performed. This line is used to distinguish between the ethnological subject and object. In Léry's text it is drawn through the difference between two literary forms, that which narrates tales of travel (chapters 1–6 and 21–2), and that which describes a natural and human landscape (chapters 7–19).

[. . .]

On the first is written the chronicle of facts and deeds by the group or by Léry. These events are narrated in terms of *tense*: a *history* is composed with a chronology – very detailed – of actions undertaken or lived by a *subject*. On the second plane *objects* are set out in a space ruled not by localizations or geographical routes – these indications are very rare and always vague – but by a taxonomy of living beings, a systematic inventory of philosophical questions, etc.; in sum, the catalogue raisonné of a knowledge. The historical parts of the text value time 'as an accomplice of our will'[7] and the articulation of *Western acting*. In relation to this subject who acts, *the other is extension*, where understanding delimits objects.

For Léry, the book is a 'History' in which 'seen things' are still attached to the observer's activities. He combines two discourses that will soon be separated from one another. One discourse is attached to science; as opposed to 'natural history' (left to the philosopher) and to 'divine history' (left to the theologian), it assumes its task, according to Jean Bodin, to be one of 'explaining the actions of contemporary man living in society' and analyzing 'the productions of the human will' insofar as it is *semper sui dissimilis*.[8] In the sixteenth century, at least for theologians, history takes for granted the autonomy of a political and juridical *subject* of actions (the prince, the nation, the 'civil order') on the one hand, and on the other, of *fields* where dissimilitudes between various expressions of man's will (law, language, institutions, etc.) can be measured. In Léry's case the subject is momentarily an 'exiled prince', a man lost between sky and earth, between a God who is disappearing and an earth that is yet to be discovered; the subject's itinerancy connects a language left vacant to the work needed to provide another effectivity for this language. Later there will be 'ethnology', when the picture of the primitive world will have acquired a homogeneity independent of the displacements of actual journeys; in other words, when the space of 'objective' representation will be distinguished from the observing judgment, and when it will have become futile to present the subject in the text of a constructive operation.

NOTES

1. Jean de Léry, *Histoire d'un voyage faict en la terre du Brésil*, ed. Paul Gaffarel, 2 vols (Paris: A. Lemerre, 1880), vol. 1, pp. 34–5; author's emphasis.
2. Ibid., vol. 1, p. 157.
3. Alphonse Dupront, 'Espace et humanisme', *Bibliothèque d'Humanisme et Renaissance* 8 (1946): 19.
4. De Léry, *Histoire*, vol. 1, p. 112.
5. Ibid., vol. 1, p. 12.
6. Ibid., vol. 1, pp. 91–6.
7. Louis Dumont, *La Civilisation indienne et nous* (Paris: Armand Colin, 1964), p. 33.
8. Jean Bodin, *Methodus ad facilem historiarum cognitionem* (1566), in *Oeuvres philosophiques* (Paris: PUF, 1951), pp. 114–15.

3

'INTRODUCTION' TO *SEA CHANGES*

Stephen Fender

[The] ideology of American emigration and settlement was first articulated in European ideas about the New World, and from the beginning these ideas were organized around the classical dichotomy of culture and nature. America represented nature and Europe culture. Upon their first encounters with the New World, the Europeans imagined it as a sort of paradise, from which the cultural accretions of the Fall working itself out through history were providentially absent. In time, particularly in British imperial theory, the paradisal model gave way to a model of settlement. Now American nature was promoted for its positive and material values, for the resources that could sustain an emigrant population and be exploited for metropolitan manufactures.

Even before the American Revolution, the American colonies (and especially Massachusetts) began to construct themselves, and to be constructed, in a posture adversarial to the Mother Country. After American independence, during the unrest that followed the Napoleonic Wars*, British progressives and conservatives began to inscribe the domestic debate for and against reform within an argument about the viability of the new republic across the Atlantic, and particularly about the wisdom of emigrating there. Though almost twice as many British subjects left their native shores for Canada, Australia and New Zealand during the same period, it was emigration to the United States that was the lively political issue.

From Stephen Fender (1992) *Sea Changes: British Emigration and American Literature*. Cambridge: Cambridge University Press.

What did the British migrants to the United States think themselves? Though skeptical of the more visionary promotional tracts written by boosters and radicals alike (especially when the propagandists had invested in American property on which they hoped to persuade their readers to settle), the emigrants were not immune to the general promise of the New World: its liberal institutions, its relative freedom from inherited class distinctions, the opportunity afforded by its cheap land to convert the one commodity they possessed in abundance – their labor – into an agrarian self-sufficiency.

From the beginning of American settlement British emigrants to North America had expressed these feelings in the rhetoric of both the paradisal and colonial models: of stripping away Old World culture and embracing the nature of the New. The Puritans who migrated to Massachusetts found in their theology of the portable faith a ready-made ideology in which to accept, propose and justify their departure from the worldly comforts of England, but they were as ready as were later emigrants to celebrate the material profusion of nature they encountered in their new home.

There were moral issues implied in both the paradisal and the colonial branches of emigration rhetoric. The paradisal model cast a cold eye on cultural institutions – in some hands it was really a satire on the Old World – and raised questions about the proper use of the leisure that life in the New held forth as a promise. The colonial model put nature to the scientific test. Its catalogs of natural profusion awaiting exploitation were also a way of authenticating the fabulous traveler's report in the material reality of the verifiable. Furthermore even the apparently neutral economic technicalities of mercantilist circulation – a guaranteed supply of raw materials for metropolitan manufacture and in turn a captive market for the finished goods in the colonies – increased value at every stage of its process, and put the unemployed to productive work. Crèvecoeur's *Letters from an American Farmer* explored both these models of emigration rhetoric, and thus gave America its first moral geography – and when that scheme was overtaken by the violence of the Revolutionary War, its first narrative to end with the protagonist lighting out for the wilderness.

So the rhetoric of emigration gave words and figures to a distinctively republican American voice. If the influential metropolitan culture caricatured American speech and institutions as degenerate, and if even some Americans began to suspect that a lack of imaginative 'association' and paucity of local social stratification would render American poetry and fiction impossible, others like Tom Paine* and Thomas Jefferson drew on the discourse of emigration to fashion a national project out of the conflict between culture and nature. In Paine's *Common Sense* Old World hierarchies and prerogatives were satirized as they had been by emigrants casting off the culture they had to leave behind, and American rebellion naturalized through the imagery of irresistible growth. Jefferson borrowed from the emigrant's natural catalog to authenticate the

American environment on the level of physical climate and nurture, disproving Count Buffon's* theory that species degenerated when transplanted to the New World with scientific-looking inventories of American animals to demonstrate the superiority of their dimensions and variety over their European equivalents.

As with the physical environment, so with the cultural. Repeatedly the proponents of a distinctly American literature, from Emerson and Whitman to William Carlos Williams, sought to establish their national cultural projects in words and arguments drawn from the rhetoric of emigration. The settlers' material nature became the poets' native materials. Like the settler, the poet answered the felt lack of American quality with an endless profusion of American quantity, thus valorizing the ideas of process and the material. The self-interrogating narrative that never comes to rest on a final, determinate interpretation, and the long poem that never ends, and also remains open to chance material encounters along its way, fashioned the emigrants' rhetoric of process into the two distinctive American literary inventions.

Characteristically the settlers described their migration as an irrevocable transformation in their personal and physical condition, the 'travail' initiating them into a new dispensation of better health, reformed manners, and sometimes even a higher spiritual state. Consequently the decision to migrate was momentous, personal and irreversible. Any reluctance to accept the new home, or inability to adapt to its demands and conventions, seemed to constitute a failure, for which the unhappy emigrant had to accept individual responsibility. In seeking to reverse the irreversible – that is, in failing to conform to the paradigm of initiation – back-migrants were thought to have disgraced the families to whom they returned, and aroused the contempt of the emigrants who stuck it out. So their stories had to be discounted in advance, and written out of the record. Conversely, the 'successful' emigrant's letter home was treasured and preserved, as the badge of the initiate.

This special drama of the rite of passage in which the experience of emigration was inscribed also contributed to the formation of the national consciousness and the literature which reflected and conditioned it. The sense of reformation is both communal (in that the process is simultaneously happening to others in the sect or sodality) and individual (in that it is motivated by personal election and conviction). This paradox is reflected in the American legal fiction of the collective singular: in the principle of the sovereignty of 'We the People' and in the very idea of an 'American character'. Novels based on the immigrant experience express the crisis of uprooting and resettlement in the imagery of adolescence, distributing the opposing values of Old World and New between the generations of immigrant parents and children. More generally the characteristic focus on adolescence in American fiction – the country's fondness for stories of good-bad boys like Huckleberry Finn and Alexander Portnoy – reflects and reinforces the national culture of the emigrant's rite of passage.

In another popular American form, the western, an individual is initiated into a higher condition of knowledge through the act of transcending the frontiers of his communal and individual culture. In the first western, and arguably the American foundation narrative, Captain John Smith is captured and his life threatened by the Indians, then saved by Pocahontas, the Chief's daughter, after which he returns to the settlers' camp to stiffen their resolve and prevent their back-migrating to England. As the frontier moved westwards, so did the drama of initiation. Francis Parkman's *The Oregon Trail* extends the narrative of the emigrant's rite of passage into a definition of American identity: as an American explores the furthest reaches of his continent, so he learns what makes up the American character, and his own.

Not everyone reacted favorably to the experience of emigration, however, or could turn its exhilarations into new forms of expression. Some emigrants – though how many is not clear, since their written remains are few and fragmentary – were disappointed with the New World as they found it. Of those who returned, some converted themselves into 'travelers', thus saving face and exploiting a ready market for hostile comments on the audacious republic. Back-migrants and literary travelers alike – and sometimes, as in the case of Mrs Trollope*, the categories overlapped – addressed themselves as much to the British political debate (and much more so to a British audience) than to anything American, but their books also disconcerted and annoyed the Americans, who took their criticisms at face value.

So for the most part the disappointed migrants either fell silent or recast themselves as conservatives on re-entry. The exceptions to this rule were the Puritans, whose general standard of literacy and respect for the word, and whose habit of semi-public self examination, ensured that they set down and preserved a fuller record than most other settlers of their motives for emigrating and their feelings on arrival. The Puritans' evidence provides fascinating insights on the choices to be made before leaving home, but also suggests a sense of personal anticlimax, a sort of spiritual backsliding, shortly after arrival. On the more public level of experience, Puritan leaders sometimes complained of the community having fallen away from its 'first love' in charity.

What the Puritans reveal, and less articulate witnesses fail to convey, is the difference between a *rite* of passage and just a passage. The rite is a ritualized journey out to the borders of the culture and back again, whereas the passage – which is what 'successful' emigration actually is – goes one way only. This expectation that the experience of emigration would be more ritualized and symmetrical – more susceptible to narrative shaping – than it turned out to be in the event, may account for the frustration and anticlimax experienced on arrival in the new setting. Significantly the characteristically American narratives of initiation, like Mary Rowlandson's* story of her captivity or Parkman's *Oregon Trail*, not only send the protagonist out beyond the frontier, but ritualize the passage by bringing him or her back as well.

So emigration could be disabling as well as enabling, could trouble the American imagination as well as stimulate and liberate it. Some of these doubts and discontents became internalized in American thought and writing. One recurrent theme is the nostalgic longing to return to a culture more settled, more architecturally and institutionally substantial, than the commonplace American reality: a reverie that always collapses of its own improbability. Another, related motif is the paradox of death in life, or old age in youth. Yet another is the mirror that gives back no image, or the window presenting no perspective. This last stands as a figure for a recurrent feature of the American literature of initiation: that it tends to elide, or even efface, the middle distance between the individual and the horizon, so that the social and political context of the immediate community goes virtually unimagined. As late as World War Two and Vietnam, American authors were still registering these most 'immediate' and 'real' experiences in terms of captivity and individual development, displacing the historical enemy with a threat closer to home, in their own ranks.

Sometimes, as with Hawthorne and Henry James, these anxieties were openly thematized, even joked about. Sometimes they were suppressed, so that they appear only obliquely, as fault lines cutting across the more orderly layers of narrative. Or again, some of these discontents, like the cultural nostalgia, were the inescapable regret for what the emigrant had to give up, while others, like the elided middle distance, represented an inevitable weakness in what was otherwise a powerful imaginative recourse for the emigrant: the narrative of initiation. The organic model of an individual's adolescent growth – the irresistible, irreversible process by which Paine naturalized the Revolution and countless emigrants proclaimed their assimilation to their adoptive country – was and remains a powerful enabler of both individuals and societies.

But the organic development of the individual must not be mistaken for human history. Thanks to the rhetoric of emigration, American identity has often been modeled as a form of personal evolution. This is as true of much canonical 'American literature' as it is of Frederick Jackson Turner's* influential thesis that the ever-receding (and now vanishing) frontier has always conditioned the American character. However invigorating, the analogy is also dangerous. Unlike countries, individual organisms grow old and die. Except through a distorting haze of nostalgia, their past is always as irretrievable as any lost childhood, and their future limited to their natural lifespan. A country, on the other hand, can review and analyze its past, and renew itself in social and political interaction. The threat in the emigrant's impulse to move 'westward the course of empire' lies in its hidden apocalyptic agenda: when the land runs out, so does time itself.

4

'THE REWARDS OF TRAVEL'

William Stowe

Celebrants of the rites of travel were clearly aided in their offices by guidebooks, which in turn offer evidence about the evolution of travel practices and attitudes. Many guidebooks also provide explicit commentary on the ultimate purpose of the ritual, the boon to be gained by its practice. In addition, a close analysis of these texts suggests that nineteenth-century Americans used Europe and European travel in less overt and explicit ways, to assert and defend social and cultural positions of privilege and domination.

Most nineteenth-century American guidebooks claim that their version of the European tour provides a combination of pleasure and improvement far superior to anything available at home. Putnam defines the exalted pleasures of travel in explicit contrast to ordinary amusements. 'For scarcely a greater sum than is often wasted in unsatisfactory pleasures', he writes, travelers 'may glide in a gondola on the moonlit waves of the Adriatic . . . or tread the classic soils of the lava-crushed cities of Vesuvius'.[1] John Henry Sherburne makes a similar contrast between the idle life of the American watering places and the 'information and improvement' to be derived from a summer's tour in Europe, visiting 'three or four kingdoms, their capitals, institutions, and people' and enjoying 'a pleasant sail of seven thousand miles on the Atlantic'.[2] Later writers are less prim, but they still have the tourist's intellectual and spiritual

From William Stowe (1994) *Going Abroad: European Travel in Nineteenth-Century American Culture*. Princeton: Princeton University Press.

improvement in view. William Hemstreet follows up his opinion that 'Europe is the biggest show I ever went to' by advising 'all Americans who . . . are willing to pay money for substantial education, [to] go to it'.[3] Grant Allen [. . .] gives the formula a prescient pragmatic twist by suggesting that 'going about the world to amuse ourselves . . . is the way to preserve and enlarge . . . our interest in knowledge'.[4] From Putnam to Hemstreet to Allen, guidebooks sold themselves as manuals for pleasant and productive worship at the shrines of Europe. From one end of the century to the other, travelers expected to enjoy and improve themselves by following the orders of service proposed by these trusted authorities.

Guidebooks also promulgate more specific, historically determined relations between travel, knowledge, and satisfaction. Some of the earlier ones maintain the eighteenth-century tradition of the traveler as amateur natural and social scientist by defining travel as a kind of improving research. Roswell Park advises his readers that 'to *see* the curiosities of nature and of art, to *observe* the manners and customs, and to *examine* the laws and institutions of the old world, should certainly *expand the mind* and *improve the understanding* of a citizen of the new'.[5] Murray assumes that the European tourist will be interested in a detailed account of the hydrology of Amsterdam's canals and a description of a high-speed diamond polisher powered by four horses.[6] Other, more properly romantic authorities neglect description to exalt the benefits to be gained from coming to know Europe in a more spiritual way. Some years before Park and Murray, Putnam was already touting the romantic frissons available to the tourist 'beneath Buonarotti's dome'.[7] And at the end of the century Grant Allen combines the two approaches by claiming that the only real, the only lasting knowledge is that which is obtained by the enthusiastic spirit.

> Few men remember in middle life any of the beggarly stock of Greek and Latin they acquired for the moment at school or college. Why? Because they never cared for it; therefore they never learned it . . . How different is the knowledge one has drunk in with pleasure in examining some stately cathedral, some exquisite temple, some fresco of Fra Angelico's, some relief from the perfect chisel of Pheidias! Those things, and the knowledge of them live with one forever. You don't try to remember them. You couldn't forget them.[8]

The ideal tourist experience combines pleasure and instruction, exaltation and study to produce improvement. Like a ritual celebrant, the traveler returns with a boon: with knowledge, memories of exalting, ennobling experience, and a magically transformed sensitivity to history and to art.

Immediate pleasure, knowledge, and the salutary effects of exalted experience may be the most obvious benefits of travel, but they are not necessarily the most important. The rite of travel also provides its votaries with an exhilarating sense of freedom and power. Traveling is as close as most people come to truly independent action: the security of organized group travel has always commanded less prestige than the independent traveler's putative freedom; Hans Magnus Enzensberger has suggested that the *Wandervogel*'s footloose irresponsibility is so appealing because it is all that remains of the romantic revolutionary's heroic *'liberté'*.[9]

Of course, few nineteenth-century travelers used their freedom to do anything except follow the standard tourist itineraries, but within these fairly narrow limits guidebooks encouraged them to think of themselves as the knowledgeable creators of their own European experiences. Indeed, it seems to me that one of the guidebooks' most important functions was to endow the traveler with all the freedom and power of the bourgeois consumer by serving as a catalog of tempting products among which he or she was free to choose and by constructing an implied reader who felt well informed, authoritative, and ultimately superior to other tourists, indigenous peoples, and previous generations.

Most guidebooks emphasize their readers' freedom of choice, even when the number of options is limited by convention or by such practical matters as the availability of transport. George Putnam makes the tourist's freedom clear from the very beginning of his 'Notes for the Way'. After a few words on Liverpool, he lays out a number of options for the independent traveler:

> *If* you intend to visit Ireland, a steamboat goes daily from Liverpool to Dublin. A short tour *may* be made thence to Belfast, *or* to the Giant's Causeway, and *if* Scotland is an object, before proceeding to London, cross from Belfast to Glasgow: (See Tour in Scotland,)
>
> – *or* –
>
> you *may* go to Scotland via the northern counties, the lakes of Cumberland &c.[10]

More prescriptive guidebooks can also be used by independent travelers as catalogs of choices rather than strict instructions. The hortatory Roswell Park is less permissive than Putnam: his 'mays', interspersed with imperative 'wills' and simple commands, are those of a schoolmaster and really mean 'should', or 'must'. 'Here you *will* save time by taking a cabriolet to visit the tomb of la Fayette, the patriot of two worlds', he remarks at one point, apparently leaving the presumably patriotic tourist little room to object that she might prefer a second visit to the Louvre. 'You *may* next . . . visit the famous cemetery of Père la Chaise', he goes on, and then, even more peremptorily, '*Observe* the monuments of Abelard and Eloise . . . *visit* . . . the largest of the five slaughterhouses constructed by Napoleon'.[11] In his introduction, however, Park admits that the individual tourist will ultimately decide whether to follow his very good advice and suggests that it be used as what he calls a general itinerary, 'by means of which [the tourist] will be able to estimate his own progress, and proportion his own time; so as not to linger too long amid scenes of minor interest, nor pass too rapidly by those of greater importance, unless for special reasons'.[12]

Murray's *Handbook for Travellers in Central Italy and Rome* sums up this aspect of the guidebook's appeal very clearly:

> We believe that most travellers form some plan for themselves . . . and that no general rule can be laid down to which exceptions may not be taken . . . With this view, therefore, we have arranged the different objects of attraction in Rome under separate classes, observing, as far as possible, a systematic arrangement of the details. For facility of reference, there is, we are convinced, no plan which presents so many advantages; and it has this additional recommendation, that it brings within one view a complete catalogue of objects which would be scattered over various and detached parts of any work in the topographical or chronological arrangement.[13]

Murray uses the word *catalogue* here to mean exhaustive list, as in the catalog of a museum's collections or of a library's holdings, but the commercial sense of the word is at least as appropriate in this context. The guidebook shares features of the catalogs of the Library of Congress and Sears and Roebuck. The traveler is a reader and a researcher but also, and perhaps primarily, a consumer. Successful travel, in other words, combines the satisfactions of the free, imaginative construction of experience with the joys of shopping. Guidebooks facilitate both activities by describing the available attractions, experiences, and commodities and by providing practical advice on how to enjoy or acquire them most conveniently and economically.

Pleasurable though it may be, however, shopping is not a particularly prestigious activity in official nineteenth-century culture, and to become an accomplished shopper is not a widely honored ambition. It is not surprising, therefore, that the authors of even the most utilitarian catalogs of European goods, services, and sights should choose more honorific (and more masculine) metaphors to describe their texts' missions and to provide their readers with more heroic, masterful figures for the tourist *him*self. 'A man without [a guidebook]', writes W. Pembroke Fetridge in the self-serving preface to the fifth edition of *Harper's Hand-book*, is 'like a ship at sea without a compass, dragged round the country by a courier'.[14] The purchaser of *Harper's Handbook*, by contrast, will be not a passive drifter but the purposeful captain of an obedient crew, the master of a well-run ship.

Fetridge's authoritative traveler may resemble a shopper in his daily activities, but he is encouraged to think of himself as a captain of men in a more general sense. The implication that the tourist shares the masculine force and independence of the sea captain flatters the male traveler, helping the writer, the clergyman, the artist, or the student to feel that as a traveler he is filling a powerful, independent male role, and it also empowers in a backhanded way the large number of travelers who were women, by encouraging them to appropriate this same independence for themselves. By inviting all travelers, men and women, rich, like John Quincy Adams, and poor, like Bayard Taylor, white and [. . .] black, to identify with the upper-class sons of Anglo-American colonists, by encouraging the tourist to think of him- or herself as a deservedly masterful member of a deservedly dominant gender, class, and ethnic group, and by referring explicitly and disdainfully to other groups, guidebooks helped make tourist travel a profoundly empowering activity for individual Americans.

One important element in this empowerment was the tourist's notorious ethnocentricity. John Pemble provides an extensive analysis of the British traveler's sense of superiority to the 'sensual' and 'childlike' peoples of the South;[15] William Vance, in *America's Rome*, does the same for the American.[16] Fetridge's description of the 'Sicilian character' can stand for the superior attitude toward foreign 'races' most frequently adopted in American guidebooks. 'They are cheerful, inquisitive, and fanciful', he writes, 'with a redundance of unmeaning compliments, showing they are not so deficient in natural talents as in their due cultivation . . . The upper classes are incorrigibly indolent, and fond to excess of titles and such like marks of distinction'.[17] The 'natives' of Europe, and particularly southern Europe, are altogether different kinds of beings from the Anglo-American tourist: they are exotic, quaint, childlike, and even primitive in their old-fashioned delight in titles and display.

The guidebook's class assumptions can be equally overt. Dean MacCannell describes the treatment of workers as tourist attractions in nineteenth-century Paris and remarks on Baedeker's disdainful attitude toward wretches condemned, unlike his readers, to work for a living.[18] Mary Cadwalader Jones advises her readers that 'many of the nicest English people always travel third class', 'but if you are going through the "black country," or into the mining district, where there is a rough population, it will be, perhaps, wiser to choose first class'.[19] The most common treatment of the lower classes in guidebooks, however, is simply to write them out of existence. Putnam, Park, Fetridge, and Morford all mention the palaces, parks, and noble houses of London, but none so much as suggests the existence of the urban poor.

Guidebook writers encourage tourists to claim positions of dominance by exercising the economic power of the consumer, then, and by assuming the 'natural' superiority provided by some combination of actual or honorary gender, class, race, or nationality. They also empower tourists by treating their activities as ways of coming to know and hence to dominate the world. As we have seen, tourism is often understood as a form of study. Dean MacCannell relates the tourist and the ethnographer;[20] Georges Van Den Abbeele suggests that the tourist's ambitions parallel those of the theorist, since 'both theory and tourism imply a desire to see and to totalize what is seen into an all-encompassing vision'[21] Judith Adler reminds us of the scientific pretensions of early travelers, which persist well into the nineteenth century, to ' "envision" whole countries through a detailed inventory of their flora, fauna, antiquities, and monuments'.[22] Totalizing and envisioning imply domination. Tourists are sightseers: their subjugating gaze reduces individuals, institutions, artworks, and landscapes to bits of knowledge and elevates the tourists and their class, race, gender, and nation to the position of the authoritative knower. The method of the traveling gentleman-scholar, as Adler points out, was closely related to 'techniques developed to rationalize the information-gathering practices of absolutist states' and instrumental in the mercantile project of the 'European cultural and intellectual elites' as they 'sought to take title to "the whole world" then coming into view'.[23] Tourists in this sense are the not-so-secret agents of social, political, and economic domination.

One way of knowing and controlling the world is to reduce complex objects, phenomena, and experiences to sets of easily graspable facts. The most obvious manifestation of this practice is the guidebook's notorious addiction to numbers. Vasi's *New Picture of Rome*, first translated into English in 1818 and recommended to American tourists by Putnam and Park, among others, sets the tone. Its description of St Peter's moves immediately from vague appreciation to measurement and enumeration. 'The front of the cathedral' is 'magnificent'. 'To give an idea of its size, it is sufficient to say that it is 370 feet wide, and 149 high'. 'The effect produced by this front . . . is truly astonishing', 'particularly when the whole is illuminated by 4,400 lamps, and afterwards by 784 flambeaus'.[24] Murray reinforces the tourist's sense of control by presuming to criticize as well as describe: 'The façade is 368 feet long and 145 feet high; but it is more adapted to a palace than to a church, and is ill calculated to harmonise with such a structure as the dome'.[25] Osgood's *Complete Pocket-Guide to Europe* retreats from judgment but provides even more figures, presumably to help the reader grasp the church's immensity and gauge its importance: 'It cost over $50,000,000; took 176 years (the reigns of 28 popes) to build; and covers 212,231 sq. ft, being the largest ch. in the world'.[26]

Just as numbers are presumably easier to master than the complex aesthetic and spatial experience of architecture, so are simple facts, objects, and anecdotes easier to register than complex systems of economic and cultural life. Vasi again sets the tone by reducing bustling public spaces to collections of objects, some with 'interesting' stories attached. His description of the Piazza del Popolo takes no notice of the 'popolo' that presumably animates it, but rather points out the gate, the obelisk, the garden, and the two matching churches, integrates the whole as a single, satisfying 'coup d'oeil', and then adds a two-sentence history of the obelisk, from its erection 'at Hieropolis, by Sesostris king of Egypt', to its ultimate relocation here in 1589.[27] Osgood similarly reduces the bustling Piazza di Spagna to a group of commercial establishments, buildings, and monuments: 'The Piazza di Spagna is surrounded by the hotels and shops of the foreign quarter, and contains Bernini's Barcaccia fountain; Pius IX's Column of the Immaculate Conception (with 5 statues); the Palace of Spain (Spanish Embassy); and the College of Propaganda Fide (1662)'.[28]

Tourists, however, do more than visit squares and monuments, and some are even interested in the economic activities of the places they visit and the lives of the inhabitants. Guidebooks cater to their interests by reducing even these objects of interest to figures, facts, and images. Murray describes Italian economic and social life with cool detachment, treating their details as independent bits of information. 'The vitriol works of Viterbo', he informs us, 'produce upwards of 100,000 lbs, of which about one-half is exported. The salt works of Cervia, the Comacchio, and Corneto, give an annual production of 76,000,000 lbs'.[29] His paragraph on farming contains parallel figures ('the number of sheep collected on the Campagna at the season is said to amount to 600,000')[30] along with matter-of-fact accounts of the lives – and deaths – of migrant workers: 'They work in the harvest-field all day under a scorching sun, and at night sleep on the damp earth, from which the low heavy vapour of the pestilent malaria begins to rise at sunset. Even the strongest and healthiest are often struck down in a single week'.[31]

Reducing public places, work, lives, and national customs and institutions to figures and 'objective' descriptions is one way of turning them into information, of coming to 'know' and, presumably, to 'master' them. The combination of what the tourist actually sees and the information that the guidebooks provide produces something that the tourist is eager to call knowledge and to use as a basis for establishing himself as an authority. Having seen a building or a group of peasants and read an explanation of their composition, history, and function, the tourist credits himself with having 'experienced' and so, by unjustified extension, understood them. Having negotiated the omnibus system, found a hotel, changed money, and bought some gloves, the tourist claims to know Paris.

Another, related way of establishing one's authority is by assuming a central and usually superior position in relation to one's surroundings, of placing oneself, like Stevens's jar, upon an eminence and forcing the slovenly wilderness of the 'foreign' world to surround it. The most obvious way to do this is to climb a hill or a tower. Guidebooks invariably recommend the ascent of the Campanile or the towers of Notre Dame or the heights of Fiesole to the connoisseur of 'views'. Georges Van Den Abbeele traces this practice back at least as far as Montesquieu, who always began his visit to a city by climbing the highest tower 'pour voir le tout ensemble',[32] and relates it to the tourist's inveterate 'desire to see and to totalize what is seen into an all-encompassing vision'.[33] The *Satchel Guide* proposes a more pleasant means to a similar end, suggesting that a ride on the top of a London omnibus – making the self the moving center of the passing panorama – is 'the quickest way of obtaining a general view of its most remarkable features'.[34] Jones gives the very same advice and provides another image of the tourist as a centered, ordering perceiver and knower (as well as underlining her ethnic and class assumptions) when she suggests that 'if the next Sunday after church, during the season, you will take a chair at Hyde Park corner while some of the handsomest men and women in the world, belonging to the English upper classes, walk up and down, you can form a good idea of the mighty strength of our common race'.[35] Sherburne suggests studying maps as a more private way of centering oneself, obtaining a grand, synthesizing vision of the 'tout ensemble', and 'mastering' the lay of the land or the layout of the city and makes it very clear how such study can liberate and empower. 'The tourist, immediately upon his arrival, should step into one of the numerous bookstores, and for a shilling purchase a neat pocket map'. He should then study the map until he has a clear picture of the layout of London in his head. This 'will enable him to move about the city and see all that is to be seen without asking many questions'.[36]

These examples suggest that at least one image of the ideal tourist is the unseen seer who dominates the world around her by observing it, processing it, and ultimately comprehending it. The purpose of the map and the guidebook is precisely to make this process possible. With a guidebook in hand and a map in mind, one is an independent viewer of the passing scene, possessing the necessary information to understand what one sees and to move through it without impinging upon it or being impinged upon by it.

NOTES

1. George Palmer Putnam, *The Tourist in Europe* (New York: Wiley and Putnam, 1838), p. 5.
2. John Henry Sherburne, *The Tourist's Guide* (Philadelphia: G. B. Zieber, 1847), p. 14.
3. William Hemstreet, *The Economical European Tourist: A Journalist Three Months Abroad for $430* (New York: S. W. Green, 1875), p. 2.
4. Grant Allen, *The European Tour* (New York: Dodd Mead, 1900), p. 2.
5. Roswell Park, *A Hand-Book for American Travellers in Europe* (New York: G. P. Putnam, 1853), pp. 9, 10–11; Stowe's emphasis.
6. John Murray, *Hand-Book for Travellers on the Continent* (London: J. Murray, 1843), pp. 47–8.
7. Putnam, *Tourist in Europe*, p. 5.
8. Allen, *European Tour*, p. 5.
9. Hans Magnus Enzensberger, 'Eine Theorie des Tourismus', in Enzensberger, *Einzelheiten* (Frankfurt/Main: Suhrkamp, 1962), p. 156.
10. Putnam, *Tourist in Europe*, p. 11; Stowe's emphasis.
11. Park, *Hand-Book*, p. 94; Stowe's emphasis.

12. Ibid., p. 73.
13. John Murray, *Handbook for Travellers in Central Italy and Rome* (London: J. Murray, 1843), p. 263.
14. W. Pembroke Fetridge, *Harper's Hand-book for Travellers in Europe and the East*, fifth year (New York: Harper and Brothers, 1866), p. v.
15. John Pemble, *The Mediterranean Passion: Victorians and Edwardians in the South* (New York: Oxford University Press, 1988), pp. 67, 142.
16. See William Vance, *America's Rome*, 2 vols (New Haven: Yale University Press, 1989), vol. 2, pp. 139–60.
17. Fetridge, *Harper's Hand-book*, pp. 379–80.
18. See Dean MacCannell, *The Tourist: A New Theory of the Leisure Class* (New York: Shocken, 1976), pp. 57–76, esp. p. 64.
19. Mary Cadwalader Jones, *European Travel for Women: Notes and Suggestions* (New York: Macmillan, 1900), p. 89.
20. MacCannell, *The Tourist*, pp. 177–9.
21. Georges Van Den Abbeele, 'Montesquieu touriste; or, a View from the Top', *L'Esprit créateur* 25 (1985): 67.
22. Judith Adler, 'Origins of Sightseeing', *Annals of Tourism Research* 16 (1989): 14.
23. Ibid., 21, 24.
24. Marien Vasi, *A New Picture of Rome and Its Environs in the Form of an Itinerary* (London: Samuel Leigh, 1818), pp. 381, 382, 383.
25. Murray, *Handbook for Central Italy*, p. 337.
26. James R. Osgood, *Osgood's Complete Pocket-Guide to Europe* (Boston: James R. Osgood, 1883), p. 351.
27. Vasi, *New Picture of Rome*, pp. 3–4.
28. Osgood, *Osgood's Complete*, p. 343.
29. Murray, *Handbook for Central Italy*, p. xiii.
30. Ibid., p. xv.
31. Ibid.
32. Van Den Abbeele, 'Montesquieu touriste', 65.
33. Ibid., 67.
34. *The Satchel Guide for the Vacation Tourist in Europe* (New York: Hurd and Houghton, 1872), p. 59.
35. Jones, *European Travel for Women*, p. 109.
36. Sherburne, *Tourist's Guide*, p. 78.

5

'INTRODUCTION' TO *IMPERIAL EYES* AND 'HUMBOLDT AS TRANSCULTURATOR'

Mary Louise Pratt

'INTRODUCTION' TO *IMPERIAL EYES*

Ethnographers have used this term ['transculturation'] to describe how sub-ordinated or marginal groups select and invent from materials transmitted to them by a dominant or metropolitan culture. While subjugated peoples cannot readily control what emanates from the dominant culture, they do determine to varying extents what they absorb into their own, and what they use it for. Transculturation is a phenomenon of the contact zone. In the context of this book, the concept serves to raise several sets of questions. How are metropolitan modes of representation received and appropriated on the periphery? That question engenders another perhaps more heretical one: with respect to representation, how does one speak of transculturation from the colonies to the metropolis? The fruits of empire, we know, were pervasive in shaping European domestic society, culture, and history. How have Europe's constructions of sub-ordinated others been shaped by those others, by the constructions of themselves and their habitats that they presented to the Europeans? Borders and all, the entity called Europe was constructed from the outside in as much as from the inside out. Can this be said of its modes of representation? While the imperial metropolis tends to understand itself as determining the periphery (in the emanating glow of the civilizing mission or the cash flow of development, for

From Mary Louise Pratt (1992) *Imperial Eyes: Travel Writing and Transculturation.* London: Routledge.

example), it habitually blinds itself to the ways in which the periphery determines the metropolis – beginning, perhaps, with the latter's obsessive need to present and re-present its peripheries and its others continually to itself. Travel writing, among other institutions, is heavily organized in the service of that imperative. So, one might add, is much of European literary history.

In the attempt to suggest a dialectic and historicized approach to travel writing, I have manufactured some terms and concepts along the way. One coinage that recurs throughout [. . .] is the term 'contact zone', which I use to refer to the space of colonial encounters, the space in which peoples geographically and historically separated come into contact with each other and establish ongoing relations, usually involving conditions of coercion, radical inequality, and intractable conflict. I borrow the term 'contact' here from its use in linguistics, where the term contact language refers to improvised languages that develop among speakers of different native languages who need to communicate with each other consistently, usually in context of trade. Such languages begin as pidgins, and are called creoles when they come to have native speakers of their own. Like the societies of the contact zone, such languages are commonly regarded as chaotic, barbarous, lacking in structure. (Ron Carter has suggested the term 'contact literatures' to refer to literatures written in European languages from outside Europe.)[1] 'Contact zone' in my discussion is often synonymous with 'colonial frontier'. But while the latter term is grounded within a European expansionist perspective (the frontier is a frontier only with respect to Europe), 'contact zone' is an attempt to invoke the spatial and temporal copresence of subjects previously separated by geographic and historical disjunctures, and whose trajectories now intersect. By using the term 'contact', I aim to foreground the interactive, improvisational dimensions of colonial encounters so easily ignored or suppressed by diffusionist accounts of conquest and domination. A 'contact' perspective emphasizes how subjects are constituted in and by their relations to each other. It treats the relations among colonizers and colonized, or travelers and 'travelees', not in terms of separateness or apartheid, but in terms of copresence, interaction, interlocking understandings and practices, often within radically asymmetrical relations of power.

[. . .]

'HUMBOLDT AS TRANSCULTURATOR'

'The Indians', reads the passage [from Alexander von Humboldt's* *Personal Narrative*], 'fixed our attention on those beautiful red and golden yellow woods'. On the Orinoco a *corregidor* who 'gave us three Indians to go in front and open up a path' proves in conversation to be 'a likeable man, cultivated in spirit'.[2] A few lines later on that very path, a missionary bores Humboldt with anxious monologues on recent slave unrest. Such traces of the everyday interaction between American inhabitants and European visitors suggest the heterogeneous and heteroglossic relationships that produced the Europeans' seeing and knowing. Brought to the surface by narrativity, the 'merely personal', as Humboldt called it, raises a challenging question: What hand did Humboldt's American interlocutors have directly and otherwise, in the European reinvention of their continent? To what extent was Humboldt a transculturator, transporting to Europe knowledges American in origin; producing European knowledges infiltrated by non-European ones? To what extent, within relations of colonial subordination, did Americans inscribe themselves on him, as well as he on America?

Such questions are difficult to answer from within bourgeois, author-centered ways of knowing texts – which is why it is important to ask them, not just of Humboldt but of all travel writing. Every travel account has this heteroglossic dimension; its knowledge comes not just out of a traveler's sensibility and powers of observation, but out of interaction and experience usually directed and managed by 'travelees', who are working from their own understandings of their world and of what the Europeans are and ought to be doing. For instance, Humboldt prided himself on being the first person to bring guano to Europe as a fertilizer, a 'discovery' that eventually led to the guano boom which by the end of the century caused a war between Peru and Chile and brought the latter's economy into total dependence on British bankers. Of course, Humboldt's discovery consisted of coastal Peruvians telling him of the substance and its fertilizing properties. Who knows what their assumptions and expectations were? The conventions of travel and exploration writing (production and reception) constitute the European subject as a self-sufficient, monadic source of knowledge. That configuration virtually guarantees that the interactional history of the representation will turn up only as traces, or through the 'travelee's' own forms of representation, such as autoethnographic materials of the sort mentioned at points throughout this book.

What have been documented are Humboldt and Bonpland's [Aimé Bonpland, Humboldt's fellow explorer] encounters with Spanish American intellectuals, whom they actively sought out. In sealing off its empire from outsiders, Spain had left the rest of Europe in profound ignorance of American indigenous history, culture, and language, as well as American botany, zoology, and mineralogy. These matters had continued to be studied within the Americas, however. (Is it necessary to repeat that universities in Peru and Mexico date from the sixteenth century?) Humboldt and Bonpland, we are told, went far out of their way to meet American naturalists like [José Celestino] Mutis in Bogota; it was Spanish American intellectuals who put them in touch with Inca and Aztec antiquity. To a great extent in his archeological essays, Humboldt was transporting to Europe an American scholarly tradition dating back to the first Spanish missionaries, and sustained by Spanish, mestizo, and indigenous intellectuals. Humboldt's year in Mexico (1803–4) was spent almost entirely in the intellectual and scientific communities of Mexico City, where he studied existing corpuses on natural history, linguistics, and archeology. On his return to Europe, he followed up assiduously on what he had learned, tracking down forgotten Amerindian manuscripts, such as Maya codicils, that since the Habsburgs had been gathering dust in libraries in Paris, Dresden, the Vatican, Vienna, and Berlin.

In some sectors of creole culture, then, a glorified American nature and a glorified American antiquity already existed as ideological constructs, sources of Americanist identification and pride fueling the growing sense of separateness from Europe. In a perfect example of the mirror dance of colonial meaning-making, Humboldt transculturated to Europe knowledges produced by Americans in a process of defining themselves as separate from Europe. Following independence, Euroamerican elites would reimport that knowledge *as European knowledge* whose authority would legitimate Euroamerican rule.

NOTES

1. Ron Carter, 'A Question of Interpretation: An Overview of Some Recent Developments in Stylistics', in Theo D'haen (ed.), *Linguistics and the Study of Literature* (Amsterdam: Rodopi, 1986), pp. 7–26.
2. Alexander von Humboldt, *Personal Narrative of Travels to the Equinoctial Regions of the New Continent*, tr. Helen Maria Williams (London: Longman, 1822), vol. 3, p. 178.

6

'TRAVEL WRITING AND ITS THEORY'

Mary Baine Campbell

INTRODUCTION

'Travel literature' is the significantly *generic* descriptor that has succeeded the Modern Language Association Bibliography's pre-1980s 'travel, treatment of'. But as a tool it cannot complete a search for relevant critical and theoretical materials. Very early in the contemporary resurgence of interest in travel writing, relations with the analysis of ethnography, thus with the history and function (and future) of anthropology in the West, and with postcolonial theory generally, became vital and generative. The interest in travel writing – across a wide political spectrum – was part of the necessary reimagining of the world first occasioned by the post-World War Two resistance movements and wars of liberation in the former European colonies, as well as by the waves of immigration that followed. It is a vivid shock to walk into the room-sized stained glass globe of the world (1935) suspended in the Mother Church of the Christian Scientists in Boston. Not only because, with loud metaphorical resonance, you can hear the whispers of people on the far side of the glass world as if they were speaking in your own ear, but also because the various pieces, each a different jewelled colour, belong to a world on the point of explosion. Much of the work of observing, interpreting, articulating the explosion of that world, as well as the historical development of the imperialised world that led to it, was done through

From Peter Hulme and Tim Youngs (eds) (2002) *The Cambridge Companion to Travel Writing.* Cambridge: Cambridge University Press, pp. 261–78.

recovery and analysis of people's writings about 'foreign' and especially 'exotic' places in which they had travelled and lived: as colonial masters, pilgrims, explorers, ambassadors, ambivalent wives, roving soldiers, ecstatic cross-dressers, conquistadores, missionaries, merchants, escaped slaves, idle students of the gentry and aristocracy, 'adventurers', and alienated modern artists.

During the same period theoretical models were developing which would help to launch illuminating readings of texts once considered 'subliterary', of mainly archival use for narrative history, or just boring. These models came mostly from France (including *départements* such as Jacques Derrida's* Algeria and Frantz Fanon's* Martinique), Eastern Europe, Britain, and the United States, increasingly since 1980 enriched and sometimes transformed by work from South Asia, the Caribbean, and Africa. These readings in turn fed back into theory, producing unexpectedly out of what at first, in the 1970s, was mainly rhetorical, semiotic, deconstructive, and even psycho-analytical forms of attention, the more *engagé* programme of postcolonial theory. From formalist beginnings came a technique of close but 'suspicious' reading ideally suited to texts that were, in another sense of the word, notably suspicious themselves. From the 'close reading' championed especially by the American New Critics* and the rhetorical analysis invigorated in the 1950s and 1960s by the widely read work of Kenneth Burke* and the linguist Émile Benveniste* emerged, by way of Michel Foucault*, the practice of discourse analysis: this aimed, not at the individual productions of a single canonical author, but at the collectively produced 'discourse' surrounding and constituting a particular matter of social interest or action (and not necessarily limited to written or even verbal texts). Hayden White's *Tropics of Discourse: Essays in Cultural Criticism* (1984), aimed more at historiography than at travel writing, was a milestone in theorising and modelling the analysis of both 'discourse' and specific examples of non-fictional representation.

One result of academic attention to travel writing in recent decades has been the wider dissemination among the political classes of critical views of colonialism and the imperial powers, once of Europe, more recently of the United States, Russia, and China. History, including ancient history, composes itself now from different images, different facts, and most importantly, different and multiple points of view. Students in most English-speaking countries are asked to read against the grain of what they are now regularly taught to see, at least at the post-secondary level, as situated and ideological texts, and they are also enabled to study a wider range of texts, produced by a wider range of authors and 'cultures', than they had before.

But much is left to be done in the realm of engaged criticism and theory. Recent attention to globalisation, diaspora, 'nomadism', and cyberspace is showing us the need for new and powerful theoretical work to replace, rather than simply supplement, the polemics and models produced by an academic collectivity concerned mostly with locatable cultures, bounded nations, and the imperial past. Where *is* 'India', now that it is divided into three hostile states, and has produced a huge diaspora mostly of educated professionals with access to public speech? Where is 'Kurdistan'? How do we talk about the Jews as a nation, very few of whose members live in the state of Israel – and some of whom are Arabs? What does 'Chinese' mean? What is the percentage of 'Americans' in California? Where do the people of the Philippines live? The Cubans? What is the USA to resident Puerto Ricans? What was London in the eyes of its nineteenth-century Irish immigrants? What is '*English* literature'? Questions of travel, as the American poet Elizabeth Bishop titled her famous book, and even of 'space', but not so much of place. The old motifs of the journey – home, departure, destination, the liminal space between – have lost their reference in the lived experience of most people who are not tourists.

Literary critical work on travel writing, or relevant to the reading of it, has continued along with and sometimes between the same covers as the work of historical and cultural revision. As a kind of writing, 'travel writing' provokes certain kinds of essentially literary questions and formulations. Most interesting here are works of literary criticism that find themselves directly facing issues of power, knowledge, and identity as a consequence of the very nature of the formal matters raised. Formal issues that have been fully explored with relation to travel writing in recent decades include the nature and function of the stereotype, lexical matters such as the hidden etymologies so well excavated in Peter Hulme's *Colonial Encounters* or William Pietz's papers on 'fetish', the subjective presence of the author(s) in texts of knowledge, truth value in narrative writing, the independent or hard-wired shape of narrative itself, the rhetorical nature of 'fact', 'identification' in reading (with its consequences in social and political life), the representation of time, inter-cultural 'translation', and the function of metaphor and other figures.[1]

A text that generically proffers itself as 'true', as a representation of unaltered 'reality', makes a perfect test case for analytical work that tries to posit or explain the fundamental fictionality of all representation. Considerable relevant work on our topic, then, is to be found in the pages of *Representations*, a journal started by literary critic Stephen Greenblatt and art historian Svetlana Alpers at Berkeley in the early 1980s. Other interdisciplinary journals whose origins can be traced to the theoretical movements and mergers referred to, and which are particularly fruitful with papers on topics related to travel, travel writing and ethnography, include *Ariel*; *Diaspora*; *Gender, Place, and Culture*; *Journeys*; *Studies in Travel Writing*, as well as (less regularly) the various volumes and collections that issued from, especially, the Essex conferences and symposia on the sociology of literature, the Centre for Contemporary Cultural Studies in Birmingham, the School of American Research in Santa Fe, and anthropologist George Marcus's series *Late Editions*.

A major source of information and theory related to travel writing and its valences with colonial and postcolonial history and geography, not to mention literary concerns with subjectivity and authorial perspective, has been the diverse work of feminist theorists and historians. Many travel texts were discovered, rediscovered, or revisited in the course of bringing back into print and public discourse the European and American women writers of the last three or four centuries, so many of whom wrote autobiographically, whether at home, abroad, or on the frontiers of expanding nations like Canada or the United States. Some of the most celebrated of the non-English include the fourth-century Galician pilgrim Egeria, the sixteenth-century Spanish transvestite Catalina de Erauso, French feminist Flora Tristan in Peru, Swiss adventurer Isabelle Eberhardt (who lived and travelled as a man in North Africa), and the Danish writer Isak Dinesen, sometime wife of a plantation owner and author of *Out of Africa*: since 1980 especially, their writing has been republished and much discussed, even made into movies. Their works have also served as case studies, first in the production of an alternative history of free and mobile female actors, as well as later in their problematic relation to 'colonial discourse', a wake-up call to the initially androcentric assumptions of postcolonial theory. Imperial women travellers such as Lady Mary Wortley Montagu and Mary Kingsley offered particularly provocative occasions for the complication of women's history during the period in which gender studies was coming to the foreground as a more rigorously theorised branch of the wider cultural study of 'difference' than was women's studies per se.

The works of the women and cross-gendered writers above, and those of countless more obscure writers – diarists of the Raj, of the American frontiers, of pilgrimage, of diplomatic and sometimes military and maritime life, as well as contemporary ethnographers and memoirists of the cultures of diaspora and war – have also helped critics of literature and of culture to open up the complexities of the master-slave paradigm, which at first dominated critical discussion of modern travel writing in a crude form: the West vs the Rest. It has been an important advance to realise that 'the Rest' had its own various power politics and forms of observation, into which usually oblivious Western desires could be plugged, and that the power of colonial masters was not as absolute or deracinating as the masters themselves, or even some of their guilty descendants, believed. The shock with which people began to realise that travelling or displaced women did not comfortably fit the profile of 'Western oppressor' being so subtly and powerfully constructed by postcolonial theory seems peculiar now (which is not to say that women did not have various uses in turn for the structure of colonial oppression in which they had some power, privilege, and mobility). And the study of their work as writing, as records, as narratives, has provided considerable material for discussion of the gendered nature of subjectivity and the positionality or 'situatedness' of all knowledge.

TEXTS AND TOPICS

The rest of this chapter will discuss, briefly, some major works in different parts of our collective field, along with a few individual topics and terms of critical-theoretical import. In the scholarly literature related to these topics and terms students can find formative discussions of the literature of travel and ethnography and its interpretation by contemporary intellectual culture. The academic disciplines that have had most to say or made most cogent use of the recent flowering of interest in the large corpus surveyed in this book are literary and cultural studies, history (including art history and history of science), anthropology, geography, and area studies, as well as various interdisciplinary alliances and projects among them. So many disciplines provide an inconveniently large number of subtopics and key themes for consideration, and I will pay particular attention mostly to the fields and inter-fields in which I am at home: literary and cultural studies, particularly pre-modern, in relation to the histories of anthropology and geography.

Though such statements are never absolutely true, the 1978 publication of Palestinian literary critic Edward Said's starkly titled *Orientalism* – almost contemporaneous with Arab anthropologist Talal Asad's edited volume *Anthropology and the Colonial Encounter* and American feminist philosophers Sandra Harding's and Helen Longino's first papers on 'standpoint epistemology' – initiated for the English-reading public an epistemological shift that would transform the study of culture and cultures. Said had been reading Foucault, and found in the concept of 'discourse' a magic key to the problem of Western imperial domination of 'the East':

> My contention is that without examining Orientalism as discourse one cannot possibly understand the enormously systematic discipline by which European culture was able to manage – even to produce – the Orient politically, sociologically, militarily, ideologically, scientifically, and imaginatively during the post-Enlightenment period.[2]

It is certainly not the case that those interested in travel writing jumped immediately on the bandwagon of Foucault (as modulated in those days by critics familiar with such Marxist* thinkers as Antonio Gramsci, Louis Althusser, and Pierre Macherey). But even quite traditional and empirical studies of sub- or non-literary writing that represented places not-home, 'elsewhere', foreign, and exotic, began to proliferate in indirect relation to a new programme of thought whose outlines were emerging from works such as Said's. The study of what we know and how we know it – not to mention who 'we' are – broke loose from its somewhat rarified moorings in philosophy departments and became a vital task for all disciplines as the experiment of empire came to be seen as failing, and indeed the centre did not hold – if it had ever existed.

Said's main target was a kind of multi-disciplinary area studies that included the region of his birth and upbringing (in Palestine and Egypt) among its objects of authoritative knowledge. (It is hard now to remember that the word 'orientalist' was once quite neutral in connotation for most Western European and North American academics.) But of course many of these late eighteenth- and nineteenth-century orientalist texts were composed 'in the field', or as a result of intensive foreign travel, and are what we now call travel writing as well as academic contributions to geography, linguistics, and anthropology. Not only did those who wrote and critiqued ethnography take note of Said's and Asad's interventions, but so did those of us whose discipline at the time was understood to be the re-presentation of texts with occult meaning: 'doing readings of' mainly 'great' (hence intentionally complex) works of literary art or at least of rhetorical intricacy. Said took sophisticated hermeneutic methods normally used to approach the high literary texts he taught in the department of English and Comparative Literature at Columbia University and applied them to non-poetic and non-fictional works, helping to open up the field of literary studies to an apparently endless supply of new and socially salient texts. Among the most interesting and fruitful of these newly approachable corpuses was that loosely gathered under the name of 'travel writing'.

Much early work, both before and after the new spotlights were first shone on the imperial texts of information, was given to traditionally literary questions of genre and tradition, voice and fictionality. Although these topics may seem quaint from the point of view of the highly articulated theoretical advances of the 1990s, they were useful to the theoreticians who began the construction of our current methods of reading – useful not as mere objects of conceptual repudiation but in fact as minesweeping tools and empirical groundwork for the development of reception histories (important to a discourse analysis that presumes to historical illumination). An early and widely cited essay by Jenny Mezciems, ' "'Tis not to divert the Reader": Moral and Literary Determinants in Some Early Travel Narratives', by its very title instructs social scientists and theoreticians about what they require from literary historians and critics.[3] The sense of travel writing as a genre was, where it manifested itself, often crude and restrictive, but the articulated concept of a corpus or 'tradition' was in fact useful, especially to social historians, in showing contemporary readers how to be proficient at reading *with* the grain of older accounts. Without that we cannot do the 'deeper' work of reading against it. Ambivalent texts of 'false consciousness', or political 'unconsciousness' have much of the complexity of modernist art itself, though it is not aesthetic complexity, and Anglo-American literary criticism was by the late 1970s a highly developed tool for responding to complexity. Literary criticism, one could say, mapped out the textual terrain more cogently represented by discourse analysts and postcolonial theorists. Foucault's complaint that criticism was 'commentary' and that commentary merely repeated a text was perhaps insufficiently grateful to the patient work of discovery performed in many a deconstruction or rhetorical analysis. The discomfort prestigious theory feels in relation to 'empirical' or descriptive critical work with texts is not unrelated to the discomfort felt for so long by critics in relation to subliterary texts, texts that seem – as colonial travel writing does to its feminist theoriser Sara Mills – 'all surface'.[4] That they can seem that way now is a mark of the field's achievement: early readings of individual texts were often laughed out of court for their level of detail and their apparently paranoid decoding of imperialist rhetoric and its key tropes.

One very influential work of what could be called rhetorical criticism, by the French classicist François Hartog, was translated into English in 1988 as *The Mirror of Herodotus: The Representation of the Other in the Writing of History*. Although it took the form of a scrupulously close reading of a single *logos* in Herodotus's *Histories*, its method and some of its terminology were to become widespread, disseminated in North America particularly by the editorial and critical work of the dean of New Historicism, Stephen Greenblatt. His series for the University of California Press, 'The New Historicism: Studies in Cultural Poetics', brought out this translation of Hartog's book as one of its first volumes. Herodotus, 'Father of History' and 'Father of Lies', whose first books are accounts of mostly Mediterranean and Eastern European geography composed from the authority of the writer as traveller, is to the philosophically minded historian a fascinating scandal at the historical root of his vocation. Issues that haunt discussion of travel writing in evolving forms, in particular the truth value of representations, inexpressibility and 'translation', and the difficulty of imagining or representing the Other, are central to this consideration of the urban Greek writer's discussion of the nomadic Scythians – who share the same 'oriental' enemy with the cosmopolitan Greeks, and with Darius's and Xerxes's Persians.

Hartog points to Herodotus's uses of the strategies of negation and, more importantly, inversion, to handle the problem of the inexpressibility of the Other – in this case the nomadic other, the person who is by negation just unimaginably *apolis* (cityless), but seen through the lens of inversion is a nomad whose *aporia*, or disconnectedness – spatially but also, Hartog implies, in terms of representation – is a strategy for survival: 'the Scythians' only advantage is their *aporia*, the fact that there is no *poros* (bridge) by which to reach them, so they remain impossible to seize'.[5] In Hartog's words, 'It is not hard to see why travellers' tales and utopias frequently resort to this method [of inversion], since it constructs an otherness that is transparent for the listener or reader: it is no longer a matter of *a* and *b*, simply of *a* and the converse of *a*'.[6]

Although Hartog's Scythians are presented as simply an example of the functioning of inversion and of a submerged structure of cultural symmetry in the *Histories*, he has in fact chosen for his study sample the most basic form of cultural otherness represented in Western ethnographic writing: that of the non-agricultural, and therefore spatially unfixed or unlocatable people. Herodotus's

Greece saw the nomad (in this case Scythian) as 'primitive', just as Shakespeare's England saw the Algonquians (actually farmers of both crops and fish as well as hunters) and as high modernists saw, with detached approbation, the Bedouin of North Africa. In anthropologist Hugh Brody's widely read experimental ethnography of the Inuit people of northern British Columbia, *Maps and Dreams*, he describes himself during a mapping and ethnographic research expedition commissioned by the government discovering that these supposedly illiterate and nomadic hunting people did indeed have maps and a definite sense of, as well as knowledge of, 'territory'. But this knowledge was as narrative as it was spatial, and indeed was hard to reduce to graphic signs, because of its fluidity and temporality, and the irrelevance to it of what literate peoples think of as 'borders'. Brody reproduces some survey maps on which hunters have drawn lines representing their various routes in different seasons and over time, and also transcribes part of a conversation in which he is told about a kind of map-dreaming, in which the maps show the trails to heaven. The white European academic deals with the difference of the nomadic by, apparently, loosening his own psychic borders and being voluntarily indoctrinated into a different and more narrative form of spatial knowledge. He 'goes primitive', to use Marianna Torgovnick's phrase from her discussion of the function of travel and the exotic in modernism, but in the interests of knowledge and translation, rather than in pursuit of strangeness and aesthetic shock.[7]

'Nomad' became a more and more important – and metaphorical – term in French post-structuralist theory (especially in the work of Gilles Deleuze and Paul Virilio), as well as a persistent source of connection between travel texts and such canonical texts of Western culture as Exodus, the *Odyssey*, the *Aeneid* and other culture-founding Euro-Asian narratives of homeless wandering – in which civilisation is always represented as the end and salvation of the nomadic life. (The one non-indigenous American 'nation' included in Laguna Indian Leslie Marmon Silko's anti-epic novel *Almanac of the Dead*, among the gathering masses of newly awakened peoples repressed and oppressed for so long by European invasions of the Americas, is 'the homeless'. Ironically, this nation is largely made up of veterans of the last great US imperial adventure, the war – 'police action' – in Vietnam.) The postmodern concept, and fact, of 'displacement' has brought the attention of critics and theorists in the 1990s back with a vengeance to questions Hartog handled in almost structuralist fashion in his treatment of the foundational Western case of representing the – nomadic, inexpressible, elusive – Other.

This nomadism may involve some projection: a lost traveller's feel for the locational structure of the space he or she negotiates without real language skills or shared experience is easy to imagine as sliding towards the sense that his or her hosts, too, are lost, excessively unpinned. But it is also true that the Western sense of property and sovereignty – some of it in fact first articulated in early American encounters – is far from universal, and rooted in the historically specific circumstances of late medieval Europe, when for a number of reasons (including climate) agriculture finally began to produce surplus, and with it the bureaucratics of finance and property. The written archives modern historiography depends upon are of relatively recent vintage in European cultural history, but they have made it difficult for Euro-American historians to produce historiography that is *not* adapted to archival sources. Representation of the nomadic is a fundamental limit case for cultures shaped by agriculture, writing, bureaucracy, and the archive. Thus its riveting interest for contemporary theory, in a globalised world where tens of millions of people are officially 'displaced persons' travelling without will, desire, or intention – without the (perhaps imaginary) emotional bedrock, then, of the earlier subjects of travel: the exile, the pilgrim, and the (pre-Second World War) immigrant.

Much of the theoretically informed writing on travel and travel writing has had to do with imperial periods of the later eighteenth, nineteenth, and early twentieth centuries, in which the geographical surveying of the globe as well as the anthropological investigation of its non-metropolitan or 'cityless' (*aporoi*) peoples produced so much knowledge in the service of so much desire for power and wealth. Historians and historicist literary critics, like Francis Jennings and Michael Nerlich, as well as historical anthropologists and ethnohistorians such as James Axtell and Marshall Sahlins, concentrated also on the early, pre-imperial formation of ideas of European hegemony and the development of venture capitalism.[8] Columbus imagined colonial exploitation of labour and resources before he ran into a single actual resource in the Caribbean, and wrote his first report on the voyage – from shipboard – to Queen Isabella's Keeper of the Purse, extolling the benefits of such exploitation for funding a new Castilian offensive against Muslim control of the Holy Land. Pope Alexander VI was soon to divide the globe between Spanish and Portuguese sovereignty, in a move codified by the Treaty of Tordesillas (1494), and the push to empire was in the making. Dutch jurist Hugo Grotius and others were developing the field of international law, in part to decide issues of sovereignty and property rights in places subject to the Pope's treaty.

This early period of imperial aspiration on the part of nations themselves only barely established enough to expand is important to the understanding of the colonial world, even to its dissolution and neo-colonial reconstitution, but difficult to work into social and cultural theory which must explicate a model in its state of function rather than its early stages of development. Marxist theory is the least impeded by the diachronic dimension of the problem, and some literary Marxists have done helpful work that includes the corpus of travel writing in its narratives: I am thinking especially of East German critic Michael Nerlich, author of *The Ideology of Adventure: Studies in Modern Consciousness, 1100–1750*, an account of the combined development of 'adventure capitalism', colonialism, and literary romance, and the literary historian Michael McKeon's *Origins of the English Novel, 1660–1740*, which represents the novel as a mediator of social and epistemological tensions in the world of a newly mobile and acquisitive bourgeoisie and a newly empirical science. A new genre for a new historical phase, the early novel – in McKeon's account – combines the features and content of such emergent factual genres or modes as travel writing, criminal biography, and 'natural philosophy' with older romance and religious narrative forms to produce its 'power both to formulate, and to explain, a set of problems . . . central to early modern experience'.[9] McKeon's narrative, like Nerlich's, takes him back to the twelfth century, a period in which, as I have mentioned, Western European lordships began dealing with the problem and opportunity of surplus, and politically unified regions to develop agricultural markets and, by the fourteenth century, money economies based on gold.

A number of influential works on travel writing or (proto-)ethnography in the special situation of Europe in the so-called Age of Discovery* appeared in the 1980s, importing post-structuralist and cultural materialist thinking into the increasingly dense context of travel writing as a literary or at any rate textual phenomenon. Essays by New Historicists Stephen Greenblatt and Louis Montrose in the United States, among others, set the stage for considerable work, still ongoing, with the texts of English explorers in North America, as well as canonical English writers' use of them in the nation-building project under way at home. Their initial interest in historicising and materialising the referents and contexts of Shakespeare's plays and Spenser's *Faerie Queene* gave way quickly to an interest in the exploration texts themselves. Greenblatt's *Marvelous Possessions*, a reading of a number of late medieval and early modern works of travel and acquisition in exotically distant places, marked a climax of this kind of work, which on a Foucauldian* ground and fortified with the insights of anthropological theorist Pierre Bourdieu*, studies cultural 'moments', events, and documents as if they were literary texts, and with the same tools.

Greenblatt and New Historicism owe a great deal to the impressionistic but extraordinarily sensitive work of the French historian and post-structuralist Michel de Certeau, who from a more Lacanian* angle composed a couple of essays that arrived in English translation in the later 1980s: 'Montaigne's "Of Cannibals": The Savage "I"' and 'Ethno-Graphy: Speech, or the Space of the Other', a reading of Jean de Léry's* seventeenth-century travel report on his journey to French Brazil with the colonial entrepreneur, Villegagnon. These, along with an essay on the early eighteenth-century anthropological theorist and Jesuit missionary Father Joseph Lafitau, combine rhetorical, linguistic, and psychoanalytically inflected forms of attention to produce – in the unclaimed lineage of Frantz Fanon – a historical psychology of alterity, for early modern and modern Europeans in the process of creating what the historian refers to as ethnology. 'What travel literature really fabricates is the primitive as *a body* *of pleasure* . . . At the same time that it creates a profit, the voyage creates a lost paradise relative to a body-object, to an erotic body. This figure of the other has no doubt played a role in the modern Western *episteme*, more crucial than that of the critical ideas circulated through Europe by travel literature'.[10]

Historians have repeatedly questioned the thinness of empirical research in American New Historicist work, which operates by close readings, or what anthropologist Clifford Geertz calls 'thick description', of fragments and individual moments or events – biopsies, as it were. But the work is compelling for students and readers of the literary (not necessarily the High Literary) in the depths it opens up, and its unusual ability to make connections across scales and registers, between social realms and discourses normally not thought about in the same breath. New Historicist work 'travels'. A rich, even climactic gathering of papers in this vein came out in a special issue of *Representations* (Winter 1991) entitled 'The New World', since reissued as a book, *New World Encounters*. It is dedicated to de Certeau, and concludes with a translation of the late historian's research proposal with regard to travel literature, made to the Centre national de la recherche scientifique in 1978, from which the essays mentioned above are offshoots (though the proposal was rejected!).

Somewhat less problematic to most historians has been the work of European professors of literature who work mainly or partly with factual or information-bearing texts: Peter Hulme and Frank Lestringant offer a number of particularly good examples of theoretically informed and interdisciplinary handling of such texts, from the earliest period of exploration to, in the case of Hulme's *Colonial Encounters*, the last days of the Enlightenment. Hulme's treatment of cannibalism, one of the most frequent and telling motifs of exotic travel writing (from early Greek texts to nineteenth- and even twentieth-century ethnography), has helped engender a great deal of thinking and analysis, from the very literary – Philip Boucher's *Cannibal Encounters* (1992) – to the anthropological – William Arens's recent 'Rethinking Anthropophagy' (1998).[11] Lestringant has written several trenchant articles on the topic himself, especially in its configuration with eucharistic symbolism and the religious wars of Reformation and Counter-Reformation Europe, and a monograph titled simply *Cannibals*. It is a topic that invites analysis of the rôle of the imaginary (including Lacan's Imaginary) in the production of knowledge, even strategic knowledge, and more broadly, of discourse. Arens's case is that cannibalism is simply imaginary in the standard sense of the word, that it has almost never been practised by anyone, only narrated of 'foreigners'. Lestringant takes no position at all – the 'reality' quotient of the practice is not once broached in his book-length treatment of the topic. For Hulme, introducing the collection, it most pertinently 'exists as a term within colonial discourse'. 'For us, the overriding questions remain, why were Europeans so desirous of finding confirmation of their suspicions of cannibalism? and why does cannibalism feature so insistently as a contemporary trope in different kinds of writing?'[12]

The pressures that hold in place such a persistently flamboyant image of 'otherness' are clarified to some degree through a discourse analysis touched by the psychoanalytic theorising of Frantz Fanon, and less directly but perhaps as deeply by Jacques Lacan's model of object relations as well as his linguistically oriented analysis of the 'language' of the unconscious. Feminist refinements and challenges to Lacanian thinking have helped make its valences with the social and collective more available (as in Jane Gallup's *Reading Lacan*), and a number of postcolonial social and literary theorists have taken the matter of encounter with a sentient Other as ground for far-reaching theoretical models of historical action, for example Gayatri Spivak ('Can the Subaltern Speak?' among much other work), and Homi Bhabha.[13] However nervously we might encounter explanations of history that are located too firmly in individual psyches or the fuzzy notion of 'culture(s)', they are a good approach for the unravelling of travel writing, which is produced not only by the culture or society of the person who writes it and the situation which gives her the authority to speak but also by the writer, *a writer*, someone who does indeed have a psyche (whether that amounts to a Self or a 'unified subject' is not the issue), and whose book is constructed to make its effects through an impact on other (culturally or socially produced) psyches. The job of postcolonial theory has been in part to get us to see how those effects are made, especially where they are produced and/or operate unconsciously, and to provide a picture or pictures of the particular, historicised, unconscious within and without them.

The linguistic turn within anthropology led to the famous editing collaboration of critic James Clifford and anthropologist George Marcus, *Writing Culture: The Poetics and Politics of Ethnography*. Along with Mary Louise Pratt's later book, *Imperial Eyes*, Clifford and Marcus's *Writing Culture* has become a kind of textbook in how, and for what purposes, to analyse accounts of foreign or 'exotic' places written by people, especially of the West or 'developed world', who have some kind of authority of speech. Like the projects of the New Historicism, this collection, the ultimate result of an Advanced Seminar at the School of American Research in 1984, is concerned with the loss of 'unchallenged authority' in a once-authoritative anthropological canon and its genres. Its essays set out to dissect ethnographic texts and the situations of their production with the fine tools of literary and rhetorical analysis: the consequences, it would be safe to say, have helped to unsettle the classic account of modernism in the arts as well as the scientific confidence of ethnography. The very fact that rhetorical tropes and allegorical structures can be uncovered or simply pointed out in ethnographic texts has revealed to two generations of scholars and social scientists that ethnographic writing was a kind of representation as wedded to an inherited medium and the associative rip tides of the unconscious as is poetry or political propaganda. Johannes Fabian's searing, almost melodramatic *Of Time and the Other* put a similarly rhetorical-allegorical approach to ethnography to work for a polemic – centred on the ahistoricity with which 'Other' cultures are represented in ethnography – that seemed to leave no morally imaginable future for anthropology at all. A more contemporary and upbeat approach to that despair has been to turn the lenses of anthropology back towards 'home', wherever that may be for the anthropologist or her institution. London novelist Iain Sinclair's finely detailed and historically dense account of his V-shaped traverse of London, *Lights Out for the Territory*, is both a literary masterpiece Sinclair considers a novel and a case of postmodern, one might almost say reverse, ethnography that points to a future for the social science of the Other after all: we have met the Other and – as usual, but now we admit it – s/he is Us. And who might that be? Even the past is still unwritten.

NOTES

1. See William Pietz's articles on 'The Problem of the Fetish', published in *Res* in issues 9, 13, and 16, especially 'The Problem of the Fetish II: The Origin of the Fetish' (Spring 1987): 23–45.
2. Edward Said, *Orientalism* (New York: Pantheon Books, 1978), p. 3.
3. Jenny Mezciems, ' "'Tis not to divert the Reader": Moral and Literary Determinants in Some Early Travel Narratives', *Prose Studies* 5: 1 (May 1982): 1–19.
4. Sara Mills, *Discourses of Difference: An Analysis of Women's Travel Writing and Colonialism* (London: Routledge, 1991), p. 11.
5. François Hartog, *The Mirror of Herodotus*, tr. Janet Lloyd (Berkeley: University of California Press, 1988), p. 199.
6. Ibid., p. 213.
7. See Marianna Torgovnick, *Gone Primitive: Savage Intellects, Modern Lives* (Chicago: University of Chicago Press, 1990).
8. See Francis Jennings, *The Invasion of America: Indians, Colonialism, and the Cant of Conquest* (Chapel Hill: University of North Carolina Press, 1975); James Axtell, *The Invasion Within: The Contest of Cultures in Colonial North America* (New York: Oxford University Press, 1985); Michael Nerlich, *Ideology of Adventure: Studies in Modern Consciousness, 1100–1750*, vol. 1, tr. Ruth Crowley (Minneapolis: University of Minnesota Press, 1987); Marshall Sahlins, *Historical Metaphors and Mythical Realities: Structure in the Early History of the Sandwich Islands Kingdom* (Ann Arbor: University of Michigan Press, 1980).
9. Michael McKeon, *Origins of the English Novel, 1660–1740* (Baltimore: Johns Hopkins University Press, 1987), p. 20.
10. Michel de Certeau, 'Ethno-Graphy: Speech, or the Space of the Other: Jean de Léry', in *The Writing of History* (New York: Columbia University Press, 1988), pp. 226–7.
11. For Arens's essay, see *Cannibalism and the Colonial World*, ed. Francis Barker, Peter Hulme and Margeret Iversen (Cambridge: Cambridge University Press, 1998), pp. 39–62.
12. Peter Hulme, 'Introduction: The Cannibal Scene', ibid., p. 4.
13. Spivak's 'Can the Subaltern Speak?', originally published in 1988, is most readily accessible in *Colonial Discourse and Post-Colonial Theory: A Reader*, ed. Patrick Williams and Laura Chrisman (New York: Columbia University Press, 1994), pp. 66–111. Homi K. Bhabha's early essays of the 1980s are reprinted in his *The Location of Culture* (London: Routledge, 1994).

GLOSSARY OF TERMS

Abrams: M. H. Abrams (b. 1912), literary critic of Romanticism. *The Mirror and the Lamp* (1953) distinguishes between an (eighteenth-century) conception of literature as mimetic, and Romantic theories of the imagination's creative power. [E]

Addison and *The Spectator*: Joseph Addison (1672–1719), English politician and writer. The urbane essays of his journal *The Spectator*, written with Richard Steele*, became an influential form of social and literary commentary, and a model of good style.

Adorno: Theodor Adorno (1903–69), German Marxist critic of the arts and member of the Frankfurt school. Principal works include *Dialectic of Enlightenment*, *Aesthetic Theory* and *The Culture Industry*. [E]

Age of Discovery: period of world exploration by European adventurers between the fifteenth and seventeenth centuries, fuelled by technological innovations from the Renaissance.

Alien and Sedition Acts: four laws supported by the Federalists in 1798 in which the United States Congress restricted immigration and internal dissent.

American Renaissance: F. O. Matthiessen's term in his 1941 book of that name for the mid-nineteenth-century literary works of Hawthorne, Melville, Emerson and Whitman.

Babel: the linguistic 'Fall of Man', whereby people became unable to understand each other's languages. In the biblical book of Genesis, God confounds the languages of the peoples who were building a tower at the city of Babel.

Bakhtin: M. M. Bakhtin (1895–1975), Russian literary critic and philosopher whose work on the novel collected in *The Dialogic Imagination* (1981) has influenced structuralists, post-structuralists and semioticians. [E]

Baudelaire: Charles Baudelaire (1821–67), prominent French poet, translator and critic of the nineteenth century. [E]

Benveniste: Émile Benveniste (1902–76), French linguist best known for his work on Indo-European languages.

Bermoothes: 'Still-vexed Bermoothes', Shakespeare's *The Tempest*, I. ii. 229; 'Bermoothes' are the Bermudas.

Bissette: Cyrille Bissette (1795–1858), Martiniquan abolitionist leader in France; editor of *Revue des Colonies*.

Black Atlantic: a term popularised by Paul Gilroy's book of the same name which reads the history of colonial and postcolonial black identity within the spatial coordinates of Atlantic crossings between England, Africa and the Americas. [E]

Bourdieu: Pierre Bourdieu (1930–2002), French sociologist whose concept of 'social space' has been influential in fields such as anthropology, aesthetics and cultural studies. [E]

Bryant: William Cullen Bryant (1794–1878), US Romantic poet and journalist.

Buffon: Georges-Louis Leclerc, Comte de Buffon (1707–88), French naturalist, biologist and author, whose fifteen-volume *Histoire naturelle* (1749–67) advanced a theory of New World degeneration.

Burke: Edmund Burke (1729–97), Whig Anglo-Irish politician, political philosopher and author; his major contribution to aesthetics was *A Philosophical Enquiry into the Origin of our Ideas on the Sublime and the Beautiful* (1757).

Burke: Kenneth Burke (1897–1993), US literary critic of the Modernist period; author of *A Grammar of Motives*, *A Rhetoric of Motives* and *Language as Symbolic Action*. [E]

Calvinist (theology): theology and practice developed under the influence of John Calvin (1509–64), with Martin Luther* the major theologian of the Reformation of the Christian Church in the Renaissance. His *Institutes of the Christian Religion* became the foundational text of Puritanism in Britain and America.

Césaire: Aimé Césaire (b. 1913), expatriate from Martinique, proponent (with Léopold Senghor) of the négritude* movement. [E]

Charlotte Temple: highly-popular American seduction and sentimental novel published in 1790 by Susanna Rowson.

Chateaubriand: French writer and politician (1768–1848), considered to be the founder of French Romanticism.

Chesterfield: Philip Dormer Stanhope, Earl of Chesterfield (1694–1773): see *Letters Written by the Late Rt Hon. Philip Dormer Stanhope, Earl of Chesterfield, to his Son*, 6th edn, 4 vols, J. Dodsley, 1775.

Child: Lydia Maria Child (1802–80), US novelist and activist in women's rights, abolition and Indian rights.

Chomsky: Noam Chomsky (b. 1928), linguistician associated with transformational-generative linguistics, proponent of 'deep structures'. Influential in linguistics, psychology and (latterly) political commentary. [E]

Chronotopes: term coined by M. M. Bakhtin* denoting the interconnectedness of space and time, literally translated as 'time-space'.

Common Sense (British school of): philosophical tradition which emphasised common sense both as wide consensus and as universally accessible human attributes; advanced as an antidote to scepticism. Its major proponent was the Scottish philosopher Thomas Reid (1710–96).

Congreve: William Congreve (1670–1729), comic playwright of the English Restoration.

Deconstruction: tradition of philosophy and literary criticism originating with the work of Jacques Derrida. [E]

Derrida, Derridean: (referring to the work of) Jacques Derrida (1930–2004), French cultural critic and literary philosopher famous for verbal play and theories of deconstruction. [E]

Dewey: John Dewey (1859–1952), US philosopher and cultural critic whose work in epistemology focused on pragmatism.

Fanon: Frantz Fanon (1925–61), Martiniquan critic of decolonisation and its psychology; author of *Black Skin, White Masks* (1952) and *The Wretched of the Earth* (1961). [E]

Fechner: Gustav Fechner (1801–87), German experimental psychologist.

Fish: Stanley Fish (b. 1938), US literary theorist who has advocated the importance of 'reader-response' in the interpretation of texts. [E]

Foucault, Foucauldian: (referring to the work of) Michel Foucault (1926–84), French post-structuralist critic of power, order and discourse; influential in both the arts and social sciences. [E]

Fugitive Slave Laws: put in place by the United States Congress in 1793 and 1850 to allow for the return of slaves to the state from which they had escaped.

Fulbright: in 1945, Senator J. William Fulbright (1905–95), introduced a bill in the US Congress proposing the use of funds from surplus war property for international student exchange. Today the US Department of State funds grants allowing students, known as Fulbright Scholars, to study outside the US.

'Generated soul': refers to a line from W. B. Yeats' poem 'Coole Park and Ballylee, 1931'.

George: Stefan George (1868–1933), German poet and translator who revolted against realism and was made a national poet by the Nazis after his death.

Glossolalia: language that strikes the listener as unknown or meaningless.

Goethe: Johann Wolfgang von Goethe (1749–1832), prominent German Romantic poet, dramatist and cultural critic, notably cosmopolitan in outlook. His *Sorrows of Young Werther* (1774) achieved massive popularity.

Gould: Glenn Gould (1932–82), Canadian pianist and musician.

Grégoire: Henri Grégoire (1750–1831), French Roman Catholic priest and revolutionary leader; his *De la littérature des Nègres* (1808) attacked the European colonial system.

Hanoverian succession: in 1714, the Stuart Queen Anne died without an heir and the British throne passed to George I of Hanover. Jacobite uprisings against the Hanoverian succession in 1715 and 1745 were attempts respectively to put James Stuart and Charles Edward Stuart on the throne.

Hegel, Hegelian: (referring to) Georg Wilhelm Friedrich Hegel (1770–1831), German philosopher. In his *Phenomenology of Spirit*, consciousness is understood through a dialectic between master and servant where only by acknowledging the Other can one be made self-aware. Because one feels threatened by the Other, a master-servant relationship develops. [E]

Heidegger, Heideggerian: (referring to) Martin Heidegger (1889–1976), German philosopher of phenomenology and existentialism whose work influenced deconstruction, hermeneutics and postmodernism. [E]

Humboldt: Alexander von Humboldt (1769–1859), eighteenth-century German naturalist and explorer.

Hume: David Hume (1711–76), Scottish philosopher, one of the British empiricists (following Locke and Berkeley); major works include: *A Treatise of Human Nature* (1739–40), *Enquiry concerning Human Understanding* (1748), *Enquiry concerning the Principles of Morals* (1751) and *Essays and Treatises on Several Subjects* (1753–4).

Idealists: philosophical movement of German Romanticism developed from Kant's work of the 1780s and 1790s as well as the revolutionary politics of the Enlightenment. Key thinkers were Fichte, Schelling, Schleiermacher and Hegel. [E]

Illuminati conspiracy: a conspiratorial secret society believed to be attempting to control world events.

Jerome: Saint Jerome (c.347–419/420), translator of the Bible from Greek and Hebrew into the Latin Vulgate.

'John or Jonathan': monikers denoting Britain (John Bull) or America (Jonathan).

Kabbalistic: Jewish mystic writings.

Kant: Immanuel Kant (1724–1804), German philosopher whose work bridged the rationalist and empiricist traditions of the eighteenth century. Major works include his three Critiques: *Critique of Pure Reason* (1787), *Critique of Practical Reason* (1788), *Critique of Judgment* (1790). [E]

Kingston: capital town of Jamaica.

Kleist: Heinrich von Kleist (1777–1811), German writer and dramatist who attacked rationalism in form and content.

Lacan, Lacanian: (referring to) Jacques Lacan (1901–81), French psychoanalyst and psychiatrist, responsible after Freud for the dialogue of psychoanalysis with other disciplines. [E]

Léry: Jean de Léry (1534–c. 1613), Huguenot, Calvinist Minister and author whose travels influenced Michel de Montaigne and Claude Lévi-Strauss.

Lewis: R. W. B. Lewis (1917–2002), Pulitzer-prize winning American literary critic whose *The American Adam* traces the Adamic theme in American literature.

Linguistic sign: in *Cours de linguistique générale* (*Course in General Linguistics*) Ferdinand de Saussure* claimed that language can be analysed as a formal system of organised difference; the linguistic sign is the basic unit of a given language at a given time. [E]

Locke, Lockean: (referring to) John Locke (1632–1704), empiricist philosopher whose *Essay Concerning Human Understanding* (1690) advanced the proposition that all ideas are formed from combinations of impressions of the external world. His political philosophy was influential in the foundation of modern liberalism.

L'Ouverture: Toussaint L'Ouverture (1743?–1803), a self-educated slave freed before the uprising of 1791, who became the liberator of Haiti from the French.

Lukács: Georg Lukács (1885–1971), Hungarian Marxist and literary critic, influential on modern theories of class consciousness and on the genre of the novel. [E]

Luther: Martin Luther (1483–1546), German Protestant reformer who first translated the Bible into German; with Calvin*, the major theologian of the Reformation.

Mallarmé: Stéphane Mallarmé (1842–98) French symbolist poet and critic [E]

Man: Paul de Man (1919–83), Belgian deconstructionist and literary theorist.

Manifest Destiny: a phrase coined by John L. O'Sullivan (1813–95) in reference to the annexation of Texas; it referred to the providential right Americans felt they had to possess the whole continent.

Marx: Karl Marx (1818–83), German philosopher and revolutionary famous for his foundational work on socialism and communism. [E] He published the *Communist Manifesto* (a political tract arguing for proletarian revolution) with Friedrich Engels in 1848.

Marxist: work informed by the philosophy or politics of Marx and his later interpreters. Marxist cultural criticism emphasises the determining influence of the material conditions of production on literary or artistic work.

Matthiessen: F. O. Matthiessen (1902–50), US literary critic whose influential book *American Renaissance* (1941) focused on the development of mid-nineteenth-century American literature.

Mexican-American War: fought between 1846 and 1848, marked by the American sense of Manifest Destiny* and resulting in the sale of California and New Mexico to the US and the recognition of the annexation of Texas.

Michaux: Henri Michaux (1899–1984), twentieth-century Belgian writer, painter and poet.

Middle Passage: the intermediate route of the slave trade (which originated and ended in Europe) where Africans were taken from Africa to be sold in North and South America and the Caribbean.

Mill: John Stuart Mill (1806–73), nineteenth-century English philosopher and political economist in the tradition of the British empiricists.

Montaigne: Michel de Montaigne (1533–92), Renaissance humanist writer, often considered as the inventor of the personal essay. Florio's translation of Montaigne into English appeared in 1603.

Nabokov: Vladimir Nabokov (1899–1977), Russian-US author who wrote in both Russian and English; most famous for *Lolita* (1958); he also translated many works from Russian, including a four-volume edition of Pushkin's *Eugene Onegin*.

Napoleonic Wars: series of wars during Napoleon's reign in France from the beginning of the nineteenth century until 1815 when Napoleon was defeated at Waterloo.

Négritude: literary and cultural movement of the 1930s headed by Aimé Césaire*, Léopold Senghor* and Léon Damas which positively reclaimed the word *Nègre* for the united efforts of the African diaspora against French hegemony.

Neoplatonism: system of philosophical and religious thought emphasising elements of Platonism and Aristotelianism as well as oriental mysticism.

New Critics: dominant mid-twentieth-century critical school emphasising close reading; primary figures include: T. S. Eliot, F. R. Leavis, William Empson, I. A. Richards, Cleanth Brooks and John Crowe Ransom. [E]

New England Renaissance: otherwise termed the 'American Renaissance'* in the book of the same name by F. O. Matthiessen*.

Nietzsche: Friedrich Nietzsche (1844–1900), German philosopher who challenged traditional structures of Christianity and humanist philosophy. [E]

Orpheus: in Greek legend, Orpheus was the principal representative of poetry and song.

Ortega y Gasset: José Ortega y Gasset (1883–1955), Spanish philosopher who emphasised, *contra* Descartes' 'cogito ergo sum', that life is the sum of the ego and circumstances.

Ossianism: fascination with Celtic myth following the 'discovery' by James Macpherson of epic poems of the third-century bard Ossian; Macpherson's controversial 'translations' of *Fingal* (1762) and *Temora* (1763) were the subject of long-running literary battles concerning authenticity.

Over-Soul: Emerson's Idealist essay 'The Over-Soul' defines the term as: 'that Unity, that Over-soul, within which every man's particular being is contained and made one with all other'.

Paine: Thomas Paine (1737–1809), Englishman whose pamphlet, *Common Sense*, was credited with helping to spark the American War for Independence.

His *Rights of Man* (1791–2), supporting the French Revolution, was also a reply to Edmund Burke*.

Pannwitz: Rudolf Pannwitz (1881–1969), German philosopher, poet and writer.

Pantisocracy: utopian governmental system of Romantic conception in which all rule equally.

Parrington: Vernon Parrington (1871–1929), US historian best known for his three-volume intellectual history of America, *Main Currents in American Thought* (1927–30), in the third volume of which he argued that the American Civil War divided American thought irretrievably into 'before' and 'after'.

Pastoral: a type of literature popular since the Renaissance, dealing with themes of simple rural life and often used to critique contemporary culture.

Peacham: Henry Peacham (1546–1634), English Renaissance writer and curate whose *Gardens of Eloquence* (1577) was influential in rhetoric.

Peirce: Charles Sanders Peirce (1839–1914), considered himself a logician but is now known as a philosopher and founder of American pragmatism. [E]

Picturesque: a variant on the sublime, the picturesque was popularised by William Gilpin in both verbal and visual forms that emphasised compositional elements 'suitable for a picture'.

Pindar: (522 BC–443 BC) the greatest of ancient Greek lyric poets, Pindar composed his Third Pythian Ode to celebrate the victory of Hieron of Syracuse at a horse race.

Pléiade: la Pléiade, a group of sixteenth-century French Renaissance poets who championed French as a suitable language for literary expression.

Plutarch: (46–127) Greek historian, biographer and essayist who became a source for Shakespeare.

Poésie concrète: concrete poetry, a form of writing in which the typographical arrangement of words on the page is significant in conveying meaning.

Puttenham: George Puttenham (c. 1530–90), author of *The Arte of English Poesie* (1589).

Quincey: Thomas de Quincey (1785–1859), English essayist and critic famous for his autobiography, *Confessions of an English Opium-Eater*.

Reeve: Clara Reeve (1729–1807), popular British novelist; her *The Old English Baron* written after the style of Walpole's *Castle of Otranto* influenced Shelley's *Frankenstein*.

Rilke: Rainer Maria Rilke (1875–1926), important German lyric poet; he also translated work by others, including the sonnets of Louise Labé, a sixteenth-century French poet.

Romantics, Romanticists: refering to German Romanticism (1790s–1850), it proceeded from the work of Schiller and Goethe* and emphasised the union of poetry with metaphysics. See also Idealists*. [E]

Rorty: Richard Rorty (b. 1931), US pragmatist philosopher and cultural critic whose *Philosophy and the Mirror of Nature* (1979) targets the idea of knowledge as a mental mirroring of a mind-external world.

Rowlandson: Mary Rowlandson (1635–1711) wrote *A Narrative of the Captivity and Restoration of Mrs Mary Rowlandson*, an extraordinarily-popular Indian captivity narrative which offered a paradigm for an American literary genre.

'Rule Britannia': James Thomson's (1700–48) poem, included in the masque *Alfred* (1740) became the basis for this British patriotic song.

Saussure: Ferdinand de Saussure (1857–1913), Swiss linguist who emphasised the arbitrary relationship in language between the sign and that which it signifies; a progenitor of twentieth-century structuralism. [E]

Schlegel: Karl Wilhelm Friedrich von Schlegel (1772–1829), German Romantic poet, scholar and critic.

Schleiermacher: Friedrich Schleiermacher (1768–1834), theologian and philosopher, known for his work in hermeneutics and on translation.

Senghor: Léopold Senghor (1906–2001), expatriate from Senegal, proponent (with Aimé Césaire) of the négritude* movement. [E]

Sentimental fiction: also called 'domestic fiction', the 'sentimental novel', or 'women's fiction', eighteenth- and nineteenth-century sentimental fiction aimed to educate the moral sentiments through emotionally-rendered scenes.

Shaftesbury: Anthony Ashley Cooper, 3rd Earl of Shaftesbury (1671–1713), philosopher in the tradition of Locke*, known for his ideas concerning a 'moral sense'.

Speech act: a speech act emphasises that speech connotes action; prominent theorists include J. L. Austin and John Searle. [E]

Stamp Act (1765): passed by the British Parliament in 1765, it required American colonists to pay a tax on imported newspapers and other documents.

Steele: Richard Steele (1672–1729), Irish essayist, dramatist, journalist and politician; editor of *The Tatler* and, with Addison*, *The Spectator*.

Sublime: aesthetic theory emphasising the grandeur of nature and a response of awe, prominent in the eighteenth century through Edmund Burke's *A Philosophical Enquiry into the Origin of our Ideas of the Sublime and Beautiful* (1757). John Keats used the phrase 'egotistical sublime' to describe Wordsworth's poetic style, which he saw as overly preoccupied with the poet's self.

Swedenborg: Emanuel Swedenborg (1688–1772), Swedish scientist, philosopher, mystic and religious thinker, influential amongst mid-nineteenth-century American intelligentsia.

Symbolism: a late nineteenth-century literary movement originating in France, in reaction to Naturalism and Realism; Stéphane Mallarmé* and Paul Verlaine as well as Edgar Allan Poe (translated by Baudelaire) were influential in the movement.

Tintern Abbey or Mont Blanc: William Wordsworth's poem 'A few lines written above Tintern Abbey' (1798) and P. B. Shelley's poem 'Mont Blanc' (1817).

Transcendentalist: philosophical and aesthetic movement centred in Concord and Boston, Massachusetts in the mid-nineteenth century. Emerson's essay 'The Transcendentalist' first defined the word as 'Idealism as it appears in 1842'.

Translatio studii (et imperii): Latin phrase indicating that civilisation flees a decadent society for an innocent one, usually by moving west.

Trollope: Frances (Fanny) Trollope (1779–1863), English author whose account of travels in America, *Domestic Manners of the Americans* (1832), became notorious for its outspoken criticism of American society.

Turner: Frederick Jackson Turner (1861–1932), US historian whose 'frontier thesis' was first articulated in 1893.

Union: between Scotland and England in 1707, when the Scottish parliament voted to dissolve itself in favour of parliamentary union with England.

Voss: Johann Heinrich Voss (1751–1826), German poet and translator.

War of 1812: (1812–15) between Britain and America waged largely at sea, as America sought to gain sea power and sovereignty over its western territories.

War of the Spanish Succession: (1701–14) war between Austria and France for the Spanish throne after the death of the last Habsburg king Charles II; at the end of the war, the Treaty of Utrecht established a balance of power in Europe.

Weltliteratur: 'World literature', coined by Goethe* in 1827, the basis for the discipline of comparative literature.

Williams: Raymond Williams (1921–88) Welsh Marxist academic, novelist and critic. [E]

Yacine: Kateb Yacine (1929–89): Algerian writer resident in France.

INDEX

Adamism, 101
American holocaust, 236
American Studies
   and Cold War, 1
   integrationist impulse of, 45
'anxiety of influence', 77, 90–2
'area studies', 2, 78
Atlantic, 4, 58–9, 145

Black Atlantic, 58, 123, 139 *passim*
borders, 2, 49, 323

Canada, 38
capitalism, 46
captivity narratives, 273, 301
Circum-Atlantic, 236
collection, 124, 157
colonialism, 122
   and *The Tempest*, 122, 126 *passim*
Common Sense philosophy, 253
comparative literature, 7, 80 *passim*
   and literary unification, 76, 81
congener, 10
'contact zone', 284, 313
contagion, 124, 158
copyright legislation, 19, 23 *passim*
   and American Copyright League, 23
   and authorship, 28
   and English authors in the US, 29
   and International Copyright Association, 27
   and literary aristocracy, 26, 28–9
   and literary history, 24, 26
   and piracy, 25, 28

cosmopolitanism, 3, 5–6, 21, 53 *passim*
   and the local, 56
   and the nation, 56
   contradictions in, 55
   definitions of, 53–4
cultural earliness, 100–3
cultural insiderism, 141
cultural lateness, 99–100

'deep time', 124–5, 160 *passim*
deterritorialization, 228
diaspora, 137–8, 145
differance, 123, 132–3
difference
   cultural, 89 *passim*
   ethnic, 141

eloquence, 221 *passim*
emigration, 282, 298 *passim*
   and national identity, 299–300
   as disabling, 301
Enlightenment, 55
epistolary exchange, 264
ethnography, 283
exceptionalism, 1, 45, 58, 219
exile, 71, 282–3, 285 *passim*
   definitions of, 286–7

frontier, 2, 45, 302

genre, 124, 152, 218, 233
   and exceptionalism, 256 *passim*
   and travel, 233–4
global technology, 31–2, 46